THE NIXONS:

A FAMILY PORTRAIT

EDWARD C. NIXON

AND

KAREN L. OLSON

BOOK PUBLISHERS NETWORK

Book Publishers Network
P.O. Box 2256
Bothell, WA 98041
Ph 425-483-3040

Printed in the United States of America

LCCN 2008943469
ISBN10 1-935359-05-3
ISBN13 978-1-935359-05-0

Nixon, Edward C.

   The Nixons : a family portrait / Edward C. Nixon and Karen L. Olson.
   -- 1st ed. -- Bothell, WA : Book Publishers Network, c2009.

      p. ; cm.

      ISBN: 978-1-935359-05-0
      Includes bibliographical references and index.

         1. Nixon, Richard M. (Richard Milhous), 1913-1994.
      2. Presidents--United States--Biography. 3. Nixon family.
      4. Milhous family. I. Olson, Karen L. II. Title.

Editor: Vicki McCown
Cover Design: Laura Zugzda
Interior Layout: Stephanie Martindale
Indexer: Carolyn Acheson

Cover photo (l-r) Ed, Gay, Dick, Pat, Clara Jane, and Don Nixon. Courtesy of Clara Jane Nixon.
Permission has been requested but not yet granted for photos on pages 132, 194, 200, 237, and 303.

*Dedicated to generations yet unborn
and to those parents and teachers who
will lead them with absolute honesty.*

CONTENTS

FOREWORD

The complexity of Richard Milhous Nixon is legendary. This book unravels some parts of the mystery with a portrait of the 37th President's ancestral roots and family life that manages to combine fraternal loyalty with human fascination.

Life as seen from the inside of the Nixon-Milhous families has never before been written. The cast of characters is almost Shakespearean in its historical colour and personal depth. At the beginning of the story, in and around the Nixon's Mom n' Pop grocery store in rural California, we learn about the versatile but irascible father Frank Nixon and his "rough Appalachian ways"; the still deep love of his wife Hannah, whom neighbours called "a Quaker saint"; the redoubtable poetry loving matriarch of the clan, Almira Milhous; and the charismatic eldest son Harold who died of TB on his mother's 48th birthday, the second loss in the family as 7-year-old Arthur Nixon also passed away from the same disease.

Ed Nixon and his co-author Karen Olson capture the poignancy and the passion of these tragedies together with the hardscrabble yet ambitious poverty of the future President's upbringing. When the Nixon family set off for Dick's graduation at Duke University in 1937,

Ed is amazed by the expenditure on gas for the long drive. "I had never before noticed Mom and Dad spending money on something that was not a necessity," he writes.

Dick is a good older brother and mentor to his youngest sibling. The age and experience gap between them is bridged by many personal bonds and episodes. From the White House years we get accounts of Tricia's wedding, rides on Air Force One, official banquets for Arabian princes and Apollo astronauts, and an understanding of the President's private friendships with Bebe Rebozo, Bob Abplanalp and Gavin Herbert. There is not much on Watergate. The subject is apparently "not important"—surely a euphemism for too painful—for the brothers to discuss.

Despite this and other curious omissions from the Nixonian passion play of personal and political dramas, this book is an enthralling read, full of rare insights into Milhous-Nixon family life. Some of the glimpses are quirky, others unconventional. The end result is a portrait of the 37th President and his roots, which goes deeper in intimacy and understanding than the writings of most political commentators.

❧Jonathan Aiken

Jonathan Aitken is a former British Member of Parliament, who served in the Cabinet as Treasury Secretary and Defence Minister. He is the author of *Nixon: A Life*, which won The Churchill Prize for political biography in 1993.

ACKNOWLEDGMENTS

Authors of non-fiction books often thank an extensive list of collaborators. For me to acknowledge the countless people who contributed to this long story, however, would require a total recall from my memory banks. I am grateful to so many that such an effort would risk slighting those inadvertently omitted.

I especially wish to thank my wife Gay Lynne and our daughters Amy and Beth for their stories and for the many hours they spent reviewing the manuscript. Cousins, nieces, and nephews also constitute a special group, all of whom had a vital part in verifying significant details of chronology and dialogue.

My family is very large, but friends, associates, and acquaintances comprise an even longer list. Many of their names appear in the index, and they deserve thanks for all their encouragement and suggestions.

This book has been a labor of love underway for at least twenty years, but until 1998, when Karen Olson volunteered to join the effort, I was getting nowhere. Therefore, I wish to extend my deepest gratitude to my coauthor Karen and her husband Dennis Olson.

I also wish to thank my friends Bruce Herschensohn and James Humes, who wrote testimonials for the back cover, and Jonathan Aitken, who wrote the Foreword and also a testimonial.

Under publisher Sheryn Hara's leadership, Vicki McCown, Laura Zugzda, Stephanie Martindale, Carolyn Acheson, and the entire Book Publishers Network team patiently collaborated with the authors to bring the work to fruition. Such dedication to service deserves special recognition as a model of great teamwork.

Finally, I wish to acknowlege Tricia Nixon Cox and Julie Nixon Eisenhower, my nieces, for permitting us to quote from their father's extensive writings.

INTRODUCTION

Relying on
Research to Reveal Heritage
Memories to Recount Lives
Questions to Review Legacy
Persuasion to Renew Hope

⌁Edward C. Nixon

Strangers at the airport, at the restaurant, on the street often stare at my profile. Some hear me speak. The bold ones ask, "Are you related to Richard Nixon?" Others simply inquire, "Are you related?" I guess my nose and voice are dead giveaways.

For some people, meeting me is one degree of separation from meeting my famous brother. Reporters, autograph seekers, and people naturally curious about my life want to know, "What was it like growing up as Richard Nixon's brother? How did being related to the President affect your life?"

To answer accurately, I'd have to say Dick was more than a brother. Because we never shared a boyhood, he assumed the role of assistant father and mentor. At the time of my birth, he was seventeen and getting ready to start college. But he realized he could be an important influence in my life, and he took his self-imposed responsibility seriously, always listening to his kid brother. I considered Dick to be outgoing with his ears—not with his mouth. Through thought-provoking questions, he encouraged me to learn and solve problems. More than anyone else in the family, he could stand back from a contentious situation and give impartial and convincing advice.

Frank and Hannah Nixon raised five sons—Harold, Dick, Don, Arthur, and me—in a close-knit family, teaching us the importance of religious faith, traditional values, and a strong work ethic. Family life revolved around Dad and Mom's store, the Quaker church, and family gatherings. In many ways, Dick's rise from humble beginnings to the presidency of the United States epitomizes the American dream—a dream in which my family and I participated.

Yet, I've done nothing to deserve public notice except to be related to a celebrity. Although not well-known in my own right, I've lived all my adult life in the shadow of one of the most influential and controversial men in the twentieth century, and such proximity has led me down paths I otherwise would not have trod. When Dick became President, doors opened that put my family and me in the midst of exciting and historic endeavors and gave us access to national and foreign leaders everywhere we traveled. Suddenly, heads of state, reporters, and business leaders sought my opinions both on Dick's presidency and on environmental issues. As the President's brother and a geologist, I welcomed the chance to share my view of the Earth in many developing countries.

While my family and I are truly grateful for the many opportunities we've had, there also have been times of grief and pain. With fame comes risk. What happens when the celebrity falls from favor and is fairly or unfairly attacked in the press? What impact does that have on the family?

Over the years, friends and acquaintances have urged me to write the stories about Dick and our family that I've told in public speeches and privately. My brother Don, too, would often say, "We've got to write a book."

In August 1997, I wrote a few letters of inquiry to New York publishers but received no encouragement on my book proposal. Then on December 3, 1998, I heard my niece, Julie Nixon Eisenhower, speak at the Richard Nixon Library and Birthplace. At the luncheon following her speech, an acquaintance asked me how I was coming on my book.

I told him, "I haven't made any progress. I need a writer to help me get it moving."

At that point, Karen Olson, the lady sitting next to him, jumped up and said, "I'll help you!"

I learned that Karen had her own story of meeting my brother and that she lived not far from me in the Seattle area. After hearing her describe that meeting, our collaboration began in earnest.

Because memories, some more than seventy-five-years-old now, are fragmentary and fallible, I have tried to confirm my recollections with family members and friends who participated in the events. Karen also did extensive research on the people and occurrences mentioned in the book. I included dialogue only when my memories of those conversations are vivid or when quotations appeared in published sources. Conversations with family members were easy to reconstruct; I can still hear them talking in their distinctive manner.

While volumes have been written about Dick's life, this book includes never-before-published material about him, our family, and my own life from a perspective only I can give. In some instances, *The Nixons: A Family Portrait* sets the record straight, correcting the errors that have been written and disseminated. Readers seeking tell-all gossip, however, will be disappointed. No, Dick did not share with me any revelations on Watergate. Instead, we discussed matters that seemed to us far more important.

In this book, I have attempted to answer the many questions that pique people's curiosity. I share a positive view of the Nixons, examining our heritage and the influence it had on all of us. I also recount the experiences I had with Dick during my youth and adulthood. Through these anecdotes—snapshots, so to speak—my goal is to give readers a personal portrait of Dick and our family. I hope people will consider Dick's character, accomplishments, and legacy in a new light. Finally, I hope to rekindle interest in what Dick taught this nation. The wisdom and knowledge he left us certainly bear upon the challenges we face today.

~: CHAPTER 1 :~
STORIES OF OUR HERITAGE

All families are defined by their stories. It is the oft-repeated
tale that fashions the family culture and, if the stories are
inspiring enough, fashions the family sense of purpose.[1]

~:Stephen Mansfield

We all have one feature in common: ancestors, even if we didn't know any of them. Some of us have had the privilege of a relationship with all four grandparents, and a few have known their great-grandparents, but beyond that, we just hear tales from our elders about those who have gone before us. Unlike my brothers, I knew only one of our grandparents, because I was born so late in our parents' lives. The grandparents were all born before 1853—a rather remarkable fact from our vantage point in 2008.

My brothers and I grew up hearing stories of our ancestors, who left us the legacy of their heritage. Dick was especially fascinated by history—family history as well as that of the world. Although my other brothers and I didn't share his love of world history, family history was real to us and therefore interesting. Our parents, aunts, uncles, and grandmother made it come alive through their stories. As we sat and listened to them reminisce, we marveled at the hardships our ancestors faced and gained an appreciation of how easy we had it with our modern conveniences in the 1930s and 1940s.

---

1 Stephen Mansfield, *The Faith of George W. Bush* (Lake Mary, FL: Charisma House, 2003) 4.

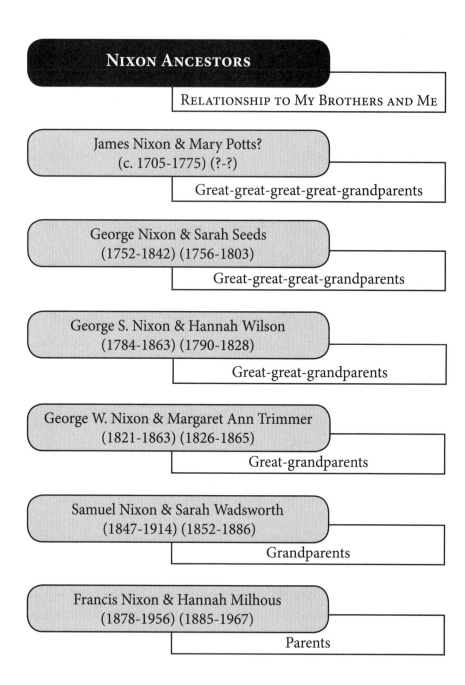

NIXON ANCESTORS

RELATIONSHIP TO MY BROTHERS AND ME

James Nixon & Mary Potts?
(c. 1705-1775) (?-?)

Great-great-great-great-grandparents

George Nixon & Sarah Seeds
(1752-1842) (1756-1803)

Great-great-great-grandparents

George S. Nixon & Hannah Wilson
(1784-1863) (1790-1828)

Great-great-grandparents

George W. Nixon & Margaret Ann Trimmer
(1821-1863) (1826-1865)

Great-grandparents

Samuel Nixon & Sarah Wadsworth
(1847-1914) (1852-1886)

Grandparents

Francis Nixon & Hannah Milhous
(1878-1956) (1885-1967)

Parents

Genealogical facts certainly add to the knowledge of our identity, but perhaps more important is the family lore passed down from generation to generation, connecting the young to their elders and ancestors. And our elders taught us that we, in turn, should honor our heritage by leaving a worthy legacy to future generations.

THE NIXON CLAN

One can only speculate about the origin of our Nixon ancestors. Historians tell us the earliest Nixons were of Scottish descent. Hundreds of years ago, "Nixon" originated as a patronymic surname meaning "son of Nick or Nicholas," and was spelled in a variety of ways, making bloodlines difficult to trace. No one has been able to find our direct line in European records.

In the fourteenth century, Nixons appeared as a branch of the Armstrong clan in southern Scotland. As part of the infamous Border *reivers* (robbers), Nixons and Armstrongs plundered rival clans, as well as the English living near the border between Scotland and England. Raiding, arson, kidnapping, and murder were the reivers' accepted way of life—and the only means of survival—until the end of the sixteenth century.

In his book, *The Steel Bonnets: The Story of the Anglo-Scottish Border Reivers*, George MacDonald Fraser commented on the coincidence of the 1969 U.S. presidential inauguration in which Richard Nixon, Lyndon Johnson, and Billy Graham, likely descendants of three Border reiver clans, stood side by side, separated from their warring ancestors by thousands of miles and many centuries. Fraser noted that all three resembled their forebears in physical appearance, and he singled out my brother as a classic example.[2]

In her genealogical research, my daughter Beth found the Armstrong clan intertwined with the line of William "Braveheart" Wallace (ca. 1272-1305), the liberator of Scotland and enemy of the brutal King Edward I "Longshanks" of England, a distant ancestor on our Milhous side. She speculates that somewhere along the line, a relationship existed between Wallace's family and ours. We believe

---

2 George MacDonald Fraser, *The Steel Bonnets: The Story of the Anglo-Scottish Border Reivers* (London: HarperCollins Publishers, 1995) 1-2.

our Nixon forefathers played a part, at least, in Wallace's fight to liberate Scotland.

❧ ❧

In 1603 upon the death of England's Queen Elizabeth, King James VI of Scotland, ascended the English throne, whereupon he added the title of King James I of England. He fulfilled his dream of uniting the countries of England and Scotland into Great Britain but, in the process, gained the animosity of both Englishmen and Catholics. Several attempted to assassinate him.

A devout and learned Protestant, King James feared that Catholic-controlled Ulster (modern-day Northern Ireland) would rebel against the crown. In an attempt to weaken their influence, he confiscated their land and established the Ulster Plantation, so Protestants would have a permanent colony on the island. He granted land to those who settled there. Many Scots, including my ancestors I've been told, took King James up on his offer. Because the settlers maintained their Scottish culture, Presbyterian religion, and loyalty to the King of England, the native Irish naturally resented their presence.

During King James' reign, British settlers also began to colonize the New World. About one hundred years later, James Nixon, the first Nixon in our recorded lineage, settled in Brandywine Hundred[3], New Castle County, Delaware, three miles north of the present city of Wilmington. Dad told my brothers and me that our fourth great-grandfather James sailed for America to flee religious persecution in Northern Ireland. The first documentation we have is James' deed dated 3 April 1731 for the purchase of a one-hundred-acre farm in Brandywine Hundred. Then in 1734, he bought an adjoining one hundred acres. The deeds listed his profession as cooper, or barrel maker. He died on July 26, 1775, leaving his belongings to his wife Mary, sons George and James, Jr., daughters Elizabeth and Mary, and their husbands. Beyond these scant facts, we have only family lore.

When Dad would meet with one of his siblings—Ernest, Walter, or Carrie—they spent much of their time repeating the wonderful blend of tales they had heard growing up about Nixons settling the land

---

3   A "hundred" was a British tax division consisting of one hundred families.

and fighting for freedom. Knowing Dad and his siblings, I'm sure they embellished some of the details. As accuracy decreased over time, the embellishments became the story, and family legends were created.

One of the stories Dad told us is that James had traveled with his brother from Northern Ireland to America. They had a bit of an argument as to which direction they would go upon reaching the shores of the New Land. James' brother decided to go south to get warm. James, on the other hand, stayed in Delaware, where he and Mary raised their children.

Their sons George and James, Jr., both fought in the Revolutionary War. Lieutenant George Nixon crossed the Delaware with General Washington to fight in the Battle of Trenton. Eventually, the brothers and their descendants migrated west, settling in Pennsylvania for a while before moving on to Ohio.

George's son, George S., however, remained in Pennsylvania, where his son George W. was born in 1821. His wife, Margaret Ann Trimmer Nixon, bore ten children, including our grandfather, Samuel Brady Nixon. During the Civil War, George W. fought on the side of the North as a private in the 73rd Ohio Volunteer Infantry, Company B.

My brothers and I heard the verified story of how Richard Enderlin, a brave eighteen-year-old private, risked his life to bring aid and comfort to George W. Nixon, our great-grandfather, as he lay dying on the Gettysburg battlefield near the Confederate line. On July 1, 1863, Private Nixon had fallen in battle, and though he cried for help, no one dared come to his aid. To cross the battlefield during the day would have meant certain capture or death. That night, however, Private Enderlin snuck across the open field amidst enemy fire and dragged Private Nixon back to Union territory. Unfortunately, he died two days later—one of the last men to lose his life at Gettysburg. He is buried there at the National Cemetery.

Because of his heroism in rescuing Private Nixon and other acts of bravery at Gettysburg, Enderlin was soon promoted to the rank of sergeant and in 1897 received the Medal of Honor. Our family remains grateful for Enderlin's bravery and compassion, enabling our ancestor to receive care and die with dignity.

~ ~

Uncle Ernest, Dick, and Pat at grave of George W. Nixon
Gettysburg National Cemetery, 1953

✌Family album

My brothers Dick and Don and I many times wished we had recorded our "Old Man" telling amusing stories about his family based on his vivid memories of childhood. His direct manner of speaking and colorful, rustic descriptions captivated his audience and generated many smiles. However, Dad's avoidance of the abundant tragedies in his past has left many gaps in my own efforts to reconstruct the family history. And sadly, many of his stories about his parents were lost when Dad and his siblings passed on.

I do know that Grandfather Nixon taught school, farmed, and belonged to a Methodist church in Vinton County, Ohio, and the family lived in Swan Township not far north of McArthur. In the southeastern part of the state, Vinton County is situated at the northern reaches of Appalachia, an impoverished area during my ancestors' lives. Unlike the glaciated flat land in northern Ohio, Vinton County is hilly and rough, a difficult place to farm with the tools available in the nineteenth century. But the land was affordable, and with our forebears' strong work ethic, somehow, they managed to eke out a living.

Sarah Ann "Sally" Wadsworth Nixon, our grandmother, also taught school. Family lore has it that she was a distant relation to Henry Wadsworth Longfellow. Her brother, Robert Franklin "Frank" Wadsworth, whom I met in 1946, always made a point of mentioning their family's relationship to the famous poet, but I can find no confirming evidence. I don't think our Wadsworth line had a lot of poetic instinct, except for Dad's use of simple rhymes in many of his entertaining stories.

When I was sixteen, Dad showed me the house where he had lived with his parents. He choked back the tears when he viewed that Appalachian shack. Emotion welled up as he recalled his childhood. "Just look at that," he said, pointing to the hovel that once had been his home.

I wondered how our grandparents and their five children—Irene, Walter, Frank, Carrie, and Ernest—could have survived in those cramped quarters. Inspecting the house, I imagined how the wind must have blown right through the cracks in the rough clapboard walls.

Nevertheless, our grandparents always resisted accepting charity in favor of finding any kind of work that able-bodied people could do.

Samuel Brady Nixon
Frank Nixon's father
⌁Family album

Sarah Ann "Sally"
Wadsworth Nixon
Frank Nixon's mother
⌁Family album

They figured they were much better off than many families who really needed assistance. They instilled that work ethic in all their children, especially our father, Francis Anthony "Frank" Nixon.

Dad was born December 3, 1878, just thirteen years after the end of the Civil War. He said his parents gave him his middle name in honor of Anthony Wayne, one of George Washington's valiant generals in the Revolutionary War. His troops had nicknamed him "Mad Anthony" because of his tactical rashness. I suppose that appealed to Dad, for he delighted in explaining to all he met the connection with his namesake. People would ask him, "Who were you named for?"

"Mad Anthony Wayne; Anthony's my middle name," he would respond with pride.[4] He even suspected the famous general was a distant relation through the Wadsworth line.[5]

I never heard whether the name Francis had any particular significance. Dad always went by Frank, except on official paperwork.

When Sally became ill with tuberculosis, Sam packed up the family belongings in a covered wagon and drove his family south to the Carolinas and Georgia, hoping the warmer climate would cure her illness, but she grew sicker. In desperation and financial distress, Sam took the family back to Ohio.

Dad vividly remembered the Christmas of 1885. His mother, who was in the last stage of the disease, entered their small living room with a white sheet or some sort of cloth draped over her head, pretending to be Santa Claus, I suppose. Dad's brother Ernest, at age two, screamed when he saw the ghost-like stranger. Dad was scared too, but he remained silent. Walter, their older brother, however, caught on quickly to the sheeted figure's identity.

Somehow their mother had saved enough money to buy seven oranges from Florida—an extravagance in those days. She squatted down on the floor and rolled five oranges to her children, keeping the remaining two for her husband and herself. The whole family peeled

---

4 Throughout the book, I use the word *pride* in the sense of satisfaction or elation, not self-importance. Dad and others in our family were not arrogant.

5 Genealogical research has not verified an ancestral connection between the Wadsworth line and Anthony Wayne, although the Waynes resided in Chester County, Pennsylvania, at the same time as many of my father's ancestors. Perhaps some fought alongside Mad Anthony Wayne. Alternatively, Dad's parents might have named him after Anthony Trimmer, his maternal great-grandfather.

the precious fruit together. Dad never forgot it. That was Christmas to him: simple, straightforward, not an overabundance but something unforgettable and full of meaning—gifts given out of love and sacrifice. That was also Dad's last strong memory of his mother. She died a few weeks later on January 16, 1886, at the age of thirty-four, when Dad was only seven.

Dad's life was tough. After his mother died, the family fell apart. His grieving father remained at home with the younger children. Poverty stricken from caring for his terminally ill wife, Sam couldn't support all his family, so he sent the older children away. Elihu "Lyle," Sam's youngest brother, and his wife Alice, who lived in Richland Township, took Dad in to raise him along with their two young daughters. A son and another daughter were born to Lyle and Alice while Dad lived with them. Walter left home to work for neighbors to earn a living. Irene, Dad's eldest sibling, must have done likewise before she married, had children, and eventually died of tuberculosis like her mother.

Four years later, Sam's situation had improved enough so that Dad could move back to his father's new home. But for Dad, the homecoming was not a happy one. In 1890, Sam had married Lutheria Wyman, a woman just fifteen years older than Dad. She treated him harshly with physical beatings to accompany her frequent tongue lashings. Two years later, in 1892, Sam and Lutheria had a son named Hugh, who benefited from a little extra attention and some special protection from his mom. Nevertheless, Uncle Hugh's gift of good humor secured his popularity with the rest of the family.

At the time Dad grew up, many children quit school as soon as they could master the fundamentals of reading, writing, and arithmetic. Most never went past the third or fourth grade. That's all they needed for the majority of farm and city jobs in the nineteenth century. In 1885, the eighth grade was considered upper level education. Dad attended school only through the sixth grade. Despite his brief exposure to formal education, he learned the skills necessary for survival.

Dad loved to tell a story about the last year of his formal education in the one-room schoolhouse near MacArthur. The children were so rowdy that the school couldn't keep a teacher. One would come in, work a week or so, and leave. Finally the school board hired an older gentleman, a big strapping retired cowboy. On his first day of school, the kids took one look at him and snickered to each other, "Oh, another new one. We can really have fun with this old guy."

However, this teacher had a different approach to classroom management. He sat down at his desk as the kids filed in. As soon as he rang the bell, he whacked a big stick to catch their attention. Then, much to the children's dismay, he pulled out his six-gun and laid it on the desk.

"If any of you students act up, this is going to be used," he threatened. "Now sit down and shut up until I ask you to speak." Silence settled over the classroom, and the boys and girls remained quiet the rest of that day—and to the end of the school year. None of them wanted to see what would happen if they stepped out of line. Even the bullies and pranksters didn't make a peep.

At home Dad's situation continued to deteriorate. He thought his stepmother much too harsh to put up with, so shortly after Hugh's birth, he left home and drifted from job to job for the next several years. As a young teen, he could do the work of a grown man. A jack-of-all-trades with an incredible work ethic, he held a variety of jobs, including glassworker, potter, housepainter, potato farmer, ox team driver, sheep rancher, telephone linesman, carpenter, roustabout in the oil fields, and streetcar operator. The 1900 U.S. Census lists Dad and his brother Walter as servants and laborers on the Charles Blunck farm in Larimer County, Colorado.

One event during Dad's roving years stood out in his memory. As I recall Dad telling the story, he was taking care of a local farmer's sorrel stallion in 1896. He happened to be in Columbus, Ohio, with the horse when he heard an announcement of a parade in town for Ohio Governor William McKinley, candidate for President against Grover Cleveland. More people were needed to participate, so Dad was invited to join in at the back of the procession. Dad had that horse curried down and polished with soft soap. With his braided mane, the stallion looked fit for a king. As McKinley's carriage passed by to take its place at the front of the parade route, McKinley spotted the magnificent creature and stopped.

"Young man," he smiled, addressing Dad, "that's the most beautiful horse I've ever seen. I want you to ride right behind my carriage. Would you do that?"

"Yes, sir," Dad answered, a bit in awe of the famous man.

Whereupon McKinley asked, "Are you going to vote Republican now?"

"Yes, sir, I will when I'm old enough." Dad was only seventeen.

"Good for you," McKinley nodded in approval.

I remember Dad telling us that William McKinley deeply influenced his interest in politics—and he never got it out of his system. The story illustrates what little compliments from celebrities can do. Meeting McKinley was a life-changing experience for Dad. There he was, a dirt-poor farm boy noticed by the governor of Ohio—and the future President of the United States.

That incident cemented Dad's decision to become a Republican, the party to which he was leaning, because he felt President Cleveland's economic policies had plunged the country into a depression. A maverick in his family of Democrats, Dad was the first of the Nixons to vote Republican. And in Colorado in 1900, he did vote for McKinley for his second term.

Never staying put for long in those days, Dad returned to Columbus in 1904 and took a job as a streetcar motorman. In the open, unheated vestibule where he stood, his feet and hands stung from frostbite in the wintertime. All his adult life, he complained of having contracted chilblains from that job.

Dad delighted to tell us about his one successful venture into lobbying. He approached a local candidate for a statewide office, explaining the hazards of working on the streetcar. In return for the man's promise to get the vestibules fixed if elected, Dad offered to support his campaign and to rally other motormen. With their help, the candidate won, and he fulfilled his promise. The open vestibules eventually were enclosed, but not soon enough for Dad. By the time the government finally responded, he had already moved on.

Discouraged by the long delays in the political process in Columbus, Dad migrated to Southern California in 1907 and got a job as a Pacific Electric Railway motorman. In sunny California, he no longer had to worry about frostbite. He often reminisced with pleasure about

Frank Nixon, motorman on Pacific Electric Railway's Red Car, Whittier, CA, 1907

∽Family album

MILHOUS ANCESTORS

RELATIONSHIP TO MY BROTHERS AND ME

Thomas Milhous & Elizabeth ?
(1637-?) (?-1708)

Great-great-great-great-great-great-grandparents

John Milhous & Sarah Mickle
(1669-?) (?-?)

Great-great-great-great-great-grandparents

Thomas Milhous & Sarah Miller
(1699-1770) (1701-1775)

Great-great-great-great-grandparents

William Milhous, Sr. & Hannah Baldwin
(1738-1826) (1748-1825)

Great-great-great-grandparents

William Milhous, Jr. & Martha Vickers
(1783-1874) (1786-1873)

Great-great-grandparents

Joshua Vickers Milhous & Elizabeth Price Griffith
(1820-1893) (1827-1923)

Great-grandparents

Franklin Milhous & Almira Park Burdg
(1848-1919) (1849-1943)

Grandparents

Hannah Milhous & Francis Nixon
(1885-1967) (1878-1956)

Parents

his days driving the interurban "Red Cars," as they were called, from Santa Fe Springs into Los Angeles and back out to Whittier. At that time, Whittier was an important freight and commuter location, and this route was one of Pacific Electric's most extensive lines. Electric streetcars were the way to get around in those days—a mass transit system before automobiles, trucks and cheap gasoline took over.

THE MILHOUS CLAN

My mother's side of the family has been better documented than my father's side. Internet genealogists have traced the various branches back to Mayflower passengers, Plantagenet kings and queens of England, and the line of Scottish king Robert the Bruce. More recent ancestors are detailed in the book on our family history: *Descendants of William Milhous, Jr. and Martha Vickers* compiled by our cousin, Eloise Milhous Price.[6]

Just before the Republican National Convention in August 1968, Jessamyn West McPherson, a second cousin and well-known author, wrote to me, summarizing the Milhous family history as epitomizing the American melting pot and the march toward freedom:

> They left Germany because of religious persecution for the freer climate of England.
>
> In England, they helped Cromwell depose a king.
>
> In Ireland, they associated themselves with the movement that emphasized the authenticity of each man's inner light.
>
> When Penn had established his colony of brotherly love—and it was that, the Quakers were the only people who recognized the rights of the Indians and lived in peace with them—they, the Milhous family, moved to Pennsylvania.
>
> They have been on every frontier since then: Ohio, Indiana—and now the vast frontier, California. (They would not go south because of slavery.)
>
> It is fitting that Richard be in the forefront of that march begun so long ago.

6 Eloise Price, *Descendants of William Milhous, Jr. and Martha Vickers*, 7th ed. (Coulterville, CA: Self-published, 1996).

Our earliest known Milhous ancestor, Thomas, born in 1637, his wife Elizabeth, and their son John joined the Society of Friends (Quakers) in Timahoe, County Kildare, Ireland. John's son Thomas and his wife Sarah Miller Milhous answered William Penn's call to immigrate to the New World to find religious freedom.

Oddly enough, Thomas and Sarah Milhous settled on a two-hundred-acre farm in Pennsylvania in 1730—just eleven miles north of Wilmington, Delaware, and eight miles from where the James Nixons settled the following year. Like James, Thomas was a cooper. No record exists connecting the Nixon and Milhous families during that period, but their paths certainly could have crossed. Even more interesting, Dr. Raymond Martin Bell, a Washington and Jefferson College professor who researched President Nixon's ancestry, discovered that ancestors in one hundred of his lines on both sides of the family lived at one time or another within seventy miles of Wilmington.

Eventually, our Milhous ancestors migrated west to Ohio and then Indiana. Jessamyn wrote her best-known novel, *The Friendly Persuasion*, about Indiana Quakers based on the lives of our great-grandparents, Joshua Vickers Milhous and Elizabeth "Eliza" Price Griffith Milhous.[7]

Joshua, born the end of 1820, became a nurseryman, specializing in fruit tree stock. In 1847, he married Eliza, a preacher. Although women preachers were rare in other denominations at that time, they were common among Quakers, who believed in and practiced equality. The Griffiths were a well-established American family of Welsh descent when the Milhouses arrived. In fact, our Griffith ancestors had sailed to America in 1682 on the same ship as William Penn.

Because the Republican Party was founded on opposition to slavery, Joshua strongly supported the party's candidates. He attended the 1876 Indiana State Republican Convention. That year Rutherford B. Hayes, a Republican, won election as President.

Joshua and Eliza's son Franklin, born November 4, 1848, in Mt. Pleasant, Ohio, grew up immersed in the Quaker faith with its aversion

---

7 Jessamyn West and my brothers all knew Great-Grandmother Eliza Milhous, who moved to Whittier, California, in 1906 at the age of seventy-nine.

to armed conflict and opposition to slavery. When he was five years old, the family moved to a farm in Jennings County, Indiana. He and his family stood among the crowd to hear Henry Ward Beecher, the eloquent Congregational minister and abolitionist, preach against slavery at the Vernon County Courthouse in 1860.

The Civil War posed a dilemma for the peace-loving Quakers. Should they bear arms? Franklin's uncle, William Milhous (1811-1884), an early abolitionist, helped transport escaped slaves to Canada as a "conductor" on the Underground Railroad. But William also served in the military, performing special duty at General Nathaniel Banks' headquarters in Strasburg, Virginia. After returning to his First Regiment, he was captured in 1862 by Confederate troops under the command of Stonewall Jackson and incarcerated in the notorious Libby Prison in Richmond. Later, the Confederates moved him to Harrison Landing, where he was exchanged for Rebel prisoners and sent to Washington, D.C.

The Milhous family highly valued education. Franklin attended Moores Hill College, a Methodist school, near Cincinnati. As a German major, he displayed such a talent for the language that he taught at the college after graduating. Later he taught elementary school.

Musical ability ran in the Milhous family, and Franklin was especially gifted. He joined music groups in college, played the concertina and the organ, and sang in the church choir. Throughout his life, music remained an avocation, and he encouraged his children to develop their musical talents.

A genial young man, Franklin developed a reputation for being kind, understanding, and a good listener. He fell in love with a teacher at Hopewell Academy named Sarah Emily Armstrong, whom he married in 1872. The young couple purchased land near the Milhous family farm and orchard in Sycamore Valley. Like his father, Franklin became engrossed in planting and tending his orchards and selling nursery stock. Three children were born to Franklin and Sarah: Griffith William, Mary Alice, and Emily. Then tragedy struck when Sarah died in 1877, and nineteen days later, baby Emily died and was buried next to her mother. No record or story remains to tell us why they met untimely deaths.

Franklin Milhous family, Indiana, 1890
Hannah in front of her bearded grandfather, Joshua Vickers Milhous
⌁Family album

Franklin Milhous family's new home in Whittier, 1897
⌁Family album

Franklin was not destined to be a widower for long, however. In 1879, he married Almira Park Burdg, a teacher at Hopewell School and daughter of long-time family friends. Almira, our grandmother, was born September 16, 1849, in Damascus, Columbiana County, Ohio, to Oliver Burdg and Jane Hemingway Burdg. When Almira married Franklin, she eagerly assumed the role of mother to his two surviving children. Together they had six daughters, Edith, Martha, Hannah (our mother), Elizabeth, Jane, and Rose Olive, and a son, Ezra Charles. Franklin and Almira raised all nine children with the same moral training and treated them equally, while recognizing each child's individuality. From all accounts, our grandparents were exemplary role models, teaching their children the tenets of the Quaker faith. They encouraged a strong communal spirit and selfless dedication to the service of others as a way of life. In the home, they lived their faith with quiet reverence, hard work, thrift, tolerance, compassion, and patience.

Franklin and Almira believed travel to be educational as well as fun for the family. Every summer, they organized an excursion with some or all their children. Franklin and Almira were drawn to the small California Quaker community named "Whittier" after the Quaker poet and abolitionist, John Greenleaf Whittier. Although Whittier never visited the town and had no connection to it, the city fathers thought his name would lend an air of culture and piety. The Quaker church and schools, including Whittier Academy (which later became Whittier College), made the town an attractive location for a family raising their children in the faith.

By 1897 the Milhouses had moved west, although Franklin returned to Indiana twice a year for seven years to manage his Indiana nursery business. In Whittier, the Milhous family prospered. Our grandfather found the mild climate ideal for horticulture. He planted a citrus grove and took on responsibilities in the community and church. The children grew up in a happy home filled with religious teaching, music, and friendly social gatherings.

✌ CHAPTER 2 ✌
OPPOSITES ATTRACT

While our parents didn't disclose many details to us boys about their courtship and early life together, the story I heard Dad tell was this: As a bachelor living alone in California in 1907, Dad sought social events to attend. Single and in good shape, he wanted to find a young lady with whom to share his life. He soon discovered that in Whittier, the only place to meet people was at church. Although raised a Methodist, he would go to services at any church in those days. It did not matter to him as long as the congregation was friendly. One Sunday he decided to attend the Whittier Friends Church. Sitting in back of the auditorium, he surveyed the choir, where he spotted Jane Milhous. He thought, "Gee, that's a beautiful little lady." Impressed by her melodious voice and smiling eyes, he determined to learn more: Who was she and where did she live?

A friend in the congregation—a conductor Dad knew from the Pacific Electric Railway—told him, "There's going to be a Valentine's Day party at the church. You should come and meet all the Milhous girls."

Dad accepted the invitation. It was Hannah, Jane's older sister, who caught his eye at the party, however. He liked the fact that Hannah was taller and a bit more mature than Jane and decided she was the one worthy of his pursuit. And pursue, he did. Dad asked if he could walk her home, and she gladly accepted, enjoying the attention the handsome young man bestowed on her. Upon arrival at the Milhous home, he was invited in to meet all the family.

Dad fell in love with the whole Milhous clan, and somehow they tolerated his rough Appalachian ways and very outspoken manner. As the courtship progressed, Mom's parents became concerned, however. Hannah hadn't yet finished college, and Frank was a Methodist. It was an unspoken assumption that a Quaker would marry a Quaker if the tenets of the faith were to prevail in the relationship. Mom's sisters didn't consider Frank a worthy match for Hannah and tried to discourage the relationship. They argued that he lacked the educational and social standing of the Milhous family.

Nevertheless, despite Frank's shortcomings, love won out in a true case of "opposites attract," and Hannah accepted his marriage proposal. On his part, Dad eventually yielded to the friendly persuasion of the Milhous family and joined the Friends church by his own decision, of course; Quakers would never force their beliefs on anyone.

Dad and Mom wed on Thursday evening, June 25, 1908, only four months after they met. The Reverend Lewis Hadley, Mom's uncle, officiated at the ceremony at the East Whittier Club House attended by about 130 relatives and friends. Hannah's brother Ezra was the best man, and her sisters Edith, Jane, and Elizabeth sang a musical prelude and played the piano. Eight bridesmaids carried a chain of daisies that formed a floral aisle through which Mom's father escorted her to her awaiting groom.

In the journalistic style of the day, the *Whittier News* printed an article titled "Milhous – Nixon, Brilliant Event." The reporter wrote:

> The bride was handsomely gowned in white organdy and wore a veil and carried a shower bouquet of Shasta daisies. She is a young woman of charming personality and has made an excellent record as a student in Whittier college, while the groom is a successful young business man of high ideals.[8]

---

8 Excerpted from a retyped *Whittier News* article dated June 26, 1908.

Frank and Hannah Nixon's wedding photo, 1908

∻Family album

Dad and Mom's marriage, however, was not greeted with enthusiasm by all the relatives. A well-known family story tells of Olive, Mom's youngest sister, taking a paring knife and carving "Hannah is a bad girl" on the trunk of the backyard pepper tree on the very day of the wedding.

Our parents left on a six-week honeymoon by train to Ohio, Virginia, and back. Dad said their trip cost about two hundred dollars. Besides tithing to the church, he had developed a savings plan in which he tithed to himself, so to speak. For every ten dollars he earned, he would set aside a dollar, slipping it into a special fold in his wallet until the bills no longer fit; then he traded them for higher denominations. By the time he married, he had saved nine hundred dollars. The first money he spent from his savings paid for their honeymoon.

Dad wanted Mom to meet his father and family and to show her where he grew up. Because his father was in failing health, Dad felt that might be their last opportunity to visit him. Samuel Brady Nixon was living in Swan Township, Vinton County, with his second wife Lutheria, their sixteen-year-old son Hugh, and Dad's twenty-five-year-old brother Ernest, a schoolteacher.

When introduced to Mom, Lutheria, an opinionated lady, stated, "I don't like the name 'Hannah.' Here you will be called 'Mildred.'" So, all my Nixon cousins knew Mom as "Aunt Mildred," while my Milhous cousins called her "Aunt Hannah." Mom didn't mind. She would answer to either name.[9]

Returning to California with surplus from Dad's savings, the couple temporarily stayed at the Franklin Milhous home. Dad then went to work as a field hand at the Jordan Ranch east of Whittier. Harley Jordan provided room and board for his employees. Dad and Mom's first house was small and simple, quite a contrast to the spacious homes of her youth. Dad couldn't make enough to support them at that job, so with the help of his father-in-law and his own sweat equity, our parents bought into a new orange grove near Lindsay, California, about sixty miles north of Bakersfield.

---

9   Some time after Sam Nixon died of influenza on April 14, 1914, his widow Lutheria married W. V. Marshburn, father of Rose Olive's husband Oscar, who had lost his first wife. So, we had an unusual second marriage between the Nixon and the Milhous clans. Thus, Dad's stepmother became known to my siblings and me as "Grandmother Marshburn." When she was in a nursing home in Fullerton, California, in her later years, Mother visited her regularly, taking me along.

Frank and Hannah's visit to Sam and Lutheria's in Ohio, 1908
(Standing l-r) Hannah, Frank, and Walter Nixon; Merrill and his
father George Wildermuth; Ernest and Hugh Nixon
(Seated) Lutheria and Sam Nixon and Carrie Nixon Wildermuth

~Family album

I remember Dad complaining about the Ridge Route between Bakersfield and Los Angeles, a rutted dirt road before construction of the original Highway 99. Everyone dreaded the Ridge Route. Travelers couldn't run their horses along it, and they had to pack plenty of water, because sometimes the usual watering holes ran dry. Without modern communication systems or paved roads, the Milhous clan split into the Lindsay branch and the Whittier branch. Attending reunions in either location was an agonizingly slow process for those traveling long distances.

Dad and Mom soon realized that high hopes and hard work were not enough to make a living in Lindsay. Young citrus trees need a few years to mature before they produce a positive cash flow. The hard life must have been a strain on them all. Coupled with the isolation they felt in Lindsay and the difficulties of farming an immature orchard, Dad and Mom decided to return to Southern California. Besides, a new addition would soon be born to their family, so Mom welcomed the opportunity to live with her parents for a while.

On June 1, 1909, Mom and Dad's first son, Harold Samuel, was born at the Milhous home in East Whittier. The 1910 U.S. Census shows Francis A., a citrus farmer, Hanna (sic) M., his wife, and H. Samuel Nixon, their son, living in Los Nietos Township, East Whittier Precinct. The town of Los Nietos primarily served as a Mexican village housing workers for the orange groves.

Dad and Mom moved back to the San Joaquin Valley, so Dad could continue working on citrus ranches until he could find a more promising and agreeable situation. Later in 1910, they bought property fifteen miles southeast of Whittier in Yorba Linda, hoping to gain financial independence and set down roots once and for all.

José Yorba and his Spanish expedition had explored the area in 1769. It then became part of a Mexican land grant to Bernardo Yorba in the early 1800s. Jacob Sterns, a Fullerton realtor, purchased the land and then in 1907 sold it to the Janss Corporation of Los Angeles, which subdivided the property into lots under the name of Janss Investment Company. Their poster advertised "Yorba Linda Orange Land, The Best Proposition in California Today ... Choice Ranches

$250 Per Acre and Up."[10] They promised abundant water and a deep, rich soil—a stretch of the truth—but the land was cheaper than property in the Whittier area where land speculation, development, and the prospering citrus industry had inflated prices.

Yorba Linda attracted Quakers because property deeds prohibited the sale of alcohol within the community. My parents would have disagreed with historian Stephen Ambrose, who claimed the Quakers in Yorba Linda had nothing to do because the town lacked liquor establishments.[11] In those days, people had plenty to do with raising families, earning a living, and attending church socials. Recreation involved creative activities such as playing musical instruments, singing, and participating in inventive games designed to exercise the mind and body.

In 1912, my parents were among the earliest settlers in Yorba Linda. Grandfather Milhous again helped the struggling young family by setting them up with lemon trees on just over eight acres of barren land. Dad built a 900-square foot, two-story frame house on the property from a mail order catalog of plans. Some have speculated that he used a Sears or Montgomery Ward kit, but research has discounted those theories. Wherever it came from, Mother was delighted finally to have a place of her own, humble though it was.

When Dad built the house, Yorba Linda had no sewer or gas lines, electricity, or municipal water system. So, their original house lacked indoor plumbing. Mom had to hand pump water from the well to the kitchen. She cooked on a distillate stove, which used a liquid fuel such as kerosene—probably similar to a Coleman or white gas camping stove of today. Lighting the stove first required pressurizing it. Mom stored the produce in a "California Cooler," a cupboard on the north side of the kitchen with a screened opening to the earth beneath the house.

On warm summer days, a driver from the ice house in Fullerton delivered ice for the family's icebox. In the early days, workers harvested ice from Lake Arrowhead or possibly Big Bear Lake in

---

10 "A Brief History of Yorba Linda," *City of Yorba Linda* <http://www.ci.yorba-linda.ca.us/history.asp> accessed 27 April 2005.

11 Stephen Ambrose, *Nixon: The Education of a Politician 1913-1962* (New York: Simon and Schuster, 1987) 19.

winter and hauled it in large wagons to the ice house, where it was stored under straw, a good insulator. Mom would leave a sign in the window saying how much she needed—25, 50, or 100 pounds. If no one was home, the iceman would come in and place a large block in the upper compartment.

During the five years the trees were maturing, Dad had to do odd jobs to support his young family. In Yorba Linda, he gained a reputation as a builder and as someone people could rely on for help. Dad did such a good job erecting his fireplace that neighbors began asking him to build theirs too. As a volunteer, he helped construct the Friends meetinghouse, the first church in Yorba Linda. One of his contributions was the steeple, an architectural feature that did not please the more traditional Quakers visiting from the East.

Theodore Stanley, a Quaker from Ohio, objected to the Yorba Linda steeple as an "unwelcome sign of 'worldliness.'"[12] He was also alarmed to discover the church had an organ and a paid minister who preached. Even singing was considered too worldly for some of the more traditional Friends. The older Quaker ways were still practiced in some parts of the country, but over the years, Californians had developed a reputation for their willingness to try new methods at the expense of old traditions, and the Quakers of Yorba Linda were no exception.

To supplement the family income, Mother worked at a fruit packing plant and cannery in La Habra, about five miles west, close to an hour's ride on a buckboard with a fast horse. Years later, I asked her, "How can you peel peaches so fast without cutting your finger or making a mess?"

She said, "I've had a lot of practice."

I marveled at her prowess. Without automation in those days, she must have worked her fingers to the bone in those packing plants.

On the night of January 9, 1913, one of the coldest on record, Mother went into labor in their small alcove bedroom. Grandmother Almira tended to young Harold while Henrietta Shockney, a registered nurse, helped the doctor deliver Richard, the only son born in the family home in Yorba Linda. Meanwhile, Dad divided his time

---

12 Joseph Dmohowski, "From A Common Ground: The Quaker Heritage of Jessamyn West and Richard Nixon," *California History*, Fall 1994, 219.

The House Dad Built in Yorba Linda, CA [Photo taken in 1950]

~Don Nixon collection

Harold and Dick in pumpkin patch, Yorba Linda, 1914

~Family album

between operating the stove and fireplace to keep the bedroom warm and trying to keep their young lemon trees from freezing. According to Dad, his second son entered the world that evening with a powerful set of lungs and abundant black hair.

While the family was living in Yorba Linda, two more sons joined the family: Francis Donald "Don" on November 23, 1914, born at the Milhous home in Whittier, and Arthur Burdg, born on May 26, 1918, in a Yorba Linda hospital. Except for Don, named "Francis" after our father, all of us brothers acquired names of early kings of England.

Although the family sometimes didn't have enough to eat, my brothers remembered their childhood in Yorba Linda with fondness. Dick considered the town an ideal place for young boys in those days. A big attraction was the nearby irrigation canal, the Anaheim Union Water Ditch, fed by the Santa Ana River. My brothers and their friends swam in it, much to the worry of our parents, and rightly so because children had drowned there. Even Dick, who rarely got in trouble, was disciplined for taking a dip in that irresistible ditch.

Both Dad and Mom involved themselves in the close-knit Yorba Linda community, which numbered about two hundred people the year of Dick's birth. One of Dad's favorite volunteer activities was teaching Sunday school, because he saw the importance of influencing young people to live godly, worthwhile lives. Jessamyn wrote:

> Frank was not only the best Sunday school teacher I ever had, he was just about the best teacher. Frank had that prime requisite for teaching: great enthusiasm for his subject; and he aroused enthusiasm in his pupils to match. Frank was, as they now say, "with it." He related his Sunday school lessons to life about us, to politics, local and national. His class was so popular it overflowed the space allotted to it and if I could have attended it a few more years, I think I might have become a fair stateswoman myself.[13]

In turn, Dick used to say that Jessamyn's father, Eldo West, a quiet, reflective man, was his best Sunday school teacher. Eldo was the first to recognize that Dick had leadership potential, and he predicted

---

13 Quoted in Dmohowski 221.

Nixon brothers in Yorba Linda, 1922
Donald (in the tire), Richard, Harold, and Arthur

∽Family album

that one day he would be President. Unlike our father, he lived to vote for Dick in 1968 and saw him elected.

Jessamyn turned out to be more liberal-minded than Dick and loved to joke about it. She wrote to me:

> I'll tell you a funny story. Ted Weeks, former editor of the *Atlantic Monthly*, was and is a Violent Democrat. He asked me if I knew Richard. I said, 'Yes, his father was my Sunday school teacher. My father was his Sunday school teacher.' Without a minute's hesitation and with a deep growl, Weeks said, 'Well, all I've got to say is that his father was a hell of a lot better Sunday school teacher than your father.' This always makes my father laugh.

Maybe the difference between the approaches of our fathers was Frank being forcefully convincing as opposed to Eldo being quietly persuasive. I don't know what Dad would have said about that, but I know how he taught: He assigned a reading and then led a rousing discussion on the topic the next Sunday, relating the Bible stories to life and especially to politics. Teaching with zeal, Dad aimed to shape lives through his lessons.

The Nineteenth Amendment giving women the right to vote didn't pass until 1920, but that didn't prevent the women of Yorba Linda, including our mother, from participating in civic affairs. Mom became a charter member of the Yorba Linda Federation of Women, which is still in existence. In 1912, she and the other club members worked to bring electric power to the town and to establish a public park. Dick was the first baby born to a member of the federation.

Although Dad and Mom had woven a place for themselves in the fabric of Yorba Linda, making a living as citrus farmers proved too difficult. In those days, two problems hindered farming in the area: weather and soil. Located at the mouth of the Santa Ana Canyon, Yorba Linda was blasted by cold north winds blowing off the desert in winter, sometimes freezing the citrus crops in their path. Before the days of weather forecasting and radio broadcasts by the California Fruit Frost Service, farmers couldn't predict "smudge-pot weather tonight."

And unlike owners of large ranches who could afford to hire ranch hands to protect their trees, small .farmers like Dad always suffered the plight of inadequate resources to survive severe weather. Our father probably hired some help, but not the live-in type that could set out smudge pots and maintain them on cold nights. Those devastating Santa Ana winds, however, did not pose a problem once they reached the broader basin in western Los Angeles County, by which time they had spread and warmed, making the climate in Whittier more consistently moderate than in Yorba Linda.

Smudge pot
∾Courtesy of Craig Peterson

In contrast to the exaggerated claims of the Janss Corporation, the soil in Yorba Linda was porous, and the clay subsoil did not drain well, making it unsuitable for citrus trees unless they were well fertilized. Dad refused to go into debt to buy expensive fertilizer, so the trees suffered, along with the family finances. His decision was not so much a general aversion to risk but a way to avoid what he considered a foolhardy gamble.

In early 1922, the final straw occurred for our father when temperatures plummeted so low during a cold wind that all the lemon trees froze. He said, "Let's not fight it anymore. It's time to leave the citrus farming business and move to Whittier." I'm sure Grandfather Milhous also had advised Dad and Mom to move back to the warmer side in Whittier and try something different.

Dad sold a portion of the Yorba Linda property to a family by the name of Friends. Later the Yorba Linda School District purchased the last five and a half acres, and Jack Waldron, the school custodian, and his family lived there.

Meanwhile our parents bought an acre of land on Whittier Boulevard half way between Whittier and La Habra. The Boulevard occupied a section along Father Junípero Serra's trail called "El Camino Real," or "The King's Highway," connecting his chain of eighteenth century missions.

Our father foresaw the automobile being the wave of the future, so he built a two-pump gas station, the only one for miles around. On the property, he also built a small home and garage with a room above it for my brothers. Later he added a store named "F.A. Nixon—General Merchandise." The family business proved to be a more reliable source of income and certainly more profitable than his farming ventures.

As a young teenager, Harold began to suffer from respiratory ailments. An active boy, he hated to curtail his outdoor activities because of poor health. When he couldn't participate in his brothers' games, he sometimes would sit in a chair outside wearing his bathrobe and watch them play. The doctor finally diagnosed his illness as early-stage tuberculosis.

Then tragedy struck our family in the summer of 1925. Seven-year-old Arthur, whom my family described as a loving but shy boy, suddenly became very ill. Initially my parents didn't realize the seriousness of his condition. On August 10, he died from either tubercular encephalitis or meningitis, known in those days as "sleeping sickness." The same bacterium caused the dreaded and often fatal tuberculosis.

Dad blamed himself for Arthur's death, thinking God had punished him for selling groceries and pumping gas on Sundays. After losing his son, he put an end to Sunday sales and began to pour more of his energy into revivalism. Mother's great faith helped her accept his death with courage. She drew comfort from her belief that God had a plan for each person, difficult as it was to understand His purpose in calling home one so young. Mom felt guilty for having had to work long hours in the store, which kept her from spending more time with her son.

No one knew for sure how Harold and Arthur contracted their diseases. Even Dick and Don had related symptoms. Dick came down with undulant fever, possibly from bacteria-contaminated milk, and Don had a pulmonary shadow, but they both recovered. The raw milk from the family cow that Dad had bought in 1922 could have transmitted the bacterium, because bovine TB is one of the major types of tuberculosis. Doctors advised our parents to have the cow tested for disease, but they never did. Our father believed raw milk was healthier than pasteurized. Pasteurization, he thought, destroyed essential nutrients, or some such nonsense. In fact, it might have saved the lives of two of his sons.

Then in the fall of 1926, Dad and Mom sent Harold, who was in remission from TB, to the Mount Hermon School for Boys in Gill, Massachusetts, because they had worried about him having too much fun with the wrong crowd at Whittier High School and letting his grades slip. He never immersed himself in his studies as Dick did.

In 1881, evangelist Dwight L. Moody had founded the Mount Hermon School to provide a strong classical Christian education to children whose parents could not afford the tuition of private East Coast preparatory schools. The school appealed to our parents because of its emphasis on Bible study and its stern discipline. The boys started their days with a cold shower at 5:30 in the morning. By April 1927, Harold was so sick that he returned from Massachusetts with a full-blown case of TB. Mother blamed herself for having sent Harold away, fearing the cold showers caused the return of his illness. The showers most likely did aggravate his preexisting condition.

Prior to the development of antibiotics, doctors prescribed bed rest and fresh, dry air as the treatment of choice for TB, but Harold failed to cooperate. Instead, he made great efforts to live life normally and to enjoy it to the fullest. He wouldn't rest until his energy flagged. As the disease entered the secondary stage, however, he had no choice but to limit his activities. Harold and the family realized he was sick and becoming sicker; they feared he, too, would die.

Mom and Dad made great sacrifices for Harold, doing everything possible in a desperate attempt to prolong his life. Dad wouldn't accept public assistance, so first they took him to private facilities in Southern California. Harold came home briefly in 1928, but when his condition worsened that spring, Dad and Mom drove him to Prescott, Arizona, on the doctor's advice. They all felt the good, clean air and dry climate of Prescott and the high elevation would improve his health. In that era, TB patients—"tuberculars" or "lungers" as they were called—and their families flocked to Prescott in search of a cure, or at least relief. Many people, in fact, did recover. The Prescott area boasted eight TB sanatoria, including the exclusive Pamsetgaaf, an acronym for *Pure Air, Maximum Sunshine, Equitable Temperature, Good Accommodations, and Food.*

Not able to afford the twenty-five to forty dollars a week at Pamsetgaaf, Mom and Dad decided she would rent a lunger bungalow in the hills on the west side of town and stay there with Harold. For an extended period, she cooked, cleaned for, and nursed three other tuberculars, as well as Harold, to help pay the twenty-five dollars monthly rent.

During Harold's and Mom's stay in Prescott, they lived in at least two but probably three locations. The historical record is unclear as to their exact whereabouts at all times. Some local historians believe they lived on Apache Drive in the Pine Crest District in 1928 and 1929.

With an altitude higher and supposedly healthier than downtown Prescott, the entire Pine Crest neighborhood had become a colony for tuberculars and their caretakers, often family members. Some patients, however, were cared for in one of the sanatoria in town while their families lived in Pine Crest. Because just about every household in the neighborhood was somehow affected by the awful disease, the neighbors developed a supportive community.

Mom, of course, made many friends and became known in the area for sharing her delicious home-baked cookies, pies, and cakes. Years later, Grace Geissensetter Foudy and Ted Edmundson, who were children in the late 1920s and early 1930s, each having a parent with TB, recalled their fond memories of my family in Prescott.

In those days, TB patients slept on screened-in porches, even during chilly winter nights. Doctors believed the crisp night air to be beneficial. But for Mom's patients, the disease had progressed beyond the point of air doing them any good. She watched with great sadness as one by one the men in her care succumbed.

The exact chronology of my family's movements is difficult to determine, but I believe Mother returned to Whittier around Christmas 1928. On March 16, 1929, Harold wrote a heart-wrenching

Arthur (on left) at his seventh birthday party, Whittier, May 1925
∾Family album

Harold, Whittier, c. 1925-1926
∾Family album

letter to Mom from Prescott, saying he missed her care and wanted to come home.

After wrestling with the decision, Mom concluded that Harold should stay in Prescott. In the spring of 1929, she returned there instead. While Harold and Mom lived in Prescott, my parents and brothers did the best they could to spend time together and to keep the business going. Occasionally, Mom traveled back and forth between Prescott and Whittier with Dad, Dick, and Don, who drove over on some weekends and during school holidays.

Dick and Don spent part of the summers of 1928 and 1929 in Prescott. The time was no vacation for Dick, who worked at whatever job he could find, including plucking and dressing chickens for a butcher shop and working as a janitor at a swimming pool. Don's photo collection included a picture postcard of the Frontier Days Rodeo where Dick also worked as a barker selling tickets to a sideshow. But in spite of the hard work and Harold's illness, Dick developed a fondness for Prescott and enjoyed the friends he made there and the hikes and horseback rides in the beautiful hills forested with ponderosa pines.

ᨠ CHAPTER 3 ᨡ

IMPROBABLE NEWS

Around the time of the 1929 stock market crash, Mom learned she was pregnant at age forty-four. A new baby would certainly complicate matters. The family was already stressed both financially and emotionally because of Harold's illness.

Dad reacted with shock and disbelief to the improbable news. "The doctor must have made a mistake!" When reality set in, they decided she couldn't continue caring for TB patients, so Mom left Harold in Prescott at the Clows Rest Home on Copper Basin Road. He lived in one of the six or so tubercular cabins surrounding the home of Marshall and Johanna Clow and their son Marshall, Jr. Harold and Charles H. Stuart, who undoubtedly suffered from TB as well, boarded with Merrill H. and Lena Prant, according to the 1930 U.S. Census.[14]

Mom returned to Whittier around Christmas 1929 to await my birth. By the time I arrived on May 3, 1930, Mom had turned forty-five and Dad was fifty-one.

My three oldest brothers had been born at home—Harold and Don at Grandmother's in Whittier and Dick in Yorba Linda—but

---

14 The 1930 U.S. Census for Prescott Justice Precinct, Prescott, Yavapai County, Arizona, erroneously lists Harold as "Charles" Nixon, but all the other identifying information is correct.

Clows Rest Home,
Prescott, AZ, c. 1930
✌Sharlot Hall Museum
Photo, Prescott, AZ

Dad and Eddie,
Whittier, 1930
✌Family album

Mom and Eddie, 1930
✌Family album

Mom decided that at her age a hospital delivery would be safer for both of us. In those days, women did not receive prenatal care, and childbirth was risky. Giving birth to four sons had already taken a toll on Mom physically, because all my brothers weighed over ten pounds—unusual by today's standards. In those days, fat babies were considered healthy babies. Dr. Raymond C. Thompson attended my birth at Murphy Memorial Hospital in Whittier. Not to be outdone by my brothers, I weighed in at a robust ten and a half pounds and measured twenty-one inches long.

After four boys, my parents had wanted and fully expected a girl, whom they planned to name "Patricia." Instead, they had to come up with a boy's name upon my arrival. True to their tradition of choosing the name of an English king, they selected "Edward," the name of seven prior monarchs. I've been told we descended from the three Plantagenet King Edwards, but I doubt our parents knew that. In addition, Edward, Prince of Wales, who became King Edward VIII in 1936, was the talk of the day at the time of my birth, and Mom told me Harold had suggested that name in case I turned out to be a boy. My parents never revealed to me why they gave me the middle name "Calvert."

Following the custom of those days, Dad had bought a baby-sized silver ring and sterling cup in anticipation of my birth. Seeing he had yet another son instead of his first daughter, he had the cup and ring engraved with a very ornate " $\mathcal{E}$ " rather than a " $\mathcal{P}$."

The record is unclear, but I believe Dick spent part of the summer of 1930 in Prescott keeping Harold company while Mom cared for me. Dick talked about living with the Marshall Clow family, and Theodore "Ted" Edmundson confirmed that memory. I imagine Harold had been terribly lonely without Mom, so having Dick nearby would have cheered him up. Ted, who was eight years old in 1930, remembers Dick as "a fun guy" who liked Mrs. Edmundson's chocolate cake and rode horses almost every day with his older brother Garland.[15]

In September 1930, Harold convinced Mom and Dad to let him come home to Whittier, where he stayed until 1932. When his condition worsened, he and Mom returned to Prescott. There she again

---

15 Theodore Edmundson, phone interview by Karen Olson, 25 June 2008.

cared for Harold and other TB patients in a four-room house in the Pine Crest District, I believe on Yavapai Drive. The electricity and indoor plumbing made life a little easier for the sick young men. Mom, of course, found it difficult to be away from her family in Whittier and to leave me in the care of others. She had an awful lot to juggle with a terminally ill son, a toddler, two teenagers, and a demanding husband, but she handled her obligations with characteristic grace, longsuffering, and determination.

During that time, Dad, Dick, and Don primarily raised me. When I was an infant, Harold "Hal" Schuyler, a neighbor boy about ten years old, came over and kept an eye on me when my dad and brothers couldn't. Many years later, he told me he had been my first babysitter. He probably tired of changing dirty diapers, so my cousin Alice Milhous, Uncle Ezra's third youngest of nine children, took over at some point.

Mom, Dick, and I spent time in Prescott with Harold in the summer of 1932 while Dad and Don held down the fort in Whittier. I vaguely remember at the age of two going to Prescott with my dad and brothers. Throwing snowballs during a late-season snowstorm was a new and exhilarating experience, and I've loved snow ever since. My other clear memory is of the big round boulders behind the house. Rocks impressed me even at that tender age.

My family described the fourteen-hour trips between Whittier and Prescott as grueling. Having no air conditioning in those days, they would set out about 10 p.m. to avoid the sweltering desert heat. Even at night, the air remained hot, so my family kept the wind blowing through open windows. On that twisting road, dust would fly everywhere, especially through our windows. I would sleep most of the way, but when Dad drove up the Oatman grade along Route 66 in the Black Mountains of western Arizona, I would invariably wake up. Then Dad would complain, "That dirt road's as bumpy as an old washboard!"

Later in 1932, our parents brought Harold home for the final time. I think he knew he wasn't going to survive. Homesick, he wanted to spend his remaining days with his entire family in Whittier, enjoying the time he had left. He even proposed to Edith Hudspeth, a young lady in Whittier whom Mom much admired. Our cousin

*Mom in the snow in
Prescott, c. 1928*
∾Sharlot Hall Museum
Photo, Prescott, AZ
Grace Geissensetter Photo
Collection

*Harold and Eddie,
Whittier, 1931*
∾Family album

Jessamyn noted that they were engaged, but Harold was gone before the wedding could take place. Later, Edith married Douglas Brannon, brother of Don's friend, Herman Brannon.

In August 1932, Jessamyn too received the dreaded diagnosis of terminal TB and was admitted to a sanatorium. But unlike Harold, she followed her doctor's instructions and stayed in bed—for ten long, agonizing years. During what she called her "horizontal years," Jessamyn wrote *The Friendly Persuasion*, developing her literary talent into a career as a famous novelist. I'm sure my family wondered whether Harold would have recovered if he had been as compliant a patient as Jessamyn.

~: ~

Later that year, I remember Harold bringing home a red scale-model racing car about ten inches long—vintage Indianapolis 500. He had borrowed it from a friendly store owner uptown just to show me. He rolled the little car across the floor, and, of course, I eagerly tried to grab it. But Harold said, "You can't play with that now. You must wait until you're a little older."

My introduction to delayed gratification was a disappointment. I never saw the car again.

Another early memory was of Harold swooping me up in his arms when he heard airplanes flying overhead. He would rush outside with me to watch them. Harold loved planes. Later, I heard he went on a tour with somebody in one of those old barnstormers and then convinced the pilot to give him flying lessons. He loved the thrill of adventure, living life to the fullest as long as he could.

Harold and Dick were very close, having gone through school together and working together in the family store. In spite of their differences, or perhaps because of them, Harold and Dick truly enjoyed each other's company. They were a good deal alike in initiative, enthusiasm, and facial features, although Harold had blond hair and blue eyes and more closely resembled Dad, while Dick took after Mom with his dark complexion.

But in talents and personality, they were a study in contrasts. Harold was mechanically gifted and was an irrepressible, spirited soul. He liked to play practical jokes, was wild about horses and rodeos, and loved to fly. And he loved the girls. Didn't like boys so much, unless they were willing to compete in some way, one of the few traits he and Dick shared.

Dick admired Harold greatly and looked up to him as the older brother. He described Harold in the vernacular of the day, saying, "He was a gay blade" (a dashing young man). Dick, on the other hand, was studious, serious, and shy by nature. A lady's man, he wasn't. Despite his innate intelligence, he preferred to engage the talents of others when faced with mechanical challenges.

While I have snapshot recollections of Harold alive and cheerful, I have no memories of his death or funeral. Mom and Dad probably shipped me out to the Marshburns to stay with my cousin Teddy, so I wouldn't be underfoot during that sad occasion.

Curious to know about Harold and Arthur when I was a little older, I asked Dick and Don about them, but they either kept silent or told me very little. "Those were hard times," Don said. "You should be glad you were too young to understand." On other subjects, he freely shared his opinions.

The full impact of Dick's loss of Harold's death did not hit me until Christmas 1966, when I spent the holiday with Dick and his family in New York. Dick and I, along with Pat, Tricia, and Julie, were enjoying a quiet evening in their apartment. While we were reminiscing, I asked him what he remembered about Harold.

After a long pause Dick said:

It's not easy but I'll try. As you know, Mom did all the baking of fresh pies and cakes for the store. Harold had recently heard of a new electric mixer that might lighten her workload. He decided we should buy one of those new gadgets for her birthday. The mixer cost thirty dollars, an unheard of price at the time, but Harold was convinced we should try to make her life a little easier. Somehow, we scraped the money together, and planned to buy the mixer when I returned home from school on Monday, the sixth of March. Harold was so sick that I suggested we wait, but he insisted. So I bundled him up, helped him into the car, and drove three miles to Whittier Hardware.

The next morning, as I stood in front of the bathroom mirror, one side of my face freshly shaven, the other side covered with lather, Harold appeared at the door, quite upset, and insisted I leave for school that minute.

"But I'm not ready," I protested.

"I don't care. I'm not feeling well and need the bathroom. Just leave. Get out of here."

So I left. I learned later that Harold had sent Don off to school in the very same manner.

At that point in the story, Dick's voice broke, and the rest of us sat in awed silence, wondering whether we should let him continue. We had no choice.

That day—March 7—was Harold's last, and he apparently knew. When the time came that morning, he walked downstairs and found Mom in the kitchen. He asked her to hold him, telling her that was the last time he would see her before she got to heaven. He died in her arms.

Later that evening, I gave Mom the mixer.

Dick had to excuse himself from the table. He still bore evidence of that tragedy thirty-three years later as he persisted in telling the story through everyone's tears.

↝ ↜

It was bad enough for Mom to lose a son, but to lose him on her birthday was an additional crushing blow, but she received comfort by focusing on the lessons God taught her in the midst of suffering—namely understanding and compassion. She felt it wrong to question God's will. One way Mom dealt with her grief was to help care for Jessamyn, who still suffered from TB. Jessamyn always loved Mom for showing her so much compassion and dedication during her time of need.

For our father, Harold's death almost caused his undoing. Previously he had lost his mother, sister, and Arthur to TB. Losing a second son was nearly too much for him to bear, but yet he realized life had to go on. He had to continue working to support the rest of his family. Work was his therapy, and he rededicated himself to Christianity. Feeling God had punished him again by taking Harold away, he renewed his commitment to revivalism. He would drive our family to Los Angeles to attend revival meetings led by well-known preachers such as Aimee Semple McPherson, a Pentecostal evangelist who emphasized faith healing, and "Fightin'" Bob Shuler, a Methodist minister who railed against alcohol consumption and corruption in high places. I could see how each of those preachers would have appealed to Dad.

Of course, Harold's death had a strong impact on Dick as well. Not only did he lose his best friend, but suddenly he was thrust into the role of eldest son. My parents turned to him for stability, Don looked to him for advice, and I regarded him as a second father figure. Dick felt a need to take care of everyone else, probably at the expense of taking care of himself, and he assumed more responsibilities at home, work, and school.

On March 10, 1933, just a few days after Harold's death, the ground started to rumble at 5:54 p.m. Dick picked me up. Not knowing the severity of the earthquake, he opened the door and we looked out at a strange scene—telephone wires and power lines dancing and poles wobbling back and forth. Safe in Dick's arms, I did not feel any of the rocking. He said, "Look outside! Look outside! We'll stand right here in the doorway to see what happens."

I watched, fascinated by the movement of the earth. Perhaps this display of nature's power piqued my interest in what would be my life's pursuit: geology. Of course, as a young child, I had no conception of the danger and destruction caused by the estimated 6.25- to 6.4-magnitude earthquake. One hundred twenty people lost their lives, mainly in unreinforced brick buildings that collapsed. More than $50 million in property damage occurred. [16]

Later, I heard the story about Dad and our next-door neighbor, Isaac "Slim" Craddick, driving to Long Beach to check on Mom's sister Jane Beeson, her husband Harold, and their family, who were living

---

16 "Long Beach Earthquake: 75th Anniversary," *Southern California Earthquake Center.* <http:www.scec.org/education/08-307longbeach.html> accessed 4 September 2008.

near the quake's epicenter. Mother was upset and concerned about their safety, so Dad and Slim got in the car, and Dad drove like a wild man to check on them.

Afterward he said, "We came to a wide crack in the highway and just jumped right across it." Good thing they didn't crack the wheels. Dad and Slim witnessed a lot of destruction along the way, but in Long Beach, they found the Beesons safe.

⌒ ⌒

Dick's graduation in 1934 near the top of his class at Whittier College led to a summer of big decisions. His application to Harvard fell by the wayside when the recently established Duke Law School in Durham, North Carolina, offered him a full scholarship. The Harvard prospect strongly appealed to Mom and Dad, but the financial challenge convinced Dick to accept the Duke offer. The money saved would allow Don to join Dick in North Carolina and attend Guilford College, a small liberal arts school founded by the Society of Friends in Greensboro, about fifty miles from Duke.

Thus, I watched two of the most important people in my life drive off to college in the fall of 1934, accompanied by Phil Martin, Dick's friend from Whittier College, who was going on to seminary in Pittsburgh. I would be without the companionship of my brothers until they returned in the summer of 1935. At that time, Don quit school, deciding he could be more usefully occupied at the family store. Determined to become a top-notch lawyer, Dick continued at Duke Law School until he graduated.

OUR FAMILY CULTURE

Every family has a culture that sets it apart—somewhat like a corporate culture. In our family, Dad, Mom, my brothers, and I were both kin and collaborators. As the top management, Dad and Mom imparted their guiding principles about family, faith, work, education, and politics, and they established the norms of behavior expected of us sons. They shared a strong work ethic, religious conviction, and passion for education. Yet they gave us the freedom to explore and develop our own very different personalities and talents.

Through all the years Dick, Don, and I spent with our parents, we never witnessed a serious disagreement that divided them on family matters. When one gave a directive, the other agreed, and we knew the final word had been spoken. Both of them were disciplinarians but with different methods of enforcement. Although they took great pride in us, they were also our severest critics.

My brothers and I learned at an early age that we had to respect our parents, teachers, and other adults. We Nixon boys had to address adults by "Mr.," "Mrs.," or "Miss" as a matter of respect, even though Quakers, including children, traditionally shunned honorifics. First name familiarity in dialog might be heard among contemporaries, but our parents taught that seniority always called for formal recognition.

Mother earned a reputation as an extraordinary lady. Dick called her a saint, and so did Dr. Billy Graham when he delivered a eulogy at her funeral. Life must have been very hard for her, but she never focused on her own sorrows. She grieved for everyone in their times of grief, but only at the death of close family and friends did she display her emotions. She personified compassion—always kind and very sensitive to others' feelings. To anyone in distress, Mom would offer assistance. As a great people handler in the best sense of the term, she would carefully weigh the effect of her words, never fanning the flames of a disagreement or perpetuating an argument. And she had the patience of Job—a tremendous asset in raising five sons.

Some writers have pitied Hannah Nixon as being a weak woman dominated by an overbearing husband, but that was far from the case. Mom exhibited much strength of character, and Dad was devoted to her. In her own quiet way, she had a remarkable ability to state her point and to gain agreement—even from Dad.

Unlike Mom, Dad was opinionated and vociferous, but he tolerated others' views—as long as he had a chance to express his own and to try to correct theirs. Some psychobabble authors, though, have made far too much of his boisterous character and quick temper, painting him as an angry, abusive father who psychologically and physically damaged his sons. "That is why Richard Nixon turned out the way he did," they claim.

That's pure nonsense. Dad was no tyrant and shouldn't be judged by current-day standards; corporal punishment was the norm when Dad and his sons were growing up. Like many fathers, he would swat his sons with his hand or a strap. I think he regretted that later, but he always administered justice swiftly and fairly, never doing anything permanently deleterious to our backsides or to our young psyches. With his admonitions to "Wake up, stand up straight, and do it right," he was trying to get our attention, and he certainly did. Boys can be pretty mischievous, and his sons were no exception. My brothers and I got into mischief as if it were our second nature.

Dick and I didn't challenge Dad like Harold and Don did, however. Being more argumentative, they would engage Dad in verbal battle. Dick took after Mom in his desire to avoid unpleasant confrontations. His attitude was, "Take responsibility and support the Old Man." As he grew, Dick spent much of his time studying and tending to his chores, rather than getting into trouble. He and I weren't on the receiving end of much of Dad's discipline. Mom's look was enough to keep us in line.

Most of my punishments consisted of solitary confinement in my room to give me time to ponder my infraction or failure to perform a duty. I must admit that my times of seclusion often included recesses out my window before my parents viewed me emerging repentant from my room.

Although Dad was a no-nonsense kind of guy, he had a more overt sense of humor than Mom. He could tell amusing stories better than anyone I knew. His great memory for details and talent for achieving whatever reaction he sought made him the center of attraction at family reunions and other gatherings.

Another memory is of Dad lighting our natural gas hot water heater by hand. More than once, he singed all the hair on his head when the heater backfired. However, he seldom complained. Even when Slim Craddick kidded him about "shaving" his eyebrows, he would respond, "My natural gas heater's a whole lot better than trying to heat my bath water in a five-gallon can on top of the stove, and five gallons ain't enough anyway!"

No one could match Dad's determination. Once he started a project, he just wasn't happy until he finished it. One time he and his brother Walter completed a house—foundation, framing, plumbing, wiring, insulation, roof, everything—in one month. The house then served as a rental for new residents joining the growing community of Whittier.

Although the family business occupied much of Dad's time, he still maintained an intimate involvement in our community. In the 1930s, community spirit was rampant in Whittier; everyone pitched in, especially Dad. Whenever anyone needed help, he was available and eager to share his solution.

Dad took a keen interest in the goings-on in town. By the mid-1930s, the population had grown to a point that people worried whether fresh water supplies would be sufficient for the future. Accordingly, Dad became excited about the new well for the city on the Murphy Ranch north of Whittier Boulevard. I'm not sure whether he helped dig the well, or whether he was just an avid spectator offering all kinds of advice. When the drilling proved successful, Dad exclaimed, "They've got a good one. Water is just gushing out!" He was so pleased, you would have thought they had struck oil.

⌣ ⌣

As is true with most boys, my brothers and I expressed our affection for each other in a matter-of-fact manner by kidding around and doing things together. Dick and Don were always very close and seemed to share a special understanding, although their natures sharply contrasted—Dick taking after Mom and Don taking after Dad. Being so much younger, I couldn't participate in a lot of their activities, but they made an effort to include me whenever possible. I never felt neglected, and I never experienced or witnessed sibling rivalry.

Don and I learned to think of Dad and Mom as the executive and legislative branches of our family and Dick as the judicial. Because he was the natural mediator in any family disagreement, we looked to Dick for advice. He had the rare ability of being able to settle an argument without indulging any personal opinion of his own. He could make an objective decision without seeming to take sides. And he did it without causing resentment.

I remember Don recalling an incident that had made him angry, because he felt Dick had wronged him. He never told me any details of the alleged affront, but I could visualize the scene. Having a quick and vocal temper like Dad, Don vented his wrath on Dick for several minutes. Dick listened calmly, never saying a word until Don had finished. Then, while Don sat in surprised silence, Dick carefully and calmly listed what seemed like dozens of events leading up to the incident. He cited specific times, places, and dates for each example and quietly closed the conversation. When it was over, Don had no choice but to agree with Dick's summary. It's no wonder he became a lawyer.

I think Dick's appreciation of a challenge must have come from Dad; he had that same determination and never-give-up spirit. During my childhood, I heard about the time Miss Ernsberger, Dick's geometry teacher at Fullerton High School, presented the class with an advanced problem and announced that if anyone came up with the answer before the next class period, that student could count on an automatic "A" in the subject. Dick never got very excited about math and had been struggling to earn a "B," but the teacher's challenge motivated him to give the subject full attention. He went home that night determined to solve the problem. He wouldn't go to bed until he came up with the answer. Finally having an inspiration close to 4 a.m., he arrived at the solution. The surprised Miss Ernsberger awarded Dick the promised "A." He was the only one in the class to solve the problem.

We all had chores to do at home as well as at the store. With his husky build, Don was well suited for heavy-lifting jobs and voluntarily assumed his duties outside the house. Of course, lots of dishes had to be washed, and we had no dishwashers in those days except for the human kind. Mom assigned that chore to Dick. Even though he didn't mind washing dishes, being seen doing "woman's work" embarrassed him. In those days, gender roles were still well defined. To protect his male image, Dick would pull down the blinds, so the other kids couldn't see him washing dishes.

Attitudes had changed by the time I was old enough to do chores. I didn't experience any stigma doing so-called "girls' work." Whether the shades were pulled down or not, I had to wash dishes, and I didn't care who saw me.

Dick and Don generally played football or baseball with friends and relatives after school and then helped Mom and Dad close the store in the evenings. What Dick lacked in athletic talent, he made up for in unrelenting willpower. In sports, he stressed abiding by the rules—strictly. Uncle Oscar Marshburn told a story of our heftier cousins ignoring the rules one day during a football game. Dick took the ball and sat on it. He wouldn't get up until they agreed to play by the rules.

My brothers would sometimes bring football teammates home for dinner, and the boys always found an unlimited supply of food at that particular training table. If Mom thought she might run out of food, one of the boys could solve her problem with the turn of a key at Nixon's Market.

A constant stream of dogs and cats found residence at our home, much to the delight of my brothers and me. The first dog I remember was Duke, Harold's huge German shepherd. Being so young, my memory of him is faint, but I know Harold really got a kick out of that dog, teaching him to perform many tricks. The whole family loved Duke. My favorite dog—and maybe Dick's too—was King, perhaps the largest Irish setter I've ever seen. Although not as clever as Duke, King had a natural ability to point. We also had a number of small dogs, but, in the days before dog leash laws, they were no match for the cars on Whittier Boulevard. I liked the cute little kittens, but Don thought cats should be left in the yard to catch mice. Dogs definitely prevailed at our house. They could come inside, although Mom preferred they stay outdoors. Dad tolerated them—indoors or out.

GRANDMOTHER AND OUR EXTENDED FAMILY

My brothers and I had the privilege of growing up in a close-knit, supportive family— extended as well as immediate. Both our Milhous and Nixon relatives stressed the importance of spending time together, and they visited often. All of us children had the advantage of many eyes watching over us and giving input regarding acceptable behavior.

Our beloved Grandmother Milhous—Almira, or "Allie," as some of her contemporaries called her—was the only grandparent I ever

Mom, Eddie, Grandmother Almira, Cousin Priscilla Timberlake
Second birthday picnic, 1932

∽Family album

King, Nixon family dog,
c. 1938

∽Family album

knew. Our family viewed her as a strong matriarch and a very special lady. I remember her management style being rather stern, but without threats. She would explain that her admonitions were guidelines to help us avoid injuries to both body and mind.

Among her thirty-two grandchildren, Grandmother displayed an understandable inability to remember all our names. She simply called for attention by saying something like, "Now, Petit (pronounced "petty"), thee needs to mind thy manners and be kind to one another!" She reserved "Petit" as a term of endearment for her grandchildren. I really had no idea what it meant, but there was never any question as to whom she was addressing.

My parents used to drop me off at Grandmother's house to play with my cousins. Aunt Olive, Uncle Oscar, and their children, Hadley, Howard, Marygene, and Ted, lived with her in the old Milhous homestead. Grandmother had the bedroom on the main floor in the back corner with an adjacent bathroom. The Marshburns occupied the bedrooms upstairs.

Following Quaker custom, my relatives always left their front door unlocked. They didn't fear people stealing their earthly possessions. Anything they had was free for the taking.

One day when I was three or four years old, my parents left me at the Marshburns. I opened their door and wandered around, calling for my cousins. As usual, my parents had not checked to see whether anyone was there, because someone was always home. But not that time. Frightened to find myself alone in the big house, I cried myself to sleep on the sofa, where Grandmother and my aunt and uncle found me when they returned.

∾ ∾

Famous for her hospitality, Grandmother made her home a place of peace, love, and good cheer. Making the most of every situation, she often reminded us to live expectantly. She demonstrated her reverence for life in everyday acts of kindness to both people and animals.

One morning after staying overnight with my Marshburn cousins, I found Grandmother at the kitchen sink holding a partially cracked chicken egg. I didn't realize it was in the process of hatching. I asked if I could help her, but she said, "No, Petit, I just want to help it live. The little chick is struggling and seems to be too weak to break out."

After Grandmother carefully removed all the shell, the fragile little chick emerged and survived, much to my surprise. Witnessing Grandmother's frequent displays of such concern more than proved her deep love for all God's creatures. She imprinted her sense of humanity on all of us.

Having inherited her father Oliver's fondness for farm animals, especially horses, Grandmother still preferred horse and buggy to modern horsepower. I remember her cow named "Bossy." With the help of Uncle Oscar, she provided the family with fresh milk. The dog Tippy, a true pet, loved to announce the arrival of visitors. The cats did their duty by maintaining a low mice population.

❧ ❧

As an ardent supporter of the Women's Christian Temperance Union, "W.C.T.U.," Grandmother displayed their sign in her front yard along the highway. "Alcohol just doesn't fit anywhere in any human life and shouldn't be tolerated except to sterilize wounds," she would say.

Dad agreed with her on that subject. He perpetually argued with Raymond "Ray" Aldrich, whose daughter Sue was my grammar school classmate. Next door to his little house, Mr. Aldrich owned a small tavern. Its location half a block from our home and market and across the street from the East Whittier Friends Church did not sit well with Dad or the W.C.T.U. ladies of the church, including Grandmother. Of course, Mr. Aldrich had every right to use his property as he did. Selling alcohol was not illegal, just undesirable in that particular location according to Dad, Grandmother, and the W.C.T.U. Despite their protests, Mr. Aldrich's business remained in operation.

Harold, Dick, and Don were exposed to the freewheeling ways of some of our neighbors and others in the community, and many of us Milhous grandchildren abandoned the total abstinence of our upbringing as we grew and went away. Nevertheless, as adults we saw the wisdom of Grandmother's strong beliefs and appreciated the need to avoid the excesses of "modern" society.

Grandmother loved to write poems and admired great poetry and great literature. It was such a part of her life that she even thought poetically. As secretary of the W.C.T.U., she wrote the minutes in rhyme. Letters to her children took the form of poems. For her, family events needed to be recorded in verse, such as this one written on April 16, 1929, which would have been the fiftieth anniversary of her marriage to Grandfather Franklin, who died in 1919.

OUR WEDDING DAY

The sixteenth day of April, was our wedding day.
Just fifty years ago now, we our wedding vows did say.
In old Grove Church, near the tall beech trees.
Any eye, a setting like that, should please.

After the marriage rites were over, the Minister set his seal,
Pronounced us a wedded pair, love in his prayer we could feel.
Then we journeyed to the Burdg home, a few rods from the door
Where a company was gathered, numbers nearing four score.
There was a sumptuous wedding dinner, and a table long indeed
Filled with the best of eats a plenty, all the guests to feed.[17]

Family gatherings and sumptuous dinners were among my strongest childhood memories. Grandmother organized every Christmas event. At these very popular reunions, all her children and grandchildren would assemble in her home in Whittier. Her seven children, two stepchildren, thirty-two grandchildren, plus a few great-grandchildren, many in-laws, and friends came from all over the Los Angeles Basin and towns as far away as Lindsay and Bakersfield in the Great Central Valley. Because my brothers were so much older, I considered her youngest grandchildren more like brothers and sisters to me than first cousins. We always enjoyed getting together.

Grandmother and the Marshburns attractively decorated their home at Christmastime. In the bay window of the living room, right next to her chair, stood an eight-foot tree almost touching the ceiling—but with just room enough for the treetop angel. Some of the more traditional Quakers disputed the appropriateness of displaying an angel, questioning whether visual representations should be made of spiritual beings, but our religion also left room for individual

---

17 Price 106.

conscience. I can't remember Grandmother, or anyone else in our family, having a religious problem with that angel. It always adorned the treetop.

Everyone brought Christmas gifts, and Grandmother always received the most, but the gifts were not lavish. The spiritual meaning of Christmas took precedence over the material. Grandmother made sure we were all aware that the purpose of the celebration was to reflect on the birth of Christ. Until her eyesight began to fail, she would read a passage from the Bible at every Christmas gathering. When she could no longer see the small print, she assigned the reading to someone else.

Christmas dinners were a sight to behold; partaking of them was even better. The Milhous women, all exceptional cooks, produced an amazing array of wholesome main dishes and irresistible desserts. All the women contributed to the dinner, cooking the food from scratch at their homes and then bringing it to the family gathering at Grandmother's house. With such a big crowd, the challenge was how to heat everything that needed to be served warm.

Someone would bring a big ham and another would contribute a turkey. Even Dad participated by supplying a beef pot roast, one of his favorite foods. He would start cooking it on low heat in the early morning, adding carrots and other vegetables to the big, flat roasting pan. We kids appreciated the candied yams because they were sweet, and of course, we had to have lots of fresh vegetables, some of it homegrown and, of course, organic.

The women always displayed a mouth-watering array of home-baked pies. I remember them discussing how to make flaky crust. Mother, who baked for the Nixon store, was known for her fabulous pies, but all the aunts in our family had learned the skills required for perfect pies. Their technique for making piecrust had been handed down from their mother. Mom and all her sisters made it the same way. Mass production bakeries and their client restaurants today can never afford to match the age-old manual techniques perfected in the nineteenth century.

Dick would rave about Aunt Olive's delicious specialty—loquat pie. The *loquat japonica*, or Japanese plum, is a marvelous little yellow fruit. A loquat tree grew right outside Grandmother's back door.

Grandmother Almira Milhous at 90

∾Family album

Because it bloomed around Christmastime with the fruit ripening in spring, Aunt Olive would can some of it for her Christmas pies.

After dinner as many as could fit rotated through the kitchen, scullery, and pantry to begin cleaning up over one hundred dinner plates and whatnot. Nevertheless, after the guests left, the Marshburns always had much more to do just to resume their daily routines.

Following Christmas dinner, everyone who had taken music lessons, including Dick, was kindly persuaded to play his or her best or favorite piece. Aunt Jane, the most accomplished female musician in the family, entertained us on the piano, and we all sang Christmas carols to her accompaniment. Uncle Griffith tried his best to get me up to speed on the piano, so I could play something at the Christmas recitals, but I didn't practice enough and lacked self-confidence. Not being sufficiently satisfied with my ability or preparedness, I usually opted not to perform. No one tried to force me.

For many years after Grandmother passed away in 1943, the Marshburns continued the family tradition of Christmas reunions. But as the older generation passed from view and their children moved away, the younger family members organized summer reunions in the Sierras where Uncle Ezra and his family had settled.

Quaker Faith

Our parents raised us boys as Quakers, and that faith was an integral part of our lives—practiced at home as well as at church and lived as well as believed. During the week, we would conscientiously study our Sunday school lessons, read the Bible, and pray in private. On Saturday nights, our parents would close the store until Monday morning, and we would look forward to the remainder of the weekend, which we called "First Day."

Sundays always meant going to Sunday school and church as a family, and that was no token appearance. Mom and Dad took us to the East Whittier Friends meetinghouse across Whittier Boulevard from our home.[18] Sunday school started at 10 a.m. and the worship service at 11 a.m. Each week during the service, we would sit on the

---

18 Dick maintained his membership at East Whittier Friends throughout his life.

East Whittier Friends Church, pre-1930

~Family album

same bench at the left rear of the auditorium. Dad said he could hear better there. The acoustics provided a bounce to his liking.

In my earliest years, Mom would bring an apple every Sunday and pare it with a knife during the service, giving me a slice from time to time to keep me quiet. Sunday afternoon, the family enjoyed a time of rest and quiet reflection.

Back in those days, many young people, including Dick and Don, were attracted to the Wednesday night Christian Endeavor meetings. Through Bible study and application, the meetings served to refresh their faith. During World War II, when I was old enough to participate, Endeavor meetings had diminished in popularity.

The Quaker church in East Whittier belonged to the evangelical branch of the Society of Friends. Our services in many ways resembled those of other Protestant denominations. Like the Friends church in Yorba Linda, our congregation paid our ministers and had a choir. Men and women sat in integrated pews, in contrast to the more conservative churches back East, where men sat on one side and women on the other.

An incident that happened more than seventy years ago remains lodged in my memory with details as vivid as if it had occurred yesterday. When I was five or six years old, Mom dressed me in an itchy wool suit one Sunday. My parents then walked me across the street and popped me into a new Sunday school class. It was not to my liking. As a shy boy, I was averse to strangers and unfamiliar circumstances. My cousins went to the Whittier First Friends Church uptown, and I didn't know any of the nine or ten kids in my class at East Whittier. At that age, I wanted to get acquainted and play with the children before being stuck in class with them. Otherwise, my shyness would prevail, and I would close my mind to any thought of serious learning.

When Ethel Walker, the teacher and pastor's wife, started to tell a Bible story, I remember thinking, "I'd rather hear it from Mom at home while wearing my comfortable play clothes." Maybe Mrs. Walker, a stiff, proper lady, narrated the story too formally, or maybe she didn't relate it to anything familiar in my life. Whatever the problem, I said to myself, "I don't need to sit here if I'm not hearing the story."

Abruptly, I got up, opened the door, and slammed it behind me. Mrs. Walker made no attempt to stop me. Perhaps she thought I had to use the restroom. Instead, I ran home across Whittier Boulevard, which had been widened from a two-lane to a three-lane highway and resurfaced with concrete, replacing the old asphalt road. The third lane in the middle eventually became known as "the suicide lane." The traffic was fast but still light that Sunday morning. Fortunately, I made it across.

When my parents went to the classroom to pick me up, they were shocked to discover I had asserted my independence and left. Hurrying home, they found me safe, wearing my play clothes.

"Why did you leave?" they asked.

"I just was not comfortable there."

I don't remember being punished, but after that, Mom and Dad kept a closer eye on me, and the next Sunday Mom dressed me in cotton. I probably inherited that independent, cantankerous streak from Dad. All of us boys showed that spirit at one time or another. Our parents had their hands full.

∾ ∾

Dad, with his boisterous nature and quick temper, didn't fit the Quaker mold, yet he did his best to acknowledge Quaker beliefs. As energetic as he was, he threw himself into church activities. I don't remember Dad teaching Sunday school at East Whittier, but he served on church committees and helped construct the new sanctuary. He expressed some pretty strong attitudes regarding appropriate use of the building. "If it's going to be a meetinghouse, then it's a meeting for worship, study, and learning." Anything like a potluck dinner in the church basement raised his ire. He didn't even want to think about such frivolity.

Mother, however, didn't have a problem with potluck dinners and other social events at church. She would say, "The point is that we get to know one another, so when we go in for serious study and conversation, we each know where the others stand."

Dad eventually came around to Mom's point of view. "Well, that might be all right."

I suspect one reason behind his opposition to potlucks was that he disliked Mom having to bake more pies, because she spent so much time baking for the store. Moreover, in case of possible disagreements,

I think Dad would have preferred to find out where someone stood during conversations on weekdays in the store, but of course Mom cringed at such noisy public displays.

By birth, breeding, and temperament, Mother was a Quaker to the hilt. She lived her religion. She would say, "A good Friend does not wear his religion on his sleeve." Instead of outward display, Friends embraced an inner light that shone through simplicity, honesty, and integrity. Mom's moral strength and devout faith affected virtually everyone who knew her. People sought her out as a peacemaker, conciliator, confidante, and true friend. She had no enemies, least of all those who may have initially envied her for having the grocery store and plenty to eat or pitied her for having an argumentative husband.

With her Quaker contemporaries and in the family, Mom would use the plain speech dialect, for example, "thee is" (rather than "thou art"). When the Society of Friends was founded in the seventeenth century, people had begun to address individuals of wealth and social standing as "you," a term of respect and deference. Quakers, who believed in equality, thought "you" was fancy and pretentious. They shunned fanciness in their quest to live a simple life, so they clung to plain speech long after it had gone out of fashion in the rest of society. In California, beginning with Mom's generation, plain speech among Quakers began to fall by the wayside. Mom and her siblings decided they would not say "thee" and "thy" to avoid embarrassing people by introducing a disrespectful amusement or a bone of contention. She and my aunts didn't want non-Quakers to feel ostracized or uncomfortable in their presence.

Traditional Quakers also shunned fanciness in dress and avoided such adornments as buttons, buckles, and jewelry. Mom and her generation didn't oppose adornments, however. They chose to blend in and not accentuate differences, focusing instead on the tenets of the Bible. In the end, what was on the inside was all that really counted.

Mom and Dad reared my brothers and me in the Quaker disciplines of piety and hard work, teaching us that good deeds should match our words, but they never tried to force their convictions on us. Rather, they gave advice and set examples, believing that religion should be a source of strength and not a burden to us. We prayed before meals (most often a silent grace), read the Bible every day, and memorized scripture, but tolerance was stressed over doctrine. They taught us to be guided by our convictions, hopefully tempered by sound moral training in our youth.

THE FAMILY BUSINESS

Working together at the Nixon service station and grocery business helped shape our family identity and strengthen our bond. A major portion of the family effort revolved around the business during my childhood. We functioned as a corporate unit, and we all had valuable roles to play. While Mom and Dad spent long hours in the store, Dick and Don took turns caring for me in my early years. Later, I participated along with them.

By the time I came along, the family had settled into the place I knew as home for my first eight years. With our business and living quarters connected, we didn't have a commute. Dad had built the house and remodeled it continually after they moved to the corner of Santa Gertrudes and East Whittier Boulevard in 1922. He built additional rooms to provide more space for his growing family. The main floor included a bedroom and bath, a long living room/dining room, and a kitchen/dinette. To reach the four bedrooms and bathroom over the detached garage, we had to go outside and up a covered stairway.

I slept up there on a small cot at the foot of my parents' bed. I vividly remember the morning of May 3, 1935, when my dad roused me, saying, "Eddie, wake up. You're five years old today!" And then he went to work. I got up as usual, went downstairs, and found Mom fixing breakfast.

Extremely talented with his hands, Dad built or added on to nearly every house we ever lived in and every place of business. He relished being able to accomplish any physical task that other men could do. "If you decide to do anything any other man can do, it might take a little longer, but you can do it," he would advise us. Dad recognized that some people had an innate talent or more education, and others had to work at it. Living by that philosophy, he always worked hard to better himself and his family.

The family business began as a service station. In their younger years, Harold and Dick helped pump gas. Then Dad added a few groceries for the convenience of customers. As the Whittier population grew, the grocery part of the business expanded and thrived, while the service station soon demanded more time and attention than it was worth.

When East Whittier Friends built a new church building, Dad bought their old structure and had it moved across the highway to our property. That became the new Nixon's Market, which sold everything from gasoline and tires to foodstuffs and special orders for such things as dry goods and canning supplies.

One of my earliest recollections of the service station and store was during the devastating flood of early February 1935. Unusual for normally dry Southern California, torrential rain pelted the region for three days and nights, culminating in a cloudburst on February 6. Water rushed down Russell Street and across Whittier Boulevard and Santa Gertrudes like rapids. There in the foothills, the elevation was steep enough to cause the water to flow in channels. Thanks to Don, the photography enthusiast, our family has a record of the flood. I can still hear him say, "We've got to get pictures of this!" He snapped the shots from the north side of Whittier Boulevard looking at the service station, the garage, and the house behind it. The service station flooded, and so did Mom's pie and cake kitchen on the ground level of the garage. Water up to the hubcaps was one thing, but standing water in the kitchen sure made a mess for Mom, who was in the midst of baking pies. Being sufficiently above ground level, the rest of the family living quarters and the store escaped inundation.

When the rain stopped, Dad drove down to Fullerton, taking Don and me along to check on his widowed youngest sister, Carrie Wildermuth, and her two sons. Along the way, we saw the havoc that flood had wreaked. The water had wrenched a house clear off its foundation and deposited it in the middle of the street. From the perspective of a child nearly five years old, the sight was perplexing; that was not the way things should be. At the Wildermuth home, everyone had survived, but several inches of water covered their floor. Dad and Don immediately took action, helping our relatives move furniture and mop the water.

Later we learned the extent of the devastation: three hundred families lost their homes and at least eight people lost their lives. Landslides wiped out roads and railroad tracks around the area.

❧ ❧

Dad exuded boundless energy. In fact, none of us boys could keep up with him until he finally started to slow down in his late sixties. I remember the lengths to which he went to paint the entire inside of the store, which had once served as our church auditorium. First, he covered all the products with newspapers and canvas. Then he rigged scaffolding, so he could paint the very high ceiling. Working up on that scaffolding was a dangerous undertaking, especially for a man in his fifties, but he accomplished the task without incident. After painting the interior, he aired the place out when the business was closed on Sunday. All his efforts required a great deal of physical exertion, but he never complained. He genuinely relished hard work.

With Dad's willingness to tackle any job that other men could do, he would try to repair any broken equipment or structure. In the 1930s, our refrigerated meat cases operated with an ammonia compressor located outside the back of the store. A high pressure pipeline conveyed the compressed fluid into the store to the expansion coils under the displays, keeping the temperature just above freezing. The low pressure return line brought the gas back outside to the compressor. Occasionally the old pump would spring a leak around the valves. Anyone familiar with ammonia gas knows how it chokes the lungs and brings tears to the eyes, even if it's in the open air outside.

Dad knew what he had to do to repair a leak. He'd grab his tools and run around to the back, holding his breath. Then he would shut down the pump, unscrew the pipe, and run around to the other side of the store for a breath of fresh air. Holding his breath again, he would run back, install new seals in the valve, and turn the compressor on. At times, he'd have to repeat the process to get a proper seal. His determination was just unreal. He had a phenomenal will to keep going until he finished the job.

Later, the industry used Freon and other gases for refrigeration. Freon was supposed to be a great advance—a "miracle compound" of several chlorofluorocarbons. Don said, "Freon 12 is harmless. It's

Nixon's Market in 1935 flood

↭Family album

so much better because it doesn't knock you out. If you accidentally inhale some, you can still breathe and it won't hurt you."[19]

∿ ∿

Our family delighted in providing only the highest-quality meats, fresh produce, and home-baked pastry at Nixon's Market. An amazing number of people came from long distances to buy specialty items such as prime beef and daily fresh produce. Mother's pies—especially apple, cherry, lemon, and mincemeat—attracted repeat customers. She never seasoned her apple pies with nutmeg—only cinnamon—the way Dad liked them. On baking days, Mom would begin rolling pie dough before dawn while Dad assembled the ingredients. They baked as many pies as time would allow—sometimes upwards of thirty—and then sold them in the store for 25 to 35 cents each, depending on the variety.[20]

Eventually, Dad concluded that the pies were not worth Mom's time and effort. He said, "You know, the ingredients in those pies cost almost as much as we sell them for. When you add in your work, you're only making a few pennies." But they both felt the prices were too high anyway, especially during the years of the Great Depression, so they resisted raising them. Although Dad tried to discourage her from baking, people came into the store from all over the area just to snatch up one of those pies before they sold out, often before noon. It was a rare treat for our family when a pie didn't sell, and Mom could bring it home for us. She continued to bake pies for the customers despite Dad's objections.

Dick and Don started work early. Dick, who was in charge of produce in the late 1920s and early 1930s, rose before 4 a.m. to head for the wholesale market on 7th Street in downtown Los Angeles to get the pick of the day's supply. He always returned to our store with the freshest fruits and vegetables he could find.

---

19 Freon, a halogen compound gas, is colorless, odorless, nonflammable, noncorrosive, and best of all, nontoxic. But we didn't realize then that chlorofluorocarbons appear to have a destructive effect on the ozone layer in the upper atmosphere.

20 Some sources say she made fifty pies before breakfast. I don't believe she could have baked that many.

After Dick left to attend Duke University, Dad took over buying produce and managing that department. Sometimes he let me ride to Los Angeles with him—but only on days when school was not in session. I considered those times a treat, because I seldom got to ride in the truck, and I enjoyed all the activity at the old wholesale produce market—a lively, fascinating place where ethnically diverse local farmers would set up their displays before dawn. Dad and I usually loaded up the produce by 5 a.m. and headed back to the store.

While Dad was on the way to the produce market, Don got up to prepare the meat section. Dad knew the basics of butchering, but Don really became an expert. He called on the Los Angeles-based Manning's Baby Beef and the Luer Company, which marketed pork. Don especially appreciated Bill Ross, a happy-faced, red-haired Jewish fellow who drove the Luer refrigerated van to deliver sides of fresh pork, bacon, ham, and lard. Mr. Ross taught Don many tricks of the trade—how to describe the best cuts and how to market them effectively. Thanks to what he learned in the early years as the lead butcher in Nixon's Market, Don soon progressed to become a gourmet cook and a restaurateur.

At 7:30 a.m., as I headed off to school, Dad opened the grocery store for business. After school, I attended to my chores, sweeping the floors, stocking shelves, and cleaning produce. Don added meat-grinding to my list. The ground beef was not called "hamburger," because it consisted of premium cuts of meat with just the right amount of fat. Don also prepared a pet food that I ran through the grinder using scraps of beef that weren't marketable. The dogs expressed a strong preference for our pet food over the alternatives, helping make the Nixon recipe a very popular product.

After World War II when Dad was retiring, Charles L. "Chuck" Milhous, one of our many cousins, came to work at the store as an apprentice under Don. He continued as a meat cutter for the market for many years. Lyle Brumfield and Tom Seulke, another Milhous cousin, started working there. Tom eventually became the store manager and remained so for the duration of its existence. Over the years, several other extended family members and friends took jobs in the store.

George Irving, Sr., the salesman for Bishops Candy, regularly visited Nixon's Market to maintain his candy displays. Some salesmen made themselves unwelcome with pushy manners, but not George. He had mastered the art of extracting a smile from everyone. When I was a preschooler, Mr. Irving impressed me so much that I believed he was Santa's helper.

His son, George Irving, Jr., one of Don's sidekicks in the meat department, developed into a genuine expert in his own right. A few years later, I had my sights on Mary, George's beautiful blonde sister, when she came to work as a hostess in Don's new restaurant. After a few dates with Mary during the summer of 1950, I soon became acquainted with the whole Irving family—all nine of them—and cultivated friendships that have lasted to this day. The Irvings, like the Milhouses, exhibited marvelous strength and closeness as a family unit.

∿ ∿

With Mom's encouragement, our store served as a gathering place for friends and relatives. For one thing, she was the greatest listener I knew. I always suspected our thriving business resulted as much from Mom's listening skills as from the reputation for quality merchandise. She had more than thirty cousins in Southern California, and many of those in the Los Angeles basin either worked in the store or were frequent customers.

One of Mom's favorite cousins and closest friends was Grace Milhous West, wife of Eldo West and mother of Jessamyn, Myron, Clara, and Merle. They lived right up the road from the market on the other side of the church. An unusually cheerful woman, Grace displayed an infectious sense of humor. When she came into the store, she would soon have everybody laughing.

Dad, on the other hand, sometimes provoked people into yelling. I witnessed many heated conversations between Dad and some of his customers and salesmen. Often he would engage Bill Ross in political discussions. Mr. Ross, who had so often helped Don with marketing techniques, encouraged an open mind in everyone. I never saw him when he wasn't smiling. He would joke about the seeming inconsistency of being Jewish and delivering pork. "If someone else

George Brickles, cousin & produce man for Nixon's store,
c. 1940

❧Family album

wants to eat pork, that's okay with me," he'd say. "My job is about mak-ing money for my employer." On matters other than a kosher diet, however, Mr. Ross never shied away from his Jewish faith—or his left-leaning political views.

"That you're Jewish is not a problem with me," Dad said. "I don't have any problem with Jewish people. What I have a problem with is your liberal politics." And they would argue on, but I'm certain they both enjoyed the lively banter.

Mother, in her gentle way, would interrupt, saying, "Frank, you must stop talking like that. Just stop. Our customers are hearing you."

"They should hear me. They should!" he would shout.

Slim Craddick would sometimes show up at the store when Mr. Ross arrived—just to pick an argument. Mr. Craddick was a gun-sling-ing Westerner, and furtively anti-Semitic. As a young boy, I noticed he hardly ever smiled. He ran a little avocado grove and sold produce and orange juice on a roadside stand next door to our market. Mom would often give me a dime and say, "Go over and get a glass of orange juice from Mr. Craddick."

I now suspect she hoped I would keep Slim occupied until Mr. Ross left our store.

Mr. Craddick, in turn, would buy butter or bacon at Nixon's Market. He never made change. Maybe he was testing me, but at the time I suspected he just didn't know how. He'd take a bag of coins out of his pocket, empty it on the counter, and say, "Take what you need." A high level of trust existed among the neighbors.

Back in the 1930s, a few of our customers started using charge accounts. Paying by credit was not common then, but my folks were always willing to help in any way they could. Dad and Mom recorded their names and purchases in little 4- by 6-inch booklets. I can still picture the tray of record books. People paid once a month or as often as they could.

Customers would place orders by telephone, and we would fill those orders and deliver them. Our store seemed more like a commu-nity service organization than a simple mom and pop operation.

People from all over La Habra Heights and the valley below us would shop at our store. It served as a mixing bowl for the citrus growers who lived in the area—the wealthy who had built homes in the hills, migratory Mexican workers, and Japanese produce farmers from a few miles away. Mexican cooks who operated the mess halls for citrus fruit pickers at the neighboring Leffingwell and Murphy Ranches came in to shop once a week, which gave my family and me frequent exposure to the Spanish language, because they spoke no English at all.

Although Mom hadn't studied Spanish, she became a good interpreter, because Spanish is so closely derived from Latin, which she had studied. Dick and Don did pretty well with Spanish too. All of us except Dad learned a lot of words from the customers who shopped at Nixon's Market. Often they would hand us grocery lists written in Spanish. We would have to find someone to verify our translations before we could fill the orders. One of our translators was a Mexican lady, the wife of a fruit picker, who worked for Mom for a while. Being well-educated, she provided valuable assistance in bridging language and cultural barriers.

The Leffingwell Ranch had hired Mrs. Belen, a Mexican woman, to run a boarding house for the pickers. A marvelous, friendly lady with a contagious smile, she would buy one hundred pounds of pinto beans, as well as cornmeal, *manteca, manzanillas,* and, of course, Lucky Strike and Camel *cigarillos.* Dad got a kick out of her. Not understanding a word of Spanish, he would use amusing pantomime to communicate with her. A finger in his mouth meant cigarettes. Dad, however, was proud he had never put "one of those nasty things" in his mouth.

❦ ❧

For me, the family grocery business provided a good education and entertainment as well. I gained practical experience working alongside my parents and brothers. My parents modeled respect and compassion for all people, regardless of their ethnicity or economic status, and I thoroughly enjoyed the diversity of customers who shopped there. An "allowance" was a misnomer in our family. Any cash my brothers and I needed for a specific purpose required an open request to the legislative branch of the family (Mom), whereupon the executive branch (Dad) either approved the disbursement or vetoed the appropriation for lack of well-defined need. Occasionally Mom succeeded in redefining the need in irrefutable terms, and the overridden veto brought a smile to the face of the executive.

As a child, I also liked to observe others in the community at work. On hot summer days after completing my chores, I sometimes walked with my dog from the boulevard down Santa Gertrudes Street. The asphalt pavement, suffering from excessive heat, became softer and softer. About a quarter mile south of Whittier Boulevard, Santa Gertrudes petered out into a dirt road leading to the Leffingwell Ranch. From early childhood, I watched mule teams at the ranch hauling wagons loaded with crates of oranges, lemons, and grapefruit from the orchards to the packing house nearby. From there the crates were shipped to wholesale markets all over the country.

During the summer, a peculiar aroma permeated the air around the ranch, especially the mule barns. I think it came from treating the manure and mixing it with lime for fertilizing the orchards. That fertilizer was probably healthier for the trees than some of the chemicals we use today, but the undesirable odor did fill the orchards with "dairy air."

Economics determines the workforce, and in those days, Mexicans were willing to labor in the boiling heat, standing on three-legged ladders to pick fruit for the wages they received, but as far as I know, they were all legal immigrants. The ranchers much appreciated the hardworking Mexicans, and they couldn't have operated their orchards without them.

On the other hand, high school students in the area weren't attracted to the picking jobs. The smudging operations paid better, so the teenagers would light smudge pots on cold winter nights. Everyone in the orchard business would listen for the radio broadcasts of the California Fruit Frost Service. I don't know how the forecasters did it, but they could predict minimum expected temperatures right down to half a degree. When they would forecast temperatures around 28 degrees Fahrenheit, the student workers knew that meant, "Don't plan to go to bed tonight. Light the smudge pots and refill the oil." The next morning the sky would be so dark with soot that we could hardly see across the street.

Dick and Don might have worked in the orchards lighting smudge pots, but I never did. By the time I was old enough, wind machines had replaced most of the old smudge pot operations. The machines stirred the air, preventing the cold from settling around the trees.

EDUCATION

Both our parents were strong proponents of education—Dad, because he didn't have much formal schooling and wanted his sons to do better, and Mom, because her family so highly valued education that it amounted to a birthright. She had planned to become a schoolteacher, but marriage cut that dream short. In raising her sons, however, she imparted her love of learning and used her teaching skills to help us through school.

In a sense, Dad was also a teacher, and he made it clear to us that he greatly respected teachers. He would say, "You've got to learn. To make the most of life, you'll need everything you can get from schooling and then some."

I remember Dad trying to write with very phonetic spelling. On an old Corona typewriter, he would peck out memos and letters. It didn't matter to us that his spelling wasn't perfect. We could all understand what he wrote, and so could anyone else.

Dad taught me how to sound out words phonetically and to read. That's how I got in trouble with *colonel*. Much to my embarrassment, I pronounced it *co-ló-nel* in school one day. A few of the more erudite students began to laugh, but Miss Ethel Stone, our teacher, quickly set us all straight with a clear explanation of the French origin of the word and an admonition not to make fun of others' sincere efforts to read aloud.

Mother never firmly insisted on anything, but when we understood her appeal, we could hardly turn it down. One of her appeals was that each of us study Latin in high school before launching into Romance languages, and she wanted each of us to take German before delving into English literature, because so much common language in English derives from Latin and German. If we were going into life science or medicine, she said we would benefit from knowing some Greek. Having a natural talent for languages like her father, she had studied Latin, Greek, and German for two years in college.

Because of Mom's persuasion, Dick and I both took two years of Latin in high school and did very well. I'm sure she encouraged Don in that direction as well. Dick was impressed by the utility of the language. I found it to be an easy course except for having to learn a lot more cases, conjugations, and declensions than in English. Mom helped me with Latin by making me wade through it rather than giving me the answers. She probably offered Dick and Don such assistance too.

At Whittier College, Dick studied four years of French, the "diplomat's language." He was fascinated with French, perhaps because of his interest in the Revolutionary War and the participation of the French. His language skills aided in his studies of the French legal system, of which there are still vestiges in Louisiana, the only state that does not follow English common law.

As one of my first teachers, Dick taught me to value education and to respect authority. Even as a young person, he recognized the importance of discipline in creating a classroom environment in which learning could take place. When I was in grammar school, he told me that one of his most memorable teachers was Jenny Levin, who taught American history, his favorite subject. Because she wanted to ensure that her students knew the subject matter, she wouldn't allow any skylarking, jabbering or jittering. No one passed her courses without demonstrating knowledge of the people and events that shaped our country. Some parents complained that she graded too hard, however. As a result, by the time I got to Whittier High School, Miss Levin had been relegated to managing the study hall. That's what schools in California started doing with disciplinarians—moved them into positions with no teaching responsibilities.

In study hall, I would sometimes go up and ask Miss Levin a math question. She would quietly suggest an exercise to help me see patterns by solving problems on my own. When I showed her my results, she would say, "You got it. That's exactly right." She encouraged me to do better by giving me a little guidance.

Always concerned about my development, Dick would challenge me by setting up problems for me to solve and encouraging me to try a little harder. During my grammar school years, Dick would say before sitting at the dinner table, "We're out of milk. Eddie, run to the store and get a quart. I'll time you with my stopwatch." I would run as fast as I could. The next time he sent me to the store, he would challenge me to run faster, and he would time me again to see if I could increase my speed. Dick was like a coach: he appreciated competition and excellence. That led to my participation in track. In grammar school, I won the fifty-yard dash a couple of times with runs of 6.4 seconds.

When Dick played football at Whittier College, Dad insisted we attend the games. Coach Wallace Newman, a Native American, taught the team some brutal techniques. "Chief," as he was called, told the players, "Knock them down and get their attention." (That didn't go over well with our gentle mother.) The Chief had no patience with the attitude that it didn't matter whether the team won or lost. He taught fair play by the rules, but he also taught the importance of winning. Chief Newman had a profound influence on Dick—not that he made a star athlete out of him. At 155 pounds and 5 feet 11 inches, my brother lacked the physique needed to excel in football. In fact, Dick warmed the bench more than he participated in action on the field.[21] Nevertheless, the Chief inspired Dick to persevere, and the principles Dick learned in football, he applied to winning in politics and other life situations.

As a boy, I was an avid football fan. Perplexed by the name of the Whittier team, I asked, "Dick, why are they called the 'Poets'? Couldn't they have been the Lions or Tigers or Bears or something fierce like that?"

Asking Dick a question was like asking a teacher to give a test. He never gave me point-blank answers but encouraged me to think and to look beyond the surface by asking me more questions such as, "Who was John Greenleaf Whittier?"

"I don't know."

"Then you'd better find out. And, by the way, who was Henry Wadsworth Longfellow?"

From Dick I learned that poetry was part of our Milhous heritage. Grandmother wrote poems prolifically, and Dick had tried his hand at it too. At an early age, he recited poems at school and in church. He

---

21 Rev. Philip Martin told Karen Olson that he spent many hours warming the bench with Dick. He said he came to know my brother "well enough to know the thoughts of the man."

even wrote the eighth-grade class history in verse. That encouraged me to write poetry as well.

Harold, Dick, and Don attended grammar school in Yorba Linda until the family moved to East Whittier, where Harold and Dick went to East Whittier Elementary two miles west of home. Don and I, however, attended Lowell Joint Elementary School two miles east on the boundary between Orange and Los Angeles Counties—thus the adjective "Joint." Don and I had our choice because we lived almost exactly halfway between the two schools. Don decided on Lowell to stay close to his boyhood friends. The first day, my parents sent me to East Whittier, but I didn't like the school. They let me transfer to Lowell, which had the advantage of an easier commute on the school bus. The 1933 earthquake had caused some damage to the building, but repairs were undertaken, and by the time I started first grade, the school was in pretty good shape.

Lowell was slightly smaller and included grades one through eight. The other grades had their own classrooms, but grades two and three, four and five, and six and seven were combined with two grades to a room.

The students at Lowell received a very solid primary education. Mrs. Eastman, our first grade teacher, was a grand lady.[22] She smiled even while she enforced the rules. The kids responded readily to her subtle commands, thus keeping the classroom environment orderly and ideal for learning. She taught us to read but at a slower pace than educators who push the children today. In those days, teachers just let students absorb reading by exposure. If we didn't catch on as quickly as our classmates, teachers and parents didn't worry. We all learned at a pace that left no one behind, and pressure to keep up with our peers in a friendly environment seemed to achieve acceptable results.

I could read when I entered first grade, because Dad had taught me how to sound out words phonetically, but I didn't read very well—not like Dick, anyway. I wasn't as interested as he.

---

22 Mrs. Eastman came to the Nixon Library and Birthplace on her one hundredth birthday in 1990 to look for me. I've regretted ever since that I missed her on that special day.

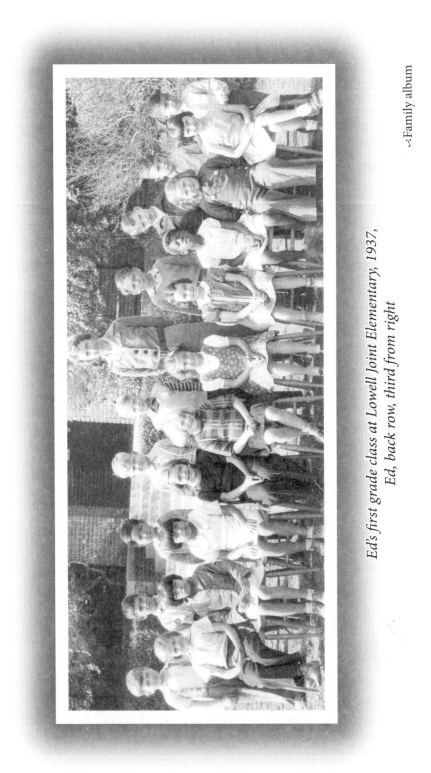

Ed's first grade class at Lowell Joint Elementary, 1937,
Ed, back row, third from right

❧Family album

Ethel Stone taught a combined second and third grade class, and Mrs. Rydell taught fourth and fifth. They were patient and persistent with each one of us, but the main reason for their success was their effective use of classroom discipline. They promptly brought the cut-ups into line and reattached them to the flow of the curriculum.

At Lowell, teachers provided the opportunity for students to explore all kinds of art: finger painting, watercolors, and other media that would be easy to clean up after school. Miss Stone gave us an assignment to take a bar of soap from home, if our families could afford it, and carve something. So, I got a cake of Ivory Soap from the store and stared at it. Having admired the sphinx of Egypt while glancing through a *World Book Encyclopedia,* I decided to carve a lion in that pose. My sculpture must have been recognizable, because my family, Miss Stone, and classmates complimented me.

"This is really good. How did you do that?" they asked.

"I don't know. I just got the idea, cut the soap away from where I thought it shouldn't be, and wound up with a lion."

After that I thought perhaps I should be a sculptor. I was at the age when people would ask me, "What do you want to do when you grow up, Eddie?"

As soon as my brothers heard of my desire to become a sculptor, they discouraged me. "No, you don't want to do that. Sculptors and artists have a hard time making a living," Don said.

"But you did really well; carve as a hobby. Meanwhile, study hard and learn a trade," Dick added.

I continued to whittle away but never created any masterpieces.

In the sixth and seventh grades, we kids had to endure a year under the watchful eye of the "tiger teacher," Jessie Stone, Ethel's sister. Because she made us toe the line and learn, we thought of her as the meanest of all teachers. Every time Johnny Spring would say or do something out of line, Miss Stone would reprimand him on the spot as if jerking his imaginary chain.

Smart little kid that he was, he'd say, "Well, it's a free country, isn't it?"

"Not while you're in my class, young man," Miss Stone retorted. "Sit down!"

And he did. The rest of us were rarely bold enough to challenge Miss Stone like that.

In hindsight, I realize she probably saved the bunch of us, shaping us up so we were prepared to continue our education. Because she disciplined us, we learned self-discipline—the most crucial element in learning.

Miss Carol Calkins taught eighth grade. As young teenagers, I and the other boys in class were beginning to notice feminine beauty. A bright young lady with very fine features, Miss Calkins caught our eye. By the end of the school year, a suitor had won her hand in marriage.

Mrs. Gladys Starbuck, the principal, team taught the unit on the U.S. Constitution with Miss Calkins. Mrs. Starbuck had truly mastered the art of teaching, as did school principals in those days. Both Miss Calkins and Mrs. Starbuck believed that knowledge of our country's fundamental legal document was a requisite for good citizenship. In fact, we had to pass the Constitution test in order to graduate.

I studied and studied and had most of the answers down pat, but a girl named Marjorie Wentz beat me on the test and came in first. I remember arguing with her about some of the answers and finally saying, "Okay. You won."

For the last fifteen minutes of every day, Miss Calkins and Mrs. Starbuck drilled us in math. The whole class would sit there and mentally process a sequence of arithmetic functions—add, subtract, multiply, divide. Elvira Rodriguez, the smartest kid in our class, was my chief competition in math. She and her younger sister Beatriz were polite, pleasant girls, respected by everyone. Ethnic prejudice at Lowell never entered my mind and for good reason: Teachers treated all students equally regardless of race or ethnic heritage. Excellence prevailed as the ultimate objective, whether in academic performance, athletic ability, or any other discipline. Some did better than others, but recognition of genuine friendship helped us all progress together.

In 1940 or 1941, some of the Lowell students were out playing ball at recess. Because of staggered recesses, I was inside with my classmates when we got word that Milo Burcham, a Whittier resident and test pilot for Lockheed Aircraft, was going to show his hometown the new P-38, a twin-engine, counter-rotating prop fighter plane.[23] He had promised his friends in Whittier, including my brother Don and Beryl Parsons, a relative by marriage, that someday he would pass over East Whittier. When the day came, we heard the plane swooping down very fast, probably about four hundred miles per hour in a low, flat dive that caused the windows to rattle. Then, right over the school, he pulled back and climbed vertically in a victory roll. Burcham later reported to his local buddies that just before leveling off, he was still making sixty miles an hour—a mile a minute, straight up—an incredible performance in those days. We were all duly impressed by his feat, which was the talk of the town for several days. Unfortunately, I missed the show that day and had to wait until the next year to get my first look at a P-38 in flight.

Mrs. Starbuck's son John flew B17s in World War II. When the Nazis shot down his plane over Germany, all of us at Lowell School, as well as the entire community, mourned his tragic loss.

EXTRACURRICULAR ACTIVITIES

Education being more than formal schooling, my learning experience also included participation in Boy Scouts. Harold had joined in his early teens when the family moved from Yorba Linda to Whittier, but the family's financial situation soon precluded further participation. Dick and Don never had the opportunity. By the time I reached scouting age, Don suggested I bypass Cub Scouts and go right into the older group. I belonged only long enough to reach First Class level at the age of twelve or thirteen. During summer vacations, Troop 475 mustered at Arbolado, the Boy Scout camp in the San Bernardino National Forest, where I earned a few merit badges such as semaphore signaling, fire management, and campfire cooking. At my last summer camp, I was inducted into the Order of the Arrow, the national honor society promoting leadership development.

---

23 The P-38 Lightning and later models were among the best all-around fighter aircraft in World War II. They were fast, powerful, and capable of performing in a variety of roles. They were deployed in Europe, the Mediterranean, and the Pacific. The first Allied fighters over Berlin flew P-38s. Milo Burcham died in 1944 while flying a P-80 aircraft.

With a membership of only about ten Scouts, the leaders had trouble maintaining Troop 475. Following the Japanese attack on Pearl Harbor, everyone felt the strain. Like today, some parents were too busy to keep their boys involved; some were transferred out of the area because of the war; and the boys themselves had competing commitments. Back then, the leaders lacked the resources needed to train the boys and supply the outings. Our Scout Master was living in Depression Era conditions, but he shared what he had and gratefully accepted the food and transportation donated by Nixon's Market, thanks to Don's generosity.

The most memorable merit badge I earned was for completing the hike to the top of Mount San Gorgonio, known as "Grayback," the highest peak in Southern California. Ted Marshburn didn't belong to the troop but eagerly agreed to accompany me. The two of us set out alone from Aunt Edith Timberlake's cabin at about 5,500 feet in the Valley of the Falls. Feeling exhausted but exhilarated, we finally reached the benchmark posted at 11,485 feet. The nearly 6,000-foot climb amounted to more than I needed for the nine-mile-hike merit badge, but the view from that elevation and the scenery along the way were more gratifying than any award. The crystal-clear sky allowed us to look down on the four other nearby peaks over 10,000 feet high. That panoramic view challenged description, leaving us with a sense of awe at the grandeur of the San Bernardino mountain range.

❧ ❧

To our family, Mom conveyed the strong Milhous heritage of music appreciation and performance, and she made sure our education included music. She taught my brothers and me that music helps prepare the mind for learning, and recent studies have confirmed she was right.

Our parents appreciated tradition and expressed their preference passively with a disapproving look or comment if we ventured too far from classical forms of music accepted through the ages. New compositions qualified for approval only when they followed or at least resembled classical patterns. Dad and Mom did not tolerate diversion into anything exotic.

Mom had learned to play the piano and expected my brothers and me to study an instrument. Harold played the clarinet—at least he was supposed to. At a very young age, Dick showed musical talent and could readily play tunes on the piano by ear. Recognizing his ability, Mom sent him to study first under Uncle Griffith Milhous, and later she placed him under Aunt Jane Beeson's tutelage.

An accomplished musician, composer, and arranger, Uncle Griffith had headed the Music Department at the Indiana Boys School before moving to Whittier. He had a great singing voice and had even made some recordings on old 78 rpm records. In teaching Dick to play the piano and violin, he found a receptive, promising student. Dick soon joined the violin section of the school orchestra, and I believe he also fiddled with Harold's clarinet.

Aunt Jane had studied at the Metropolitan School of Music in Indianapolis and became a professional pianist, organist, and music teacher. Between Christmas 1924 and June 1925, Dick lived with her and her family two hundred miles north in Lindsay. With daily lessons and rigorous practice, he became an accomplished pianist. One of his favorite pieces that Aunt Jane taught him was "Rustle of Spring" by Norwegian composer Christian Sinding. At every opportunity, Mom requested Dick to play that piece, which had been popular at the turn of the century during her youth.

Don must have taken lessons too—Mother would have seen to that. But when I was growing up, I don't remember him playing any instrument, nor does his widow Clara Jane Lemke Nixon. Don always found other things—more physical pursuits—to occupy his time. He had an ear for great performances, however, and promoted classical music appreciation throughout his life.

Uncle Griffith tried to teach me piano when I was six to maybe seven or eight years old, but my lessons suffered because of my insufficient self-discipline. Regardless of how much I practiced, I was never satisfied with my recitals. After teaching such an eager, talented student as my brother, Uncle Griffith probably felt disappointed that I didn't show the same natural ability and inclination to study music. And I thought Uncle Griffith was too stern, so I said, "I'm not doing that anymore." Mother didn't force me to continue. Now I wish she had.

As a young boy, I had a special affinity for cowboy music, what we call "country western" today. In 1935 or 1936, I was listening to some popular singer, possibly Roy Rogers, on the radio when Don came in and turned the dial to KFAC, a strictly classical station. He said, "You don't want to listen to that cowboy music. That was good for Harold, but you listen to this. You'll learn something." And I did.

Thinking back, I suspect that incident related to Harold's death. Harold was "born in the saddle," so to speak. He loved country music, but after he died, Mom couldn't bear to hear it. When Don switched channels, maybe he was defending her sensitivities, protecting her from sad memories. From that point forward, I've always preferred classical music.

For my fifth birthday, my parents treated me to the newly released *Water Babies*, an animated show recommended for young moviegoers. Of course, it appeared as a double feature, as movies did in those days. All the gunfire exchanged between the cowboys and Indians in the first movie, a Western, kept me on the edge of my seat. I can imagine the horror Mom must have felt, exposing me to violence at such a young age. By the time *Water Babies* came on, I was sound asleep, so my parents carried me out early.

As one can imagine, in a Quaker family in those days, dancing was seldom practiced. Nevertheless, Mother loved waltzes—especially Strauss waltzes. To her they were lyrical; the graceful music with movements reminded her of poetry. She didn't see many movies; few people did during the Great Depression, but she enjoyed *The Great Waltz*, the story of Johann Strauss. That was her preferred type of entertainment.

Dick believed that acting on stage fostered self-discipline and helped people express themselves more clearly. Consequently, he got involved in the local theater. In fact, he met Pat Ryan in 1938 at Whittier's Little Theater casting tryouts for *The Dark Tower*, a play by George S. Kaufman and Alexander Woollcott. Pat had the lead role, and Dick played the man who didn't get the girl. In real life, he proposed the night they met, and he got the girl two years later.

The visual arts didn't have much prominence in our home—maybe because our parents didn't have the money to spend on decorating, or maybe because Quakers weren't concerned with adorning their homes with artwork. For whatever reason, painting never fascinated me, and my brothers didn't show much interest in that kind of art either.

However, my family did have precious mementoes. The one I remember most was a tiny Dresden figurine that Uncle Oscar had bought for Aunt Olive while in Europe during World War I. As a Quaker, he did not believe in armed conflict, so he had driven an ambulance for the American Friends Service Committee in France. Aunt Olive had loaned her treasured porcelain figurine to Mom, who had just placed it on the mantel for display at our home when an unfortunate incident occurred. As boys are prone to do, I was bouncing a basketball in the living room. It went awry—straight toward Aunt Olive's figurine. Mom must have been mortified, and certainly Aunt Olive was greatly disappointed, but both remained calm. Aunt Olive reacted in her typically gracious manner when viewing the shattered remains. "It was just a thing," she reassured me.

I appreciated that my family considered material items subordinate to precious memories. Nevertheless, I deeply regretted causing the destruction of Aunt Olive's irreplaceable memento.

RECREATION AND TRAVEL

Our parents' long hours working at the store precluded regular family vacations and recreation, but during my free time as a boy, I sometimes played with neighborhood children. Mom, however, encouraged me to associate only with my contemporaries who were smart and motivated to excel. Regarding any kid who goofed off, she would advise, "Please do not cultivate that acquaintance."

Dick could judge the character of my friends just as well as Mom. For me, it seemed like I had an extra parent, protecting me from potential harmful influences. He recognized that my first cousins were the best playmates, because their parents raised them with the same religious training and good philosophy as our parents. Mom, Dad, and Dick always allowed me to play with my cousins close to my age: Aunt Olive's son, Ted Marshburn, Aunt Jane's daughter, Barbara Beeson, and Uncle Hugh's daughter, Neva Nixon. Ted, who was five months older than I, was my closest companion, until he left Whittier High School at the end of his sophomore year, when I was a freshman.

He finished high school in Barnesville, Ohio, and then returned home to attend Whittier College. At Whittier High School, Ted gave me a head start in math by simply explaining some of his geometry lessons before I took that subject the following year.

When I was in grammar school, Babe Sexton, a girl about my age, lived next door. Her real name was Janice, but her two older sisters had nicknamed her "Babe." The girls were Slim Craddick's nieces. We played out on the bales of hay, pretending they were a house or a store. Her sisters were always after us to play more "grown-up" games. Mother, aware of the girls' schemes, would run them off. She told me, "Babe's okay because she's your age, but stay away from the older ones."

Occasionally I was allowed to play with other children. Harold and Goldie Bromby's only child, Billy, was a happy-go-lucky kid, and we always had fun together. At times he would spend Friday nights and Saturdays at our place. When I was about ten years old, we got into an amusing business venture. For 25 cents a week each, Dad had given us the job of tending the chickens—feeding them and keeping the chicken coops clean. However, Billy feared that Dad might ask us to dress the chickens for sale in the store. He let it be known that removing the heads and feathers certainly was not a desirable job. Thinking we could make more money selling chicken manure, he persuaded me to help him scoop it up. When Mom got wind of our plan, she didn't want to squelch our entrepreneurial effort, but neither did she want those lug boxes of manure piled up in front of our store with for sale signs. Dick apparently paid someone to buy it and get it out of sight.

One of my closest friends was William "Billy" Lewis Harrison, son of William Henry Harrison, a respected architect, who later designed the first airport jet way. The Harrisons lived on the street below the home where we moved in 1939. On the tragic Sunday of December 7, 1941, Billy and I were tinkering with the wheels of a soapbox coaster we were building in his garage, when Mr. Harrison stepped in to tell us the shocking news he had just heard on the radio. "The Japanese attacked Pearl Harbor this morning!"

Billy asked his dad, "What does that mean for us now?"

Mr. Harrison described the probable course of events and the likelihood of the U.S. entering the war. "There may soon be shortages

Babe Sexton and Eddie, c. 1936

∿Family album

Eddie and Billy Bromby, c. 1936

∿Family album

of all the products we now take for granted in peacetime. We'll have to mobilize all the citizens of the country, and many young men will be called to serve in the Army and Navy. Building materials, machinery, gasoline, sugar, shortening, meat, and foods of all kinds will be reserved for the war effort, and goods will be rationed."

"What does *rationing* mean?" I asked Mr. Harrison. I had grown up in the hard times of the Depression, but *rationing* was an unfamiliar concept to me. His explanation was sobering. I thought only of the economic hardships we would face. It didn't occur to me that our family would soon be saying good-bye to Dick as he left to serve our country on the front.

The next day, President Roosevelt delivered his famous declaration of war speech to a joint session of Congress, and Mr. Harrison's predictions soon became reality. Additionally, Selective Service came into full effect.

⌒ ⌒

Bill, the name he went by as he entered his teen years, was a brilliant kid, who enjoyed reading encyclopedias. In fact, he introduced me to the value of reading the *Encyclopedia Britannica* while I was in the eighth grade and he in the ninth. After some initial skepticism, I soon learned how handy those books could be. He also encouraged my interest in science and showed me where to find scientific information. Smart as a tack, he had the subjects down pat and eagerly shared his knowledge with me.

In the summer of 1946, Bill and I ventured up the east slope of the Sierra Nevada Mountains. We both wanted to climb Mount Whitney, the tallest peak in the continental U.S., a challenge Dick had talked about but never had the opportunity to try. Setting out in the early morning from the end of the road, we almost reached the peak before we nearly ran out of air. The inadequacy of our clothing soon became apparent as well. Near the summit at over 14,000 feet, it's hard to get enough oxygen, and the climate is much colder than at Lone Pine in the valley 11,000 feet below. With all our book-based references, we simply had missed some essential preparations before we began our venture. Learning by experience is most memorable and, provided we survive the experience, the lessons learned serve well in planning future expeditions. "Be Prepared!" applies to life in general. It amounts to much more than a motto for the Boy Scouts.

∽∙ ∻

Because of Dad's and Mom's busy schedules at the store, Sunday afternoons following church were the only times we had for an occasional family trip. Grandmother, Mom, Dick, Don, and I were more likely to travel than Dad, who would say, "You want to go, go ahead. I haven't got time." He preferred work to social activities, and on Sundays he would rather discuss religion after the service and then expound on politics the rest of the week at the store.

On our excursions, we sometimes visited relatives in other towns and occasionally went to the mountains or the beach. I always looked forward to visiting my favorite destination—Aunt Edith and Uncle Tim's cabin in the Valley of the Falls in the San Bernardino Mountains. At an elevation of over a mile high, the cabin provided a refreshing getaway from the Timberlake home in Riverside with its stifling, hot, dry summers. In the winter, we would go to the cabin to frolic in the snow and then warm up in front of the big wood-burning fireplace. The cabin was isolated in the 1930s, but today the Valley of the Falls is a popular destination for vacationers and hikers. My cousin Betty Timberlake Paldanius now owns the small lot and original cabin.

The Timberlakes named their modest frame structure "Lot-o-Rest." It had one bedroom and an attic with several cots, where twelve people could sleep—if they got close enough to keep warm. Everyone who spent any time at Lot-o-Rest learned to cook on Aunt Edith's woodstove. There seemed to be no limit to the recipes attempted—even the famous Milhous pies and cakes.

We all appreciated the cabin's indoor plumbing, but anyone who used the toilet in the winter had to pour a little kerosene, or "coal oil," as we called it, in the bowl and tank to keep the toilet from freezing. Occasionally the temperature would drop low enough to crack the toilet regardless of the coal oil, thus necessitating its replacement. When it cracked, we used the outhouse a few steps from the rear door for the back-up plan.

The great flood of 1935—the one that had inundated our store—denuded the Valley of the Falls. I can barely remember my first visit before that flood, but I recall a beautiful valley full of towering ever-greens all the way across the valley floor from the cabin to the falls. After that flood, huge boulders and smaller rocks covered the valley, and giant trees lay on the ground like dropped pick-up sticks. The trees around the cabin had escaped damage, but those adjacent to the creek bed had all toppled. As a young boy, I saw some benefits to the changed landscape: I liked all the rocks, especially the boulders I could climb on.

Grandmother described a November 1938 visit to the cabin in verse:

Lot-O-Rest

Away up on the mountain side
Where, at times, the Timberlakes reside,
In a neat little cabin, 'most surrounded by trees
All of which are of nature's own planting
In a variety of shades any eye should please.

There are many tall pines, so green and sedate
And other small trees a nice picture to make.
A company of young folks, with birthdays near
Were invited to come to this cabin of cheer.
Entering this mountain cabin, cozy and neat,
A bright blaze from the fireplace you meet.
For the mountain air is chilly today
And a cheery, bright fire is welcome, we say.
Birthdays are ranging eleven to twenty-four
Donald, Betty, Priscilla, Marygene, the four
All seated around, with faces serene,
A table of food, e'en fit for a queen.

The number of occupants, eighteen surround it,
A company of relatives, happy and gay.
But before we partake of this dinner so luscious
We bow with thanksgiving the Lord's Prayer to say.

> After the feast some games were played
> Some went hiking the falls to see
> Thus ended a pleasant and carefree day
> As all the guests will surely agree.[24]

The trip I remember most, though, was a two-week drive across the country in late spring 1937 when I was seven years old. It stands out in my mind not only because of the momentous occasion—Dick's graduation from Duke Law School—but also because I never before had noticed Mom and Dad spending money on something not a necessity.

Dad, Mom, Don and I, along with eighty-seven-year-old Grandmother Almira, set off for Durham, North Carolina, fitting just fine in our 1936 Chevy sedan. While driving through Mississippi on U.S. Highway 20, Don spotted two little boys playing in a big cotton field on the side of the road. Dad stopped—one of his rare breaks in the long drive—and Don lined up those kids and me alongside the Chevy and took our picture.

Dad drove with the same determination as he tackled everything else. He wanted to drive nonstop to his destination. Grandmother, however, would get cramps in her feet, saying, "Frank, thee has to stop!"

"What's the matter?" he would ask.

"I just have to shake my legs."

For her especially, Dad would stop the car—or fulfill any other request for that matter.

Having graduated second in his class from Whittier College, Dick had attended Duke University's School of Law on a full scholarship, which he had to renew annually by keeping at least a B average. With the country still in the throes of the Depression, he lived frugally those three years, surviving mostly on meager wages (35 cents an hour) from working in the library and on five- and ten-dollar bills when Mom and Dad could afford to send them. Aunt Edith occasionally chipped in what she could, and Grandmother sent Dick five dollars every month, which he used to buy Cokes, Milky Way candy bars, and apples. Of all her grandchildren, she thought Dick the most likely to

---

24 Price 121.

Eddie and boys in Mississippi, 1937

❧Family album

become a leader, so she was eager to help him achieve his educational goals as a steppingstone to future service.

I'll never forget arriving at the place Dick lived during his last year of law school. Don drove us into the Duke Forest to "Whippoor-will Manor," as Dick and his friends facetiously called it. For his first two years, Dick had rented a room with classmate Bill Perdue for five dollars a month. Then in his final year, Dick, Bill, and two other law students, Lyman Brownfield, and Fred Albrink, had located a small farmhouse, or, better said, a shack in the woods near the main campus. Mrs. Henderson, the widowed landlady charged them five dollars a month. In the winter, because they had no money for kerosene, they went without heat. To keep warm, they burned newspapers in a potbellied stove. Their only source of light other than the sun was a sixty-watt incandescent light bulb hanging in the middle of the room. They studied at the law school library until it closed, returning to their cabin only to sleep. In the morning, they returned to the law library to shave and clean up.[25]

After the long drive, all of us weary travelers arrived at Dick's place in the hot, muggy, mosquito-infested woods. Grandmother napped on Dick's bed, while I tried to sleep outside on a hammock. It must have been 100 degrees in the shade with what seemed like 100 percent relative humidity. I decided then and there I would never study at Duke. Some prophet I was!

Before the graduation ceremony, Dick gave us a tour of the campus. Don also knew his way around. While attending Guilford College in Greensboro, he had visited Dick at Duke, but lack of a car curtailed his travel, and Dick spent most of his time studying and working anyway. Times were so rough in the mid 1930s that Don soon decided to return to Whittier to help support the family by working in the store and managing the meat department. I think that suited him better than academia anyway.

Following our tour, my family and I headed to Page Auditorium. I can only imagine the sense of pride Dad, Mom, and Grandmother must have felt watching Dick graduate third in the class of 1937 and receive the added distinction of induction into the prestigious Order

25 Today Duke University's Nicholas School of the Environment and Earth Sciences occupies the land where Whippoorwill Manor once stood.

of the Coif, the national legal honor society.[26] Don and I, on the other hand, found amusement as we sat in the hot balcony listening to the unfamiliar southern names being read as the law school graduates marched to the podium. When Don heard a name that particularly amused him, he would nudge me. He got my attention and I giggled.

The family—now including Dick—crowded into our car for the return trip to Whittier via the Midwestern states. Dick brought only a few possessions—mainly his clothes. He had shipped his law books and papers home as cargo.

In those days, we tried to avoid staying in motels, called "auto courts" or "auto camps," because they had a reputation for attracting unsavory clientele and often didn't meet the hygiene standards of Mother and Grandmother. In fact, Mom insisted that they inspect the rooms before staying there. If they didn't pass inspection, she would say, "We will go on a little farther."

Whenever we could, we stayed with relatives—but not just to avoid auto courts. In Pennsylvania, Ohio, Indiana, and Iowa—Quaker country—we stopped to see Nixon and Milhous relatives and got to know ones we hadn't met before. They always had a guest room, a spare bed or two—or maybe just sleeping bags or blankets. Through those visits, we became more familiar with our ancestry. Later we dubbed our 1937 journey the "heritage trip."

From Durham, we headed north to State College, Pennsylvania, to see Dad's brother Ernest and his family. He was the only one of Dad's siblings to have earned a college degree. In fact, he went on for his doctorate and then taught agronomy and plant-extension pathology at Penn State. At his home, I met Aunt Mary and cousins Alice, Ernestine (nicknamed "Dimpy" because of her dimples), and Leland Warren "Nicky." In the East, the cultural norm was for boys to wear short pants until they turned twelve. Ten-year-old Nicky didn't like the fact that I, at age seven, showed up wearing long pants. Making matters worse, in his opinion, I stood several inches taller than he.

As the adults were talking, someone suggested that Alice accompany us to California for her graduation present. She had just graduated from Penn State and wanted to see the country. The plan was for

---

26 Bill Perdue and Lyman Brownfield graduated first and second in the class respectively.

Don and Eddie
at Duke University, 1937
∿Family album

Three Generations at Duke
∿Family album

Uncle Ernest Nixon's
family in State
College, Pa, 1937
(l-r) Hannah, Dimpy,
Don, Mary, Eddie,
Ernest, Alice, Nicky,
Dick, Frank
∿Courtesy of Ernestine
"Dimpy" Nixon Noll

her to help Mom bake pies when we got home. Uncle Ernest gave her some money for the trip, and then all seven of us piled into our car. To this day, Dimpy and I cannot figure out how we ever fit. I must have sat on someone's lap.

Leaving Pennsylvania, we traveled west through Ohio and Indiana. My parents insisted we stop to see their birthplaces—Dad's near McArthur in Vinton County, Ohio, and Mom's near Butlerville, Jennings County, Indiana. I don't remember much about McArthur except Dad commenting on how much the area had changed since his childhood.

At the farm in Butlerville that Grandmother and Grandfather had left in 1897, she sat by the Rush Branch stream and with nostalgia penned the following poem:

Our Indiana Home

I'm sitting by the dear old stream
That ran below our home,
That dear old home, so sadly gone –
The one we used to own.

The little creek is much the same
As years and years ago,
The solid rock that formed the walk
Along the side clear waters flow.

And often in the summertime
Wading in the nearby brook,
The children caught their little fish
With bent pins for their hook.

Farther down, where the water's deep,
They went to take a dip,
Their city cousins thought this fun,
The best part of the trip.
How often in the years agone
The children played right here,
Waded in the water cool

Of dangers had no fear.

Here were all my children born,
The yard was so pretty and green,
Those happy days so full and gay
Of memories I like to dream.[27]

Next we took Grandmother to Seymour, Indiana, where she stayed to visit friends, and we continued our trip home. At least that gave us a little more space in the car for the longest stretch of our journey.

Just a few days after arriving back in Whittier, the phone rang at the Marshburns. My cousin Howard remembered the incident vividly. He was home alone when the call came from Western Union asking if someone could come uptown to pick up a telegram, the primary means of long-distance communication in that era. Howard hopped on his bike, pedaled up to the WU office, and raced back home to deliver the message to his mom, my aunt Olive, who had arrived home in the meantime. The telegram reported that Grandmother had contracted an acute infection that the doctors considered life threatening.

A few calls later, Dad learned of her illness and sprang into action. When he made up his mind to do something, he did it. And Dad would do anything for Grandmother. He insisted on driving rather than having Mom and Olive fly to their mother's bedside. First he enlisted my cousin Alden Beeson to load our car for the trip to Indiana. Then, he and Alden, who had a lead foot, drove nonstop with Mom, Aunt Olive, and her daughter Marygene, making the 2,400-mile trip in forty-eight hours, quite a feat in those days. Dick, Don, and my older cousins looked after me while my parents were traveling.

By the time they arrived in Seymour, Grandmother had shaken the intestinal flu and was recovering comfortably. She decided to continue her delayed excursion, traveling next to Mason City, Iowa, to see more close relatives. As she had done many times before, she traveled home by train. Dad and his group, too, returned home safely. After all the wear on the engine, he had it disassembled and examined. That engine passed inspection without any damage, thus securing Dad's loyalty to Chevrolet for the rest of his life.

---

27 Price 109.

Meanwhile, Alice enjoyed her time visiting Nixon relatives in Southern California. A pie-baker she wasn't, however. Her sister Dimpy thought we should have taken her instead. She informed us she would have been much more helpful to Mom—her "Aunt Mildred," as our Nixon cousins called her. After a few months with us, Alice returned home to State College to marry her sweetheart.

∿ ∿

Dad put in a lot of miles in 1937. Our family grocery store could finally afford a delivery van, so that summer Dad rode the train to Flint, Michigan, where Chevrolets were manufactured, and picked up a panel station wagon. Detouring to Ohio in his new vehicle, he visited Uncle Lyle, his father's youngest brother. Dad always appreciated Uncle Lyle's kindness during the difficult period after Dad's mother died. Lyle, now a widower, eagerly took Dad up on his invitation to travel with him to California.

My first impression of Uncle Lyle was of a frail old man with a mustache. He must have been seventy-seven years old. I enjoyed his visit, because he smiled often, got along with everybody, and acted like a kid seeing all the new sights in California.

Dick and Don drove Uncle Lyle down to the beach, where they took pictures of him in his pre-1920s full-body bathing suit. I thought he looked funny, but he didn't mind wearing old-fashioned clothes. My brothers and I couldn't help but be happy seeing the delight on his face as he waded into the ocean—the first time he had ever experienced the feel and smell of salt water.

Uncle Lyle had heard about Yosemite, Sequoia, and the Sierra Nevada Mountains. Because Ohio doesn't have mountains to speak of, Dad, Dick, and Don decided to take him to Sequoia National Park to see the big trees—the giant sequoias. We traveled over the Ridge Route up to Bakersfield, toward Lindsay, and up into King's Canyon. When Uncle Lyle saw the General Sherman tree, he could not believe its size. He looked up and he must have walked around that tree three times and then tried to find a piece of string long enough to encircle it. Not succeeding, he paced around the tree again and counted the number of steps. We had a hard time coaxing him away from it. He was just so impressed with that giant tree.

In contrast to my teetotaling family, Uncle Lyle was not averse to stopping in a saloon or tavern to cure what he called "gastric indigestion," so he pleaded with our dad to stop when he spotted one. Even though Dad disapproved of alcohol, he consented to stop. There Uncle Lyle ordered himself a draft of beer, downed it, and said, "Ah, I can make it all the way back home now. Let's go." So, I learned at a young age that beer does have a palliative effect.

DICK, MY MENTOR

Dick settled back into family life at our home in Whittier. I had missed him and was thrilled the three-year separation had ended. After passing the California bar exam, Dick went to work for the law firm of Wingert and Bewley, with offices on the top floor of the Bank of America Building on the corner of Greenleaf and Philadelphia Street, six blocks from Whittier College. He let me get involved in adult work by bringing me to the law office to lick stamps and run errands. At age seven, I felt significant, if not important, being able to help my older brother.

Dick's return to Whittier meant more fun for me, but it also meant more emphasis on schoolwork. Living at home during that period, he could take a more active interest in my learning. My natural inclination had always been toward science, mathematics, and technical things. While Dick appreciated that, he wanted me to have a well-rounded education, and he encouraged me toward the social arts as well, which must have been a thankless job for him in those early years. The differences in our attitudes toward education were great. Dick had always enjoyed school, finding it exciting, and he loved a good book. I, on the other hand, preferred to play outdoors and help at the store.

Mom used to say that Richard's hobby as a youngster was reading the newspaper. At age nine, he had become upset when he read about the Teapot Dome oil scandal during the Harding Administration—a case of money influencing politics. Secretary of the Interior Albert B. Fall was under Senate investigation for taking bribes for leasing the Teapot Dome oil fields in Wyoming to an oil operator without competitive bidding. Secretary Fall was eventually convicted. As Mom reported, "Richard decided then that most of all he wanted to become an honest attorney."

Dick loved history and literature, but his attempts to intrigue me with those subjects met with little success. I was baffled how he could find it stimulating to sit in a classroom or read a book when life revolved around people as exciting as those who came to our store every day. My attitude must have discouraged Dick, but with his characteristic determination, he persisted, and eventually it did some good.

Unlike many young men with kid brothers, Dick often included me on his trips and on his dates. In high school, he started dating the popular and attractive Ola Florence Welch, his first romantic interest. Together they starred in the senior class Latin play, Virgil's *Aeneid*, and then they both enrolled at Whittier College. Dick and Ola Florence usually asked me to come along on their Sunday trips to the mountains when I was just preschool aged. We would climb rocks and have picnics, and I eagerly looked forward to those outings. I liked Ola Florence very much, but Dick's and her relationship went nowhere, except into their catalogs of good friends. Maybe Ola Florence's more liberal persuasion introduced too much contention into their conversations. Whatever the reason, by the end of college, they had parted ways, and Ola found a new beau, whom she later married.

Dick was considered one of the most eligible bachelors in Whittier when he returned from Duke with his law degree. Then in January 1938, Dick's life focus changed; he met a beautiful red-haired young lady named Pat Ryan at the Whittier Little Theater tryouts for the play *The Dark Tower*. At his insistence, they began to date. Like Dad when he first met Mom, Dick knew right away that Pat was the woman for him, but unlike Mom, Pat gave little encouragement to her persistent suitor in the early days of their acquaintance.

Pat taught business courses at Whittier High School and advised the pep club. When my family and I met her, she was so full of energy and enthusiasm that all of us were immediately drawn to her. Pat fascinated me with her beauty, kindness, and athletic prowess. She won me over by saying, "Eddie, let's go to the beach." I loved that because my family seldom had time to take me. She would drive me down to Huntington Beach and race me to the sand. Although only nine years old, I was nearly as tall as Pat, but she could outrun me. That was quite an accomplishment, I thought, because with my long legs, I could beat everyone in my class. That fact alone qualified her to be my brother's wife, so I gave Dick my approval, telling him, "You can marry her if you want."

Dick and Don jointly owned a brown 1937 Chevrolet coupe. With both my brothers dating, each wanted the car every Saturday evening. Using it on alternate Saturday nights conflicted with Dick's intentions to pursue Pat Ryan at every opportunity. Many arguments over the car ensued until Dick decided he was doing well enough financially to buy one of his own. He ordered a new Oldsmobile for delivery at the factory in Lansing, Michigan, planning to travel there by train. Then he would drive the car back to California.

Dick decided to take me with him on that trip during my spring break in March 1939. He didn't have to, but as the big brother, he wanted to spend more time with me. At not quite nine years of age, I felt pleased and excited that my twenty-six-year-old brother would invite me to go along.

Don drove us to Union Station in Los Angeles, which serviced the Southern Pacific, Union Pacific, and Santa Fe lines. The station was one of my favorite destinations, with its fascinating Western motifs. I especially enjoyed the paintings of Southwest Indians and desert scenery. Whenever a relative traveled by train, our family would make a special event of going to Union Station, and Dick's and my trip was no exception. A crowd of friends and family gathered to wish us farewell.

The Union Pacific train pulled out as we waved good-bye to everyone. At Pomona, the first stop, the conductor came by, saying, "This must be your coat, young man. Your other brother brought it to the station."

I had left my coat in Don's car but hadn't realized it was missing. When Don discovered it, he decided to race the train to the first stop. I would have gotten quite a chill without my coat in March. Such thoughtfulness was typical of Don.

The thirty-nine-hour trip took us through the magnificent canyons of Utah and then across the Great Plains. We ate in the dining car and slept two nights on the coach-class seats.

During the journey, both Dick and I noticed the beautiful stewardess, who always had a friendly smile and time to chat. Dick struck up a conversation with the young lady on a number of occasions. When she got off the train in Omaha, I was disappointed, wondering why Dick let her get away. I didn't understand then the intensity of his feelings for Pat—and for her alone.

With just the two of us traveling the vast expanse of inland America, Dick and I had lots of interaction. He asked me about my schooling and what I wanted to do when I grew up. Taking advantage of many teaching moments, he gave me pointers on life. Most of all, he wanted me to understand the world. And I learned from him, because he made learning intriguing.

We proceeded to Chicago, where we changed trains to Lansing. Upon arrival there, we taxied directly to the Oldsmobile headquarters for directions. As soon as we checked in at the assembly plant, we spotted Dick's brand new Olds coupe. To keep the price to bare minimum, Dick had ordered no special accessories: no heater, no radio, just two doors, sleek body, an engine, black paint. He couldn't afford any of those extras, and he didn't need a heater in Southern California anyway. Nevertheless, that was a great car from my viewpoint. I can still remember the distinctive smell of that new car.

After a tour of the factory, Dick and I began our trip home. He gave me a map and said, "Now, Eddie, I want you to study this map. After we reach Chicago, we'll follow Route 66 all the way to California. If you find a stretch of road straight enough and long enough, I'll let you sit between my legs and steer the car on our trip back home."

I tell you, I learned to read maps right away, and I read them like crazy. I've been a map reader ever since—looking for that straight road.

From Lansing to St. Louis, Dick had to drive at thirty miles per hour to break in the engine. After that, it was full speed ahead up to each state's limit, some as high as fifty-five miles per hour or even "Reasonable and Proper."

Dick and I ate at greasy-spoon truck stops and stayed in auto courts. For two or three dollars a night, we'd get a bedroom with a shared bathroom. A very fancy motel would have cost as much as five or six dollars. Along the often deserted stretches of highway, we felt lucky just to find a place to stay, and we weren't as particular about our accommodations as Mother and Grandmother. Besides, we had no relatives or friends along the route who could offer us lodging.

Dick had a way of intriguing kids. That's why he was a great teacher. Wanting to make the journey both fun and educational for me, he stopped at several historical sites, including the Will Rogers Museum and memorial in Claremore, Oklahoma, which had opened in 1938. A Cherokee Indian, born in 1879, Will became a cowboy, movie actor, radio commentator, author, humorist, and pundit. He had met an untimely death in 1935 in a plane crash in Alaska with Wiley Post, the famous aviator. I was impressed that Will Rogers had so many talents.

Noting his quotation, "I never met a man I didn't like," inscribed on the base of his statue, I asked, "Dick, what did he mean by that?"

"Just think about it."

I pondered for a moment and then said, "Maybe he hadn't met everyone."

In the Midwest and Rocky Mountain states, I was curious about the big green brontosaurus, Sinclair Oil's gas station logo. I asked Dick, "What does that dinosaur have to do with gasoline and oil?"

"Well, perhaps it suggests all that oil in the earth came from extinct animals buried down there somewhere," he answered. "So, to that extent, paleontology connects with geology."

We entered New Mexico where the roads were long and straight. I was having a great time occasionally getting over to the driver's side and steering that car—with Dick's guidance, of course. Crossing into Arizona, I noticed an unusual site name near Flagstaff. "It says 'Meteor Crater' on the map. What's that?" He never answered my questions directly. Instead he used them as a teaching opportunity.

"I don't know," he replied. "Let's go see."

Dick veered off Route 66 onto a narrow dirt road about a quarter mile up to the rim of the crater and parked near a small rustic museum, the site of an impressive tourist facility today. An elderly gentleman with a full beard was selling bits of meteorite. To me, he looked like a hermit. At first I didn't realize the depth of his knowledge and his affection for that crater.

Looking into the huge cavity, I stood captivated by the immense hole in the Earth three-quarters of a mile wide. Then questions started popping out of me.

"What is this hole? How did they get this big, beautiful stadium out here? Where did it come from? How was it made?"

Geology not being Dick's area of expertise, he seemed perplexed too. So, he set me up to ask the questions and said, "Check with this gentleman here. Ask him where he found these bits of metal."

Realizing my big brother didn't know all the answers surprised me, but I happily followed his suggestion. I turned to the man, who said, "A meteor hit the Earth. We don't know what part of the sky it came from, but we're pretty sure a shooting star came all the way down here."

"Where did the meteor go? Has anybody found it?"

"No one knows. Geologists have drilled and surveyed but never found it. The meteor must have exploded before hitting Earth, so we just find little bits here and there."

So, I was left with the question, "How could the meteor have made such a huge crater?"[28]

As we turned to leave that incredible site, Dick bought me a small sample of meteorite for 25 cents to take home as a souvenir. That meteorite lasted less than two weeks after I showed it at school. But from that point on, I knew I would either become an astronomer or a geologist, and I've studied both ever since.

After our stop at Meteor Crater, Dick wanted to revisit Prescott, Arizona, where he had spent time with Mom and Harold. He felt close to Prescott and would return there at any opportunity. And he wanted me to see it and have true memories of where I had spent time in my earliest years.

We found the Clows' house that evening and stayed overnight. Dick obviously felt at home, and Mrs. Clow impressed me with her generous, friendly spirit—very much like our mother in character. I don't recall any other family members there during our visit.

---

28 Meteor Crater was the first impact crater to be identified and is the best preserved example on Earth. Scientists believe an asteroid about 80 feet in diameter formed the crater 20,000 to 50,000 years ago.

The Barringer Crater - better known as "Meteor Crater"
From the "World's Greatest Wonders" (1930)

∾Public domain

In the morning before continuing our journey back to Whittier, Dick took me to breakfast at the Green Frog Café in downtown Prescott. I guess I raved about the pancakes and maple syrup, because Dick kidded me about it many years later.

For a couple of months after returning to school in the spring of 1939, I begged Mrs. Rydell, my teacher at Lowell Elementary, to let our class study astronomy. I wanted to learn about the stars and see where those meteors originated. Considering the extra time and effort needed to plan such a special project, Mrs. Rydell showed no excitement about my idea. However, my classmates shared my enthusiasm after listening to my stories of Meteor Crater, so Mrs. Rydell finally instructed us how to build a miniature planetarium out of wooden lath and heavy packaging paper. We built it with an overhead dome by punching holes in the paper, attempting to approximate the look of the night sky. I don't know how much time that project took for Mrs. Rydell or whether she had to get permission to deviate from the curriculum, but her willingness to accommodate our curiosity caused me to include her among my list of great teachers. The project interested a lot of other kids in astronomy too.

✒ CHAPTER 4 ✒
CURRENT EVENTS

From our earliest years, Dick, Don, and I listened to discussions on current events, political philosophy, and business. At the dinner table, in the store, or in the car—wherever Dad was—he would instigate lively conversations, which often ended in arguments. When we were older, we participated in those exchanges. Dad got us to think, and anytime we expressed our opinions, we had better be able to defend them. I'm sure Dad influenced Dick's political views; he certainly influenced mine.

As long as Dad was in the room, his philosophy was at the forefront of the discussion. When he disagreed with people, he wanted them to correct their thinking immediately. Mother, on the other hand, was imbued with the friendly persuasion of her Quaker faith and insisted that Dad get better acquainted with his adversary before imposing his opinions with a sledgehammer. Mom's peacekeeping ways also profoundly influenced Dick, because he saw that she got her point across successfully without alienating people.

I heard rumors growing up that Mom had disagreed with Dad over the 1912 election, although women did not have the right to vote until 1920. Mom was never disagreeable, and she seldom challenged him. Therefore, the family could never confirm the suspicion that she had favored Woodrow Wilson, who was known as "the peacemaker." Most Quakers were pacifists and did support Wilson. Dad, on the other hand, strongly supported Theodore Roosevelt, who then was running as the Progressive Party candidate. Mom didn't like Teddy's belligerent nature; Dad did. Like Roosevelt, Dad believed that stopping violence, with force if necessary, was the best way to preserve peace.

Dad had a populist streak along the lines of Senator Robert La Follette of Wisconsin. Both sympathized with the small business owner and the common man. After all, Dad was one himself. He resented tactics used by big corporations and trusts, aiming to squeeze the little guys out of business by cutting prices below cost just long enough to destroy small-town customer loyalties. He encouraged everyone he knew to avoid doing business with John D. Rockefeller's Standard Oil Company and instead to trade with the independents. I can imagine how delighted Dad would have been if he had lived to see his son defeat a Rockefeller for the Republican presidential nomination.

According to Dad, big government threatened small business and the common man as much as big corporations did. He favored free and fair competition rather than government controls. He also ardently defended the Constitution. The Preamble became his life principle: "The government should 'promote the general welfare,' but it dare not provide it," he would say.

To Dad, *liberal* meant "Let the government do it." Dad would say, "Keep the government out of our private lives. It has no business there." He would never accept government welfare and didn't think anyone else should either. People needed to be self-reliant if they wanted to preserve liberty, he thought.

One example of government intruding on Dad's liberty concerned the fireplace he had built in the family's house in Yorba Linda. According to the building code, he had to have it inspected by the county. The building inspector checked Dad's work and said, "I'm not going to pass it. You'll have to take down the back wall, because you can't build a fireplace like that. An earthquake could cause these bricks to fall right off the back and onto the fire and then onto the floor. It's just too great a risk."

Thinking that a bunch of nonsense, Dad promptly launched into an argument about masonry. "The bricks won't fall, but if they're going to fall out of the chimney, they're going to fall whether the back wall is facing this way or that. They're going to spread those ashes one way or another."

The inspector got firm. "Yeah, well, I can't approve it like that, so you'll just have to tear it down."

Not to be outdone, Dad rejoined, "All right. I'll tear my fireplace down and build it the way you want. But as soon as you're gone and I get my approval, I'll tear it down again and build it back the way I want."

"Okay, you might as well keep it the way it is," the inspector relented. He signed off on Dad's fireplace.

Dad had won. He was so stubborn. Whether he was right or just convinced of it, he wouldn't back down. I suppose he passed that personality trait on to his sons in one form or another.

THE GREAT DEPRESSION

Growing up in the Great Depression, I remember people from Arkansas and Oklahoma—the Dust Bowl—driving down Whittier Boulevard in caravans of dilapidated jalopies full of kids inside and loaded with two or three mattresses on top. Dirt poor and hungry, those folks wondered where they could find work. What could they do? How could they survive? They all wanted to work, but there weren't enough jobs to go around. Occasionally single people, called "tramps" in those days, would knock on the door, hungry and looking for something to eat. They often stopped at Grandmother's house, because she had a reputation for giving to those in need.

They would ask, "Do you have some bread or something I can eat?"

"I do have something for thee, but thee will have to cut some wood on that pile out there. Could thee do that for me?" Grandmother answered. She made them work, and they did it gladly because they were hungry. That made an impression on all of us. She exemplified compassion as a means of meeting personal needs, while preserving the dignity of the needy by offering them work.

Witnessing our family's efforts on behalf of people in need during the Depression, my brothers and I saw that private help could be more effective than government aid. Mom, Dad and Grandmother were among those generous people who believed compassion was just as vital to meeting human needs as was physical assistance. Theirs was the traditional response of relative helping relative, neighbor helping neighbor, and people helping strangers in need.

One example was Mr. George Gipple, who worked as a janitor at Lowell Elementary School. He and his wife had several children, and they had to watch every penny and half penny to make a go of it. They survived with a little neighborly credit, running up quite a bill at F.A. Nixon—General Merchandise. Nevertheless, by the start of World War II, Mr. Gipple had paid it all, minus some of the debt Mom and Dad just forgave.

Dad respected Mr. Gipple's honesty and work ethic. He said, "A person like that is always worthy of help."

We were quite fortunate to have had the grocery store, so we never went hungry, but our parents made us realize that some people did not have enough to eat. Don most resembled Mom in generosity. In fact, one of his high school buddies, Herman Brannon, told a story of Don taking a couple of quarters out of the till at the store every morning and slipping them into his shoe. When Don got to school, he would quietly pass the quarters to Herman, so he could buy something to eat. Herman, a big kid, never had breakfast at his home. Realizing his friend went to school hungry, Don decided to do something about it.

Five or six of my friends in grammar school were really destitute. About 1937, the local kids were taunting a boy in our class from the Dust Bowl, because he didn't have any overalls, the current fad. It was all his parents could do to keep something on his rear, but he pestered them for overalls. His mother finally broke down and bought him some coveralls—not overalls like the other boys were wearing. He came to school, obviously proud of his new clothes, but some kid made fun of those coveralls. I befriended the boy after that sad incident. All the children in our entire family were taught to do something for those who needed help and to realize that others didn't have all the benefits we were so fortunate to possess.

Along with the waves of Depression-era migrants pouring into Southern California, our Nixon relatives from Ohio and West Virginia came to seek sustenance and employment. In California, we were blessed with plenty of food—a scarce commodity in much of the country. And our large, close-knit family took care of each other. My parents were always willing to put up relatives for the night or an extended stay.

Dad's youngest sister Carrie Wildermuth, a widow, and her sons Merrill and Floyd moved to California from Ohio about 1930. They settled in Fullerton, just five miles down the road from our house. I remember Floyd being the huskiest guy around, and Merrill, his older brother, smoking and eating meat and potatoes—didn't want anything else.

Dad's oldest brother Walter, his wife Nellie, and their daughters Thelma and Wanda also came from Ohio to live with us for a while in1936 or 1937. With Harold gone and Dick away at Duke Law School, we had plenty of room. Thelma, who was about Don's age, and Wanda, who was about eight years younger, made trustworthy babysitters, and their parents helped out in our store.

One story I remember from the time Uncle Walter and his family lived with us involved Slim Craddick. Uncle Walter and Slim often had heated discussions—frequently about our old rooster. That bird would crow at the first sign of light in the morning, as roosters do. Slim didn't like waking up that early. Tired of hearing Slim complain, Uncle Walter one day decided to cook up that rooster and make a stew out of him. He put a big pot of water on the stove to scald the bird and remove the feathers. While sharpening the axe, he heard a bang. Slim had shot the rooster—knocked its head clean off. Uncle Walter went out whistling a tune, picked up the bird, which was still flapping, and dumped it in the pot of water. He just carried on as if nothing unusual had happened. Slim was speechless for a week—and probably disappointed that he didn't get a rise out of Uncle Walter. Slim seemed to like riling people—as did Dad.

THE NEW DEAL

Around the dinner table, Dad would reflect on the late 1920s and early 1930s, expounding on how the country got into that mess and how it could get out. He felt the Depression had resulted from greed and overindulgence in the stock market. Without some kind of controls, a great crash could occur again, but Dad said the government shouldn't go too far in trying to take care of people.

During the 1930s, however, thousands of Californians jumped on the bandwagon to promote socialist pension schemes such as the Townsend Plan, "Ham and Eggs," and End Poverty in California (EPIC), all of which originated in California. As a child, I remember Dad and other people arguing about those plans. Dad felt most of them were the wrong response to the Depression, but, oddly, he did support the Townsend Plan—a dramatic departure from his philosophy. Perhaps he felt there was a limit to what compassion could do for the multitudes of truly destitute older people during that time.

The Townsend Plan was the brainchild of Dr. Francis Townsend, who had become unemployed at age sixty-six without any savings. He proposed that all U.S. citizens over the age of sixty be allowed to retire on a pension of two hundred dollars a month, provided they met certain conditions. Robert Noble called for the state government to issue scrip and every Thursday pay thirty dollars to every unemployed Californian fifty years of age and older. His plan was nicknamed "Ham and Eggs." Upton Sinclair, the socialist author and crusader, devised the twelve-point EPIC plan. He advocated giving fifty dollars a month to all needy persons over age sixty.

The argument for those plans was: "You need sustenance in order to live." But Dad said the proponents forgot that people also needed self-respect earned by producing something of value. Free-market exchange would best enhance their lives, he believed. Furthermore, none of the schemes were economically viable. No one could fool Dad by "something for nothing" promises; he knew taxpayers would end up paying for those programs one way or another.

With all the poverty and unrest in the country in the early 1930s, President Franklin Roosevelt felt compelled to take drastic action to return the country to prosperity. He modified some of the more radical proposals and established government programs that came to be known as the "New Deal."

Although government assistance existed before the New Deal in the form of state aid, veterans' pensions and poor houses, families then took much greater responsibility for the care of their elderly and disabled. Generous people in the churches cared for those who didn't have families. If church members found people hungry and in desperate need, they would bring them wood to burn for warmth and food they could survive on. According to Dad, that was the proper way to help.

The New Deal became one of Dad's favorite targets to attack. He agreed with Thomas Dewey, who first ran for the Republican presidential nomination in 1940 as an opponent of Roosevelt's programs. Dewey said that from the New Deal we got the "ABC Appetite." He could spiel off one acronym after another:

AAA	–	Agriculture Adjustment Act
CCC	–	Civilian Conservation Corps
FDIC	–	Federal Deposit Insurance Corporation
FERA	–	Federal Emergency Relief Administration
NLRA	–	National Labor Relations Act
NRA	–	National Recovery Act
PWA	–	Public Works Administration
SSA	–	Social Security Administration
TVA	–	Tennessee Valley Authority
WPA	–	Works Project Administration

Social Security, a New Deal program based on ideas from Central Europe during the nineteenth century, guaranteed assistance to people in their retirement years. Dad, however, feared people would depend too much on their government checks. He believed everyone should save and invest privately in any way possible and every way affordable.

The Works Project Administration engaged in many worthwhile projects such as building lodges in national parks and building, improving, and maintaining roads. While most of the workers were serious about their jobs, too many, however, were adept at drawing benefits from the WPA without contributing their fair share of the work. They got a reputation for preferring to lean on their shovel handles.

The aspect of these programs that Dad despised most was the growth of government. It just got bigger and bigger and more intrusive all the time. Typifying needless and excessive government meddling was the U.S. Department of Agriculture's steady stream of flyers mailed to all the food merchants, telling them how to run their businesses. During the Depression, Dad received a brochure titled something like "Instructions to Grocers and Meat Markets" on how to market an old hen. The flyer said one could make a pretty good meal out of an old hen, and "Here's how to do it." Upon reading that, Dad's face turned red. He threw the flyer down and then scribbled a note on a plain piece of paper, folded it, stuck it in an envelope along with the flyer, and addressed it to the USDA.

"What are you doing, Dad?" Dick questioned.

"I asked them to send me pictures of the guy who designed that brochure and the one who told him to send it out."

"Well, why would you want to do that?"

"Because I'm going to flush those pictures down the toilet!" Dad's reaction was "Get off my back. Don't waste my tax money on things like useless flyers."

Alarmed by the expansion of government, Dad worried that all the social and economic programs would erode people's self-reliance. He felt the government was encouraging people toward statism, and he feared Roosevelt's assistance to the able-bodied would become a crutch, eventually crippling them—and the country.

"You've got to take care of yourself and the people around you. Don't look to government to do anything you can do yourself," he would admonish.

Better Times

In May 1939, after Dick and I returned from the trip to Michigan, our parents bought a truly distinctive home about three miles from our store. Mr. S. Martin Stoody, the owner and manager of a once-prosperous oil tool manufacturing company, had built the home. During the Depression, his company went out of business. My parents saw the estate listed at an auction. Mom wondered if they would appear too elite if they lived in a place like that. Dad said, "Well, there's nothing wrong with the land, and it's a good place to live. There would be plenty of room for guests and perhaps a niece or nephew could make use of the short walk to Whittier College. Let's just buy it." His offer was accepted, and he and Mom got the house for about $9,000.

The old Stoody estate extended from the ridge of the hill above Whittier College down to the street below. Mr. Stoody had traveled the Western Hemisphere extensively and had brought back many botanical specimens, which he planted in his huge garden. Our backyard resembled a South American forest with monkey puzzle trees and other plants, especially from Chile and neighboring countries. A trail wound through the garden, following a recirculating stream and fishponds.

Compared with the small homes we had lived in, our new home appeared huge and elegant. However, from the street, passersby could not tell what a grand house we lived in. They saw only a small front yard and a one-story building with a turret on top that seemed strangely out of place; no other house in the neighborhood had one. Hidden from view were three more stories down the steep slope to the backyard. The main floor included a living room, dining room, kitchen, breakfast room, and a garage. The bedrooms were on the floor below. Finally Dick, Don, and I each had our own. The basement, which housed the furnace and laundry facilities with a large amount of space to spare, opened into the garden.

What a thrill for me to discover that the turret housed a circular observatory with a rotating roof. I considered it our home's best feature. A spiral staircase led up to the observatory from the entry hall. Mr. Stoody had installed an eight-inch reflector telescope, but he had taken it with him when he moved. He used to tell the story around town of going up to the observatory and focusing the telescope on his office in downtown Los Angeles. He claimed he could read the time on a small watch he left in the window there.

Because I was already interested in astronomy, the observatory increased my desire to learn about the universe. I said to my parents, "Boy, let's get a telescope up there."

Dad wouldn't hear of it. "No, I don't want to open that turret. It might start leaking."

Although disappointed that the view from the top would not be available, I realized that small circular room would still provide a great den for games and activities with my friends.

I enjoyed having Dick and Don living at home, but I knew my brothers were bound to move out one day. Dick was seriously pursuing Pat Ryan, and Don was not yet serious but surveying the field, as healthy young men do. I watched Dick going through his engagement process. He and Pat didn't talk much about their plans; they just decided to move ahead and do the deed. At the age of ten, I realized the imminent event would profoundly affect my life. Although happy for them, I wondered how far away they might go.

A very private young lady, Pat didn't want attention showered on her as the bride-to-be. Having had to scrimp and save to work her way through the University of Southern California, she planned a simple wedding that wouldn't put them in debt. Dick had no assets to speak of, but at least he was becoming established in a successful law practice.

The president of Whittier College, who was also a Quaker minister, officiated at the ceremony on June 21, 1940, at the Mission Inn in Riverside, California, one of Dick and Pat's favorite locations for dinner dates. I could see why. The historic building covered the entire city block. Medieval Spanish artwork and stained glass windows created a warm, colorful atmosphere. Heavy drapery in Mediterranean hues decorated the ceiling of the small chapel where Dick and Pat said their Quaker vows. Following the ceremony, the newlyweds greeted the fifty or so guests in a brief reception in the long Spanish art gallery.

Our immediate family, along with Pat's brothers Tom and Bill Ryan, her half sister Neva Renter, Neva's husband Marc, and some of Dick's and Pat's close friends attended.[29] Among the guests was Mrs. Holt, Pat's closest friend at Whittier High School, who taught a very popular Spanish class. At the wedding, Pat introduced her to me as Mrs. Holt, but I knew everyone called her "the Señora," although she wasn't Hispanic. She had an infectious smile, and when I saw her later during visits at Dick and Pat's, she always figured out how to make me smile too.

---

29 Pat's parents died when she was a teenager, her mother from cancer and her father from tuberculosis.

After the wedding, Dick and Pat honeymooned for two weeks, driving through Mexico as free spirits with no particular schedule or destination. When they returned to Whittier, my parents held a big reception for them at our home. The newlyweds invited all their friends and relatives to the party, and most of them came. The beautiful hillside garden of that old Stoody estate accommodated the guests, with room to spare. From the balcony, Strauss waltzes filled the air. Merrill Wildermuth, Aunt Carrie's oldest son, recorded as much of the scene as he could fit on one reel with his new 16-millimeter movie camera.

Dad and Mom were very happy finally to have a daughter in the family. Mom had waited so long for a girl. They had thought I would be a Patricia, and now Dick had married one.

WAR YEARS

The young couple moved to a little house on Walnut Street in Whittier, and Dick continued his law practice and Pat her teaching. Then in early January 1942, just after the U.S. entered World War II, they drove across country to Washington, D.C., where he took a job with the Office of Price Administration (OPA) to manage the rationing of rubber tires. Dad expressed his reservations about Dick becoming a government bureaucrat in Roosevelt's Administration. He thought that was probably worse than if Dick were going off to war.

Then the news came that Dick had applied for a commission in the Navy. He reported to naval officers training in Quonset Point, Rhode Island, in August 1942. Because he had a law degree and government experience, he received a direct commission as a Lieutenant JG (junior grade). His first orders were to the Naval Air Station in Ottumwa, Iowa, where he went through the initial training to help organize a naval air transport field office in an undisclosed location. Boot training was very basic and quite abbreviated in those early days of World War II, but the men took it seriously. Disappointed at being landlocked, Dick wanted to see action in the South Pacific or the North Atlantic. Applying for sea duty, he eventually did receive orders to join the Pacific Fleet, however.

As a Quaker, Dick could have applied for draft deferment or noncombatant duty, but he was not a pacifist or a conscientious objector like others of our religion. Intent on seeking a just and lasting peace, he agreed with Dad that peace between nations would come only through military strength. Anything that needed to be done for our country and the cause of justice, Dick was willing to do.

Mother and Grandmother found it especially difficult to come to terms with Dick's decision. I won't say they were upset, because true to their Quaker beliefs, they tolerated what others' consciences led them to do. Nevertheless, it was still hard on them. I'm sure they would have been happier had he taken a job as an orderly or an ambulance driver, as had other Quaker members of our family.

Dick then received orders to report for duty in San Francisco, where he would be given his overseas assignment. First, he and Pat returned to Whittier to say good-bye to the family. Our parents, Don, his bride Clara Jane, some of Dick and Pat's friends, and I met at Union Station in Los Angeles to send them off on what could have been our last time to see Dick. We tried to keep the conversation upbeat during breakfast at Union Station's Fred Harvey House, but there was no denying the sadness of the occasion. As we waved good-bye to Dick and Pat when they boarded the train, Mother held her emotions in check, as she always did. But Dad began to sob. At that point, he probably thought Dick's working in Roosevelt's Administration hadn't been so bad after all. I'm sure the thought crossed our parents' minds that they might lose yet another son. And seeing Dad cry for the first time made me aware of the seriousness of the occasion.

Before Dick left for his thirteen-month tour of duty, he gave me a challenge and incentive because, as always, he was concerned about my future. At twelve years of age, I still wasn't much of a reader; I read too slowly to get interested in the material. So, Dick made a deal with me: "For every page you read, I'll give you a 25-cent savings stamp. It doesn't matter what you read—the *Reader's Digest* or an adventure book from the library—just not comic books. Those don't count. Mom's going to be the proctor for our bargain."

Every day Mom would ask me, "How much did you read? What did you read?" And I would have to prove I had done the reading.

With that incentive, I spent a good deal of time from then on with my nose in a book. I saved those stamps, pasted them in a book, and traded them for savings bonds. By the time Dick returned from sea duty and the bonds had matured, I had saved close to $375 as a result of our deal. Moreover, I picked up some good reading habits. Seven years later, I bought a $600 used 1940 Chevrolet town sedan with the savings stamp money and some additional earnings.

While Dick was overseas, I tried to follow his movements on a map. I referred to sketch maps printed in the daily newspapers, and beyond that, I just guessed at his location. In those days, it wasn't easy to find good maps, but occasionally I located some in old *National Geographic* magazines at the home of Aunt Edith and Uncle Tim.

Our family, of course, was thrilled to receive news that Dick would return from the South Pacific in July 1944. Pat greeted him at the airport in San Diego, and soon he reported for assignment as first lieutenant at the Alameda Naval Air Station near Oakland.

When he visited at our home, I noticed all kinds of changes in his mood and demeanor. Before he left, I remember him sitting and chatting about any number of topics. He had a more overt sense of humor then. And even though that sense of humor remained a part of him, even during his last days, it was often suppressed by the events of his life. After the war, he seemed pensive, as though digesting all he had seen and experienced. He didn't want to talk about those experiences, but once in a while he would mention nights in the pouring rain and sweltering heat, crouching in a foxhole, with bombs exploding all around.

Finally, Dick divulged his wartime whereabouts to me. He had arrived first in New Caledonia to the east of Australia and then moved north to Bougainville, the largest of the Solomon Islands, where he served with the South Pacific Combat Air Transport Command, known as SCAT. Before returning to the States, he was stationed on Green Island.

Dick told a story of sharing a two-man pup tent with another officer. Feeling something crawling on his arm, he awoke in the night. After flipping it off, he grabbed his flashlight to identify the intruder. Horrified, he saw the scorpion latching onto his buddy's arm. The man's scream woke the whole camp. Although the sting immediately caused severe pain and swelling, the man recovered—much to Dick's relief.

After Dick's assignment at the Alameda Naval Air Station, the Department of the Navy transferred him to a job working on contract

Dick on Bougainville Island, 1943
◡Hannah Nixon Family Collection

settlements with the Glen L. Martin Company of Baltimore, Maryland. He and Pat moved back East in early 1945. His renegotiation of the Navy contract with the Martin Company saved taxpayers $450,000.

THE CAMPAIGN OF 1946

While in Baltimore contemplating what to do after the Navy, Dick received an invitation from Herman Perry, a family friend and president of the Bank of America in Whittier, to present his credentials and his political beliefs to the "Committee of 100," which was searching for a Republican candidate to run for Congress in the Twelfth District. Dick found that prospect of interest, so he accepted their invitation and arrived at our home for a visit that I considered much too brief.

As he prepared for the presentation to the committee, Dick seemed unusually preoccupied. Immediately he poured his attention into drafting his statement of political philosophy that he would convey to the local leaders on the committee.

When I came home from Whittier High School in the afternoons, Mom would pull me aside, saying, "Richard is studying. Don't bother him right now. He's back in your bedroom just reading up a storm and making notes." To prepare, he always kept yellow foolscap notepads handy to jot down facts and ideas.

My bedroom was on the quiet corner of the house. I tried hard to respect his privacy despite my deep curiosity.

The committee gave Dick an overwhelming vote of confidence following his presentation. Although getting elected was a long shot, he was intrigued by the possibility and quickly launched into his campaign against Jerry Voorhis, a very popular, five-term New Deal Democrat. Dick promised a "fighting, rocking, socking campaign," and that's what it turned out to be, because Dick tackled politics with the same determination as he tackled everything else.

Not long after the primary on June 4, our entire family got caught up in Dick's feverish race for the November General Election. If anything, Dad was overly enthusiastic. Everyone he met got the campaign pitch—at the store, at the service station, wherever he went. Mom in her own quiet way was obviously pleased with her son's willingness to serve the country in a peacetime capacity.

After celebrating my sixteenth birthday, I passed my first driver's license test without much trouble, so now I was legally available to drive the Nixon's Market delivery truck, a 1937 Chevrolet panel. Volunteer workers painted campaign signs and plastered them all over the truck. Dad gave me the exciting opportunity and responsibility of driving it in parades around the Twelfth District, passing through Pomona, El Monte, Whittier, Covina, and so forth. By late summer, campaign workers in the parades carried Nixon buttons and little plastic thimbles printed with "*Nixon for Congress—Put the needle in the PAC*" to toss to bystanders along the parade routes. Those buttons and thimbles became quite popular with the crowds.

Voorhis had been endorsed by the local chapter of the National Citizens Political Action Committee (NCPAC), the non-union affiliate of the Congress of Industrial Organizations (CIO), then a left-wing confederation of labor unions, even though he was ambivalent about their support. Dick made that endorsement one of his main campaign issues, because pro-Soviet Communists had infiltrated those groups.

Another main issue was the economic situation facing the district and the country. Veterans returning home from World War II faced many problems, including a lower standard of living and insufficient housing. Prices were high, the economy was stagnant, and the federal bureaucracy had ballooned under the New Deal. Dick maintained that the country needed to return to vigorous free enterprise and to turn away from New Deal socialism with its belief that the government should take care of everyone's needs. He opposed burdensome government regulations and wage and price controls. Concerned that labor-management relations had become too strident, he felt the government should establish guidelines for negotiation rather than compulsory arbitration. In addition, he emphasized that class hatred and racial discrimination should have no place in America.

Regarding foreign affairs, Dick said isolationism had failed, and the U.S. must be prepared to defend freedom if democracy was to prevail over totalitarianism. Wary of the growing influence of the Soviet Union, both in the U.S. and abroad, he felt communism had to be contained and ultimately defeated.

Too soon for me, summer and the parade season came to an end. When school opened in the fall, I was most disappointed that Dad and Mom denied me permission to drive our old truck except on weekends.

Dick's focus changed from parades to preparation for the Nixon-Voorhis debates, which seemed his greatest hope for victory. He was a good debater, no question about that, but he never considered himself so good that he could beat any opponent; he just knew his issues, and he knew what he wanted to say. Although he had learned debating skills from Dad, Dick was less opinionated and volatile when he debated. He thought it better to be thoroughly informed, convincing his audience with facts and logic.

Throughout his schooling, Dick had excelled in debate. He learned the importance of preparation in grade school. In his first debate in the fifth grade, the issue was whether it was better to own or rent a home. With Dad's coaching, Dick ably defended the merits of renting—and won. In the seventh grade, the teacher had assigned the debate topic: "Resolved: That insects are more beneficial than harmful." Dick, who took the affirmative, called Uncle Tim, an entomologist for the University of California Citrus Experiment Station in Riverside. He gave Dick information on why we need ladybugs, aphids, bees, and other insects and taught him about the balance of nature and how the brutality of one species against another has a positive effect on maintaining that balance. Dick did his research and won the debate through presentation of scholarly knowledge. In high school and college, Dick continued to debate and won awards for his skill.

I attended the four Nixon-Voorhis debates held in different locations around the district in September and October. I especially remember the fourth debate at Monrovia High School during which Dick challenged Voorhis to tell the audience what bills he had introduced in the last four years that actually became law.

When Voorhis listed only speeches and resolutions, Dick pointed out that his sole legislative accomplishment had been a bill transferring oversight of rabbit farming from the Department of the Interior to the Department of Agriculture. "I guess you have to be a rabbit to have representation from the Twelfth District in Washington, D.C.," Dick concluded.

At that moment, the overflow audience burst into laughter, and Voorhis became flustered. Throughout the debates, he had fumbled and left Dick opportunities to attack his record and socialist leanings. Dick pointed out that Voorhis had voted the CIO-PAC line forty-one out of forty-six times. The consensus in the press, including *Newsweek* magazine and local newspapers, was that Dick had scored many points with the voters in those debates.

My brother won an upset victory on November 5 by a decisive margin of 15,592 votes. I remember the elation I felt during that most memorable event in all my teenage years. However, I had no idea of the lifelong effect his win would have on Dick and the rest of us.

∿ CHAPTER 5 ∿
NEW DIRECTIONS

The euphoria of winning the election subsided as Dick prepared to join the ranks of congressmen in the nation's capital. He realized his victory signaled deep voter dissatisfaction with the excesses of many of President Roosevelt's New Deal programs and concern about Communist influence in the government. Dick was eager to tackle these issues in the national arena, yet he knew criticizing an incumbent during a campaign was easier than bringing about positive change through the slow-moving legislative process. As an inexperienced freshman congressman, he realized his influence would be limited. He would have to work long hours to learn the ropes and put forth extra effort to make an impact.

Mom, Dad, Don, and I knew that diligence and tenacity, coupled with a keen intellect, were part of Dick's nature. We were confident he would learn his new job quickly, fulfill his campaign promises, and become a highly effective representative.

Dick and Pat moved to Washington, D.C., in December 1946 to begin this new phase of their lives. My parents and I took care of their baby daughter Tricia, born February 21, 1946, so Dick and Pat could search for a permanent residence near the capital. Finding a home suitable for raising a baby was difficult because of a critical postwar housing shortage—one of Dick's campaign issues. After residing at the Mayflower Hotel in Washington for several weeks, Dick and Pat finally rented a low-cost townhouse on Gunston Road in the Parkfairfax neighborhood of Alexandria, Virginia.

Because our folks had retired from their grocery business and were planning to move back East, they offered to drive Tricia to Washington, D.C., to be reunited with her parents. Mom, Dad, and the baby arrived in time for Dick's swearing-in ceremony on Capitol Hill on January 3, 1947. My school commitments prevented me from attending, but I heard all about the event via letter and a brief phone call from my proud parents. In those days, they couldn't afford costly long distance calls for lengthy chats.

When our parents retired from the grocery business during Dick's 1946 campaign, Don was already running the meat market and handling many of the day-to-day affairs. He then took over management of the store. With Dad on the scene, however, the store wasn't truly Don's. Dad kept giving him unwanted advice. When our parents talked of moving, Don encouraged them. Their move would give him the space he needed to reorganize and expand the business.

ECHO HILL FARM

On the folks' trip back East, they began to search for a country home. Having been born and raised on a farm, Mom longed to return to rural life, and both Mom and Dad wanted to live close to Dick, Pat, and Tricia. They bought a sixty-acre farm near Menges Mills, a village in Mennonite country twelve miles southwest of York, Pennsylvania, and about eighty miles north of Washington, D.C. The purchase price of $12,500 seems like a bargain by today's standards. However, a dollar at the end of World War II was worth considerably more than ten dollars now.

Upon returning to California, Dad and Mom prepared for our move. Dad felt he needed to go back to the farm before Mom and me to remodel the house and plant the early crops. In the spring of 1947, he traveled by train to Ohio where he took delivery of a 1946 half-ton pickup at the International truck assembly plant in Springfield. Then he drove the truck the rest of the way to York County, Pennsylvania. Mom and I stayed behind so I could finish my junior year at Whittier High School.

Meanwhile, Mom and I packed up our household goods for the moving van that arrived three weeks before school let out. At the start of my summer vacation, we said good-bye to Don, and many relatives, friends, and customers, and I drove across country with Mom in our Chevy sedan filled to the top. Like many young drivers, I enjoyed the feeling of freedom resulting from a heavy foot on the gas pedal. Along the expanse of nearly deserted highways through the Southwest and heartland of our country, I made excellent time—not by speeding but by minimizing the number and length of stops. I had to accommodate Mom, however, when she would say, "Eddie, I need to stop." By averaging about six hundred miles a day, we arrived at the farm in Menges Mills close to 2 a.m. on June 4, our longest day of travel.

As we pulled into the long driveway, Mom and I could barely see the house in the total darkness. Dad was not expecting us for two more days. We were dead tired and needed to go to bed right away, but all the doors and windows were securely locked. Our frantic attempts to break in failed to awaken Dad. His hardness of hearing shielded him from all the noises I could make by tossing pebbles on the windows and flinging gravel on the walls. Finally, while Mom aimed the flashlight into the bedroom and I hammered the corner of the house with a piece of firewood, the lights came on.

When Mom stepped up on the front porch, Dad came out in his nightshirt yelling and jumping for joy. I had not seen him so happy in a long time. Although he prided himself on being independent and self-sufficient, he needed her and missed her terribly during their months of separation. Of course, Mom was also delighted to be "home" at last and reunited with her husband, but thanks to her young son's non-stop driving tendencies, she needed access to the bathroom right away.

Before my parents bought the home, they couldn't help but notice a small hog house near the front door that emitted quite a stench. They wondered why someone would have built it so close to the human abode. Then they discovered it functioned as more than a hog house: a four-hole privy adjoined the three hog stalls. When the original farmhouse was built in 1923, indoor plumbing was limited to pumped water in the kitchen. Apparently, the owner had decided an outhouse serving his family of twelve should be located just a short run from the front door.

First on Dad's home improvement list in the spring was to install a modern bathroom upstairs. How grateful we were that we didn't have to share an outhouse with the pigs! Then, during the summer, Dad decided he and I had to move the old hog house away from the front yard. Working in knee-deep muck, we cross-braced the frame of the little building and then jacked it up onto some planks. During the project, we frequently ran to the garden hose to rinse off and catch a breath of fresh air. Finally, we were able to tow the hog house on rollers to its new foundation behind the barn.

Our farm was a small-scale operation. A sixty-acre piece of land did not warrant a corporate business; it just provided us with a very healthy living. The front twenty acres and back twenty sloped gently downward to the north. In that rich, tillable soil, we grew peas, corn, wheat, barley, and rye. What we didn't use ourselves, we sold to the Farm Bureau in West York. By the time Mom and I arrived, Dad had already planted a patch of corn and harvested ten acres of early peas.

Dad had purchased a used Ford Ferguson tractor from his brother Ernest in State College, about two hours north of York. It was equipped with a hydraulic lift and several detachable implements, including a disk plow that mounted beneath the tractor. I had always thought of a plow as being a towed implement, but this one was a much more compact unit. It plowed a very clean furrow, and we used that maneuverable rig along with the other detachable tools to work the whole farm.

Also, Dad raised some Yorkshire pigs and a couple of Guernsey cows. He made sure those cows were tested for TB. After they received a clean bill of health, he felt comfortable drinking and serving the unpasteurized milk. He named the cows Joan and Deanna after the Hollywood actresses, Joan Crawford, whose face he admired, and Deanna Durbin, whose beautiful voice must have reminded him of his mother's. After trying to milk the cows, I quickly gained great respect for dairy farmers. For me it was not easy work.

Rolling hills provided a scenic backdrop for our farm. In the distance, we could view our neighbors' apple and cherry orchards as well as fields of wheat, rye, and barley. On our property to the south, across the access road to all the local farms, a shale outcrop jutted from the face of the hilltop. From one small spot just beyond the barn, when I shouted in the direction of the outcrop, my voice would bounce back to me—not immediately, but after a measurable delay. Therefore, I decided to call our place "Echo Hill Farm." After that, we told all first-time guests about that spot beyond the barn.

Echo Hill became quite an attraction for a group of underprivileged Hispanic children from New York City. Mom had read about a charitable organization seeking volunteers in the country within a day's bus ride to give junior high school students a taste of farm life.

"Frank, I think we should offer to give these children a breath of fresh air. Many of them have never been away from home, and the only green in New York is Central Park," she said.

Dad reminded her, "If the wind blows from the East, the kids will smell the fumes from the Glatfelter mill!"[30]

But Mom's persistence and persuasive arguments finally prevailed. For all his gruff ways, Dad usually went along with what Mom wanted. So, with his concurrence, she contacted the sponsoring organization, and then a representative paid us a visit. Soon we were hosting small groups of youngsters for week-long stays. Mom set up a daily routine for the children and drilled them in arithmetic and reading. Dad enjoyed exposing them to farm life: milking cows, slopping pigs, and so forth.

My job was to show the children how to calculate the distance to the Echo Hill rock by timing the echo on a stopwatch and then looking up the speed of sound in an encyclopedia article. Then to verify their arithmetic, I had them count the paces along a straight line to the rock. Never having been in the country before, the children exuded enthusiasm at each new experience, especially hearing their voices echo from the hillside.

Dad thought that bare hillside should be forested, so Uncle Ernest, a professor of agronomy at Penn State University, provided

---

30 The Glatfelter paper mill was located in Spring Grove a few miles northeast of Menges Mills.

Echo Hill Farm - 1968 Photo
1948 - 1968 - Unchanged in Twenty Years

us with pine seedlings. Our first fall at the farm, Dad and I spent the weekends planting those young trees. We set them out in a row below the rock outcrop. For a few years, voices still echoed from the hill. As the trees matured, however, the echoes grew ever fainter. Recent residents on the farm have found it difficult to locate that magic spot by the barn that once fascinated many an inner-city child.

A stream flowed along the east side of our property. I often wondered why someone had named such a clear stream "Oil Creek." Right outside the back door of our house, a fresh spring ran all year round. It flowed into a tiny stream that eventually merged with Oil Creek. Dad hung a big ladle over the spring and several times a day would drink a cup of that refreshing water. Since working on the street car in Ohio in 1906, Dad had had a lot of trouble with arthritis, but at the farm, it became less painful. He credited that "holy spring water."

Dad and I tackled a wide variety of work the first summer. By addressing the full spectrum of tasks on the farm, he wanted to expose me to all aspects of rural life. In addition to farming, he taught me a lot of carpentry skills while we built a two-car garage with a screened corncrib in the middle—Dad's design. The garage replaced an old loafing shed—a four-post shelter for cattle—which we had torn down to make space and improve driveway access. We salvaged material to complete the garage and had plenty left over to replace broken fence boards.

Mom did everything at the farm she had always dreamed of doing. In Whittier, she had become increasingly nostalgic about her early years in southern Indiana compared to life in town where she helped manage a grocery store, arose early to bake for customers, filled gas tanks, and sold tires. Moving to the farm provided her a chance to bake pies just for the family and guests, do a little gardening, write letters, and live at a slower pace. However, she certainly missed her siblings and cousins out West and some aspects of California life.

The farm lacked many of the modern conveniences we had become accustomed to in Whittier. Our farmhouse was one mile from the nearest telephone at the little country store in Menges Mills, and we didn't have home mail delivery. Sometimes just to check the mail, Mom would trudge along the old railroad track, a bit shorter and more level route than the road. If Dick needed to contact us, he would call the Menges Mills store owned and operated by Carl and Martha Stambaugh. Carl served as the U.S. postmaster for the village. If he received a call from Dick in Washington, D.C., after we had made our daily trek to the post office, he would drive over to our house and deliver the message.

To listen to classical music in Menges Mills, we had to tune in to WQXR in New York City. The radio reception was so poor out on the farm that we could only get a clear signal after sunset. I had to work on that radio to make the signal come in. Dad's hearing was failing, so he asked me to fine-tune the dial every time one of us switched on the radio.

Despite the lack of modern conveniences, the farm experience benefited us all. Dad reveled in it. Even in retirement he could not remain idle; the farm kept him busy. Mom loved country life. I spent enough time there to get a real taste for farming. Dick, Pat, Tricia, and Julie, their younger daughter, born July 5, 1948, often visited us at the farm. Dick and Pat enjoyed the quiet retreat where they could break away from the demands of public life in the capital.

Occasionally, Dad, Mom, and I made the two-hour trip down to Washington, D.C. I first visited Dick and Pat at their Parkfairfax apartment in the summer of 1947. When they had to return to their home district in California, "Nana" (Mom) would stay with the girls.

Besides family members who loved and cared for them, Tricia and Julie had an excellent nanny, Mrs. Clifford Moore, who went by "Clifford." After Dick had determined that she was thoroughly competent, dependable, and up to Pat's housekeeping standards, he offered her the job. She was a much loved and respected lady. I'm sure Tricia and Julie remember her fondly.

HERTER COMMITTEE

Dick rose to national prominence more quickly than any of us had expected. In contrast to the lackadaisical manner in which some congressmen addressed their duties, Dick took his responsibilities very seriously. The House leadership in the Eightieth Congress noted his diligence. Because Republicans had finally won a majority of seats in the House of Representatives in the 1946 election, Dick began his congressional career as a member of the ruling party, benefiting from advantageous committee appointments.

On July 30, 1947, Dick learned that Speaker of the House Joseph Martin had named him to the nineteen-member select Herter Committee headed by Congressman Christian Herter of Massachusetts. With the goal of helping Europe recover from the devastation of World War II, the committee was to conduct firsthand investigations of the conditions in Europe and report back to Congress on how the United States could provide aid under the Marshall Plan proposed by Secretary of State George C. Marshall.

At the end of August, my parents and I drove from our Pennsylvania farm to New York City and checked into the Commodore Hotel. There we met Dick and Pat before he and the other members of the Herter Committee were to board the huge ocean liner, the Queen Mary, for the first leg of their journey to Europe via Southampton, England. The Cunard line ship built in 1934 was the largest luxury liner of its day, measuring 1,019.5 feet in length.

Pat had suggested that Dick buy five tickets to *Oklahoma!*, the popular Rodgers and Hammerstein Broadway musical, which had been running at the St. James Theater since 1943. She knew Dad, Mom, and I had never attended a Broadway show. *Oklahoma!* was a superb treat for all of us, but unfortunately Dad had forgotten his hearing aid at the hotel, so to him it seemed like a silent movie. Nevertheless, he enjoyed it immensely, claiming he could hear enough to follow the story. The colorful sets and attractive cast in western costumes kept his attention and made up for what his ears missed.

The morning after that magnificent show, Dad drove us to the Queen Mary. Dick often found ways to challenge me to solve problems on my own, so he gave me the job of parking the car near the waterfront on the west side of Manhattan. I had had my license for only a year and had no experience driving in such a congested city. While I was searching for a parking space, the rest of the family boarded the huge ship. Relieved to find a spot quickly, I parked the car and then ran across the street and down the pier to the passengers' gangway. Oblivious to the enormity of the Queen Mary, I hurried to find Dick's stateroom, which, to my surprise, was empty. After about five minutes of inspecting the room and wondering whether they had given me incorrect directions, I stepped outside the door. Led by an escort, Dad, Mom, Dick, and Pat were slowly ambling toward me. They had assumed I wouldn't find a parking space and Dick's stateroom as quickly as I had, so they didn't expect to see me in the passageway waiting for them. Because of his age and lingering arthritis, Dad had taken a lot longer to complete the brief tour of the sights on board.

Mom, Dad, Pat, and I said our farewells to Dick and then disembarked. As Dick sailed off to Europe, my parents and I drove back to Pennsylvania. Pat returned to Washington, D.C., to volunteer her assistance to the overworked staff in Dick's office while he was overseas.

The Herter Committee divided the task of surveying the destruction in Europe by sending committee members to different countries. Dick's assignment was to study the effects of the war in Italy and the Adriatic.[31] He often reflected on that overwhelming experience: devastated battlegrounds, failing utilities, infrastructure crying for repair and renewal, distribution channels clogged and inoperative, and, worst of all, people maimed by war and lacking sufficient food. He had huddled in a foxhole and had seen bombing in the South Pacific, but he found it far more disturbing to observe once beautiful Italian cities in ruins than to see jungles torn apart. The trees and vegetation would grow back; it would take a mammoth effort to repair the cities to their former function and splendor, and some of the historic buildings and artwork could never be replaced. But most important, he knew the people would need time and assistance to regain their self-sufficiency and resolve. Dick believed that unless the United States came to the aid of Europe, people would starve, democratic governments would collapse, and communism would triumph. Many people, including isolationists in the Republican Party, opposed foreign aid, but Dick was convinced our nation had to help its new allies.

---

31 On two of my recent trips to Italy to assess the new Cinque Terre National Park between Genoa and La Spezia, I had the good fortune to hear firsthand memories from several elderly witnesses to Richard Nixon's visit in 1947. Their anecdotes confirmed my assumptions regarding the vital significance of the Marshall Plan in blocking the spread of communism—not only to Italy but to most of Western Europe as well. Before I departed for home, my Italian hosts arranged a telephone contact with former President Cossiga in Rome. He expressed great admiration and sincere appreciation for my brother's courageous leadership in promoting passage of the enabling legislation despite strong political resistance in Congress.

HISS CASE

While Dick's work on the Herter Committee brought him significant national recognition, the Alger Hiss case catapulted him into the national limelight. As a member of the House Committee on Un-American Activities (HUAC) in 1948, Dick participated in the investigation of Communist infiltration in the federal government. Whittaker Chambers, a former Communist spy for the Soviet Union, testified before the committee that Hiss, a high-ranking State Department official in the Roosevelt Administration, was a Communist Party member and a spy transmitting important information to the Kremlin. But the majority of the press and many government officials believed Hiss's denials. They tried to poke holes in Chambers' story and maligned him, but the more Dick listened to both men, the more convinced he became of Chambers' veracity.

Dick mulled over his options. Several times he discussed the case with Mom, because he respected her keen perceptions about people and her sense of compassion and justice; he relied on her good judgment. Finally, he came up with an idea.

"Mom, why don't you have Eddie drive you to Whittaker and Esther Chambers' farm to get acquainted. You and Esther are both Quakers, and she is going through some hard times. I'm sure you two would enjoy each other's company, and you could provide comfort to her."

Mom agreed to Dick's suggestion. She was always willing to help someone in need.

Although Mom knew how to drive, we men in the family thought she was too hesitant on the road. And I enjoyed any opportunity to get behind the wheel. I could deliver Mom to her destination much faster than if she had driven.

So, we headed off to the Chambers' farm just down the road across the state line into Maryland. At the door, I noted Whitaker Chambers' rather disheveled appearance but didn't think much of it. After all, he lived on a farm and he was at home. The Chambers were gracious and friendly hosts and greeted us as neighbors. Dick's intuition proved correct: Mom and Esther had much in common with their Quaker faith and preference for the quiet life. The two ladies formed a friendship and visited on other occasions.

As a teenager, I avoided the political scene, and I certainly wasn't interested in women's talk. I viewed the world through a different set of lenses; I was more interested in physical structures. I asked Mr. Chambers, "May I wander around your farm while the ladies visit?"

"Why, of course," he said, encouraging me to look around.

My curiosity focused on the layout of their farm, which was similar to ours, and I was quite content to inspect the Chambers' barn. In doing that, I missed an opportunity to talk with a man who played an important role in my brother's career and in the history of the Cold War. He had gotten caught up in the idealism of communism, but when he discovered its evil, insidious nature, he dedicated his life to warning the country of its inherent threats to freedom.

Back home, Mom shared her perceptions with Dick: "The Chambers are sincere, honest people. They have the best interests of the country at heart, but they have been deeply hurt by the press doubting their story."

So, Mom confirmed what Dick had concluded. I suspect he had sent us on the visit so Mom could validate his intuition about the Chambers' good character.

I remember Dick coming up to our farm after the revelation of the "Pumpkin Papers." Chambers had hidden incriminating microfilm rolls in a hollowed-out pumpkin on his property. When Dick learned of the microfilm, he worried about how to proceed with the case. "We can't prove Hiss has done anything illegal as far as a treasonous act is concerned," Dick said, "but I believe he lied under oath. Is it my duty to prosecute the perjury?"

Mom said, "You have to think it through, Richard. The law is the law, but compassion must be taken into account. There are those who will probably hate you if you prosecute, but abide by the law and follow your conscience."

So, Dick pursued the case with Whittaker Chambers as his star witness, and Alger Hiss eventually wound up in jail for having committed perjury.

Fulton Lewis, Jr., an investigative reporter who could be heard on many Mutual Broadcasting Company radio stations across the country, was one of the few in the media who had agreed with Dick regarding Hiss's guilt. Lewis was Dad's favorite commentator—the Rush Limbaugh of his day, trying to quell the rolling tide of liberalism. Lewis's opposition to Roosevelt's New Deal and Communist infiltration in our government resonated with Dad, and, besides, Lewis held Dick in high regard, which, of course, delighted Dad. He would say, "Eddie, let's see if we can hear Fulton Lewis tonight."

Out on the farm, the only Mutual station we could receive was WOR in New York City. Like the classical music station we enjoyed, WOR was so remote that we could only listen to the broadcasts after sunset, and even then it was difficult to tune in past the static.

Other reporters in the Eastern media establishment never dropped their vendetta against Richard Nixon for his part in bringing Hiss, the darling of the liberal intelligentsia, to justice. When those reporters realized Hiss was losing the case, they looked the other way, taking the spotlight off Hiss and glaring it at Dick and Lewis. Thereafter, the liberal press seemed locked into an eternal war against my brother and others who tried to expose Communist infiltrators.

Nevertheless, the case did startle some Americans out of their isolationism and complacency to the fact that Communists and their sympathizers in high places seriously threatened the security of our country. And history has proved Nixon, Chambers, and Lewis right. In 1995, the U.S. government released the Venona Project documents, decoded cables that, beyond a shadow of doubt, exposed Hiss and others as Soviet agents.

I should note that in the 1930s and 1940s, many idealistic people like Chambers were vulnerable to the appeal of socialism and communism, thinking government control would eradicate rampant poverty. The labeling of employers as oppressive villains aroused impoverished people to revolt and strike to destroy all private initiative. Some people became convinced that a prosperous, egalitarian society could be formed simply by banding together in communes and sharing the wealth.

However, by studying historical examples and observing current events, Dick and Lewis recognized that such a system would demand that government always control the means of production, distributing the resources to those in need. In the process, citizens' self-reliance would be crippled and eventually destroyed by a growing dependency on government services. The net result would always be an oppressed people. Through involvement in the Communist Party, Chambers had discovered this firsthand and turned away from the ideology to support a form of government that guaranteed individual liberty.

HIGH SCHOOL EDUCATION

While Dick was tackling issues affecting national security, I had to focus on my high school education. Changing schools at the start of one's senior year can be socially traumatic; it certainly was for me. Initially, I was struck by the great contrasts between the public schools in California and Pennsylvania. As I recall, more than a thousand students attended Whittier High School, a four-year school. My junior class was as large as the entire student body at my new school, West York Junior-Senior High, which included grades seven through twelve.

In spite of Whittier's size, I had been well established there, having known some of the students most of my life. At Whittier, I had had a broad exposure to liberal arts. Because my grades had always been near the top of my class, I was a member of the California Honor Society, which provided welcome benefits. Ten of my best friends and I had taken school trips with the Honor Society to the Los Angeles Philharmonic for concerts. Most of us found more value in classical music than in the popular alternatives.

When my parents and I moved to Menges Mills, I missed the cultural opportunities that cosmopolitan schools in Southern California provided. At West York, I had to start over at a small high school serving a mostly rural region of Pennsylvania. Some of my new classmates had never been out of the state, even though the Maryland border was only seven miles away. Clearly, I was an outsider—that "California cowboy" they called me.

Another issue was my driving: I fit the stereotype of the notoriously fast California driver. I excused my heavy foot on the pedal, saying, "I have to get to school on time, and, besides, the road is empty." I'm sure some of the teachers, as well as the Mennonites in the community who shunned automobiles altogether, wondered why this Californian had invaded their quiet country roads.

Ed's High School Photo, 1947
∿From Hannah Nixon Family Collection

At the start of my senior year at West York, I was mildly surprised by one difference in the daily routine. During first, or home, period, the teacher would announce the day's schedule, as one might expect, followed by all students saluting the flag and reciting the Pledge of Allegiance. Then they would repeat the Lord's Prayer. I had never heard the Lord's Prayer recited in a public school in California, but having been raised in a Christian home, I was not alarmed by the practice. The students in York, many of whom were Mennonites, didn't seem to mind a bit of religion to start the school day either. They accepted requirements and discipline more readily than some of the students in Whittier had.

Despite the differences, or perhaps because of them, I believe my classmates and I did receive a good education at West York High School. My initial concerns about the quality of instruction proved unfounded. Adam Martin, the principal, administered the school with capable leadership. Living only half a block from the school, he was readily available for counsel. His son David and I were classmates.

Students at West York were divided into groups—a track system. Some were channeled into college preparatory courses, others into the commercial program, and still others into manual arts. Whittier High School had even more tracks, but that school was three times larger and served a more densely populated school district.

When considering the track system, questions arise: How broad a range of subjects should be required for students to gain the most from their education? If students are not in a track, what would they gain? If they are in a track, what would they lose? Should everyone be required to take a foreign language, or all four years of English, math, and science?

On my part, I was glad to be in the college prep track. Perhaps because my parents and Dick insisted I pursue higher education, I took my studies seriously. Like Dick, I could not be bothered with frivolity, silliness, and girls—not that all girls were silly—but I was just not interested in the vanity and conformity of the dating scene. I wanted to concentrate on learning something new and demanding.

My teachers at West York High School certainly piqued my interest in learning. Miss Anna Morris, a bright, wonderful lady, taught a challenging English course, exposing me to Shakespeare in a way no other teacher had. She forced him out into the open, and we all had to digest his works or fail. I must say, I resisted, but I did learn to appreciate great literature in her class.

Miss Morris became intrigued with the idea that some of us students could write poetry if we tried, so she made some assignments. Then she selected a few of the best poems her students had written and submitted them to Ray Zaner, known as the "Poet Scout" on WSBA, a York radio station. A few of my classmates and I were chosen to read examples of our poetry on his program. I received some compliments, but as a shy teenager, I brushed them off, feeling too embarrassed to get excited about the attention.

Another of Miss Morris's assignments was to write a thumbnail sketch of our most impressive teacher, always keeping the focus on learning, of course. I considered describing my mathematics teacher, Curvin Kopp, who taught solid geometry and trigonometry. I told Dad, "He's a good math teacher—gives me the worst grades I've ever gotten in school."

Dad asked, "Well, what's his political philosophy?"

"I think he's a Communist," I replied.

"Well, then, don't write about him!"

Mr. Kopp was the only avowed Communist, or Marxist, I was aware of in my academic world. He seemed to think government should take care of everybody. So, on Dad's advice, I didn't select Mr. Kopp. Incidentally, Mr. Kopp gave me my only "C"—in solid geometry. Knowing I was the brother of an anti-Communist in Congress may have explained what I perceived as his aloofness toward me, but I did not let that perception affect my interest in math, especially spherical geometry.

For my thumbnail biography assignment, I chose to write about David Beckmeyer, my physics teacher, because we shared a fascination with physics, chemistry, and mathematics. In Pennsylvania, students took physics in their junior year, followed by chemistry in their senior year. In California, the order was reversed, so I had already taken chemistry when I enrolled at West York High. Therefore, my physics classmates were all juniors. At the start of the course, many of them weren't paying sufficient attention to learn much physics, but as the year progressed, Mr. Beckmeyer had everyone on target.

A short man with a swarthy complexion and a slight Pennsylvania Dutch accent, he assessed the situation and brought the class to attention. A no-nonsense disciplinarian in the classroom, he didn't allow students any time to goof off.

"Look," he said, "we have a lot of ground to cover. I do not have time to go over the material twice, so listen carefully, and I will ask you questions one by one before this session is over."

During the first half of the period, Mr. Beckmeyer would present physics formulas and equations. Then for the remainder of the period, he would ask questions. He wouldn't call on me, because I was eager to learn and grasped the subject matter. Instead, he would call on anyone who seemed inattentive or chatty, asking very pointed questions about the lecture. When faces turned red, those students learned to keep quiet enough to listen and learn. I felt Mr. Beckmeyer very effectively controlled class behavior while getting his points across.

J. Wesley Wise was also a contender for my most impressive teacher. He taught Problems of Democracy, an excellent civics class. In personality and methods of classroom control, he and Mr. Beckmeyer were opposites, but I liked them both. Each in his own way was a highly effective teacher, excited about his subject.

Mr. Wise wore a perpetual smile. He seemed to be entertained by students' comments. He encouraged them to participate in discussions on current events. The students in the class were all serious seniors, so when a boy or girl occasionally couldn't quite get up and running on the topic of the day, he was patient and forgiving. Using the Socratic method, he encouraged us to think. He would ask us to read a textbook passage or article, and the next day he would ask question after question. "What do you think that meant?" "What do you think they're saying?" And the students would respond.

Mr. Wise organized a one-day field trip by bus to Washington, D.C. Because some of my classmates had never been that far from home, I tried to be modest in relating what I knew about the nation's capital; I did not want to be called a "know-it-all." Our group of seniors toured the Lincoln Memorial, the Washington Monument, and the Smithsonian Museum in the old brick buildings along the mall. At the Capitol building, we briefly viewed the House and Senate chambers from the galleries. With just one day to spend in D.C., we had time to see only some of the highlights of the city. Regrettably, we couldn't fit a visit with Dick into our schedule.

In civics, one of my assignments was to write a paper on highway safety. I scoured every local library to collect background information but couldn't find sufficient material. Then I contacted Dick, who suggested I do some research at the Library of Congress. Taking his advice, I drove to Washington, D.C., in January or February 1948.

Of course, the Library of Congress contained vastly more information than the York Public Library. I found newspapers dating back to 1925 and one old book dealing with traffic problems in New York City in the 1930s. Among the suggestions for highway safety was enforcement of a twenty-five-mile-per-hour speed limit everywhere. At that time, many locales had adopted no speed limits at all. The author argued that not only would slower speed limits yield safer roads, but also that the roads would carry more vehicles per hour, thus decreasing the need for more lanes. His argument did not seem logical to me. I countered that if the traffic density was high enough to force vehicles closer together, the risk of collisions would increase. Of course, a reduced need for wider roads would save money but would also increase driver impatience, leading to road rage.

In my paper, I also speculated on the future, noting the benefits of the avant-garde Tucker car, which promised many of the safety features we see in cars today. Unfortunately, Preston Tucker's car was too far ahead of its time and never made it into production. Nevertheless, I believed then and still do that it is more inspiring to look ahead than to regret the past.

My summary noted that better driver training would do a lot to alleviate the frustration and anger of experienced drivers, who tended to become dangerously impatient, bold, and daring. Mr. Wise, an expeditious driver himself, appreciated my suggestions and gave me an A on the paper and for the course. Having a congressman in the family available to help me locate resources and to take an interest in my education proved a great asset.

During my trip to visit the Library of Congress, Dick took me on a tour of the Capitol grounds. At his office in the Longworth House Office Building, he introduced me to his staff, which he had hired with minimum delay after taking office. His secretaries, Dorothy Cox (later Donnelly), Jane Gordon (later Collins), and Betty Lewis, and his executive assistant, William A. "Bill" Arnold, were on the job full time from the outset.

From the House of Representatives gallery, I got my first view of the floor of Congress in session. To my surprise, I saw only a few members in attendance, and Congress <u>was</u> in session. One of them, the speaker pro-tem, stood at the dais. Another congressman sat in the back row reading the colored comic pages in the newspaper.

"Why aren't more people here?" I asked Dick.

"This is normal," he answered. "Much of the business is accomplished in members' offices and committee rooms, but when a bill comes up for debate and a vote, this place comes alive."

"Who's that one seated near the back?"

"That's Congressman Vito Marcantonio, a Democrat from a gerrymandered district in New York City, including East Harlem and the more conservative Yorkville," Dick explained. "He has the dubious distinction of being the only openly pro-Communist member of Congress."[32]

ON TO COLLEGE

Even while Dick was occupied with the affairs of the United States and the dire conditions in Europe, his interest in my education never waned. He persisted in encouraging me to go to college and to continue as long as I could. Also, he advised me to keep my eye on the outside world while in school. He wanted me to tackle hard questions: What makes the world go around with respect not only to physics, but also to the cultures, economics, and inclinations of society?

Dick knew I had my sights set on attending college in California—maybe Stanford where Herbert Hoover, my academic role model, had studied. I admired the man for his vision and honesty. As a mining engineer, he believed, as I did, that the Earth's surface could be improved. Being independently wealthy, he had taken only a

---

32 Both political parties were seeking someone who could defeat Representative Marcantonio, but it was not easy because of his popularity in East Harlem. A bipartisan coalition in 1950 finally brought his fourteen-year congressional career to an end.

dollar-a-year salary as President of the United States. He was a genuine patriot dedicated to preserving the national strength of the country. After Franklin D. Roosevelt succeeded him as President in 1933, he implemented the Reconstruction Finance Corporation and several of Hoover's other ideas for ending the Depression. That fact alone proved to me that the President of the United States is effectively limited in what he can accomplish unless he has Congress on his side.

Besides wanting to follow in Hoover's academic footsteps, I still considered myself a Californian and wanted to return to the state I called home. Dick had other ideas. One weekend he came to our farm and said, "Let's drive down to Duke so you can see what's available."

At first I resisted, saying, "But I want to go to Stanford or Caltech to study engineering."

Then Dick asked, "How can you be sure of a decision if your judgment is based on a limited awareness of what's available?"

Knowing it was no use to argue with Dick, I asked, "May I drive?"

The next morning, I was behind the wheel heading south with Dick. After we crossed the border from Virginia into North Carolina, Dick said, "I'll drive now. Here's the map. Direct us into Durham."

Dick wanted my education to be as inclusive as possible, and he knew Duke University could provide me with a broad liberal arts background. The university already had a worldwide reputation for academic excellence, and it was quite cosmopolitan.

"The majority of students will be from North Carolina," Dick said, "but there'll be a large number from New York, New Jersey, and Washington, D.C. All the East Coast and the Deep South will be represented as well as many foreign countries."

But Dick had another reason for wanting me to attend Duke: to expose me to viewpoints and practices we had learned were wrong when growing up—namely the persistent racial prejudice in the South. My brothers and I had been raised in a family that considered a person's worth to have nothing to do with his or her skin color or ethnicity. Our parents made us aware that we were members of the human race, no better or no worse than the "Negroes," (the accepted term for people of African descent at that time), Mexicans, or Japanese who shopped at Nixon's Market. And no one was an American with a hyphenated prefix; we were all Americans.

While Dick strongly opposed racial discrimination, he felt that in Quaker Whittier and in Mennonite Menges Mills, I had been sheltered from some of the problems facing our country. Now that I was an adult, he thought I should witness prejudice first hand as he had at Duke. I think he also hoped I would share the values of nondiscrimination with those I met in the South.

When Dick attended Duke Law School, he had been overwhelmed by the beauty of Duke Forest and the classical Gothic architecture. What impressed me was the colorful volcanic stone from local quarries used to construct those buildings.

Dick's persuasion regarding Duke proved too hard for me to resist. I applied and was accepted. As usual, I found he had guided me in the right direction.

During the summer of 1948, Dick's congressional campaign was in full swing in California. As a popular incumbent, he faced only minimal opposition from Democrat Stephen Zetterberg, a Claremont attorney. I did not get involved in the race; instead, I stayed in Pennsylvania to help on the farm and prepare for my impending move to North Carolina in the fall.

Before I was to leave home, Dad decided I should be exposed to the shenanigans that occur at political conventions. Regardless what went on in the smoke-filled rooms, he believed those delegate assemblies were an essential part of a free society. Ninety miles was an easy drive, so we headed east to attend our first Republican national convention in Philadelphia scheduled to begin June 21.

Dick also attended for the first time, but in an official capacity representing California as a delegate. Dad and I didn't see him at the convention, however, because he was occupied with his delegate duties and led an effort to include a tough anti-Communist plank in the party platform.

Dad and I managed to find our way to the convention hall. Novices at conventioneering, we didn't even have tickets but were allowed into the basement, where Dad and I watched New York Governor Tom Dewey deliver his acceptance speech on a small black and white cathode ray tube—our introduction to television. Dad could hardly believe his eyes, but he definitely understood the sound coming out of the loudspeaker—after he turned up his hearing aid. He was both amazed and thrilled by the new technology. Little did he realize that in just four years, the political career of his son would hinge on a speech broadcast on nationwide television.

Before I left for Duke, Dad bought me a tie clasp at a jewelry store in York as a graduation and going-away-to-college present. The tie clasp, which I still have, is attached to a delicate gold chain securing a square knot of two gold rods with four ruby-tipped ends. In those days, we were accustomed to wearing more formal attire than people do today. Many events called for a coat and tie. Dad would instruct slovenly young men: "Get dressed up. Put on something other than shorts. Short pants are worn only by pre-pubescent boys. Cover your undershirt. Show some pride."

Although Dad didn't say it in so many words, I felt he intended his gift to help me feel worthy of his pride, and I in turn proudly wore that small ornament on many occasions.

In the fall of 1948, I enrolled as a civil engineering student at Duke University and settled into the freshman dorm. Dorm life was awkward for me; I had trouble adjusting to unfamiliar social environments. But friendship with my West York classmate Dave Martin, along with a few new classmates from Pennsylvania, eased the transition.

One of my first priorities in Durham was to find a source of good music—something other than the locally popular country fare. Taverns seemed a waste of time, but the local diners had jukeboxes at every table; we could insert a coin to play the latest hits, some of which were good music. I didn't mind the songs being unfamiliar. Nevertheless, I still had the urge to hear compositions by Bach, Beethoven, Brahms, or other composers of their caliber. Ever since Don switched the radio station from country to classical music in 1935 or 1936, I preferred lyrical sounds played by well-disciplined performers holding rhythmic orchestral conversations between the instrumental sections under the direction of great conductors.

Finally, I found a radio station that played classical music one hour a day—WPTF in Raleigh, twenty-five miles east of Durham. So, I reserved that time for listening to something I wanted to hear. At Duke, I took no courses in music appreciation, but I did enjoy listening to classical compositions and learning to recognize themes. Later

Ed at Duke, 1949
↢From Author's Personal Collection

I could identify specific movements in the Beethoven symphonies and other classical works.

When I attended Duke, my tuition cost $350 a year, and my total expenses amounted to nearly $1,000—a lot of money in those days. My parents helped pay for the tuition, and Dick and Don helped from time to time when I needed extra money for something special: labs, books, field trips, and other expenses. After my freshman year, I supplemented the income by doing lab work for Dr. Willard Berry, head of the Geology Department, but I was privileged to have most of my time available to concentrate on geology—or what I came to think of as "those crazy rocks in my head."

During my freshman year, the national military draft, known as "Universal Military Training" (UMT), was still in effect. It continued from World War II throughout my college years and beyond, and that bothered many students who had entered college as non-veterans. The veterans were immune from the draft, but the rest of us could be called to service at any time.

Although the majority of the freshmen were right out of high school, a great number of veterans had enrolled with assistance from the G.I. Bill of Rights. They were experienced and knew why they were in college. Not much distracted them. I thought it quite an education to observe the contrast between the veterans, who had seen action in the rest of the world and were serious about their studies, and the green high school graduates, some of whom were in college for a good time.

The freshman class impressed me because, as Dick had said, "When you go to Duke, you're going to find it's quite cosmopolitan." In spite of his briefings, I was still surprised to see and meet so many international students on campus.

One of the students, Kazem Mahdavi, came from Mashäd, the holiest city in Iran, where years later in 1978 the Ayatollah Khomeini launched his Islamist revolution. Perhaps Kazem knew my brother was a U.S. congressman, for he revealed a peculiar interest in protecting me. For whatever reason, soon after we became acquainted, he said, "Anybody bother you, you let me know. I take care of it!"

Whereupon I asked, "How are you going to do that?"

He brandished a rather large Jim Bowie-type knife in response. His attitude caught me off guard. I did not understand it at the time, but then I had never before met a Muslim. I don't know what became of Kazem after Duke, but he certainly convinced me I would need a lot more education in foreign cultures.

I told Dick I had met a student from Brazil, another from Venezuela, and several representing other foreign countries. He enthusiastically supported my exposure to foreign students, saying, "You need to see the world, and you need to feel it out before you get to it. Meet people from everywhere and get acquainted with them, and don't tell them too much. Just listen."

In the winter of 1949, Dick came south for a visit. He noted that the campus looked about the same as in his student days, 1934-1937, but that my living conditions were far more comfortable than his Spartan accommodations at "Whippoorwill Manor," the name he gave to the primitive little cabin in the woods where he and Bill Perdue had survived much tougher times in law school. Remembering that cabin, I felt very fortunate indeed.

After reminiscing for a while, Dick suggested we walk over to the indoor stadium to watch the freshman basketball game that customarily preceded the varsity game. Dick was always fascinated with competitive sports. During the game, he noticed one standout player.

"Who's that fellow playing guard making those great shots?" he asked.

"That's my roommate, Dick Groat."

Walking back from the stadium to my dorm, he wanted to know all about him. "Where's Groat from?"

"Swissvale, Pennsylvania."

"Have you met his parents?"

"Yes. They're good folks and strong conservatives too."

"Is he here on a scholarship?"

"I think so, but he's too shy to talk about it much."

My brother really wanted to meet Richard M. "Dick" Groat, because he was such a talented athlete. We waited awhile in my room, but when Groat didn't arrive, we decided to get together with him in the morning, so we started down the stairs. At the first landing, we met Groat heading back to the room. I stopped him and made the introduction.

Dick Groat at Duke, 1949
From Author's Personal Collection

Ed and Dick Groat—Duke Fiftieth Reunion, 2002
∻Author's Personal Collection – Photo by classmate Floyd Guest

My brother said, "You know, you have outstanding talent, young man. You're going to be great at whatever you do. I can see that. Basketball may be a tall man's game, but at your height of 5'11"—the same as mine—I can't imagine anybody doing as well as you've done. I wish you all the best. Keep at it!"

Always alert to talent, Richard Nixon encouraged its development in everyone who displayed a gifted performance. Regardless of the sport, he was the inveterate fan, thoroughly memorizing statistics and instantly recalling great moments in past games.

Jack Coombs, the Duke University baseball coach, had wanted to offer Dick Groat a baseball scholarship. However, the only sports scholarships available at Duke then were in basketball. So, Groat came to Duke and played baseball for Coombs and basketball for his scholarship. A natural athlete, he excelled in both sports. At Duke he was a four-time All American in both basketball and baseball and was named the 1951 Helms National Player of the Year and the UPI National College Basketball Player of the Year in 1952. His Duke classmates still proudly note that his No. 10 basketball jersey was the first to be retired at the university, and his record 48 points in a single home game still stands, and Dick's 100 percent (17/17) free throw percentage for a single game still stood as of the 2004-05 Duke season.

Over the years, my brother followed Groat's impressive career in the news. After college, he was drafted by the Ft. Wayne (now Detroit) Pistons, a professional team in the National Basketball Association. At the same time, he played baseball for the Pittsburgh Pirates until 1953 when he joined the military. He returned to the Pirates as a shortstop in 1955 and went on to great fame. In 1960, the underdog Pirates defeated the New York Yankees to win the World Series. That year Groat was the National League's national batting champion and Most Valuable Player. In 1963, he played for the St. Louis Cardinals and helped them win the World Series. Later he played for the Philadelphia Phillies and the San Francisco Giants. Three times his photo appeared on the cover of *Sports Illustrated*.

During one of my brother's presidential campaigns, Groat picked me up at the Pittsburgh airport so we could participate in a political rally. I asked if he remembered that encounter back in 1949.

"I'll never forget it," he said. "That really inspired me to keep pushing. Incidentally, why do you think I met you at the airport today?"

⁓ ⁓

Because of Dick Nixon's growing prominence as a congressman and his visits to our farm, West York High School invited him to give the commencement speech in 1949, the year after I graduated. Thus began his friendship with Harry McLaughlin, a friend of our family's and a columnist for the *York Dispatch* newspaper. McLaughlin covered the story of Dick's commencement speech. A big Nixon fan, he was very pleased to have a chance to meet my brother. Subsequently, when Dick visited the farm, Harry would drive out to Menges Mills for a friendly visit, and the two of them corresponded. Harry wrote several columns about the politics surrounding the selection of Richard Nixon as Vice President and the attempt by Harold Stassen, former governor of Minnesota, to have him dumped from the ticket. In February 2007, Harry passed away at eighty-five years of age, having spent nearly seventy years in journalism.

⁓ ⁓

I wasn't interested in fraternities, but in my sophomore year, some of my friends persuaded me to pledge Lambda Chi Alpha by saying, "You know, you don't have to be like everybody else here. We're all individuals, and we might learn something from you. Come on." So, I joined, questioning every new experience, testing all things unfamiliar.

When Dick attended Duke, students didn't even consider having cars on campus. By the time I arrived, having a car at school was a privilege for those who had passed their first year with a good grade point average. I needed a car for some of the geology field trips, so I bought a 1940 Chevy town sedan with the savings stamp money I had earned for reading while Dick served in the Navy during World War II. After my freshman year, I spent most of my free time working on that car.

One of my former classmates at the fiftieth reunion at Duke remarked, "We always remember you as the guy who had his feet sticking out from under his car, working on some problem with the transmission or the clutch."

⌣ ⌢

In 1950 while at Duke, I received word that my father had been injured in an accident on the farm. On top of Echo Hill, he had brushed against a rock that diverted the tractor into a power pole. The steering wheel had whipped around, severely breaking Dad's wrist. Later I learned the bones had not been set well, so the break refused to heal properly. With no one able to maintain the farm, my parents decided to retire to a less demanding home in a warmer climate. Uncle Ernest loved to visit Florida and encouraged them to move there in the fall of 1950.

Dad and Mom bought a house in Lakeland, Florida, where they did enjoy that mild weather. I visited there only a couple of times. While in Lakeland, Dad befriended former Democratic Senator Claude Pepper and Senator George Smathers, the Democratic congressman who won Pepper's Senate seat in 1950. Dad would talk about them at the drop of a hat. All his life, he enjoyed talking politics with southern Democrats, northern Republicans, liberals or conservatives; it didn't matter. He knew where he stood and was always ready to discuss the issues, or argue, if he deemed it necessary.

⌣ ⌢

Early on at Duke, I grew dissatisfied with my engineering courses. I had thought civil engineering would provide an opportunity for outdoor activity, but I had to spend too much time doing lab work on a drafting table. Therefore, I decided to check other sciences, including forestry, because I loved the outdoors. In addition, I took some introductory biology, botany, and plant physiology classes in search of a major.

One of my favorite courses was botany, because we would take long taxonomy strolls through the Duke Forest to identify plants. The forest covered about seven thousand acres of beautiful southern pines and a wide variety of other vegetation.

Whenever I walked through that forest, I could feel my Milhous heritage. Franklin Milhous, who had been a nurseryman, used to propagate plants and sell stock up and down the Ohio River Valley. I remember thinking, "Grandfather Milhous, I wish you were here now, because I can imagine you'd really love this place." Reflecting on those days in Duke Forest, I have often thought how wonderful it would have been to walk through those woods with a grandfather I had never known, sharing one of the great pleasures of life, asking him to tell me about his knowledge of plants.

Although Uncle Ernest's wonderful stories of horticulture inspired me, plant physiology was the turning point where I said, "No, I don't want to pursue botany. I'm not ready for this degree of specialization." I decided to check other disciplines. I liked chemistry and physics, but I couldn't decide where to focus my interests.

Then I investigated one subject I hadn't studied yet at Duke—geology. Whereas Dick had always been interested in recorded human history, I was fascinated by prehistory, trying to see far back before human life to the earliest days of creation that could be read only from rocks and what was hidden within them. Dick had left me with many unanswered questions on our visit to Meteor Crater when I was nine years old: Where did the meteor come from? How was the Earth formed? What happened to the brontosaurus? What is Earth's destiny? Studying human history may reveal knowledge, but what will produce a framework of wisdom to see into the distant past and far into the future?

I took these questions to school and have pursued them ever since. By studying the distant past and piecing the data together, we might find a bridge to the present and then a clearer view of the future. But then the more we study, the more we discover how little we know.

When I met with E. Willard "Doc" Berry, chairman of the Geology Department, he said, "If you are interested in all the sciences, why don't you major in geology? You have to know a good deal about all of them and a lot about one of them. You can specialize later."

So geology it was.

Few students at that time shared my interest, however. In my class of 1952, only one other student majored in geology. With the department being so small, the university had relegated it to the women's campus. Some of the men who took the non-major courses found the location distracting. I, too, enjoyed observing attractive women strolling across the campus, but in those days, I focused on rocks.

Duncan "Dunc" Heron, who was working on his Ph.D. at the time I entered the field, taught the introductory courses, and Doc Berry was the mainspring for mineralogy, paleontology, geomorphology, and all other more advanced topics.

Doc Berry stood out as one of the most fascinating professors of my college career. His full beard and black hair gave the impression that appearance didn't matter. "Don't pay too much attention to the outer shell," he would say. "What matters is behind your eyes." And viewing his credentials or hearing him speak, we students knew he had a lot behind his eyes. He was a renowned and well-respected paleobotanist and coal specialist. He had traveled all over the world developing a substantial and very valuable library.[33]

The students considered Doc Berry a great teacher, and we all loved him. With his magnetic sense of humor, he would start each class on a lighthearted note to make us smile. Sometimes his jokes or anecdotes were a little off color, but even the girls in the class got a kick out of them. He taught us that if we could smile while plowing through difficult facts and concepts, we could grasp the topic faster and much more firmly. While leading students into a specialized topic, he would relate a story to illustrate the principle. "Get them to smile and keep smiling until you make your point. You'll do a lot better than if you make them frown." Doc Berry's philosophy certainly complemented the wise counsel my brothers and I had received growing up in the home of Frank and Hannah Nixon.

Doc Berry, who had been raised a Quaker, and his wife Dorothy ("Dot," as the faculty called her), were both religious in keeping with traditions of the Society of Friends, but evangelism was not their mission. They taught by example and allowed others to live freely, guided by personal conscience. Their liberal attitudes about how to direct young people encouraged open conversations and

---

33 The Berry library was so extensive, especially in paleobotany, that researchers came from overseas to use it. An appraiser deemed the library one of the best, if not the best, in its area of specialty in the free world. When Dr. Berry retired, he awarded his library to my classmate, Dr. C. Edward Howard, who had been developing a geology department at Campbell College, now Campbell University, in North Carolina. After Dr. Howard left the University in 1976, the Geology Department began to decline, and some of the rare books were discarded. Dr. Berry died in 1968.

Doc Berry, 1952
↖Courtesy of Professor
Duncan Heron,
Duke University

Field Trip, Carolina Geological Society, 1952
↖Courtesy of Professor Duncan Heron, Duke University

uninhibited expression in social gatherings at their home. The Berrys believed in letting us students discover pitfalls and experience logical consequences for ourselves, thus promoting a love of exploration and discovery. Only on rare occasions did they warn us against potentially disastrous ventures. Without a leader constantly guiding the group, we occasionally made mistakes, but the learning experience was well worth the risk.

One aspect I especially liked about the Geology Department was that professors did field work on a consulting basis to carry out research for corporate as well as governmental interests. Unlike professors in some fields, the geology professors had real-world experience and knowledge they could impart to their students—knowledge that would be valuable to us in future employment or entrepreneurial ventures.

Fieldwork is a basic requirement in the study of geology. I did some of mine in the backcountry of the Great Smoky Mountains and the Appalachian Mountains of Virginia, West Virginia, Tennessee, and North Carolina. Those are great stomping grounds for a geologist, because the rocks are well exposed, in contrast to the gently rolling hills and flatlands of the piedmont and coastal plain where vegetation hides most of the underlying rocks.

We students observed wealth being extracted from the earth, but the mining companies had done little or nothing to repair the huge scars left from their digging. Piles of tailings littered the landscape, especially around the old copper smelters at Ducktown, Tennessee.

On occasions when I visited Dick in Washington, D.C., he would ask, "What are you and your classmates thinking? What are you discovering?"

I filled him in about the desecration of the environment caused by careless mining practices. "The beneficiary of that wealth should be required to put something back. Maybe it's even possible for these companies to improve the environment," I suggested. Many years later in 1970, I realized how seriously Dick had considered my suggestions when his administration created the Environmental Protection Agency.

While I relished the sciences, I found social sciences and language arts quite a challenge. But I did all right and even made the dean's list one semester. However, I was not aiming for dean's lists and "A's"; rather, I sought answers to questions about planet Earth, its environment, and its place in the universe.

∿ ∿

In 1950, Dick ran for the U.S. Senate in California against Helen Gahagan Douglas and won. I did not get involved in the campaign because I was still attending Duke University. By that time, I had developed some interest in politics, however, so I joined the College Young Republican Club. In fact, I served as treasurer at one point.

Republicans in the South were an anachronism in those days and sorely outnumbered. The Democrats completely controlled governments at all levels in North Carolina, as well as the rest of the South, but I noticed that many Democrats were far more conservative than Republicans I had met in California. I wondered at the time if this dichotomy might be recognized in the future and where it would lead.

1952 Vice Presidential Campaign

In the summer of 1952, I taught the freshman lab courses in physical and historical geology and took German as a prerequisite for my Bachelor of Science degree. During that time, General Dwight D. Eisenhower, the Republican nominee for President, announced at the Republican National Convention in Chicago that he had chosen my brother, the youngest Republican Senator, to be his running mate.

Although Dick's name had floated about as one of many potential Republican candidates for Vice President, no one in our family had a clue Eisenhower was seriously considering Dick. Grandmother Almira, who passed away in 1943, had had a premonition as early as 1940, however. She said, "Someday he's going to be very, very great."

To our complete surprise, my family and I suddenly became persons of interest to the press, sharing a small corner of the spotlight shining on Dick and Pat. During my first newspaper interview, a local reporter asked me what I thought when I heard about my brother's nomination?

I managed to respond too cavalierly. "Well, I certainly wasn't expecting it. I was surprised to the point of being dumbfounded."

So, the headline read, "Senator Nixon's brother is dumbfounded." Suddenly I saw how people who read only the headlines could be misled as to the true content of the news. With that introduction to headline editors, I realized they can be magicians with political power.

Dick advised me, "Don't worry about reporters. Give them the answers you can, and do it succinctly so they can't bend your words. You don't need to tell them anything you don't want them to know. Just say, 'No comment.' Don't be rude. Keep in mind they're just trying to earn a living."

Don told me Dad shouted for joy when he heard the news that General Eisenhower had chosen Dick as his running mate. I can still imagine him exclaiming, "Ha! Now Ike's on the right track!" Initially, Dad had thought Eisenhower too closely tied to the liberal Eastern establishment. Nominating Dick, of course, put him in Dad's good graces. He thought the General must have been an excellent judge of character to recognize Dick would be an asset to his team. My guess is that Mom reacted differently. After settling into the realization of the momentous news, she would have searched for a private place to pray, asking God to grant her son an extra measure of wisdom and guidance.

Mom and Dad had moved back to California by that time and were living on Anaconda Street in Whittier. Their return to rural life on the Pennsylvania farm had brought them great joy, but those happy times were abbreviated by Dad's accident with the tractor on Echo Hill, necessitating their move to the warmth of Florida for a year. Finally, the call of the extended family had brought them back to California, and that's where reporters found them when the period of public attention overtook their lives. The news photographers frequently came to their home, and one of them shot the famous photo of Dad celebrating Eisenhower's announcement of his running mate.

Our family's initial elation turned to consternation in September 1952, however, when we read headlines blaring "Secret Nixon Fund!" and "Secret Rich Men's Trust Fund Keeps Nixon in Style Far Beyond His Salary." Reporters wrote that Nixon had an "$18,000 secret slush fund" and had profited from public service. This allegation didn't even come close to the actual facts, but liberals wasted no time putting their spin on this two-year-old resurrected story.

There was nothing secret, sinister, or illegal about the money. After his 1950 Senate campaign victory, close friends had set up a fund so Dick could pay for printing and mailing material to supporters and travel more frequently between Washington, D.C., and California. The Senate budget allowed for only one home-state trip per year. Dick and Pat were not wealthy and could not afford those political extras that would make him an effective senator and keep him in contact with his constituency. The friends limited donations to $500 per person and accepted no corporate funding. Donors received no favors in return for their contributions.

This uproar transpired while I was in Raleigh starting my first year of graduate school at North Carolina State University (NC State). Aware of the good friends who had donated to Dick's campaign and then supported him in office, I doubted that any breach of ethics or law had occurred, and I wasn't alarmed by the media furor. I felt confident the truth would eventually rise above the cesspool of hate.

But the controversy grew into a career-threatening crescendo for Dick. Newspaper editorials and politicians clamored for his resignation from the Eisenhower-Nixon ticket. The worst part for Dick, however, was Eisenhower's silence.

Dick considered his options, and after some agonizing days on the campaign trail, he decided to present his case directly to the public via television. In the early days of TV, that was a bold move. He was staking his political career on what became known as the "Checkers Speech."

When Dick addressed the nation, Mom was baby sitting Tricia and Julie in the East. Dad and I watched the broadcast with Don and Clara Jane in California.

On air, Dick disclosed his and Pat's financial worth in detail—and it wasn't much. The only gift they had received was a cocker spaniel puppy given by a man in Texas, who had nothing to do with the fund. He simply had heard that Pat wanted to get a dog for Tricia and Julie. Tricia had named him "Checkers."

Dick considered his speech a failure, partly because he felt mentally drained and partly because he went overtime and didn't give the address of the Republican National Committee where people could send telegrams. But our family and the country judged his presentation to be a great success, and he received an overwhelming display of support. Listeners looked up the address on their own and sent millions of telegrams and letters urging Dick to stay on the ticket. Those messages flooded the Republican National Committee and the Eisenhower-Nixon campaign headquarters.

The Checkers Speech was a landmark in political history, clearing the way for Dick to continue campaigning alongside Dwight Eisenhower on the substantive issues of the shaky economy, the Korean War, and Communist influence in the Truman Administration.

The polls had predicted an Eisenhower-Nixon victory. General Eisenhower, a career military man and World War II hero, was a very popular candidate. Nevertheless, in politics, anything can happen, so my family and I were relieved when the election went as expected.

On November 4, 1952, the Eisenhower-Nixon ticket won by a landslide: 55.1 percent to 44.4 percent of the popular vote, 442 to 89 electoral votes, and 39 of the 48 states. The nine states that Illinois Governor Adlai Stevenson and Alabama Senator John Sparkman carried were all in the South. For the first time since Herbert Hoover in 1928, Republicans won control of the White House, and they also controlled both houses of Congress.

❧ CHAPTER 6 ❧
INTERNATIONAL SPOTLIGHT

Barely through my first quarter of graduate school at NC State, I received an official invitation to the inauguration of Dwight David Eisenhower as the thirty-fourth President of the United States and Richard Milhous Nixon as the thirty-sixth Vice President. Driving from Raleigh to Washington, D.C., would pose no problem, assuming my old car continued running dependably, but breaking away from the academic routine did cause me some apprehension. How much time could I afford away from the well-structured syllabus of geology courses at the College of Engineering?

Dr. Jasper Stuckey, the department head and my thesis advisor, assured me, "You'll have some make-up work after the big event, and you'll need to work a little harder when you get back. But you should definitely plan to go. After all, he's your brother. You just have to go!"

1953 INAUGURATION

So, with that encouragement, I arranged to attend the inauguration. One of my former classmates from Duke, Robert L. Davis, who then was working in Raleigh as a fundraiser for the North Carolina Symphony, volunteered to travel along as an aide-en-tour to help escort some of our family and to fend off any potential disruptions from political detractors. As a U.S. Marine Corps veteran, he had a good idea of the tumultuous times about to ensue.

Aware of the traffic snarls that develop during major events in the nation's capitol, Bob parked my car for the duration at the Statler Hotel, where we stayed—just two blocks from the White House.[34] Then he volunteered as an ad hoc escort, joining the military escorts already assigned to family members, most of whom were staying at the Shoreham Hotel. His services provided several propitious detours to get us to scheduled events on time, and we were all grateful for his help.

I'd been to Washington many times, but I had never seen such congestion. The inaugural festivities packed the city with more people and vehicles than it could comfortably contain. Alphabetical streets and numbered streets, aligned in cardinal directions, intersect with diagonal avenues at Washington's many circles. This layout often confuses first-time visitors, but on that Inaugural Day, Tuesday, January 20, 1953, with the city suddenly overpopulated with strangers searching for unfamiliar destinations, cars were creeping aimlessly. One reporter lamented that it took him two hours by taxi to travel from DuPont Circle to nearby Georgetown University.

The swearing-in ceremony occurred on the East Portico of the U.S. Capitol. President and Mrs. Harry Truman and Vice President and Mrs. Alben Barkley sat in the second row, and behind them were senior senators and Members of Congress. I remember seeing former President Herbert Hoover as well. We family members, including my parents and several relatives, witnessed our first presidential inauguration from the wings of the platform.

For me, a twenty-two-year-old nonpolitical graduate school student with "rocks in my head," a myriad of thoughts ran through my mind. On one hand, I considered all the folderol a pain in the neck, but on the other hand, I was awed by my brother taking his place in history as one of only thirty-six Vice Presidents. I reflected on our humble roots and how in America great wealth and a family dynasty were not essential to attain high office.

---

34 The old Statler Hotel at Sixteenth and K Streets, Northwest became the Statler-Hilton in 1954 and is now the Capital Hilton.

Hannah & Richard , c. 1954, at Frank and Hannah's home
∿From Hannah Nixon's collection

As was the custom for Vice Presidents, Dick took his oath of office immediately before Chief Justice Frederick Vinson administered the oath to Dwight Eisenhower. The new President of the United States then delivered the first inaugural address broadcast live coast-to-coast. In his speech, he called for citizens of the United States and the world to stand firm in defense of faith and freedom.

Deviating from tradition, President Eisenhower first bowed his head in an impromptu prayer, asking the Almighty God for "the power to discern right from wrong" and the ability to govern thereby. Addressing his fellow citizens, he reminded them of the challenges at the midpoint of the century, a time when "forces of good and evil are massed and armed and opposed as rarely before in history."[35] . . . The enemies of this faith know no god but force, no devotion but its use. They tutor men in treason. They feed upon the hunger of others. Whatever defies them, they torture, especially the truth. . . . Freedom is pitted against slavery; lightness against the dark."[36]

Eisenhower then called for peace through strength:

> Realizing that common sense and common decency alike dictate the futility of appeasement, we shall never try to placate an aggressor by the false and wicked bargain of trading honor for security. Americans, indeed all free men, remember that in the final choice a soldier's pack is not so heavy a burden as a prisoner's chains. . . . Knowing that only a United States that is strong and immensely productive can help defend freedom in our world, we view our Nation's strength and security as a trust upon which rests the hope of free men everywhere.[37]

Immediately following his speech, Congress for the first time hosted a luncheon in the Old Senate Chamber of the Capitol in honor of the new President and Vice President. Meanwhile the family members rode special buses to the presidential reviewing stand at 1600 Pennsylvania Avenue. En route we dined from well-prepared

---

35 "Dwight D. Eisenhower First Inaugural Address," *Inaugural Addresses of the Presidents of the United States*, Vol. 2, (Bedford, MA: Applewood Books, 2001) 115.
36 "Dwight D. Eisenhower First Inaugural Address" 117.
37 "Dwight D. Eisenhower First Inaugural Address" 118.

box lunches. Awaiting the arrival of President Eisenhower and Vice President Nixon, our military guide escorted us to our assigned second-row seats on the left side.

On the reviewing stand, Dick introduced me to President Eisenhower—my first face-to-face meeting with him. I was sure he had had enough handshakes for one day, but as Dick had told me, his grasp was firm and full of sincerity—no limp dishrag in that man's right hand.

An estimated one million people lined the streets to watch the largest such event in U.S. history—a four-and-one-half-hour procession of 73 marching bands, 59 floats, military vehicles, horses, and even elephants. In honor of former General Eisenhower and the other retired five-star military officers present, 642 aircraft, representing all branches of the military, flew over the parade route. Although Eisenhower had requested a shorter event, the Inaugural Committee overruled.

The celebration concluded that evening with traditional formal events in more than one ballroom around the city. The Inaugural Committee provided transportation for my parents and their immediate family (minus Dick and Pat) from their hotel to the inaugural ball in the Armory. The President and Mrs. Eisenhower, alternating with Dick and Pat, appeared briefly at each ballroom. This, the first of the nine inaugural balls I have attended, ended near midnight with all our family sharing happy smiles.

Early the next morning at breakfast, I said good-bye to our relatives at the Shoreham and caught a ride to the Statler Hotel where Bob Davis had parked my car for the duration of our stay. Standing in line at the garage, I spotted the famous comedy duo, Bud Abbott and Lou Costello, and told them how much I enjoyed their routines. I remarked that Dick appreciated their famous baseball comedy act, "Who's on First?"

The garage attendant finally delivered my car, and Bob and I headed back to Raleigh. I had some catching up to do as I got back into the swing of petrology, petrography, sedimentation, and stratigraphy.

DICK'S FIRST TERM AS VICE PRESIDENT

The U.S. Constitution prescribes only a few duties for the Vice President: He is to serve as president of the Senate but can only vote in case of a tie; he is to receive the states' electoral vote tallies for presidential elections and open these certifications in the presence of both houses of Congress; and he is first in line of succession in the event the President dies, is removed from office, or cannot discharge his duties. John Adams, the nation's first Vice President, called the vice presidency "the most insignificant office that ever the invention of man contrived or his imagination conceived."[38] With such an easy job description, some Vice Presidents faded into the shadows of history. Not Dick.

As Vice President, my brother was no figurehead, merely attending ceremonial functions on behalf of the President. With Eisenhower's blessing, Dick helped transform the office into a meaningful position—that of an assistant President ready to take charge if anything happened to the President. Moreover, for the first time in history, the Vice President was an integral member of the executive team. Eisenhower encouraged Dick to assume more responsibilities than had any prior Vice President.

Having had more experience in politics than President Eisenhower and having the energy and fortitude of a young man, Dick became a leader in the administration and a newsmaker in his own right. Eisenhower wanted his Vice President to be well-informed on all the issues, which suited Dick just fine. He tackled his new responsibilities with the same diligence and intelligence that he invested in all his prior endeavors.

In their courtship days, Dick and Pat had dreamed of traveling to foreign lands, but they could not foresee that one day those dreams would be fulfilled beyond all their expectations. President Eisenhower realized that Dick had a talent for meeting with heads of state, as well as mingling with citizens of foreign lands, so he sent Dick and Pat on goodwill trips to Asia, the Far East, Central America, and the Caribbean. More than any prior high-ranking official, Dick walked among the crowds, shaking hands and talking with people on the street and in shops.

Pat, too, had a knack for connecting with the common people and for charming dignitaries. She won hearts wherever she went.

---

38 "John Adams." <http://www.whitehouse.gov/history/presidents/ja2.html> - 17k, accessed 6/19/08.

On September 24, 1955, Eisenhower suffered a heart attack while in Denver. With the Constitution being unclear as to the Vice President's role when a President became too ill to perform his duties, Dick was in a politically precarious position. He didn't want to appear as if he were usurping power, yet he had to assume responsibilities of the office and assure the press and public that business was being conducted as usual. When Eisenhower recovered, he expressed appreciation to Dick for his skillful handling of affairs.

Graduate School

Near the end of my first year of graduate school in 1953, I had convinced myself that my best course of action would be to enlist in the military rather than wait for the draft to catch up to me. I could pursue my long-time interest in flight training and afterward focus on what I wanted to do with my life, including completion of my academic work at a school in California.

However, Dick encouraged me to do otherwise. He arranged for me to meet with Dr. Abe Zarem, a physicist from Pasadena who specialized in piezoelectric phenomena and optics. He also served on President Eisenhower's Science Advisory Board.

Dr. Zarem sat down with me in his temporary office in the Old Executive Office Building in Washington, D.C., and ran through a pro and con evaluation of my prospects. He said, "If you quit school now, you run the risk of never finishing your degree after military service, and your earning prospects would be reduced. If you continue with your education and at least get a master's degree, the difference in your earning power would be substantial."

When he illustrated the statistical difference in income and the opportunities for more meaningful jobs available to somebody with a master's versus somebody who stopped short, I said, "I see your point. You've persuaded me to continue."

Dr. Zarem said, "Ultimately, you should go on to get a Ph.D., because that's the 'union ticket' to teaching. To teach at the university level, you really need the Ph.D."

My next task was to figure out where to complete my graduate study, so I discussed visiting potential schools with Dr. Zarem. I told him that Dr. Berry had suggested Emory University in Georgia or Johns Hopkins.

"Well, why don't we just drive up to Baltimore in the morning and talk with Milton Eisenhower, the President's brother, who's currently president of Johns Hopkins," He suggested.

"That's an excellent idea. How do we arrange it?"

Dr. Zarem immediately placed a call through the White House switchboard and made the appointment for the next day.

We met with Dr. Eisenhower at the appointed time. He had already arranged to introduce me to Dr. Ernst Cloos, a distinguished geology professor at Johns Hopkins.[39] Dr. Cloos did not try to convince me to attend Johns Hopkins, but he certainly reinforced Dr. Zarem's appeal for me to continue my studies.

Soon, I returned to Duke for further counseling from Dr. Berry. After I told him of my meetings at Johns Hopkins, in his friendly, humorous manner, he said, "Why don't you just continue what you started over at NC State? You've already made the adjustment, and you can keep your teaching assistantship there to help pay the way."

My doubts removed, I decided to finish my two-year program at NC State for a Master of Science degree in Geological Engineering. During the next academic year, I completed my course work and continued with my teaching assistantship, instructing the freshman labs in physical geology.

Housed in a quaint little building called Primrose Hall, the Geology Department at NC State consisted of only six faculty members. The basement of the building was set up as a laboratory, and a life-sized replica of a Tyrannosaurus Rex skull greeted all who entered. Displays of extraordinary fossils and spectacular mineral crystals often attracted students with little or no background in geology. However, those introductory displays disguised the real world of work. Unless initially curious students developed a love for the hard labor of serious study with long hours staring through a microscope at microfossils or thin sections of rock, they wouldn't continue down that path.

I had already decided I didn't want any part of looking at microfossils in the search for petroleum reserves. The demand for

---

39 Dr. Ernest Cloos was the brother of the late Dr. Hans Cloos, who had written a famous book on the attractions of geology titled *Conversations with the Earth.*

private automobiles had skyrocketed after the end of World War II, but as early as 1950, I believed an alternative energy source could be developed to reduce the consumption of fossil resources. With the increasing demand for fuel, the limited supplies of oil would eventually be depleted. After watching my good friend Bill Harrison experiment with hydrolysis using a battery, two electrodes, and a jar of water, I began to think of ways to use hydrogen and oxygen as portable fuels.

Everybody pooh-poohed the idea, saying, "You'll be burning a lot of fossil fuel to get the energy needed to extract the hydrogen from H_2O. So, what are you gaining?"

"One day there will be a way," I insisted.

᭡᭡   ᭡᭡

During my years of graduate study, Dick continued to encourage my educational endeavors. Every chance he got, he would ask about my activities and education. He wanted to know, "What do you do on your weekend field trips?" "What are you learning?"

In response to his terse questions, I would ramble on about my field trips in the Appalachians.

Dick's questions gave me the opportunity to educate him about the environment, as I had while at Duke. Being in politics, he didn't have the opportunity to get inside a coal mine or on a drilling rig in an oil field, but he was always interested in and receptive to what I said about the environment.

"To understand those things, you, as a public official, need some exposure, even if it's second hand," I advised. Expanding on what I had told Dick when I attended Duke, I said, "In my field work, I visit old abandoned mine sites, some of which are rather dangerous holes in the ground. Tailings piles are left just as they were when the site was abandoned. I think we should try to clean up some of that mess. When a mining company takes wealth out of the earth, part of that wealth ought to be used to restore the site to a condition as good as or better than what nature gave us. If companies leave scars, they should repair them and make the land attractive again. They should give nature a chance to recover."

᭡᭡   ᭡᭡

Taking Dr. Stuckey's advice, I wrote my master's thesis on the geology of the northwest corner of Chatham County, North Carolina, a rural area about seventy square miles. Although the State had sponsored investigations there in the past, Dr. Stuckey felt further study of a copper deposit was warranted. As it turned out, I made no encouraging discoveries regarding the copper, but I learned enough to suggest closer study. The professors judged my thesis and oral response sufficient to pass muster for the Master of Science in Geological Engineering degree.

WORKING AS A ROUGHNECK

After graduating from NC State in 1954, I considered applying to Stanford University in California to pursue a Ph.D., but first I had to earn some money to continue my education. Late that summer, I took an entry-level job as a roughneck for the Santa Fe Drilling Company in the Signal Hill oil field near Long Beach, California. After the rigors of academia, working in the oil field seemed like a vacation. I enjoyed the regular, dependable routine.

An oil drilling crew consists of several levels of workers. The chief of operations, called the "tool pusher," is responsible for each contracted project. The driller, who reports to the tool pusher, directs all the field work. When adding another section of drill stem, mechanical specialists are assigned duties like manning the blocks at the top of the derrick. The lowest pay grades in the crew, some with experience and some greenhorns (like I was), are called "roughnecks" or "roustabouts"—a job my dad also did long ago. Either name applies to the ditch diggers and mechanics working around oil rigs.

On the Signal Hill job, the whole crew admired and respected the driller, a man nicknamed "Sonny." He was present on all critical transitions, e.g., extracting drill stem to retrieve a stubborn bit or reentering a new drilling phase, no matter on which of the three 8-hour shifts they occurred.

In those days, numerous oil wells and old wooden derricks still covered Signal Hill. When I joined the company, I was assigned to a driller's crew of about fifteen men working 24-7 in three shifts. The project involved redrilling an old 5,000-foot oil well to enhance the flow that had become sluggish. We completed the drilling about a month after I was hired.

To reestablish a live pumping oil well, we first had to clear the site by removing the two halves of the large steel derrick and all the drilling equipment. During the night and early morning hours, the crew on graveyard shift had lowered the derrick on its side onto jack stands. By the time I arrived on my morning shift, a mobile crane was already on site and attached to the upper section of the derrick. In order to separate the two sections, the crane would lift the upper part away as soon as the bolts were removed from the midsection. Up on the rig, I unscrewed the nuts with a large wrench and then popped out the bolts. As soon as I had removed the last bolt, I crawled toward the jack stand supporting the lower section to climb down from the derrick.

While I was still holding on, the young mobile crane director signaled "all clear" to the crane operator controlling the upper half of the derrick. The premature movement caused a steel ladder to drag across my left hand. In spite of the shock and pain, I somehow managed to lower myself to the ground. Seeing that the ladder had shattered three fingers of my left hand, practically amputating the middle finger, one of the company managers hustled me to the emergency unit at Bixby Knolls Hospital, a small Seventh Day Adventist hospital near Signal Hill. Dr. William Wright patiently realigned the bones, stitched up the long wound on my palm and middle finger, and encased my whole forearm in a cast. With great skill, he reconstructed my hand in about three hours.

While I was in the hospital, Dick made a special trip to check on my condition. The hospital staff was all agog, scurrying around with excitement and seeking autographs when the Vice President arrived.

Dick and I had a good visit as I tried to put his mind at ease regarding my injury. "Well, I never really wanted to play the piano like you anyway," I told him. "I've got other goals I can pursue now. After taking time off to recover, I'd really like to fly helicopters."

Although concerned, Dick was upbeat as usual, encouraging me to stay positive and to avoid losing sight of my goals.

During my week in the hospital, I learned that Sonny, the driller, had become very distraught over my accident. Some people were convinced his anguish led to his fatal heart attack. I was deeply saddened and stunned by the news of his premature death.

⌁ ⌁

Following release from Bixby Knolls Hospital, I returned home to recuperate at my parents' place on Beach Boulevard in La Habra, California. When I had recovered sufficiently, my cousin Chuck Milhous, some of my former Whittier High School classmates, and I decided to visit Edith and Tim Timberlake's cabin in the Valley of the Falls. Chuck drove six of us there in his new Studebaker Champion.

Aunt Edith had said, "Anytime you want to use the cabin, just let me know. I'll leave the key out for you." So, we stopped by the Timberlake home in Riverside, picked up the key, and continued on to the cabin called "Lot-o-Rest." My friends went hiking. Having the use of both hands, they could navigate the rocks and boulders, which I couldn't do. Still in a cast and feeling like a useless one-armed paper-hanger, I stayed at the cabin and wrote the following poem:

GUESTS

From Appalachian hills and chigger-laden downs,
From grimy, busy mills and smog-infested towns,
From the steamy, humid face of ivy-covered walls
To this rocky, quiet place in the Valley of the Falls
Another move, at best, could never overtake
This jaunt to Lot o' Rest as guest of Timberlake.
So with thanks, we can't express in epistolary lines
We leave with gratefulness for the oasis in the pines.

Ed Nixon
Nov. 21–24, 1954, Whittier

MILITARY SERVICE

The Selective Service eventually reached my name in the fall of 1954, but what a sense of timing! I was left facing the military draft with my left arm in a cast from fingertips to elbow. Obviously, that meant a one-year deferment. I wondered how to make the most of my lost time. Then came Dr. Zarem to the rescue. At that time, he was residing in Pasadena where he had co-founded Hycon Aerial Surveys. Based partly on his recommendation, the company hired me as a full-time cartographic draftsman. I continued there into the summer of 1955.

Meanwhile, I had decided to pursue my persistent interest in flying helicopters. The Navy appealed to me more than the other branches, largely because Pat's brother Tom was a Naval Aviator. So, I visited the Office of Naval Officer Procurement (ONOP) in Los Angeles. I filled out the applications, took the tests, and waited a couple of weeks for acceptance and orders to Pensacola, Florida. My one-year deferment had not yet expired, so what happened next caught me by surprise.

On Friday afternoon, July 24, 1955, Mom noticed a four-inch article in the *Whittier News* indicating the Vice President's brother had been drafted. That was news to me! Even though I once again resided in California at my parents' home, I had registered on my eighteenth birthday with the draft board in York County, Pennsylvania, a much more conservative area. When I finished my master's degree, the draft board decided I had had enough schooling and should go into the service now. Later, if I so desired, I could return for more education.

Knowing I seldom paid attention to newspapers, Mom told me about the article. Aware of how much error crops up in daily news articles written by reporters seeking a scoop, I preferred to find more carefully written information in weekly news magazines.

"Have you seen anything in the mail from the Selective Service?" I asked her.

Mom scanned Friday's mail but found nothing. If my brother hadn't been Vice President, I wouldn't have been forewarned about being drafted, and the greetings from the Selective Service would have arrived in the mail before I could accept orders to Pensacola for flight training. So, after reading the article, I immediately called the ONOP in Los Angeles, where my application for flight training was pending, and explained my predicament.

The officer in charge said, "Don't worry. If you haven't received anything in the mail, your draft notice isn't official yet. Report here at 07:00 tomorrow morning, and you'll be going to boot camp in San Diego."

That Friday afternoon was a flurry of activity at our house as I prepared to leave with only a toothbrush and razor. Early Saturday morning, July 25, 1955, as I was departing the recruiting office, the officers encouraged me, saying, "Once we get the approvals and notice of acceptance, we'll pull you out of boot camp and send you down to Pensacola."

No such luck! I completed all thirteen weeks of boot camp before receiving orders to flight training. No favors were forthcoming, but I hadn't expected or wanted special advantage anyway. I actually appreciated the opportunity to enhance my physical condition with rigorous training and to experience a few things that only a seaman recruit could fully understand. There I was, a twenty-five-year-old in the midst of all those homesick young bucks moaning about losing their hair and their individuality. I found it quite amusing that they made such a big deal out of an inconsequential matter.

During initial indoctrination, we received government-issue uniforms, including stiff, new boots, and we soon learned the reason for the name "boot camp." We were taught how to march and then perform a multitude of daily routines. In the organization of Recruit Company 351, I was designated the educational petty officer, a nominal title for the oldest man in the group.

Living in close quarters with sixty seaman recruits for thirteen weeks of rigorous training provided an environment conducive to an esprit de corps that crossed all boundaries of race and religion, including Islam—Filipino style. Our camaraderie and spirit reached a peak as we prepared for our graduation on Friday, October 21, 1955.

When the commanding officer at the Naval Training Center (NTC San Diego) learned the Vice President of the United States would be attending the boot camp graduation ceremony, he directed his yeoman to find the official Vice President's flag. The yeoman and a chief boatswain's mate searched through the entire storage locker but found only a picture of the flag in a book. So, the night before the ceremony, the two men painted a bed sheet to match the photograph. In the morning, they carefully hoisted the still tacky flag. When Dick arrived, it was flying along with the Stars and Stripes. That improvised flag must have looked enough like the real thing—at least nobody noticed it wasn't. While Dick was having coffee with the NTC commanding officer after the ceremony, the story broke to great laughter.

Dick heartily congratulated me on my acceptance to flight school. Our brother Harold had tried flying back in the barnstormer days, and Dick had told me stories of Harold's love of flying. His fascination with flight must have rubbed off on me; I had dreamed of flying ever since I could remember. Dick would encourage me, saying, "You've always wanted to fly, and you know you can, so do it."

Pat's brother Tom also called to express congratulations. He was sure I would qualify and soon be flying increasingly expensive aircraft. He said, "Just remember that before you even take your first solo flight, no matter what dollar value the government places on that equipment, it's not worth a nickel if you're in trouble. Don't hesitate to bail out!"

Fortunately, I never had to follow his advice.

On October 25, 1955, I arrived in Pensacola, where I awaited arrival of forty-three other Aviation Officer Candidates—"AOCs" as they called us. On October 30, AOC Class number 38-55 officially formed, and that became our identity for the next sixteen weeks of preflight training. Beginning at dawn, we drilled with calisthenics before breakfast and then submitted to seemingly endless bodybuilding exercises. We also spent time in "the tank" (the swimming pool) with endurance training and lessons on various emergency procedures such as escape from the submerged Dilbert Dunker, a plane crash simulator. Most of us were capable swimmers, but a few landlubbers had difficulty even floating.

Beyond the strong emphasis on physical fitness, the daily preflight syllabus included four or five classroom hours on such subjects as naval history and orientation, principles of flight, navigation, meteorology, and more. In the evening hours, we completed our homework, reviewing missed items on exams or attending our popular sessions called "stupid study."

The Navy had introduced the AOC program to attract college graduates directly into flight training regardless of prior military experience. Upon completing our sixteen weeks of preflight school before starting actual flight training, we were commissioned as ensigns. In contrast, the older program, called "NavCads," required successful completion of preflight and primary flight training before the cadets could become commissioned officers.

AOC Class 38-55 was the first full class at Pensacola with all members holding college degrees. Many more AOC classes followed ours, but the NavCad program continued alongside for several years, enlisting any applicant at least eighteen years old and fit to fly. They could receive a commission short of having a college degree once they finished preflight and primary flight training.

BLIND DATE

While we were in flight training, Jim Collins, my roommate, suggested that four of my friends and I visit New Orleans, a popular destination for Navy men on liberty. He had other commitments at that time, but he had called his friend Nicky, a student at Sophie Newcomb College, the women's college of Tulane University, to ask her to arrange dates for the five of us. Any healthy young man would jump at such a suggestion, and my friends and I were no exception. So, on May 18, 1956, a liberty Friday, we began the five-hour drive on old U.S. 90, anticipating a fun-filled weekend touring New Orleans with blind dates.

At the Josephine Louise House, the women's dormitory known as "J. L. House," or "Jail House," we entered the parlor and called for Nicky in anticipation of meeting our prospective dates—unaware of a drama occurring upstairs upon our arrival. One of the coeds, eighteen-year-old Gay Lynne Woods, was just finishing her sophomore year at Sophie Newcomb College. During exam week, she had been staying at the Jail House with a good friend, Sally Duren, to avoid lost time commuting to and from her home in Algiers on the West Bank of the city—an hour-and-a-half trip each way by bus, ferry, streetcar, and a final bus. In each direction, she would read German. Her professor assigned about fifty pages a day to read and translate.

That Saturday, Gay had just returned from taking a German reading knowledge exam, which students had to pass to graduate. Having good grades in the course, she felt confident about her grasp of the grammar and vocabulary. As she read the questions, however, she soon realized she couldn't pass. Although she could translate every word literally, the translation made no sense. The entire exam consisted of idioms—something about an old woman on a bicycle in a haystack. About half an hour later, she gave up in disgust, threw her blue book into the collection box, and stomped off.

Back at the dorm, Gay was furious that the professor had given such a tricky exam. She felt it didn't reflect her knowledge of the German language. Gathering her books and clothes, she thanked Sally for letting her stay at the Jail House and said good-bye. As she turned to leave, Gay bumped into Nicky blocking the doorway.

"Where are you going?" Nicky asked Gay.

Peeved, Gay replied, "I'm going home."

"You can't go!"

"And why not?"

"Because there are five guys downstairs who've driven five hours from Pensacola to meet girls. We're all going out this evening, and you're needed."

"I am not interested!" Gay protested. "They're probably all short brunettes anyway, and I only like tall, blond guys."

Nicky persisted, "Gay, you're not going anywhere except downstairs to meet the guys. I need your help!" Gay tried to maneuver past her, but Nicky grabbed her belongings and threw them all over the bed and the floor.

With no interest in going on a blind date, the unhappy young lady, dressed in pedal pushers, a T-shirt, and tennis shoes, went downstairs with Nicky, Sally, and Angela. I noticed Gay's long, red hair flying in the breeze from a nearby fan. Fire flaming in her eyes, she was obviously out of sorts.

There we stood facing four girls—five guys all over six feet two inches tall. Gay didn't even listen to the names of the first two black-haired fellows. The next one in the middle, I had dark brown hair. She half listened when I was introduced, hearing something like "ixon." The fourth guy Gay and I don't remember, but the last one was a blond-haired young man named Nels. Gay decided to make the best of the situation by focusing on him.

The girls' job was to show us the Tulane campus and get acquainted. With Nels on one side of Gay and me on the other, we headed out. Gay remembers that Nels wasn't particularly talkative but that I conversed more readily. After a lengthy stroll around the expansive grounds of the men's Tulane campus on one side and the women's Newcomb campus on the other, we entered Casimento's, a little restaurant-bar, for a beer. The nine of us sat in adjoining booths.

Gay detested beer so ordered a milk shake. I don't know what the other girls ordered, because I was looking only at Gay. Sitting across from her, I could see she was full of spirit, and something behind her eyes made me curious. But she ignored me; she had made sure she sat by Nels. Thinking about an evening date, which no one had even mentioned yet, Gay asked, "Nels, what do you like to do when you go out in the evening?"

He replied, "Well, I like to get drunk and groove to the music."

Gay thought, "Forget you, fellow. You're out of my life."

Then she turned her attention to the guy across from her—me! By the time we left Casimento's, I had my sights set on that young lady. As when Dad met Mom and Dick met Pat many years earlier, I sensed something special about Gay upon our first encounter. At that point, she still didn't know my name, but she later told me she found me fun to talk to and very interesting. Both of us being science majors, we had a lot in common. She was in the chemistry program with the goal of teaching, and I had majored in geology. We both had studied Spanish and German. The more we talked, the more we discovered mutual interests.

When we finished our drinks and stood up to go, I asked, "Could I walk you back to your dorm?"

Gay said, "Sure, it's just a couple of blocks."

At the Jail House, we were about to say our farewells. Gay, thinking we were all going out for the evening, wondered why no one had yet mentioned it. She looked me straight in the eye and asked, "Are we going out tonight or not?"

I replied, "Do you want to?"

"Nicky told me we were all going out tonight, but I haven't heard a word about it from anyone."

"I'll pick you up here at 7:30. I have a car."

"Wait a moment while I phone my parents to tell them I'll be home much later than planned." Gay's dad, Vernon Woods, answered, and I heard her explain, "A group of us are going out tonight, and it should be fine. I'm going with an interesting guy."

When her dad asked the name of her date, Gay thought quickly and said, "It's Tom Dixon. Now, Dad, don't worry, I'll be fine."

Gay promised him she wouldn't stay out too late. Then she told me good-bye and went to dinner in the dorm where the girls were all abuzz about the Vice President and his brother. Not being interested in politics then, she barely knew Richard Nixon was the Vice President and didn't have any idea what they were talking about.

After dinner, Gay went upstairs to get organized. As a guest in the dorm, she had only T-shirts, pedal pushers and tennis shoes. Up and down the hall she went, borrowing a dress, a slip, nylons, high heels and makeup. Then she showered, tied her hair into a neat ponytail, and got dressed. When I saw her, she looked pretty good in all those borrowed clothes.

Gay was ready at 7:30 when I called from the lobby, but no other guys had returned with me. I suppose none of them had struck a mental match as I had. Because I had been driving around trying to gain some familiarity with the city while she was at dinner, I asked if we could stop briefly at a place I'd passed called "Meal-a-Minute." While I ate a tuna sandwich, Gay sipped a Coke.

In the French Quarter, we strolled up and down Bourbon Street and spotted two of the guys who had toured with us during the afternoon. Gay wondered why they were walking without dates. After we sampled a famous Pat O'Brien's "Hurricane," a mixed drink served in a large glass shaped like a hurricane lamp, she informed me she still couldn't stand any kind of alcoholic beverage, so we returned to our sidewalk excursion.

"Gay, would you mind if I called the other girls at the dorm?" I asked. "We could pick them up, and they could walk around with us?"

"That's very nice of you to think about them, and yes, you should call them." We found a pay phone, and Gay told me the number while I dialed.

When one of the young ladies answered, I said, "Hello, this is Ed Nixon. Gay and I were thinking you might like to join us here in the Quarter." That's how Gay finally learned my name—and realized my identity.

The girl accepted the invitation, so Gay and I drove back to the university for her and another of the young ladies. We had refreshments and then walked with them around the Quarter. After I took them back to the dorm, Gay collected her belongings off the bed and the floor and returned the items she had borrowed. She came downstairs wearing her pedal pushers and carrying her pile of books and clothes.

We began the long trip to Algiers on the south side of the Mississippi River, the so-called "West Bank." While I drove through town down Canal Street to the ferry dock, we talked. Gay acted as my tour guide, explaining facts and items of interest about the city, the river, the ferry, and the trip in general. Crossing the river took only about twenty minutes, but Gay often had longer ferry rides when the current flowed faster or at times when commercial shipping clogged the waterway. Once in Algiers, I drove about ten minutes or so to Gay's home across the street from the Mississippi River. Gay pointed out that the levee along the river is the only hill in New Orleans, and because the city is mostly below sea level, land along the river's edge is the highest ground in town. She invited me in, but both her parents had already gone to sleep. By then it must have been around midnight.

Gay and I sat in her dad's office just inside the back door, talking and drinking coffee into the wee morning hours—until she heard her mother's feet hit the floor. Frantic, Gay said, "You'd better go—and now before my mother finds us! But please come back and meet my family for dinner tomorrow."

I promised to return Sunday afternoon and stay for dinner. I wanted to meet her parents and an aunt who would also be there.

Before leaving, I kissed Gay on the cheek. Expecting the imminent appearance of her mother, she didn't respond. I later told her, "I wasn't sure if I'd kissed you or the concrete block wall of the house." We waved good-bye and off I went to my lodging for the night.

The next day I returned to meet Vernon and Louise Woods, Gay's parents; Joy Linda, her sister; and Mae Travia, her aunt. Gay and I hardly got a moment to talk that day. The adults were all impressed by my manners and intelligence, she told me. Later in the evening, I rejoined my fellow travelers and returned to Pensacola.

Did I see Gay again? Yes, every weekend until July when she flew to Oregon to spend the rest of her summer vacation with her dad's brother and family in Tillamook. When she returned in August, our visits resumed. She went back to school, and whenever liberty would allow, I drove five hours each way just to see her.

1956 REELECTION CAMPAIGN

In 1956, while I trained at Pensacola and dated Gay in New Orleans, President Eisenhower and Vice President Nixon were running for reelection. All Dick's campaigns involved drama, and this one was no exception. Former Minnesota Governor Harold Stassen led an effort to dump Nixon from the ticket, citing a questionable poll indicating Dick could hurt the President's chances for reelection. Having fought hard for issues he believed in, Dick naturally had gained political enemies. Part of the dump Nixon effort was motivated by potential 1960 presidential candidates trying to prevent him from being Eisenhower's heir apparent. Stassen, a perennial presidential candidate, wanted Eisenhower to replace Dick with Christian Herter, then governor of Massachusetts. Herter, however, denied any interest in the vice presidency and was, in fact, embarrassed by the unsought attention.

I couldn't break away from flight training to attend the Republican National Convention in San Francisco that August. Mom and Dad were taking care of Tricia and Julie while Dick and Pat were at the Cow Palace arena. The folks had hoped to drive the girls to San Francisco as the convention got underway. However, Dad's arthritis and gout caused him so much pain that he couldn't travel.

Early the morning of August 22, the day scheduled for the vice-presidential balloting, Dick received a call at the convention from Dr. I. N. Kraushaar, our parents' family physician. Dad, who was seventy-seven years old, had suffered a ruptured abdominal artery and wasn't expected to live. Family took precedence over politics, and Dick, Pat, Don, and Clara Jane left the convention right away to be at his bedside. Dad preferred to be treated in the comfort and privacy of his home in La Habra rather than in the hospital.

Meanwhile, Marine Lieutenant Joe Beno had orders to take a cross-country training flight from NAS Pensacola to the West Coast in an F-80 jet trainer. The military called those flights "RONs" (Remain Overnight). Upon landing, the pilot would check into bachelor officers' quarters and then return to base the next morning. With a two-week temporary leave granted, I joined Lt. Beno on the flight in the student seat. Don drove out to the air base and brought us both to East Whittier where Lt. Beno enjoyed an unusual overnight stay at Don's, beginning with Don preparing steaks and Clara Jane doing the trimmings. The next day, Lt. Beno headed back to Pensacola, and I proceeded to Dad and Mom's house for the duration of my emergency leave.

When Dad, who was in an oxygen tent, saw Dick, he rallied and regained some of his feistiness. Worried about Stassen's effort to dump his son, Dad scolded him for leaving the convention, saying, "You get back there, Dick, and don't let that Stassen pull any more last-minute funny business on you."[40]

Dick didn't leave that day but watched his nomination with Dad and the rest of the family on television. Dad, of course, was thrilled Dick had weathered that political storm. He was renominated by a delegate vote of 1,323 to 1.

When Dick asked if he could do anything to lighten his spirits, Dad made one request: "If there's anybody I'd like to talk to, it's Fulton Lewis, Jr." Dick made a call to Lewis, our father's favorite radio commentator. Dad perked up and really beamed when he heard Lewis's familiar voice. I could not hear what Mr. Lewis said to Dad, but the conversation made him unusually happy.

The following day, Dad and the doctor assured Dick that he had improved enough for Dick to return to the convention the next day to deliver his acceptance speech. Dad practically ordered him out the door. Although aware his life was slipping away, he remained steadfast in his goal to vote in the November election and to see his son reelected. That was not to be. He clung to life until September 4.

On the day of Dad's funeral, East Whittier Friends Church hosted an overflow crowd. Afterwards, riding along in the funeral procession, I felt an odd mixture of emotions. Of course, my family and I grieved our loss. I realized my mother's deep pain as she now faced her remaining years without her life partner. But as I reflected on Dad's life, a long subdued pride began to emerge. Yes, Dick had attained high honors in service to the country we all loved, yet a less apparent but still remarkable fact was how much our poorly educated

---

40 Richard Nixon, *RN: The Memoirs of Richard Nixon* (New York: Grossett and Dunlap, 1978) 176.

father had attained in the face of long odds throughout his life. He sincerely had believed in the American dream. And considering his humble beginnings in Vinton County, Ohio, he certainly did achieve his dream: business and home ownership with the ability to provide a comfortable living for his family and an education for his children. And beyond his wildest dream, one of his sons had risen to the second highest office in the land.

It suddenly became clear to me: Dad's home community had come to attention, and scores of people were rendering him solemn honors—hats off, waving flags, and even saluting the casket along the highway to Rose Hills Cemetery northwest of Whittier, his final resting place.

Two months later, President Eisenhower and Dick handily won reelection, carrying forty-one of the forty-eight states with a margin of 57 percent nationwide. Dad would have been proud.

1957 INAUGURATION

I had already decided that marriage was around the corner, so I invited Gay to be my guest at the second Eisenhower-Nixon inauguration. Her parents gave their approval and encouraged her to attend. There she met my family for the first time: Mother, Don, Clara Jane, Richard, and Pat Nixon. Gay appreciated that my family greeted her with warmth and sincerity; they never put on airs, even on such an occasion. And my family made it evident that they thought highly of Gay.

January 20, the inauguration date established by the Twentieth Amendment to the Constitution in 1933, falls on a Sunday four times a century, and one of those occasions occurred in 1957. Congress had passed an act in 1792 stating that public inaugurations would take place on the following Monday if the date (at that time March 4) fell on a Sunday to avoid conflict with church services. So, for President Eisenhower's and Vice President Nixon's second term, a solemn private ceremony took place in the East Room of the White House on Sunday. There, Chief Justice Earl Warren administered the oaths of office. Because this private event was restricted to immediate family members, Gay spent time with some friends from California.

On the following day, Gay and I were seated together for the public ceremony on the East Portico of the U.S. Capitol. In his second inaugural address, President Eisenhower spoke of "The Price of Peace" in the face of the threat of international communism. He inspired the crowd by saying:

> So we voice our hope and our belief that we can help to heal this divided world. Thus may the nations cease to live in trembling before the menace of force. Thus may the weight of fear and the weight of arms be taken from the burdened shoulders of mankind. . . . May the light of freedom, coming to all darkened lands, flame brightly—until at last the darkness is no more.[41]

Marian Anderson, the famous mezzo-soprano, sang at that event, and what a privilege it was to hear her stirring performance.

The inaugural parade followed the public event at the Capitol, and again the Eisenhowers and Nixons were all seated in the presidential reviewing stand at 1600 Pennsylvania Avenue in front of the White House. Tricia and Julie met David and Anne Eisenhower, the President's grandchildren. That was the first chance David and Julie had to size each other up. With her right eye black and blue from a sledding accident, Julie felt quite self-conscious.

Sitting in the reviewing stand watching what seemed an endless procession, Pat's brother Tom turned to me and said, "Eddie, that same company of military cadets must have gone around the block three times. How many military academies do you suppose there are in the United States?" Later we read 17,000 marchers had participated in the parade that day.

That evening, I danced at an inaugural ball for the first time, and I hardly ever dance. It seems I misled Gay into thinking I enjoyed dancing as much as she did. Nevertheless, I appreciated the fine music and being able to share the event with the lady I loved.

The next day, Gay and I flew back to the Gulf Coast to continue our normal pursuits, she to Tulane and I to Pensacola.

---

41 "Dwight D. Eisenhower Second Inaugural Address," *Inaugural Addresses of the Presidents of the United States*, Vol. 2, 124.

Dick's Second term as Vice President

In his first term, Dick had proven himself to be a capable, hardworking Vice President, and Eisenhower rewarded him with increased policy-making responsibilities in his second term. On the domestic front, Dick worked for the passage of civil rights legislation. Many people today do not realize how passionately Dick favored expanding civil rights for blacks. A respect for all people, regardless of ethnicity, was an integral part of our Nixon-Milhous heritage, and Dick made that a priority in his public service.

Dick supported the bill that became the Civil Rights Act of 1957 more vocally than did President Eisenhower. On the Democratic side of the aisle, Senators Lyndon Johnson, Hubert Humphrey, and John Kennedy all opposed strong legislation. The purpose of the statute, the first civil rights law since the post-Civil War Reconstruction, was to ensure voting rights for minorities and to create authority for the establishment of a civil rights office in the Department of Justice.

In November 1957, Eisenhower suffered a stroke that affected his speech but not his mental ability. Dick did not have to assume the duties of the presidency then. Instead, he reassured the anxious public that the President would recover and that the government was carrying on.

Dick's role in foreign relations also increased during his second term. I never traveled with him on official trips, but we kept in contact by phone on a regular basis, mostly with regard to family matters, and I followed his journeys in the news.

On many occasions, Dick's and Pat's lives were in jeopardy because of his opposition to communism. Their most dangerous trip was a goodwill tour of Latin America in May 1958. In Argentina, Uruguay, Paraguay, and Bolivia, friendly crowds greeted them. In Peru, however, angry demonstrators protested their visit with anti-American and anti-Nixon epithets. Then in Caracas, Venezuela, on May 13, a violent mob nearly killed Dick and Pat by hurling stones at their vehicles. Riding in a car behind Dick's, Pat watched in horror as rioters tried to attack her husband.

When the news broke, Mom was taking care of Tricia and Julie in Washington, D.C. I was in training with my squadron at Ream Field, preparing to depart on the 1958 squadron cruise. To the relief of us all, Dick and Pat arrived safely at National Airport on May 14.

In July 1959, Dick and Pat made their famous trip to Moscow with a delegation of U.S. government officials, reporters, technicians, and television experts for the opening of the American National Exhibition and meetings with Soviet Premier Nikita Khrushchev, also the Soviet Union's Communist Party leader. The exhibition was part of a cultural exchange that the Eisenhower Administration hoped would ease Cold War tensions.

Dick had prepared extensively for his discussions with Khrushchev, who had a reputation for being a bellicose bully. Even on diplomatic occasions, he would curse and badger his opponents, trying to provoke them to lose their temper. Dick was the ideal U.S. official to dialogue with Khrushchev. From youth, Dick had had practice controlling his emotions while dealing with vociferous people. With his keen legal mind, he quickly perceived weaknesses in others' arguments. Therefore, I had no doubt my brother could handle Nikita Khrushchev.

When Dick and Pat arrived in Moscow, the government reception was cool, if not downright rude. No diplomatic protocol was followed. No bands played the countries' national anthems. No crowds greeted the Nixons. In fact, there had been no publicity informing the citizens of the Vice President's arrival.

The next morning, Dick rose early after a restless night and decided to visit the well-known Danilovsky produce and meat market. He knew that on his official tour in Moscow, he would be shown only what Khrushchev permitted him to see. However, Dick wanted to meet average Russian citizens unfettered by government officials controlling where he went and with whom he talked. From his days driving our family truck to the Los Angeles produce market early in the morning, he knew the market would be the best place to meet farmers and grocers at that hour. Dick took along his Secret Service agent and a Russian policeman who served as chauffeur and interpreter.

Realizing the identity of the visitor, crowds quickly thronged around Dick. In contrast to the cool government reception, the people showered him with expressions of friendship and pressed him for details of life in America; they did not view the United States as an enemy. Their warmth buoyed Dick's spirits and helped him prepare for his meetings with Khrushchev. Moreover, the people gave Dick hope that the two nations would one day be at peace.

Later that morning, Dick met privately with Khrushchev, whom he found to be every bit as belligerent as he was reputed to be. Dick remained courteous but didn't back down. He knew that bullies don't respect people who capitulate.

One of the points of contention was the annual Captive Nations Resolution (Public Law 86-90) that Congress had passed shortly before Dick's trip. The resolution called for the President to proclaim the third week of July 1959 Captive Nations Week in solidarity with the people enslaved by Communist imperialism, specifically those under Soviet Union domination. Enraged, Khrushchev accused the United States of an act tantamount to threatening war. He griped that the resolution stunk. Dick calmly explained the facts, traded a few barbs, and tried to change the subject. Finally, Khrushchev let the matter drop.

In the afternoon, Dick and Khrushchev previewed the American Exhibition scheduled to open that evening. RCA had set up a model television studio to illustrate the first color television taping operation. Gil Robinson, an engineer with the U.S. Department of Commerce, showed Dick how to operate the equipment and invited the two men to record greetings to exhibition attendees. Dick pushed the button to start the recording and said, "Mr. Secretary, look up above."

Astonished to see himself on the monitor, Khrushchev's jaw dropped, and for once he was speechless—but only momentarily. He quickly began a theatrical harangue against U.S. technology, claiming the Soviet Union would reach America's level in seven years. "When we catch up with you, in passing you by, we will wave to you."[42] He was playing to the camera with a pretend hand wave to the United States.

Then Khrushchev tried to goad Dick with another tirade against the Captive Nations Resolution. Dick refused to take the bait. Remaining calm, he stressed the need for a free exchange of ideas and peaceful competition between the two superpowers.

---

42 Nixon, *RN: The Memoirs of Richard Nixon* 208.

A few steps down the aisle, they came upon a full-sized model of a $14,000 middle-class American home where the now famous "Kitchen Debate" took place. Khrushchev refused to believe an average family could afford such luxuries as those contained in the kitchen, but Dick insisted an average steelworker could buy that house. Khrushchev continued his one-upmanship: Everything the U.S. could do, the U.S.S.R. could do better.

The conversation turned to a heated exchange on the merits of each other's washing machines, but both Dick and Khrushchev knew that beneath the superficialities, they were actually debating capitalism versus communism. Once, they even jabbed fingers into each other's chest to make their points.

Discussing the merits of each country's washing machines, Dick maintained, was better than competing on the strength of missiles.

Khrushchev responded, "Your generals say we must compete in rockets. Your generals say they are so powerful they can destroy us. We can also show you something so that you will know the Russian spirit. We are strong, we can beat you."

[Dick] replied, "No one should ever use his strength to put another in the position where he in effect has an ultimatum. For us to argue who is the stronger misses the point. If war comes, we both lose."[43]

While the debate and subsequent exchanges veered far afield from typical diplomatic fare, Dick and Khrushchev ended with an agreement that peace served the best interests of all nations. And surprisingly, Khrushchev seemed to enjoy debating with Dick, who, as an equal opponent, held his ground.

Back home, President Eisenhower praised Dick's performance, and Dick received widespread acclaim in this country and abroad for being able to handle the Russian dictator.

After visiting Moscow and other Soviet Union cities, Dick and Pat passed through Poland, a country at the crossroads between Central and Eastern Europe. Although the Communist government of Poland hadn't announced their visit, somehow the citizens found out. In Warsaw, Dick and Pat received a rousing reception from throngs of people tossing flowers, cheering, and even grabbing Dick's hands and

---

43 Nixon 209.

kissing them. Time after time, Poland had been overrun in wars from both the East and the West. Dick admired the strength of the Poles in the face of conflict, and he appreciated their culture. In turn, they applauded Dick's tough stand against communism. Every time he visited Poland, he received similar rousing ovations, especially in Warsaw. Dick helped cement the relationship between the Polish people and Americans, and they are still one of our strongest allies.

ENGAGEMENT AND MARRIAGE

Meanwhile, in February 1957, Gay was selected as Queen of Janus, her dad's Mardi Gras Carnival Club, and I was her escort, an ensign in white tie and tails, Navy style. After the Mardi Gras ball at dinner that night, February 14, 1957, I gave her the engagement ring, which she eagerly accepted.

On March 7, I received my Navy Wings of Gold, the cherished medal proudly worn by all designated Naval Aviators. Gay and Donna Kern, another officer's fiancée, traveled to Pensacola to pin the wings. In keeping with Navy tradition, married men had their wives pin the medals; single men could choose a girlfriend, mother, or someone else. The ceremony departed from strict military protocol, because usually an officer awarded the honors.

June 1, 1957, the morning of our wedding, Dick flew down from Washington, D.C., with his military aide, Major Don Hughes. Tricia and Julie remained in Washington with their mother to avoid missing their final days of school.

The Vice President's visits always attracted media attention, and the occasion of our wedding was no exception. The local Republican organization sent an official delegation of party dignitaries to greet Dick at the airport just after Mom and I met him. He told supporters he thought Florida would become the first Republican state in the South. The Eisenhower-Nixon ticket did carry Florida in 1952, and 1956, so there was evidence of the Democrats losing their stronghold.

After Dick shook hands with some spectators at the airport, the Secret Service drove Dick, Mom, and me to the Naval Air Station escorted by county and city police.

Ed and Gay at Mardi Gras Ball, February 14, 1957
❦Vernon Woods' Personal Collection

Gay and I had a traditional Navy wedding in the Pensacola Naval Air Station Chapel at 4 p.m. Ted Marshburn was my best man, as I had been at his wedding to Mary Louise Delkin in 1953. Our wedding party also included Gay's aunt Lucille, her mother's youngest sister, as the matron of honor, and Ensign Don McCurdy, Donna Kern's intended, as my head usher.

R. E. Elliott, the Navy chaplain, was quite a character. When he introduced himself, he said he hailed from "Chitlinswitch," Georgia—a non-existent town. "Chitlinswitch, Georgia. That's where I come from." He was trying to get us to smile, so we would pay attention to what he had to say. I don't know his denomination—probably Southern Baptist—but he had no problem performing a Quaker wedding in which we recited our personal vows without repeating them.

At the conclusion of the ceremony, Gay and I exited the chapel under an arch of crossed swords held by eight fellow officers in the Navy tradition. Afterward, a reception was held at Mustin Beach, the Officers' Club for the Pensacola Naval Air Station.

Although Dick stressed that he was there purely for family reasons, he couldn't escape the press and politics. Reporters interviewed him at the reception. He told them he supported President Eisenhower's budget, especially sufficient funding for national defense and security. Regarding Gay, Dick said I had married the prettiest bride he had ever seen. After he planted a kiss on her cheek, some of Gay's Delta Zeta sorority sisters from Sophie Newcomb College asked him to sign autographs.

Vice Admiral Austin K. Doyle, Chief of Naval Air Training, hosted Dick and members of the family at a dinner party that evening. Whenever Dick visited military installations, he would meet with the commanding officer to discuss military needs and national defense issues.

On our honeymoon, Gay and I drove across country to California in my 1954 yellow, stick shift Buick Century, towing a forty-foot house trailer—our first home together. We checked in at NAAS Ream Field, the helicopter base for most of the West Coast antisubmarine and utility helicopters at Imperial Beach between San Diego and the Mexican border.

Once we had settled in, Gay and I continued our honeymoon, driving into Baja California to see that barren land. Both of us had

"Nixon-Woods Marriage at Pensacola Naval Air Station"
Arch of Swords, June 1, 1957
❧Time & Life Pictures: Joseph Scherschel, Photographer
Permission obtained from Getty Images

studied Spanish, but neither of us had mastered the language well enough to converse with native speakers who knew no English. Against the advice of the locals, we drove a little beyond Ensenada. Gay was fascinated with seashells, so we spent time beachcombing. In all of two days, we turned around and headed back. Sleeping in our car parked on the beach had sounded romantic, but it sure wasn't comfortable. Nor was the area reliably secure.

Shortly after returning to our new home, I took Gay to visit Lot-o-Rest in the Valley of the Falls. Because it had been one of my favorite childhood retreats, I had often told Gay about it, and I wanted her to experience the beauty of the place. Mom, Aunt Edith, and Aunt Martha accompanied us. Together, the three sisters provided Gay with some essential training on the proper construction of a Milhous cherry pie, from the crust up, baked in a wood-fired stove. I considered that a valuable skill for my new bride. Gay has been baking pies with the Milhous ladies' recipe ever since with some actual improvements of her own added later, courtesy of a Tupperware crust recipe.

Training for a Tour of Sea Duty

For me, learning the intricacies of helicopter antisubmarine missions and gaining skill flying the big Sikorsky H-34 consumed most of the remainder of 1957. The H-34 was a monster compared with the Bell and Piasecki aircraft at the helicopter flight school at Pensacola's Ellyson Field.

One morning in the spring of 1958, LCDR Glen H. Wallace, my helicopter plane commander and pilot, and I, his copilot, were returning from a training flight at sea. Approximately fifteen miles off the coast of San Diego, I spotted green smoke from an emergency flare on the water and then noticed a downed pilot floating in a raft. An F-9 Cougar fighter plane had flamed out at 10,000 feet. The pilot had ejected safely at 7,000 feet. Cold and slightly injured, he was reluctant to abandon the raft for a hoist into our helicopter. Besides, getting him into our aircraft proved challenging. The helicopter rotor downwash was blowing the pilot's raft. The rough conditions at sea and the increasing winds hindered our rescue efforts, but Danny Jones, our sonar man, crouching in the open side hatch, patiently talked us into

The Hudspeth Rescue Crew -
Glen Wallace, Danny Jones, and Ed Nixon, spring 1958
❧U.S. Navy Photo

position and hoisted the man aboard. We made our way back to Ream Field and transferred LCDR Hudspeth to the care of Navy corpsmen from his fighter squadron based at Miramar Naval Air Station.

Rescuing a downed aviator at sea is a gratifying experience, to say the least. A thank you call from Mr. Hudspeth closed the case as far as I was concerned. But our flight crew and I also appreciated receiving recognition from the Chief of Naval Operations and the Sikorsky Company's award of a "Winged S" pin presented to each crew member.

On June 4, 1958, about a week before departing on my first and only active duty Navy cruise to the western Pacific, our daughter Amelie "Amy" was born. My six-month absence was hard on our family, especially Gay. I know from experience that military spouses, regardless of gender, deserve great appreciation for what they sacrifice.

Gay's parents came out to San Diego from New Orleans and soon drove her and Amy back to their home in our old yellow Buick. In the fall, Gay returned to Newcomb College to finish her senior year. She graduated with the class of 1959 with a Bachelor of Arts degree in Chemistry.

Upon completing my six-month West Pac Cruise, I returned to San Diego in early December 1958 and was greeted with orders to report to Ellyson Field in Pensacola as a helicopter flight instructor. So, I bought a Rambler Rebel station wagon and proceeded east with Bill Tate "Tater," a squadron mate, who was as eager to get home to his wife in Mississippi as I was to rejoin my wife and new daughter. As I recall, we drove nonstop. After dropping Tater at his home, I celebrated Christmas in New Orleans with Gay and six-month-old Amy.

Then in January 1959, while Gay was completing her final semester at Newcomb College, I proceeded alone to Pensacola to begin my new assignment at Ellyson Field. Eventually, I also instructed classes in helicopter operations and engineering and served as the Training Division Officer at Ellyson Field, a job I held until the summer of 1960.

Amy Nixon at six months following her dad's Navy cruise,
December 1958
    ⌁Vernon B. Woods Family Portrait Collection

NROTC Instructorship

In May 1959, two joyous events occurred: Gay graduated with a Bachelor of Arts degree in chemistry, and she and Amy moved to Pensacola, so finally we could be together as family.

Before completing my tour as a helicopter flight instructor at Ellyson Field in the summer of 1960, I considered volunteering for two more years beyond my five-year active duty obligation. On April 14, 1960, Elizabeth "Beth," our second daughter, was born at Pensacola Naval Air Station Hospital. Soon after, I requested an NROTC instructorship at the University of Washington in Seattle. I had always wanted to live in the Pacific Northwest—as far away as I could get from southern heat and swamp mosquitoes, so I welcomed receipt of official orders that came through with my first choice.

Arriving in Seattle, Gay looked at me and said, "August is a hot month in the South, and here it's actually cold!"

"Coming out of the tropics, the Pacific Northwest is indeed refreshing," I agreed, remembering what Ben Lemert, professor of economic geography, had told the class during my freshman year at Duke: "If you travel to an area with the same type of climate as where your ancestors originated, you'll be comfortable there." He said North Carolina and the South had an Asian coastal climate, California an African desert climate, and the Pacific Northwest a climate like Northern Europe. So, being of Northern European descent, I felt right at home in Seattle.

1960 Presidential Campaign

The presidential primary campaign was well underway when I received orders to the University of Washington. As Vice President, Dick was the logical successor to President Eisenhower and the leading Republican contender. Although Dick had often been deemed shy—not an asset in politics—I would describe him as contemplative to the distraction of some who wanted to see him emote. On the positive side, he was a gifted orator, a diligent officeholder, and an inveterate campaigner. His trips abroad representing the United States gave him valuable experience in foreign affairs and friendships with heads of state.

Although military duty precluded any official role for me in Dick's 1960 bid for the presidency, I did attend the 1960 Republican National Convention. Just before the convention in Chicago on July 25-28, I was at an orientation seminar at Northwestern University in Evanston, Illinois, to prepare for the teaching job at the University of Washington. Mom and Gay joined me in Chicago. We watched the proceedings from a box where we sat with Don, Tricia, and Julie.

Dick won the nomination unanimously. Out of a list of six candidates for Vice President, he selected Henry Cabot Lodge, U.S. Ambassador to the United Nations, from Massachusetts. Lodge was more liberal than Dick, but Dick thought he would balance the ticket with his broad national appeal.

In his acceptance speech, Dick spoke of building a better America and world in which the dreams of millions would be realized. He said, "Let the victory we seek . . . be the victory of freedom over tyranny, of plenty over hunger, of health over disease, in every country of the world."[44] He also stressed that he was a more experienced candidate, especially in foreign affairs, than his Democratic opponent, John F. Kennedy.

Dick pledged to convention delegates that he would campaign in all fifty states. He fulfilled his promise but in hindsight realized he should have concentrated his time on the states with the greatest number of electoral votes. The constant traveling overtaxed him physically.

In September and October, Gay and I watched the four televised Nixon-Kennedy debates from our living room in Seattle. Although Dick was skilled in debate, candidates had to be all made up with perfect hair and face paint to appeal to the vast television audiences. Dick said, "I don't need any of that stuff. I'm just going to talk." Those who listened to the first debate on the radio judged Dick the winner. Those who saw it on TV thought Jack Kennedy won. The makeup artists actually won, and vanity triumphed.

Dick and Jack were both very talented politicians, and, contrary to what many people assumed, they enjoyed a congenial relationship

---

44 Nixon, *RN: The Memoirs of Richard Nixon* 217.

in spite of their political differences. They both entered Congress in 1947. In the course of their work on the Labor and Education Committee, they established an enduring friendship.

Although Kennedy did not bring it up, an issue that unfairly surfaced in the 1960 campaign was our brother Don's financial dealings. In 1956, Nixon's Incorporated, his restaurant chain, needed to secure an investment loan in order to keep operating. Don had expanded his business holdings from the market to five successful Nixon's Restaurants, including one at Disneyland. The loan required collateral, and Don secured that from friends of Howard Hughes', the wealthy aviation pioneer, movie producer, and industrialist. The Hughes Tool Company made the loan to Don's corporation. For Don to get the loan, he used Mom's commercial property on Whittier Boulevard as additional collateral. His corporation went into bankruptcy, however. Governor Goodwin Knight apparently had encouraged the California Commissioner of Corporations to delay approvals so long that prospective investors backed away. Because of that, Don was forced to default on the loan. When taking his company public, too much red ink spelled trouble for him.

Always looking for a scandal related to Richard Nixon, some in the media insinuated that Don had approached Dick to ask Hughes for a loan to Nixon's, Inc., and that Hughes got special favors from the government in return for the loan. Nothing of the sort ever occurred. Dick had nothing to do with Don's business affairs. When the corporation failed, our mother's property was taken as compensation. The $205,000 loan was then satisfied by the assumption of a $400,000 piece of property. Mother then had no real estate asset left other than the house she lived in. Don not only suffered financially, but he also felt the controversy perpetrated by hatemongers contributed to Dick's defeat in 1960. He never forgot that hurt and anger.

When the election results came in, Dick lost by a slim margin—about 113,000 votes nationwide. He received 49.6 percent of the popular vote. The electoral total was 219 for Nixon and 303 for Kennedy, but with a shift of only 11,000 votes in Texas and Illinois, where substantial evidence indicated vote fraud, Dick would have won. I think he was convinced the election had been stolen, but the most important consideration to him was the country he loved and the Constitution he respected. He saw no reason to drag the United States into a legal battle. "No way will I try to overturn the results! This election stays as it is, stolen or not," he said.

In *Six Crises*, Dick wrote:

> I could think of no worse example for nations abroad, who for the first time were trying to put free electoral procedures into effect, than that of the United States wrangling over the results of our presidential election, and even suggesting that the presidency itself could be stolen by thievery at the ballot box.[45]

When Dick and Jack met at Key Biscayne after the election, I gathered that Jack needed to talk for the healing effect it might have on their feelings and friendship. Dick never commented to me personally about what happened there, but in *Six Crises* he devoted four pages to their discussions on the porch of the villa at the Key Biscayne Hotel before parting "on cordial terms."[46]

---

45   Richard Nixon, *Six Crises* (New York: Doubleday and Company, 1962) 413.
46   Nixon 410.

⌁ CHAPTER 7 ⌁

CAREER CHANGES

Following John F. Kennedy's inauguration on January 20, 1961, Dick faced unemployment. For the first time in fourteen years, he was no longer a public servant. Too young to retire at the age of forty-eight, he still wanted to play an active role in domestic and foreign affairs and felt he had much more to give to his country.

Whittaker Chambers, Dick's friend from the Alger Hiss days, wrote to Dick in February 1961:

> You have decades ahead of you. Almost from the first day we met . . . I sensed in you some quality, deep-going, difficult to identify in the world's glib way, but good and meaningful for you and multitudes of others. I do not believe for a moment that because you have been cruelly checked in the employment of what is best in you, what is most yourself, that that check is final. It cannot be. . . . You have years in which to serve. Service is your life. You must serve. . . . [47]

Thus, Dick began what my family and I called "the Interregnum," the eight-year period between the vice presidency and the presidency

---

47 Nixon, *RN: The Memoirs of Richard Nixon* 238.

when Dick was trying to determine where and how he could best use his talents. First he moved back to California to take a job with a Los Angeles law firm. Pat, Tricia, and Julie joined him in June after the girls finished the school year in Washington, D.C. Their lives then returned to some semblance of normalcy.

CONTINUING AT THE UW

Meanwhile, I continued teaching at the University of Washington as an Assistant Professor of Naval Science responsible for the first-year classes of midshipmen from 1960 to 1962. During that time, the Bureau of Naval Personnel selected me to lead the Freshman Curriculum Clearing House and suggest revisions to the basic course. Not being a naval historian, I found the task difficult, but I received valuable assistance from fellow instructors at three other universities around the country. We succeeded in revising the curriculum for the freshman course, *History of Sea Power and Naval Orientation*, published in 1962.

While teaching at the UW, I received a notice from the Bureau of Naval Personnel directing instructors to avoid reaching for lofty ideals. The message boiled down to: "Don't try to teach leadership to the first-year midshipmen; teach management."

I wondered who came up with an idea like that. American Naval officers had maintained a proud tradition of strong leadership for 185 years. The more I thought about the directive, the more convinced I became of its error. Then I selected topics for class discussion, giving the course content my own flavor. I noted historical examples of management failures when leadership was lacking.

In an interesting article in the March 2001 issue of *Alaska Airlines Magazine*, airlines chairman John Kelly confirmed what I had tried to convey in describing Admiral Lord Nelson's "Band of Brothers" and his promotion of a common habit of thought among the ship captains in his fleet.[48] Nelson's interactions with the captains under his command reveal an essential ingredient of his great success as a leader. Day after tedious day, searching for the French fleet carrying Napoleon's invasion force eastward across the Mediterranean, Nelson

---

48   John Kelly, "Let's Get Rid of Management," *Alaska Airlines Magazine*, March 2001: 7.

wasted no time fretting about the unknown location of the French fleet. Every quiet evening he brought one or two of his captains aboard his flagship to dine and discuss tactics for all kinds of battles at sea. So thorough were these indoctrination sessions that when the British fleet finally discovered the French warships anchored in Aboukir Bay in the Nile delta, the Band of Brothers executed their tactical moves to perfection without need of complicated signals from the flagship. Each captain knew what his crew was expected to accomplish, and together they achieved a great victory.

When mutual trust is developed through resolution of potential arguments, we can lead and trust each person to manage his or her own well-defined tasks and responsibilities. Self-discipline yields the most beneficial results for everyone. Thus, I questioned the Navy's new notion that executives should emphasize management of subordinates at the expense of striving for a common habit of thought. Before launching tactical plans, questions must be asked and answers thoroughly heard without condescension. Successful leadership does not automatically result from a charismatic reputation.

A couple of officers applauded my ideas, but I received no further comment from the Navy on management versus leadership. Meanwhile, I continued teaching as I saw fit.

ᨁ ᨁ

Unlike Dick, I didn't get passionate about politics during that time. However, Ronald Reagan's radio speeches did spark my interest. While I was teaching at the UW, one of my fellow instructors at the University of South Carolina forwarded a copy of Reagan's speech, *Encroaching Control,* delivered at the Phoenix Chamber of Commerce on March 30, 1961. I remember that speech vividly. For me, Reagan was the first public figure, besides my brother, who articulated political thought that matched our family's philosophy of opposition to big government. Reagan's words reminded me of Dad's. Both men were independent, self-reliant, and concerned that expanding government would weaken this country.

Reagan's speech so impressed me that I included it on the midshipmen's reading list when we discussed self-reliance versus government dependency. Two of the young men in my class, however, held opposing views. After they openly complained about the reading assignment, I followed the department chairman's orders and acknowledged the students' objections. I told all four of my classes, "No more political philosophy, but I hope all of you will try to think beyond one lifetime. If we let the government do it now, will future generations have to depend on the government doing everything?" Today, following the department chairman's orders would be called "yielding to political correctness." In the 1960s, we called it "muzzling the military."

～∴ ∴～

In one of my lectures to the midshipmen, I brought up some basic, enduring questions: "What is the most common cause of wars throughout history? What divides people to the point they become belligerent and behave violently against one another?" I gave them some suggestions to think about: "Is it topography? Is it a river or a mountain range that divides people? You live on that side of the mountain; you stay there. I live on this side; you leave me alone. Does that isolation over time lead to two cultures becoming so different they cannot blend? Does racial hatred, religious differences, greed for resources, or political conflict cause most wars? If wars are fought in self-defense, is that acceptable? Is it respectable? Is it admirable?"

At the time I taught naval history, the public recognized the need for a strong navy. But I wanted each midshipman to study the philosophy of war and why nations or tribes get into conflicts that result in military action. Moreover, after nations have entered a conflict, how do they end it in a way that ensures an enduring peace?

In our family, we were encouraged to apply the lessons of our Quaker heritage, believing that a carefully nurtured conscience would lead us to determine the best course to follow. We were instructed to seek the truth in all questions of potential conflict and to contemplate quietly the issues of war and peace. Dick always encouraged me to think about what we could do to make the world a safer place and, in so doing, to aim for a durable peace.

Dick and I both concluded that military action is sometimes justified to stop aggressors who refuse all offers to negotiate and who have already caused loss of innocent lives. To prevent massive losses, those aggressors must be stopped decisively. From a historical perspective, the controversial policy of unconditional surrender appears more effectively to bring lasting peace than does a negotiated settlement, as shown by the defeat of Nazi Germany and Imperial Japan.

Looking ahead, however, we must somehow avoid the petty quarrels and fanatic beliefs that lead to violent conflict. In the course I taught, I encouraged the students to look beyond military history and tactics and to search for strategies that would help prevent local disputes from escalating into full-scale war. International student exchanges can promote understanding of cultural differences, but they may not always conquer fanatic intolerance, which seems to me the most common cause of violent conflict.

My students responded with heartfelt discussion, especially in light of the American traditions on constitutional government and liberty they had been studying. Regarding freedom of religion, they agreed that there are limits to tolerance and that fanatic intolerance deserves eradication.

MOM—GOODWILL AMBASSADOR

Dick and Pat had many opportunities to travel, both in and out of public office, and they encouraged the rest of our family to expand our horizons as often as possible. To Dick, one's education was incomplete without some familiarity with the United States and the rest of the world. He had visited all fifty states, meeting people from all walks of life. He didn't limit his appearances to town hall meetings or public relations visits with the mayor and local officials, as many candidates and politicians do. Instead, Dick stressed the importance of getting acquainted with people face-to-face in service stations, grocery stores, and diners. By meeting citizens where they worked, shopped, or socialized, he would more likely learn their true opinions and gain wisdom useful in formulating public policy. He respected their hard-earned knowledge and their part in maintaining America's free enterprise system. After all, he had seen workers oppressed under the tyranny of dictatorships.

I'm sure Dad also influenced Dick to be responsive to "the common man." A grocer himself, Dad would always engage other grocers,

Hannah Nixon, Goodwill Ambassador, Quitandinha, Brazil, 1961
᭜Courtesy of Helen Hunter McGee, Moral Rearmament Sponsor

because he wanted to know how they were conducting their businesses. He didn't hesitate to tell them if he thought they could do it better. That's where Dick and Dad differed. Dick always tempered his words and displayed the mild manners he learned from Mom.

I don't think Dick ever expected Mom to travel overseas though. She had only flown once and didn't particularly like the experience, but when Moral Rearmament (MRA) invited her on a trip to South America in 1961, she gladly accepted upon hearing the purpose of the journey. Mom supported the MRA's opposition to militarism and its promotion of world reform through moral and spiritual forces of honesty, purity, unselfishness, and love—all strong values of the Quaker faith.

Helen Hunter, Mom's good friend and MRA sponsor, accompanied her on Varig Airlines to Rio de Janeiro, Brazil. Such a long journey was very hard on her at age seventy-six. Nevertheless, she enjoyed the trip immensely. From Rio they traveled to Quitandinha, where they were met by representatives of student groups from Cochabamba, Bolivia, and Caracas, Venezuela—cities where angry Communist-led mobs had demonstrated during Dick and Pat's goodwill tour in 1958. The students had prepared a program for Mom's benefit to express regrets for those incidents. Mom told them she was deeply grateful to all who welcomed her and for the opportunity to accept their apologies in person. She turned out to be a goodwill ambassador in her own right, and all the family was proud of her efforts and her stamina in making the trip.

1962 CALIFORNIA GOVERNOR'S RACE AND AFTERMATH

Back in California, Republican Party officials and political friends soon began pressuring Dick to run for governor against the incumbent, Edmund G. "Pat" Brown. Dick went against his better judgment and entered the race; his heart was not in it. He couldn't even devote the necessary time to the strategy phase of the campaign, because he had to meet the publisher's deadline for his first book, *Six Crises*.

Then on August 8, Dick went on a family vacation and book-signing tour to Seattle and Victoria, British Columbia—where he couldn't campaign for votes. I didn't see Dick and his family during that visit, because I was the officer in charge of a group of NROTC midshipmen on a familiarization trip to the Naval Air Station at Corpus Christi, Texas.

When Dick, Pat, Tricia, and Julie got off the plane in Seattle, Sally Raleigh, *Seattle Post-Intelligencer* reporter for the Women Today Section, interviewed Pat. She told Ms. Raleigh that the family planned to contact Karen Anderson (now Olson), a thirteen-year-old girl who had written to the former Vice-President, saying she was disappointed she could not see him when he came to the Seattle World's Fair.[49] Karen recently had surgery on her feet and couldn't walk during recovery. In 1959, she had become interested in Nixon's stand against communism and supported him in the 1960 campaign. Being incapacitated, she thought she would miss her one opportunity to meet her political hero.

In Raleigh's article, Pat said Dick would visit Karen at her home if his busy schedule allowed. The Andersons, however, didn't receive their newspaper that morning. Karen's mother, Lillian "Pat" Anderson, learned of the possible visit when her friend Bobbie Roslund called after reading the article. In the afternoon, an advance man phoned the Andersons to schedule the visit for the following morning.

While Pat, Julie, and Tricia toured the fairgrounds on August 10, Dick arrived at the home of Russell and Pat Anderson in a white World's Fair sedan accompanied by fair officials. Karen, her family, friends, reporters, and photographers were waiting outside. After introductions, Dick set everyone at ease with fatherly attention to Karen, her ten-year-old sister Kendra, and the neighborhood children and friends invited to the event. He asked each child about his or her life aspirations. Karen said, "I don't know for sure, but I like Spanish."

Dick responded with a few words in Spanish and then told Karen she should be a writer. Complimenting her on her writing ability, he said he couldn't visit everyone who wrote to him.

Mrs. Anderson then invited the guests inside for refreshments. Dick continued to talk with the children, encouraging them to read and study. "You think the kid next to you is a lot smarter. That's not true. Most of us are pretty equal. Study makes the difference.

---

49   Sally Raleigh, "Here's Pat Nixon," *Seattle Post-Intelligencer*, 9 August 1962: Women's Section, 6.

Richard Nixon visits Karen Anderson, her family, and friends, Seattle,
WA, August 10, 1962
~Printed with permission of The Seattle Times. Richard S. Heyza, photographer

Richard and Karen in
the Anderson home
~From Coauthor's
Personal Collection

"Get in a lot of homework. Read. Read that book." [50] He pointed to the Bible on the Andersons' coffee table and told of his faith and friendship with Billy Graham, noting that he had been to the Nixon home for dinner recently.

As Dick prepared to leave, he advised the children, "When you think things are going against you, you get out of that the good things . . . It's that way all our lives. When you're deprived of something, it makes you understand what you're missing and about other people and helps you enjoy the good things even more when you're able to have them again."[51]

On his way to the car, Dick turned back, telling Karen to keep her spirits up and to keep fighting.

Years later, John Holya, one of the visiting neighbor children, reflected on my brother's visit, saying, "What I remember most was that he said, 'Get an education, and you can become anything you want. Stay in school and learn.' It was a very important message to me. 'Never give up. Keep going through the educational system. Work hard at learning.'" Taking the advice to heart, John became an attorney.

❧ ❧

During the 1962 campaign, I was still on active duty in the Navy and teaching at the University of Washington. Because I voted in the state of Washington, I did not get involved in California politics.

In early 1962, Captain Gerdon relieved Marine Colonel Colley, the Professor of Naval Science at the UW who had served in that role during the 1960 campaign. Both professors admonished against political involvement of government employees under the Hatch Act, so I remained aloof once more.

All the enlisted men assigned to our NROTC unit at the UW seemed sure Dick would win, but I said, "Don't count on it. This is politics." And sure enough, he lost by 297,000 votes out of nearly 6 million cast. Pat Brown had succeeded in painting Dick as an opportunist intent on using the governorship of California as a steppingstone to the presidency.

---

50 "Seattle Girl Visited by Pen Pal—Nixon," *The Seattle Times*, 11 August 1962: A1.

51 Eleanor Bell, "'The Biggest Day in Her Life': Nixon Visits Seattle Girl Kept at Home By Ailment," *The Seattle Post-Intelligencer*, 11 August 1962: 14.

Concluding his concession speech, my brother told reporters, "You won't have Dick Nixon to kick around anymore , because, gentlemen, this is my last press conference…"

In hindsight, Dick realized he shouldn't have said that, but at the time he couldn't foresee ever running for political office again. After all, he had lost the governorship of his home state by 184,000 more votes than he lost nationwide in 1960. How could he recover politically from the stigma of being a two-time loser? He saw no way.

IN THE PRIVATE SECTOR

Then Dick entered a period of reflection, devoting himself to spending more time with his family and getting a better handle on the world— the whole world. Dick, Pat, Tricia, and Julie moved to New York in 1963. There he joined the Wall Street law firm of Mudge, Stern, Baldwin, and Todd, which later became Nixon, Mudge, Rose, Guthrie, and Alexander. His position gave him the opportunity to travel and immerse himself in international affairs. The move also allowed Pat and the girls a partial respite from inquisitors. Perhaps New Yorkers were either less curious about celebrities than Californians or simply too busy in the fast-paced life in the Big Apple to notice.

∿ ∿

When I finished my two-year tour of duty at the University of Washington in September 1962, I transferred to the Naval Reserves. Having completed seven years on active duty, I continued drilling as a reservist one weekend a month, or sometimes two, depending on whether we had aircraft to fly. Designated Naval Aviators in the Ready Reserve were eligible to fly an extra weekend per month to help maintain proficiency, but aircraft, fuel, and service personnel were not always available to conduct a worthwhile training drill.

Shifting to civilian employment, I began my new job with Pacific Northwest Bell Telephone Company (PNB) on November 12, 1962, as a communications consultant and marketing department salesman. Next came an administration personnel assistant job in which I coordinated the company's personnel assessment program, evaluating craftsmen for promotion to management.

On November 23, 1963, Jack Mullin, head of the personnel department, interrupted a spirited group evaluation session with shocking news from Texas: President Kennedy had been shot. On that tragic note, we adjourned, no longer able to carry on our meeting. A somber atmosphere surrounded us as we departed the building. Brief comments revealed a mixture of disbelief and overwhelming sorrow. Thoughts flashed through my mind that my brother could have been the one riding in that limousine, had he won the 1960 election.

⌣ ⌣

Thirteen months after I joined Pacific Northwest Bell, Bill Braunworth, an executive at AT&T, invited me to apply at Bellcomm, Inc., a Bell Labs affiliate in Washington, D.C., for a job as a technical employment supervisor. The new company grew out of a nucleus of managing directors on loan from Bell Telephone Laboratories to work on Project Apollo, the first U.S. manned space flight to the Moon and back. President Kennedy had begun the program in response to the Soviet Union's successful launch of Sputnik in October 1957.

Dick had also addressed the need for space exploration in his campaign for the presidency. Therefore, when I learned of the opportunity, I asked him, "Do you think I should take this job that everyone sees as a Kennedy project."

"Don't be concerned about that," Dick assured me. "If I'd been elected, I very likely would have proceeded in the same direction. You've always been interested in astronomy and space. I've known that since the early, early days. This sounds like an ideal opportunity for you. If it suits you, take it!"

I flew back to Washington, D.C., for interviews and learned that the people I would be working with had far more technical training than I, because the draft had interrupted my plans to obtain a Ph.D. Nevertheless, Bellcomm hired me in February 1964, and I moved to D.C. My family followed shortly after the end of the school year. At Bellcomm I supervised the recruitment and placement of technical specialists to work on Project Apollo. The company was under contract with the Office of Manned Space Flight, NASA Headquarters. Recruiting was already well under way, and applications were pouring in from every top university in the country—Cal-Berkeley, MIT,

Case Western Reserve, Caltech, Purdue and countless others. From those interviews, I became aware of which schools, according to the high standards of Bell Labs, had the best reputations in certain specialized fields. In addition to the young graduate students, Bellcomm employed many scientists and engineers already experienced in a wide range of disciplines in industry and government.

In the course of helping to staff a new company, I had the privilege of interviewing more than two thousand brilliant young scientists and engineers. Out of that pool, the company assembled a team of approximately five hundred experts, and Bellcomm became known as the "Conscience of Apollo." Those experts were directly involved in the check-off lists, giving the go-ahead or veto for all the countdowns to launch. They reviewed the entire work of the subcontractors to search for flaws and potential problems. Whether a launch was a go or not depended on whether Bellcomm or any of the other members of the countdown team had found anything out of order.

Working on Project Apollo, I was struck by the fact that when we get off this Earth and move fast enough to break out of orbit, heading far into space, we can look back at the whole beautiful picture. Apollo 8 astronauts Frank Borman, James Lovell, and Bill Anders saw Earth as a magnificent sphere—mostly blue and white—floating in the blackness of space on that first flight to circle the Moon in December 1968. One of my favorite mementos is a photo of Earth taken from Apollo 8 that Anders personally autographed. Subsequent flights proved we were well on the way to President Kennedy's goal of landing a crew on the surface of the Moon and returning them safely to Earth within the decade.

My predecessor's secretary soon departed after I joined Bellcomm, so the company hired Sara Currence, a graduate of New York's Katie Gibbs Secretarial School. She and I had many friendly arguments over such inconsequential details as the proper abbreviation for *Northwest* (*N.W.* or *NW*), and we often discussed the need to abolish useless technical decorum. An incredible secretary, Sara deserved much credit for the long hours and dedication she brought to the job.

While I was working for Bellcomm, Gay's parents suggested that Amy and Beth spend a year attending Aurora Academy, a very fine, private day school near their home in New Orleans. Gay and I thought the girls would benefit from the experience with family and school. So, Gay opted to stay with the girls at her parents' home and taught a full year of math at a public junior high school there.

~: :~

During that time, I visited New York on several occasions and stayed with Dick and Pat in their apartment on Fifth Avenue. In December 1966, Dick mentioned his interest in advances in tape recording technology, mainly for music. His friend, William P. Lear, who developed the Lear Jet, had also invented the eight-track tape players for cars and executive planes.

Dick asked me, "What do you think of these eight-track players?" He often asked my opinion on technical or scientific matters.

"Well, the eight-track player is a neat package," I said. "And it's probably going to sell very well for a while, but there should be a way to make it more compact by using smaller cassettes. Nevertheless, I think we should support interim successes like this tape player. We can promote new technology best by buying the products that give us what we want for the moment. Later on, someone is bound to develop a better product—a smaller, higher-quality, and more cost-effective system."

Dick then asked, "What kind of system do you have at home for playing good music?"

"Some technically inclined friends introduced me to AR, the trade name logo for "Acoustic Research," a company that builds very fine audio speakers. They conducted a stage demonstration with a live performance behind the curtain and a recording on a reel-to-reel tape played back on an AR sound system. Half the audience on the other side of the curtain couldn't tell the difference between a live performance and the tape. It was a fifty-fifty split, and that's what you want. You don't want an artificial system that sounds better than the live performance or vice versa."

"That's quite impressive. Why don't we get a couple of those speakers and put them in here. Can you set up a stereo sound system for me?"

"Sure," I said.

So, I went shopping in New York City, where I easily found the components. Then I wired Dick's study for sound. We both appreciated the classical music played cleanly—free of white noise. Dick played 33⅓ and 45 rpm records, the common media at the time. Pat would let us know when the volume reached a level too loud for her ears, but even she agreed the music sounded great.

On the last evening of my visit that December, Dick suggested we go for a walk.

I agreed. As Dick and I strolled down one side of Park Avenue and back up the other, we enjoyed the colorful Christmas lights and decorations, which seemed especially brilliant that night. And I felt a sense of elation, noting that Dick seemed so happy with his life in Manhattan.

We stopped on East 57th Street to purchase a Christmas gift for Pat—a rare bird sculpture by Edward Marshall Boehm (1913-1969). Dick and Pat had already seen it and both liked it. As I recall, the life-sized porcelain bird was yellow, a color Pat loved. I expressed surprise at the price, but he made the purchase without hesitation. Obviously, he had made his decision many days before.

Then at a music store, Dick bought a complete recording of Tchaikovsky's *Swan Lake* on Urania Records. *Swan Lake* reminded Dick of his trip to Moscow as Vice President where he had witnessed a performance of the work by the Bolshoi Ballet. Although he already had quite a collection of classical records, including another version of *Swan Lake*, he said, "I'd like to hear all of them, because there are themes in the complete versions that are missing in the suites."

On our walk back to his home, Dick started questioning me. "What do you see as the most common feature in a great leader? For example, what do you think is the most important attribute, characteristic, or capability that a President should have?"

I wondered what he had in mind, asking me questions that I thought people should be asking him. During that year, 1966, he had spent a lot of time campaigning for Republican incumbents and challenger candidates for Congress, so perhaps he was just sizing them up as potential nominees. The prospect of Dick running for President again did not occur to me until the following summer.

Not sure how to respond, I said, "I'll have to think about that."

After reflecting awhile, I remembered the session on leadership versus management in the class I taught at the University of Washington NROTC. I said, "You might not understand why I would say this, but I think a President must be a great teacher, because in the broadest sense, what is a leader?"

"A teacher? Why a teacher?"

"First of all," I replied, "a successful leader, like a great teacher, must look around and think about the masses of people he has to lead. He has to make sure they understand his frame of reference, so he can persuade and convince them that what he is trying to do is right for them and their future."

Dick said, "That's very interesting. I'm not sure I would have used the word *teacher*, but in the concept of Socrates or somebody who asks a lot of questions and takes leads from them, that's probably right. That's an idea that should be brought forth someday."

And indeed, Dick was a great teacher, always searching for answers to enduring questions and encouraging others to search as well. Not satisfied with partial answers, he nevertheless showed patience with those who made unsatisfying attempts. When a stubborn know-it-all or reluctant learner was finally persuaded to search harder, Dick would encourage and praise that person. He would seek common ground with dissidents but never would compromise with bullies.

One skill Dick tried to teach me was how to remember the names of people I met in brief encounters. He once explained his technique for remembering details about a newly introduced acquaintance. He would look intently into the person's eyes while making sure of the pronunciation of his or her name, repeating it aloud two or three times before dropping his gaze. Then he would ask about the person's hometown, members of the family, and as many personal notes as the receiving line schedule would allow. Often he encouraged me to try his suggestion, saying, "Don't ever neglect your memory. It's very important to remember and get the details firmly planted, so you can associate them with future events."

Dick frequently complimented me on my memory, but I never developed the ability to recall the names of brief acquaintances the way he did. I remain convinced that he had developed a specially trained memory bank designed for instant random access. Dick was no savant, but he had a phenomenal memory. Everyone marveled at his ability to recall not only a person's name years after a receiving-line introduction, but also unique details about the person's identity—certainly a useful skill for a politician.

⁓ ⁓

Gay and the girls returned from Louisiana to our home in Virginia the end of the 1967 school year. Renting is a temporary solution to housing needs, so we decided to look for a place to buy where we could establish roots. We found two suitable houses, one in Maryland and one in Virginia across the street from a school where Gay had often substituted. On Friday, the day after we had made an offer on the Virginia house, the school offered her a permanent job teaching math.

Bellcomm, however, announced on Monday morning that a position had opened in Seattle and asked if I wished to return to Pacific Northwest Bell. I called Gay and asked her to join me for lunch in Lafayette Park across from the White House. Our discussion in the park that day ended our plans to settle in the East. We withdrew our offer on the house, and Gay declined the teaching position.

So, in August 1967, I left my friends at Bellcomm and moved my family back to Washington, our favorite state. I rejoined Pacific Northwest Bell as a commercial staff supervisor on a job that involved preparing monthly views and forecasts of annual expense and force requirements. The commercial department budget covered about one thousand employees.

Soon after we moved into our new home in a suburb of Seattle, both Dick and Don called, informing me that Mom appeared to be approaching the end. Her health had been declining rapidly, so she had entered the Beverly Manor convalescent home in East Whittier. The care she was receiving was as good as any, but losing her independence deprived her of easy access to her friends, many of whom she felt needed more help than she. For as long as I could remember, she had pleaded with me to protect her from ever having to move into a "rest home." The world of modern mobility took her sons too far away, however, and she had no choice but to seek unwanted assistance. I am still filled with regret when I remember her fervent pleas.

Our mother, Hannah Milhous Nixon, passed away on September 30, 1967.

The moving van with our household effects from Arlington, Virginia, had arrived in Seattle only a few days earlier. Don advised me to buy four tickets to Los Angeles. He met us on arrival and brought us to his home in Newport Beach.

The next day at the memorial service at East Whittier Friends Church, we greeted neighbors, relatives, and friends and heard two of Mom's favorite local preachers, Charles Ball and George Jenkins, deliver moving eulogies, followed by the inimitable Dr. Billy Graham, who had gladly responded to Dick's personal invitation to speak. Interment followed at Rose Hills Cemetery alongside her beloved Frank, who had preceded her by eleven years.

1968 PRESIDENTIAL CAMPAIGN

Shortly after I rejoined PNB, journalists and political pundits began speculating that Dick might make another run for the presidency. All his voluntary campaigning on behalf of GOP candidates in 1964 and 1966, plus world travel as a private citizen generated much attention in the press.

Then in 1967, he embarked on four study trips overseas: first, to Europe and the Soviet Union with Robert Ellsworth, an attorney and former congressman from Kansas, who had expertise in foreign affairs and defense; second, to Asia with Raymond K. Price, a former editorial page editor of the *New York Herald Tribune*; third, to Africa and the Middle East with Patrick Buchanan, a former editorial writer and at that time a speechwriter and researcher on Dick's staff; and fourth, to Latin America with his friend Bebe Rebozo, a businessman of Cuban descent. On the trips, Dick met with world leaders and updated his knowledge of foreign affairs. As a result of his trip to Asia, Dick wrote a noteworthy article for *Foreign Affairs* titled "Asia After Vietnam," in which he introduced the idea of establishing dialogue with the People's Republic of China.

I still didn't know for sure what Dick planned to do, but I wanted him to know how I felt. So, one day in November 1967, I took time off to drive to Portland, Oregon, where he was scheduled to address a group of businessmen. Dwight Chapin, one of the earliest members of Dick's team, greeted me in the lobby of the Benson Hotel and led me up to Dick's room.

I said, "Dick, I'm out of school and out of the Navy now, so this time around, I'm not constrained by the Hatch Act from participating in politics. I want to become more involved in your campaign if you decide to make a go of it."

Dick paused for a moment and then said, "Well, I think you could be very helpful. We just need to find an appropriate niche for you. If I decide to make another run, I'll ask Bob Haldeman to set up a headquarters organization. In any event, I'll let you know."

Sure enough, in Manchester, New Hampshire, on February 2, 1968, Dick announced his intention to run. Later that month, I flew back to New York and joined the Nixon for President Committee as the mail operations manager. Someone had already decided a brother would make an ideal surrogate correspondent. Of course, Dick couldn't respond personally to every letter he received. That alone would have been his full-time job. I, on the other hand, could respond directly to letters addressed to the candidate.

Again, Gay stayed at home, managing household affairs, teaching junior high math full time, and parenting the girls, who were attending elementary school.

The committee opened its national headquarters in the former American Bible Society building at 450 Park Avenue in midtown Manhattan. Annelise Anderson, Ph.D. in Criminal Law from Columbia University, and her husband, Martin Anderson, Ph.D. in Economics from MIT, had arrived earlier to help set up the organization, including the policy for handling mail. By the time I came on board, Annelise had already drafted several sample letters and suggested methods to evaluate whether the flood of incoming mail called for specific replies or general responses. She and Martin also addressed position papers on issues such as crime and urban affairs, monetary policy, science and technology, and, in fact, any issue the candidate needed to contemplate. In my job managing the mail, I worked closely with them both throughout the campaign.

One of my first tasks was to find a reliable, dedicated, competent assistant willing to work many long days for the next nine months straight with very few breaks. I knew that keeping up with me might seem too demanding to many job applicants. Such a strong spirit permeated this campaign that staff and volunteers alike routinely and willingly worked over eight hours a day and on holidays.

I could think of only one person who possessed all the qualifications to meet the challenge: Sara Currence, my former secretary at Bellcomm. I don't remember how we tracked her down, but we did so expeditiously. She readily accepted my offer to join me on the campaign in New York.

Sara had what Dick referred to as "an iron butt," a very useful quality in politics and in administrative/secretarial work. She also had a remarkable motivation to work. Everyone noticed it. She would sit there hour after hour, sorting, typing, and filing as long as anyone had something that needed to be done "before tomorrow."[52]

With the head start provided by Annelise Anderson, I was able to organize and direct the correspondence department at the campaign headquarters. The job included developing a mail analysis system for reading and responding to the large volume of miscellaneous letters addressed to Dick.

The mail kept pouring in at an ever-increasing rate. At the peak of the campaign, about seventy-six loyal volunteers read, analyzed, and categorized the letters. I answered them with a brief cover letter on behalf of my brother according to his stated positions, and I enclosed reprints of his official position papers. Sometimes I appended a handwritten personal note. We tried to respond to everyone whose letter warranted a reply, and very few went unanswered. The staff estimated that we sent out about 150,000 letters with my signature, which gradually deteriorated to the point I could hardly write my name anymore.

Vietnam was certainly the hottest topic in the mail. Some wrote, "Don't give in! Stand up for freedom!" Others said, "Surrender! Withdraw immediately!"

Of course, my brother wanted peace, but not at any price. Dick insisted that the U.S. be mindful of history and actions of preceding

---

52 On my recommendation, William Safire, one of Dick's speechwriters, hired Sara after the election. He soon reported to me that she exceeded his expectations. She went on to serve under the administrations of Gerald Ford, Jimmy Carter, Ronald Reagan, George H. W. Bush (as Deputy Executive Clerk), and Bill Clinton (as Executive Clerk of the White House). By the time she retired after twenty-eight years of service in the White House, Sara Currence Emery probably knew more about the executive filing system than anyone on staff.

Lead Volunteers, New York Headquarters,
1968 presidential campaign
L-R - Shirley McWhorter, Kay Odell, Sara Currence Emery,
Ann Volz Higgins, Georgia Lyons, Tara Donahue, Marilyn Madden
∾Courtesy of Charles Markey personal photo collection

Presidents: Truman had been the first to commit U.S. advisors to the Vietnamese government, which was then controlled by France, in an attempt to prevent a Communist takeover. Eisenhower had continued to supply advisors. The French had withdrawn in 1954, and the country was divided into North and South Vietnam. Kennedy had expanded American military presence in South Vietnam. Johnson had ordered an enormous increase in troop strength on the advice of Secretary of Defense Robert McNamara.

Dick, who was painfully aware of that history, said to me, "We must honor our commitment to our allies and the people trying to maintain their identity as a free, democratic society. Although the South Vietnamese government has internal problems, the country at least is on the free side of the world and opposed to Communist oppression. Therefore, we must stand firm and not give in. Our sudden withdrawal from South Vietnam would precipitate a bloodbath and the collapse of the country. That, in turn, would endanger neighboring nations in a domino effect, resulting in Communist control of the region, as former Secretary of State John Foster Dulles predicted. I believe that to end the war, the U.S. would have to train the South Vietnamese, so they could defend their own country."

Many people writing to Dick noted that our country seemed irretrievably divided. The events of 1968 made it one of the most tumultuous election years in U.S. history: Martin Luther King, Jr., assassinated in Tennessee in April; Robert F. Kennedy, the Democrat frontrunner, assassinated on the eve of his primary election victory in California in June; and antiwar and civil rights protesters in the streets in increasingly violent riots. Despair prevailed as the voting public observed the seemingly hopeless situation facing the next man to lead the country.

Dick, however, was determined to set a new course toward peace with honor in Vietnam and law and order at home. On a whistle stop in Ohio, he spotted a young girl along the tracks holding up her hand-painted sign that read, "Bring Us Together." That simple message set the tone for the weeks that followed, and in noting that one sign, Dick made it famous.

Convinced that her father was the man who could bring us together and bring creative changes to the White House, Tricia suggested "Open a New Window" from the Broadway musical *Mame* as the campaign theme song. She knew her father could gain more popular support using optimism in his persuasive appeals, whittling away at brick walls, opening new doors, bringing people together, and keeping liberty alive. He wanted to bring new ideas to bear on old problems. Tricia's idea for the theme song wasn't selected, but I certainly liked her suggestion. It would have appealed to a bright new generation of young voters, and I'm certain the concept remained firm in Dick's thinking.

In answer to the question of whom could best lead America in that tumultuous time, the campaign selected "Nixon's the One" as the slogan. Dick approved the choice and was doubly happy with the music and lyrics that Vic Caesar, musician and part owner of Caesar's Forum, a supper club in Phoenix, Arizona, composed in May 1968. Wherever Dick went on the campaign trail, that song would be played. And "Nixon's the One" wound up on many thousands of bumper stickers and campaign buttons.

∿ ∿

On two occasions during the 1968 campaign, the managers scheduled me to appear at a political rally. At one event in New Jersey, I shared the podium with William F. Buckley, Jr., noted conservative columnist, author, and founder of *National Review*, to address an audience of American voters of Eastern European heritage. As the main attraction, Mr. Buckley delivered his speech and then departed for another event. His exit brought me a sense of relief as I approached the podium to deliver my speech. Gone were the jitters I had felt, thinking the distinguished orator, known for his perfect grammar and pedantic style, would be evaluating my every word. I could now relax and speak in my own casual style, which I'm sure those recently naturalized citizens in the audience appreciated.

In my speech, I emphasized my brother's popularity with the Czechs, Poles, Hungarians, and other Eastern Europeans. Having seen the destruction in those countries after World War II and understanding the perils of communism, Dick had a special rapport with Eastern Europeans longing for their homelands to regain freedom and independence. He always received an especially enthusiastic reception when traveling through Poland. Thousands of people would pour into the streets tossing flowers in his honor. I didn't have to say much to persuade that group in New Jersey. They all enthusiastically supported Nixon and responded with warm applause and cheers to whatever I said.

On the other occasion, the schedulers asked me to attend a fundraiser in Westchester County, New York, along with California Lieutenant Governor Bob Finch, Dick's longtime friend and former aide. But the bus we were on, along with several other vehicles in our caravan, never reached its destination due to a traffic snarl caused by an accident on the road ahead. For more than an hour, we sat in gridlock.

Trying to avoid boredom during that ride, I perused the only reading material at hand—a *Roget's Thesaurus*. I thought about how the country seemed to be drowning in glib, divisive commentary emanating from the opposition's overemphasis on notions of "a generation gap." So, with the help of Roget, I jotted down an alliteration of words beginning with the letter "G." Upon returning to my office, I polished off the alliteration, which needs to be recited aloud for its full impact.

THE GALLANTRY GAP

Alliteration in G

Ghastly ghosts would gallivant and gladly grout our graves
Were it not for grace and grandeur.
So, gear your gait to a glossy glide and never ever gallop.
Evade the grinning graduates where the gesturing gypsy goes.

Avoid the gruesome guile
of a gullible guiltless guise,
for a gallantry gap is growing
in gray ambiguous gaiety.

Cast off the grouchy grumbling grudges,
the grasping greed and the gluttonous graft
that generous gentry pose.

Abstain from gobs of gooey gums
and grazing greens with gastronomic gravy.

Elude the gaudy groovy grossness
of gawking gazes and glaring glances -
the garrulous goose with gregarious greasy nose.

Forestall the gabby grapevine
of gasping gushy gossip -
the gleeful giggles and gloating guffaws.

Scrub the grimy grit of grubbiness
and glib graffiti prose.

Circumvent the groggy groups
of giddy goofs in gatherings on the ground.

Quit the guild of gore and ghouls and guttural gurgling groans
that gives us gangs of grisly goons all grimly gripping guns
in great gargantuan shows.

Ignore the gorgeous gauzy gowns and garishly girdled garments -
the gaping garb of gangling girlish glamour.

Shun the glowing gleaming glistening globes
and glassy gems that glimmer.
We've galaxies all around us
and gigantic gulfs to close.

Seek not the gain of grants and gifts
nor goals of golden glory.

Beware of gambling games and gallery gags
and guesses and gimmicks too,
for the genesis of generals
and the germane gist of giants
are germs that genius sows.

So guard and guide the groping grooms
and greet the genteel guests,
for what calls more for higher score
than grades on the gallantry test?
The genial gentleman knows!

One weekend in the middle of summer 1968, Dick called me to a conference to meet with some of his most trusted aides and analysts at Montauk Point on the east end of Long Island, New York. As I recall, a diverse group of advisors sat around the table sounding off. The meeting reminded me of a TV talk show with a cross section of views from around the country. Dick wanted the participants to compare notes and consider the important issues that people expected him to address during the campaign. Because I was reading the mail, I had a good idea about concerns at the grass-roots level, so he asked me to report on what the letter writers were saying, asking, demanding.

Dick was eager to hear all sides, and he seemed especially interested in domestic issues. Whatever the people found most troubling would have to be concisely addressed with convincing arguments. Of course, foreign affairs issues on all fronts, not just Vietnam, called for clear thinking and succinctly stated positions. To cover the broad range of vital issues was a mammoth task requiring the best available minds.

In addition to issues, Dick's campaign had to focus on organizational strategy, which included setting up special groups of voters for Nixon. The Committee formed associations of actors, comedians, singers, musicians, sports figures, racecar drivers, youth, Italians, Poles, Czechs, and even the Amish. People with recognizable names who could attract press coverage headed each group. One organizer was Robert "Cy" Laughter from Dayton, Ohio. A noted industrialist, philanthropist, and founder of the Bogie Busters Golf Tournament, he organized Sports Figures for Nixon. These organizations and many others developed their own posters, bumper stickers, and buttons. Occasionally, the leaders asked me to attend group rallies, where I had the privilege of meeting many celebrities whom I never would have met otherwise. After all, I wasn't the candidate and wasn't well known, except for the shape of my nose and my last name.

Between the meeting at Montauk Point and the Republican National Convention in Miami, Dick called me to meet at his home on Fifth Avenue to ask if I had any suggestions regarding candidates for a vice presidential running mate. The political pundits had been speculating on his choice. Names mentioned included Governors Nelson Rockefeller of New York, George Romney of Michigan, Ronald Reagan of California, Mark Hatfield of Oregon, John Volpe of Massachusetts, John Love of Colorado, and Daniel J. Evans of Washington; Senators Charles Percy of Illinois and John Tower of Texas; Congressman George H. W. Bush of Texas; and Mayor John Lindsay of New York. Following conventional wisdom, Dick sought to balance the ticket. Because he was a native Californian living in New York, he and others leaned toward somebody from the Mid-Atlantic States or the South.

Dick said, "You lived down there in suburban D.C. for a few years. What do you think of Ted Agnew? How do the people of Maryland feel about him? Is there any reason he shouldn't be on the ticket?"

"I really don't know much about Agnew," I responded, "but people seem pretty happy with him as governor, and he speaks well. But, just like all your other prospects, he might be vulnerable in some way I'm not aware of."

Dick then asked me about a couple of other elected officials. He, of course, consulted all his top staff regarding the strongest prospective running mate. I didn't have any undue influence. Ultimately the decision was Dick's.

The Republican National Convention began on August 5. Unlike recent conventions, the nomination was not a "done deal." Dick faced serious challenges from Rockefeller and Reagan. Several favorite sons had also thrown their hats into the ring. All the campaign teams scrambled to buttonhole delegates.

Following the old convention tradition, candidates took delegates on yacht cruises and tried to get their assurance of a vote. I joined the party on some of those cruises and became acquainted with delegates. I introduced myself to those who seemed aloof. Although not inclined to perform as a social mixer, I did my best to seek out the quiet delegates (rare in politics) and to make sure they were not wavering on the fringes of the pep rally.

On one of the hospitality cruises, Gay and I met U.S. Representative George H. W. Bush. I readily identified with him as a fellow Naval Aviator. Speaking of superlatives, I noted that before the end of World War II he had become one of the youngest, if not the youngest, Naval Aviator to wear the wings of gold. I told him, "My only claim to fame was being known as the skinniest aviator in the Navy."

Gay also served as a social mixer for the Nixon campaign. On one of her excursions around the circuit of hospitality suites, she spoke with Nancy Reagan. Regrettably, I didn't have that opportunity. When I asked Gay her impression of Mrs. Reagan, she described her as genuinely friendly—not aloof at all.

Don and Clara Jane hosted one of several Nixon hospitality suites in the Miami Beach hotels, and that suited their personalities perfectly. No matter where they were or whom they were entertaining, they always exuded enthusiasm. Visitors crowded their suite, in part because of the attractive atmosphere they had created and in part because their humorous, lighthearted conversations put their guests at ease.

At the convention, Jackie Gleason made his presence known to everyone passing his way with that famous greeting, "How sweet it is!" Even Colonel Sanders volunteered his best fried chicken to the delegates. The "Kentucky Colonel" provided a great photo op. I doubt whether any who saw that smiling gentleman in his famous white uniform refused to pose with him.

∻ ∾

Meanwhile, Karen Anderson, whom Dick had visited in Seattle in 1962, and her friend Rose Zier, both college students, had flown from Seattle to Miami on August 3, hoping to see Dick nominated. The girls arrived in Miami without convention tickets or a place to stay. To no avail, Fran Cooper, a Washington State delegate and former Republican National Committeewoman, had strongly advised the girls against making the trip, suggesting they watch the proceedings on TV.

As Fran had warned, the major hotels were full, so Karen and Rose took a bus from the airport to the Miami YWCA, where they spent the night in a clean but drab room with only a bed, desk, and straight-backed, unpadded chair. No matter. The girls were on an adventure and were proud of their first accomplishment—finding lodging.

The next day, Karen and Rose explored the glitzy delegate hotels along Collins Avenue. Making the rounds of hospitality suites and state delegations, they were befriended by delegates from Illinois staying at the Marco Polo Hotel. One of them invited the young ladies to spend the night there and gave them tickets for the opening night of the convention. Eventually Karen and Rose found a room for ten dollars a night at the Caravan, a small motel on the beach closer to the convention center.

Then Karen contacted Fran, who told the girls to come to the Fontainebleau Hotel to pick up extra tickets she had for the August 7 and 8 convention proceedings.

Although I don't remember our first meeting, Karen recalls sharing a ride in the hotel elevator with John Erhlichman, one of Dick's campaign aides, and me.

After picking up the tickets, Karen and Rose ate lunch in the basement of the Fontainebleau. With the restaurant so crowded with delegates and other guests, the girls agreed to share a booth with an Italian reporter. At the restaurant, they talked with Congressman William Bates of Massachusetts, who sat in the next booth. Karen told him the story of Nixon visiting at her home. After lunch, Congressman Bates saw Karen, Rose, and the reporter on the corner trying to hail a taxi. He offered them a ride to the convention. When Rose got out of his car, she forgot to pick up her camera.

At the convention, Karen and Rose participated in a floor demonstration as Nixonettes, wearing red and blue shift dresses with a large white "N" in the center. They also worked in the Nixon press room. After obtaining official badges, they were able to attend a meeting my brother held with delegates.

∿ ∿

Dick's years of hard work during the mid 1960s in support of the Republican Party and its candidates paid off with a first ballot convention victory on August 7. Senators Barry Goldwater, John Tower, and Strom Thurmond helped deliver their delegations to the Nixon column.

The following evening, August 8, Dick delivered his acceptance speech, calling for new leadership, because the nation's leaders had failed to bring the Vietnam War to an end, failed to manage the economy, failed to control lawlessness, and failed to provide equal opportunity for all citizens. Then, after describing the plight of America's disadvantaged children, he concluded on a personal note:

I see another child tonight.

He hears a train go by at night and he dreams of far away places where he'd like to go.

It seems like an impossible dream.

But he is helped on his journey through life.

A father, who had to go to work before he finished the sixth grade, sacrificed everything so that his sons could go to college.

A gentle Quaker mother, with a passionate concern for peace, quietly wept when he went to war but she understood why he had to go.

A great teacher, a remarkable football coach, an inspirational minister encouraged him on his way.

A courageous wife and loyal children stood by him in victory and also defeat.

And in his chosen profession of politics, first there were scores, then hundreds, then thousands, and finally millions who worked for his success.

And tonight he stands before you—nominated for President of the United States of America.[53]

Dick's speech touched me deeply, bringing tears to my eyes. I could picture my brother as a child lying in bed in the house our father built in Yorba Linda, listening to the train whistle, and dreaming of the day he, too, could see the world. Although he didn't mention Grandmother Milhous that night, she had inspired Dick, as she had me, to travel, get acquainted, and employ friendly persuasion along life's pathways—the Quaker way. As Dick spoke, I thought of the cross-country trip I took with Grandmother and my parents to attend Dick's graduation from Duke Law School in 1937 and my train and car trip to Michigan and back with Dick in 1939. On those trips, I witnessed the vastness and beauty of the United States with the most important people in my life—my family.

As Dick finished his speech to the thunderous applause of delegates, alternates, and guests, red, white, and blue balloons floated down from nets attached to the ceiling.

Spotting Karen and Rose among the crowd exiting the convention center, Congressman Bates caught up with them and returned Rose's camera that he had found in his car. Then he asked, "Would you like to go to a party with me?"

The girls hesitated a moment because of their casual dress and painful sunburns from lying on the beach that afternoon. But they said yes. Congressman Bates kept the destination a secret.

Torches lined the entry to the South Seas-style waterfront restaurant, and a man in a white uniform checked Congressman Bates' invitation and credentials. He told the employee that Karen and Rose were his guests. Inside, the girls felt uncomfortable when they noticed the elegant ladies in cocktail dresses, and then, to their amazement, they saw Richard and Pat Nixon greeting people in a reception line. Congressman Bates had taken them to an exclusive private party in honor of Dick's nomination. Even I wasn't invited.

～ ～

---

53 Nixon, *RN: The Memoirs of Richard Nixon* 315.

Riotous antiwar demonstrations plagued the Democratic Party Convention in Chicago on August 26-29, shocking the nation. Vice President Hubert H. Humphrey survived the chaos and won the nomination to oppose Dick in the 1968 race, but the convention violence severely hindered his ability to unite the party.

My brother held Vice President Humphrey in high regard. While disagreeing with his liberal views, Dick respected him as a solid thinker, a loyal American, and a good man. In no way did he want to sabotage anything worthwhile the Johnson-Humphrey Administration had started. Dick's primary goal was to lead the nation to victory with honor in Vietnam. Beyond that, he hoped to honor what all his predecessors had done to the extent he could agree, because they had acted in good faith and goodwill. For the most part, Nixon and Humphrey disagreed over how best to accomplish goals regarding conduct of the war.

As the campaign entered the final stretch in October, I returned to York County, Pennsylvania, the place my parents and I had called home from 1947 to 1951. Of all my campaign stops, I enjoyed that the most—landing in a field on our former farm in a helicopter and renewing old acquaintances. Carl Stambaugh, the Menges Mills postmaster, and his wife Martha greeted us on arrival. Mr. and Mrs. Sterling Myers, the current owners of the farm, rolled out the welcome mat for Gay and me, as well as for the photographers and the press, who descended on their property. The Myers children, Norma, Kathy, Sam, and Carol, also made us feel very welcome. Even the Chester White hogs greeted us with friendly grunts.

On that trip, I also visited my alma mater, West York High School, and reunited with some of my former teachers, including Chuck Richards, my track coach, who laughed heartily as we reminisced about my unorthodox style of high jumping. I continued my campaign tour through the county, participating in ribbon-cutting ceremonies to open Citizens for Nixon headquarters in Dillsburg, Hanover, Red Lion, and York.

Later that evening, a crowd of more than a hundred friends, former neighbors, and classmates gathered to hear me speak in downtown York. In the midst of the noisy reception, Anna Morris, my former English teacher, then about eighty years old, took my arm and

*Ed and Gay
at Echo Hill
Farm*

*Speaking at Rally in
York, PA*

*With Classmate, Bob
Dolheimer York, PA 1968*

whispered in my ear: "Would you come up to my apartment when you've finished here?"

I promised her I would. Then I spoke briefly to the crowd, conveying my view of the upcoming election and comparing my brother's campaign with those of George Wallace, who spread racial distrust, and Hubert Humphrey, whose policies would be a continuation of the Johnson Administration's. In contrast, I told the audience that a vote for my brother would be a vote for a future with hope.

Following my speech, I visited Miss Morris in her apartment as she had requested. She handed me a fifty-dollar bill "to help your brother win the election." I was deeply touched by her generosity.

∽ ∾

Toward the end of the campaign, I became concerned that the volunteers and I could not answer all the correspondence the U.S. Postal Service kept delivering. The last week before the election, Terry Woods, niece of Dick's longtime secretary, Rose Mary Woods, relayed the welcome message: Dick suggested we cease and desist and pack up the unanswered mail for processing at the White House in the event he won the election.

When the campaign drew to a close, Dick, all our family, and his supporters endured a long vigil the evening of November 5. Everywhere I went that night in New York, "the city that never sleeps," I encountered many of the campaign volunteers from my small group waiting to celebrate. Some were watching returns at the Waldorf-Astoria, while others went to the Plaza, the Sherry-Netherland, or the Hotel Pierre in Midtown Manhattan. For a while, the election was too close to call, but late in the evening, trends looked positive for Dick as state after state fell into his column.

Early the next morning, Dick finally achieved the victory that had eluded him in the close decision in 1960. The Nixon-Agnew ticket won the electoral vote by 301 to 191 and the popular vote by 812,415 votes—43.3 percent compared to Humphrey and Muskie's 42.6 percent. George Wallace and Curtis LeMay, the American Independent Party candidates, received 13.5 percent (nearly ten million votes) and won five southern states with 46 electoral votes.

I believe that victory meant more to Dick than any other in his lifetime, even his first election to Congress in 1946 and his landslide reelection in 1972. After the deep disappointments of 1960 and 1962, he now had the opportunity to lead the country he loved to a brighter future. Our whole family had high hopes for him.

AWAITING DICK'S INAUGURATION

In the meantime, Julie and her fiancé David Eisenhower had decided to forego a White House wedding. On December 22, 1968, a month before Dick's inauguration, they were married at the Marble Collegiate Church in New York City. Dr. Norman Vincent Peale officiated in what was destined to be an American family success story, still going strong after all these years of marriage. Gay, Amy, Beth, and I attended along with close friends and family—Eisenhowers, Nixons, and Ryans—from all over the country.

The next day, Gay, Amy, Beth, and I attended the Radio City Rockettes' Christmas show at Rockefeller Center. One of Don's close friends, who had performed there in years past, had invited us, thinking my young family might never again have such an opportunity—and he was right. In brightly colored costumes, the Rockettes danced a synchronized routine of cancan kicks with amazing agility. We were more impressed by the action on that elaborate stage than by any production we had ever seen.

After the show, we toured backstage. Our guide told us, "The secret of the Rockettes' perfection is that the costumes are measured from the floor up. The eye is drawn to the hemline and the girls' legs, so no one notices that some are taller or shorter. It's a perfect optical illusion."

He also showed us the mechanics of the stage. On the back third, two separate moving circular floor ramps could turn in the same or opposite directions as well as up or down. At the front, a straight, moving causeway could transport horses with carriages, people walking dogs, or other live animal performers. The stage section could function like a treadmill so animals or dancers could walk normally and stay on stage long enough to finish a scene. The mechanics were all quite technical, but the results were pure magic, providing our family a lifetime of memories.

❦ ❧

With Dick elected President in such a surprising political comeback, reporters eagerly sought Don's and my reactions. We agreed to an interview with Mike Wallace, correspondent for CBS's *60 Minutes*. In a hotel room in New York City, Don and I sat on a sofa while Wallace questioned us from his perch in front of the camera crew. As I recall, the interview went like this:

"Now that your brother is President-elect, how will you address him?" Wallace asked.

Don matter-of-factly stated, "Dick."

I tried a more formal approach, saying, "If I were to introduce my brother to someone he didn't know, I'd say, 'Mr. President, I would like you to meet Mr. John Parker. Mr. Parker, this is my brother, the President.'"

"Well, I suppose that's the way we might introduce him to a stranger, but to me, he's Dick," Don added.

As Don and I prepared to greet the next four years, or more, with a brother in the White House, wariness tempered our excitement. We knew that words spoken in haste to reporters or political enemies could be used to embarrass the President. Reflecting now on that Mike Wallace interview, I believe it stands in contrast to numerous later encounters with the press in which reporters too frequently aimed at provoking controversy. Behind Mr. Wallace's friendly questions and inquisitive tone, I didn't sense that he intended to create something newsworthy from our innocent reactions. Of course, as Dick had often reminded us, too many media folks make their living by developing sensational stories from innocuous quotations.

~: CHAPTER 8 :~

A BROTHER IN THE WHITE HOUSE

With those unforgettable events in New York and Miami behind us, my family and I returned home for Christmas. Meanwhile, preparations for the biggest event in our lives—Dick's inauguration as the thirty-seventh President of the United States—reached a frantic pace. Dick's key staff from the just-concluded campaign called in experts to form the 1969 Inaugural Committee. Organizing the week-long festivities of a presidential inauguration demands meticulous attention to myriad details, and every presidential transition challenges the best in those involved in the planning and execution.

Dick made sure our entire extended family received invitations, and every member that could attend eagerly accepted. Because I knew all the invitees on our side of the family, Dick suggested I be in charge of identifying those guests and ensuring they received appropriate attention. However, I was not familiar with Pat's family beyond her siblings, Bill and Tom Ryan, Neva Renter, and Matt Bender. Fortunately, Ned Sullivan, one of Pat's cousins from New York, volunteered to join forces with me, and together we soon became the designated coordinators for hosting the relatives as well as many close friends.

To prepare for this massive reunion, I traveled back to Washington, D.C., a week early. Gay stayed home with our daughters to minimize their absence from school. After I left, a reporter from *The Seattle Times* called to ask about our family's plans for the inauguration. Gay explained the situation, and the reporter thanked her for the information. The next day, Gay spotted the article in the paper. One paragraph divulged that I had already left for D.C. to greet arriving relatives, while Gay and the girls would not be leaving home until the next weekend. To some that might have seemed innocuous and inconsequential—a mere statement of the facts—but not so for our family. Gay was furious to discover all our names and our complete address included in the article. There she was, alone with two young daughters, and the Seattle newspaper with the largest circulation had advertised our family's travel plans and the exact location of our soon-to-be empty, unprotected home for the entire readership to see.

Having already suffered some vandalism to our home and car following Dick's election and hearing of threats communicated to the girls at school, Gay felt increasingly compromised and insecure. She called the newspaper to ask why so much personal information had been published.

The surprised reporter said, "Most readers would consider it an honor to have their name and address in the paper."

"Well, I think it's an open invitation for burglars, more reporters, and demonstrators to come on out to our house," Gay stated. "Is the paper so short of news that inviting troubles might create a story for you?"

Of course, the reporter denied any such intention, but Gay was not at all pleased with her response. She felt the woman had dismissed her concerns and failed to acknowledge the problem. We canceled our subscription.

1969 INAUGURATION

An unusually snowy winter in the Pacific Northwest presented a major navigational obstacle. Snowstorm after snowstorm had blanketed the region. By the time Gay, Amy, and Beth were ready to leave for Washington, D.C., about twenty inches of snow had accumulated, blocking our driveway and rendering the surrounding streets treacherous. Under normal circumstances, the beautiful winter scene would have delighted my family, but they watched in dismay as the snow continued to fall. Without assistance, there was no way they could make it to the airport in time for their flight. They feared they would miss the momentous family event and the opportunity to witness history in the making.

Hearing of their plight, Al Glandt, our good-hearted local police chief, volunteered to help. He called Gay and said, "I have to take care of you folks. I'll pick you up in my police car and take you to the airport, so you won't miss the inauguration."

But the last city block to our house proved too difficult for even his chain-equipped car to negotiate, so Chief Glandt trudged through deep snow up the street and on up our driveway to help Gay and the girls with their luggage. Upon returning to the car, he discovered a flat tire. What could he do but jack up the car, change the tire, and reinstall the chains while Gay and the girls huddled in the snow, watching his determined progress. Then, with no time to spare, he drove them down the freeway to the airport with siren blaring and lights flashing. They made the flight, thanks to Chief Glandt.

Meanwhile, my cousin Marygene Marshburn Wright had arrived early in Washington, D.C., for the inaugural events. I enlisted her help because she, too, knew most of the family members. She and I worked with Evlyn Dorn, Dick's former secretary, and her daughter Roberta to keep track of "who was who" and where they were staying. [54]

My list included 205 aunts, uncles, nieces, nephews, cousins, and in-laws, many of whom flew on a chartered Braniff plane from Los Angeles to D.C. to attend the inauguration. Gathered together, all those relatives resembled a big family reunion at Grandmother's house—but much larger because the Nixons, the Ryans, and Gay's parents and sister joined the Milhous clan.

With the size of our group posing a significant logistical challenge, we appreciated the military planning to ensure that everyone arrived at the proper location on time. The 1969 Inaugural Committee headed by J. Willard Marriott assigned a military aide to each of our families: Don and Clara Jane Nixon plus their three children; Ed

---

54 Evlyn Dorn was Dick's first legal secretary in Whittier in 1937.

and Gay Nixon plus two; Tom and Dorothy Ryan plus four; Bill and Marie Ryan plus two; Pat's half sister Neva and her husband Marc Renter; and her half brother Matt Bender. Aides also escorted and assisted aunts, uncles, and groups of cousins. The committee provided buses and vans for the designated groups, thus keeping a semblance of order among so many people unaccustomed to attending a presidential inauguration as guests of the incoming President.

Through all the comings and goings, my family and I gained a further appreciation of the mammoth tasks confronting security personnel, including the Secret Service, police, military, and security guards. They had to ensure that everyone stayed ahead of schedule—not just on time. They also had to make sure everyone was in place while they surveyed the crowd for suspicious behavior before the arrival of the President, Vice President, and their immediate families. Knowing this helped us understand the enormous pressure on those responsible for security. We knew we had to follow the rules to the letter.

A Coast Guard lieutenant commander from Wyoming escorted Gay, Amy, and Beth during the inaugural events. The girls fell in love with that young man. He was a true officer and gentleman—sincere, courteous, helpful, and kind.

"How in the world did you become interested in the Coast Guard when you're from Wyoming?" they asked him.

He replied, "Well, not everybody knows that Wyoming is landlocked, and I'm impressed that you do!"

A young Marine major assisted Don and Clara Jane with their three children, Lawrene, Donnie, and Ricky. Don was accustomed to running the show for all kinds of social events, but this one overwhelmed him. Maybe just what he needed was someone to give him orders that he would gladly respect and appreciate. They all got along quite smoothly, thanks in part to Don's positive determination to cooperate with the well-disciplined but good-natured major. New friendships blossomed readily in Don's family.

As a promoter of classical music in our family, I insisted that Amy and Beth go with Gay and me to the inaugural concert at Constitution Hall, where we joined Don and Clara Jane. Eighty-three-year-old Uncle Ernest and his two daughters, Alice Linton and Ernestine "Dimpy" Noll, sat right behind me. Anna Moffo, the beautiful young soprano, sang a familiar aria after which the audience roared for an encore with prolonged applause. Uncle Ernest, who still appreciated shapely women, leaned over as she curtsied and said, "Wow! Look at that. She didn't even have to sing."

On Monday, the day of the inauguration, we donned our warmest clothing to shield ourselves as best we could from the typical frigid January weather in Washington, D.C. Taking our seats with the congressional delegation on the east front steps of the Capitol, we looked out over the crowd filling the park, sympathizing with those standing in the cold.

As the presidential swearing-in ceremony began, Pat held two heirloom Milhous Bibles. Dick placed his hands on them, while Chief Justice Earl Warren administered the presidential oath of office for his fifth and final time. Then Dick addressed the large crowd and a worldwide audience in an inaugural speech televised and broadcast by satellite.

In Dick's words, I could hear the influence of our Milhous and Nixon heritage. From the Milhous side, he stressed peace. One of his favorite passages was:

> The greatest honor history can bestow is the title of peacemaker. This honor now beckons America—the chance to help lead the world at last out of the valley of turmoil and onto that high ground of peace that man has dreamed of since the dawn of civilization.[55]

In the tradition of our Quaker ancestors, Dick called for people to look within for an answer to the crisis of spirit that plagued our nation and for a return to the "basic things such as goodness, decency, love and kindness."

I thought of Mom when Dick said:

> We cannot learn from one another until we stop shouting at one another—until we speak quietly enough so that our words can be heard as well as our voices.[56]

---

55 "Richard Milhous Nixon First Inaugural Address," *Inaugural Addresses of the Presidents of the United States*, Volume 2, 133-134.
56 "Richard Milhous Nixon First Inaugural Address" 135.

How she would have loved to hear him deliver that message as the new President of the United States.

Then I heard Dad's influence coming through:

The American dream does not come to those who fall asleep. But we are approaching the limits of what government alone can do. Our greatest need now is to reach beyond government, and to enlist the legions of the concerned and the committed. [57]

In keeping with Dick's inaugural theme "Forward Together" and our family's firm commitment to racial equality, he said:

No man can be fully free while his neighbor is not. To go forward at all is to go forward together.

This means black and white together, as one nation, not two. What remains is to give life to what is in the law: to ensure at last that as all are born equal in dignity before God, all are born equal in dignity before man.

As we learn to go forward together at home, let us also seek to go forward together with all mankind.[58]

Dick concluded his address with this inspiring challenge to all Americans:

Our destiny offers, not the cup of despair, but the chalice of opportunity. So let us seize it, not in fear, but in glad-ness—and, "riders on the earth together," let us go forward, firm in our faith, steadfast in our purpose, cautious of the dangers; but sustained by our confidence in the will of God and the promise of man.[59]

Following Dick's speech, I became a bit apprehensive, because no inaugural official had instructed me what to do next except to keep our groups in touch with our escorts. I couldn't find anyone who

---

57 "Richard Milhous Nixon First Inaugural Address" 135.
58 "Richard Milhous Nixon First Inaugural Address" 136.
59 "Richard Milhous Nixon First Inaugural Address" 138.

knew the next move. Who had the master plan for exiting the scene and moving to the next venue? It seemed the original plans had been revised, and protocol differed from what I remembered of the 1953 and 1957 inaugurations.

To my great relief, I then discovered that the escorts had proceeded to our respective vehicles. Congressional staff soon intercepted us and guided the family groups smoothly to the next stop—the presidential reviewing stand—well before the parade got underway. From that vantage point, not only did we have a better view than the crowds on foot, but also we were spared the sight of antiwar demonstrators out in full force to protest along the parade route to the White House.

After a long line of floats and bands had passed in front of us, Tom Ryan made the same observation he had at the inaugural parade of 1957: "Some of those military units must be marching around the block several times!"

The seemingly endless parade also prompted Uncle Ernest to ask, "Could someone lead me to a toilet?" A uniformed officer responded, escorting him up the long temporary boardwalk to the main entrance to the North Portico. Uncle Ernest soon returned to his seat with a big smile, exclaiming, "Now, I've finally arrived! I just relieved myself in the White House!"

I was so glad Uncle Ernest had the opportunity to witness his nephew's inauguration and to see the White House. He passed away two months later.

Following the parade, we departed to our respective lodgings to prepare for the inaugural ball later that evening. My immediate family and Gay's parents attended the event in the Capitol Hilton Ballroom, one of several sites designated for the growing number of guests at these ever-popular formal events.

Gay had designed and sewn gowns for Amy and Beth made of crushed velvet with long lace sleeves: royal blue for Amy and deep red for Beth. As we headed down to the ballroom, the girls had their photograph taken in the hallway with Colonel Sanders of Kentucky Fried Chicken, who was also attending the inauguration. Amy remembers dancing with Donnie Nixon, her twenty-three-year-old cousin, standing on the toes of his shoes, while he waltzed her around the dance floor.

The day after the inauguration, all 205 relatives and in-laws gathered for a brief reception in the State Dining Room with delicious hors d'oeuvres followed by a personal tour of the White House.

Even during his political years, Dick maintained his sincere interest in all the family and made a point of keeping up with recent events. Bill Wright, Marygene's husband, recalled that Dick always remembered what people told him concerning family members. Dick surprised us many times by his ability to recall obscure details that we had forgotten long ago. He seemed to enjoy total immersion in details.

Passing through the receiving line at the inaugural reception, Joy Woods, Gay's sister, also was surprised by Dick's great memory. She had not seen him since Gay's and my wedding eleven years earlier. Recently, Joy shared with me the following story:

> On the day of my only sister's wedding in June 1957, I was eleven and a half years old. I had cried throughout the wedding and reception. Dick came up to me and asked why I was crying. I replied, "Your brother is taking my sister away, and I won't see her again for a long time."
>
> In 1969, when I went through the receiving line at the inaugural reception for the family, Dick gave me a big hug and said, "I see that you have stopped crying." By that time I was twenty-three years old and marveled at his memory.

To cap off the reception, Dick guided Aunt Jane to the Truman piano in the East Room and asked her to play Christian Sinding's "Rustle of Spring," one of Mom's favorite melodies. Aunt Jane had taught him that piece when he stayed with the Beeson family for piano lessons as a child. If Mom had lived long enough to attend his inauguration, Dick knew she would have requested it.

Teasing and Torment at School

Beth went back to school, eager to share her inauguration and White House experiences with her teacher and classmates. Her teacher, however, never gave her that opportunity. Perhaps the woman feared the other students would feel envious or inferior. Or perhaps animosity

The President up close—with Ed and family
~White House Photo

"Hi, Uncle Dick"—Beth
~White House Photo

toward President Nixon motivated her. Whatever the reason, for the rest of the school year, she would not call on Beth whenever she raised her hand in class.

As parents, Gay and I expected our daughters' teachers to be aware of the feelings of everyone in the class, not favoring one student over the others, but we were appalled to learn that teachers sometimes singled Beth out for ridicule and at other times ignored her because of her relationship to my brother. To this day, Beth carries emotional scars from the mistreatment she received, and her classmates missed an opportunity to learn something new and inspiring from her.

Many years later, Beth aired her bitter school memories:

> Third grade, eight years old, I was beginning to develop a sense of self. Our class performed a play that year. I think it was *Sleeping Beauty*. I was cast as the wicked witch and totally lost myself in the part. Offstage, however, I was a decidedly vulnerable and painfully shy child who came across as naive. I had one loyal friend, Kathy, but as the school year dragged on, I found myself attracting and entertaining many enemies.

> Since my uncle was running for President in 1968, the first Tuesday in November was a huge event for our family. My maternal grandparents visiting from New Orleans helped take care of my sister and me. Mom was working as a math teacher and helping my dad campaign for his big brother, Richard Nixon. Things were so positive and upbeat at home that I felt it would be wrong to complain about things at school. Besides, how could I even express what I felt?

> At first, I didn't realize how very wrong things were in the classroom and on the playground. My teacher told me she was excited I had been assigned to her class because I was a Nixon, and Richard Nixon, my uncle, was running for President that very year. From my desk in the center of the room, I witnessed a mock election organized by my teacher. I was nominated to pose as one of the two presidential candidates, but the teacher said that we couldn't have a Nixon

running as a Nixon or a Humphrey, because it might prove difficult for me to write a good speech or to be unbiased. Her disparaging remarks were heard loud and clear by my classmates. Our little election involved numerous speeches, and the process went on for two to three weeks, if I remember correctly. Each morning she would discuss what she had read in the newspapers and heard on the TV news. Obviously, she detested anything Republican and would make unkind remarks to any student who said or asked anything "Nixon like," even during the speeches. She blatantly beat down my classmates, using me as an example to the point that no one dared sit in any of the desks near mine. They didn't like it either but respected her as an authority figure, just as I did. I wasn't the only kid who saw her throw my ballot disgustedly into the trash.

What was I to think? The teacher was my role model and leader. She made it abundantly clear that I belonged in the class merely as a tool, setting an example of what not to be. Her hatred was palpable. I believe that if she could have gotten away with it, she would have beaten me with a whip in front of my class.

At home I was nurtured and valued. My parents cheered me on and told me I should be proud to be a part of what was going on. I could not find the courage to tell them they were so wrong. I was a thorn in the side of the whole world. I was ashamed that I was such a bad person. So I said nothing to the people who could have helped me. I hid bruises I got on the playground from other kids shoving me into walls or throwing rocks at my back. I quit going to recess. The library became my sanctuary. The lunchroom was awful because I had no one to sit with.

When Uncle Dick won the election, my teacher seemed to let up a bit. She asked the class to write letters to the new President and asked me to deliver them. I got to go to the inauguration in Washington, D.C. It was incredible to witness such a big ceremony. When I handed Uncle Dick the letters from my class, I almost apologized. I felt ashamed that my whole school hated him and me so much. But I didn't want to hurt his feelings. He thanked me for bringing them, saw tears shining in my eyes, and gave me a concerned look. He just waited to see if I had something to say. I looked down, said "Bye," and walked away.

Upon returning to school, silly me, I was pretty excited to bring a bag of "stuff" for show and tell. I raised my hand and held it up. My teacher called on every one of my classmates, some of them twice. She even called on students who had not brought anything. I knew she would eventually get to me. She knew I had some things to share, because I had told her that morning. The bell rang. Class was dismissed. I sat in my desk and looked through the show and tell things my mom had helped me pack. There was a tiny silver plate with the Presidential seal, a squished bouquet of flowers from a White House garbage can, a plaque, an embroidered hand-kerchief, and a toy mouse with a corn kernel glued to its paws. One of Dad's friends had bought the little mouse for me on impulse.

I missed the bus. I didn't cry. I was disappointed in myself that I wasn't good enough. I was ashamed. I walked home through the woods that day and sneaked into the house to unpack the bag. Later I gave the bag back to my mom, who asked, "Oh, how did show and tell go?"

"Fine."

Things remained "fine." Actually they got quite a bit worse during 1972-1974. In junior high, kids would jeer, make up mean jokes, and ask me stupid questions all through class. Many teachers openly encouraged this; some even joined in. A few were kinder, but the political climate was such that few dared to openly defend me or offer assistance.

My junior year of college, I tried a new tactic at a new school. I simply told people that I was not related to "that Nixon." For the first time since second grade, I had tons of friends, was invited to parties, and finally began dating! I discovered to my surprise that there was nothing wrong with me. There never had been.

"Every President exercises his executive privileges; Nixon just got caught." I'm more than a little tired of that line. Nixon did whatever he did. He did not discuss his actions with me. I only spoke to him four or five times in my life. I neither know nor care what was or is on the Watergate tapes. I never did.

The press published ugly stories, and nobody cared. The schools displayed mean attitudes, and no one even looked up. People are finally talking to me about their bad behavior. I run into folks who went to school with me who tell me they remember and are sorry they weren't nicer. They were afraid of being treated like I was. "I would have shot myself if I were you, but I'm glad you didn't!" I don't blame anybody except the media. Looking back now, I realize it all happened over thirty years ago, and lots of fools still want to flog a dead horse; go figure.

Amy, too, told Gay and me stories of being teased and tormented at school because of being President Nixon's niece. Unlike her sister, however, Amy tried to deflect her detractors. She gained quite a reputation for using coarse language—the kind one might hear in wartime aboard a ship under attack—no holds barred. The anomaly of tough talk spewing from the mouth of this beautiful girl often shocked her new acquaintances. The few friends she would tolerate supported her famous uncle, the President of the United States.

Later, Gay and I learned that our daughters were not the only ones who suffered. Dick's and Don's children also faced unkindness from classmates and teachers.

WHITE HOUSE INVITATIONS

OFFICIAL DINNER HONORING APOLLO 11

While state dinners were customarily held at the White House, Dick initiated a program of "taking the White House to the people." After returning from their eleven-day global goodwill journey, Dick and Pat hosted a dinner at the Century Plaza Hotel in Los Angeles on August 13, 1969, to honor the Apollo 11 astronauts and all the personnel and primary contractors who helped achieve the goal of landing astronauts on the Moon. The hotel had the capacity to serve many more guests than the White House could—over 1,400 foreign dignitaries, U.S. officials, and governors in addition to those who had worked on Project Apollo.

Grateful and humbled to have received invitations from the White House for the gala, Gay and I arrived early and found a quiet corner from which to observe the targets of the media floodlights. Don and Clara Jane mingled with guests in the foyer, exercising their great skills as friendly mixers. When the ballroom doors opened to announce that dinner was about to be served, Gay and I entered right away and found our assigned table. As was the custom at state dinners, spouses were seated apart but at the same table. If I recall correctly, we sat with an ambassador and his wife from an Eastern bloc country.

Afterward, Gay and I discovered that Don and Clara Jane had the misfortune of arriving at their table too late; two other people already occupied their seats. How that happened, we never knew. Those people could have made an honest mistake. Or, with tickets in high demand and a packed house that evening, they might have been on a wait list and been seated while Don and Clara Jane were engrossed in conversation outside. Rather than make a scene, my brother and his wife graciously exited without experiencing the extraordinary dinner and delightful ceremony.

When Dick learned of the unfortunate incident, he made sure Don and Clara Jane would be treated fairly in the future. He saw to it that they received invitations to two state dinners, the same number of official dinners that Gay and I attended.

Apollo 11 banquet guests, August 13, 1969
(l-r) Rose Mary Woods' escort, Bill Ryan, Rose Mary Woods, Marie
Ryan, June Rogers, Dorothy Ryan, Tom Ryan, and Matt Bender

~White House Photo

BROADWAY IN THE EAST ROOM: *1776*

One of our favorite White House events—a production of the Broadway musical *1776*—took place on February 22, 1970, as the second in a series of cultural performances entitled "Evening at the White House." Staging a Broadway show at one end of the East Room required a great deal of preparation, including construction of a stage. Sherman Edwards had written the music and lyrics telling of the Continental Congress in Philadelphia and the events leading to the signing of the Declaration of Independence. Although the production was hyped up, the story remained true to fact, incorporating many of the very words penned by John Adams, Thomas Jefferson, and Benjamin Franklin. That night, nearly 250 government officials, military officers, their wives, and others obviously appreciated the history set to music.

The delightful—marvelous, in fact—performance made the hair stand up on the back of my head. I said to Dick, "This is just the way history ought to be presented." He agreed.

After the show, the actors and performers wanted to go out to eat, as they would in New York City. Because I had worked in D.C., someone said I would know the local restaurants. But when I had lived there, I avoided the late-night scene. Besides, the city did not boast nightlife like New York; most restaurants had closed before the end of the musical. I searched until someone gave me a tip on an Italian bistro on Connecticut Avenue that stayed open late. The taxi driver found the place with no trouble. Then I realized that almost any taxi driver could have solved my quandary immediately. Anyway, the members of the cast who hung in there with me enjoyed D.C.'s rare late-hour pizza service.

STATE DINNER HONORING PRESIDENT AND MADAME POMPIDOU

Soon after taking office, Dick had embarked on a mission to improve the relationship between the United States and European nations. During his meetings with President Charles de Gaulle in France in February 1969, he tried to strengthen the alliance that had become estranged over U.S. involvement in the Vietnam War during the Johnson Administration. The two world leaders discussed foreign policy issues and planned for de Gaulle's visit to the United States the following year, but that never occurred. De Gaulle resigned later in 1969, and Georges Pompidou was elected to replace him.

On February 24, 1970, President and Madame Pompidou arrived in Washington, D.C. That morning Gay and I attended the impressive ceremony with full military honors on the South Lawn of the White House, where Dick formally welcomed the Pompidous.

At the grand dinner that evening—Gay's and my only state dinner at the White House during Dick's presidency—we sipped French wine and dined on French cuisine served on gilded place settings made in France. Gay sat between White House Chief of Protocol, Bus Mosbacher, and a French pilot, Commandant Aubrey, who shared in a lively discussion comparing the differences between American and European customs with respect to dining. The dinner concluded with toasts by Dick and President Pompidou in which they extolled the historical and current friendship of the United States and France and their common ideals and destinies in pursuit of freedom and democracy.

President Pompidou loved earthy music and cigars. When Dick hosted world leaders, he sought to provide what they would enjoy, so Peggy Lee, one of the top female vocalists of all time, entertained that evening. Unfortunately, she had imbibed a bit too much beforehand and had trouble remembering her lines. Seeing her distress, Dick came to her rescue, standing behind her to hold her up, so she could finish her performance. Everyone applauded at the end, hopefully making her feel better.

That night after a brief tour of the First Family private residence floor, Gay and I stayed in the rose-colored Queen's Bedroom across the hall from the famous Lincoln Bedroom. Queen Elizabeth and several other queens had slept in that four-poster bed, but Gay could not sleep all night, so she sat up and wrote notes. In a letter to Amy and Beth, she described the beautiful, historic mansion.

I later learned that Dick had to pay for our stay, including food and staff time. It did not come out of any taxpayer money, but rather out of his salary.

SUMMONS TO THE WHITE HOUSE

About the time of our daughters' spring break in 1971, we received a call from Rose Mary Woods, who was working with Dick at La Casa Pacifica, the "Western White House," in San Clemente, California. She said, "Your brother would like you to bring your family down to LAX. We'll pick you up and take you out to the El Toro Air Base. Then you'll ride on Air Force One."

Surprised, I asked, "What's this all about? Where did this come from?"

"We'll tell you when you get here." She would say no more.

So, we packed and arranged to fly to Los Angeles. At El Toro, as we boarded Air Force One, Dwight Chapin, one of Dick's closest aides, showed me a letter Beth had written to Uncle Dick, unbeknownst to Gay and me, after returning home from the 1969 inauguration. For two years, it had sat in the dead letter file in the White House mailroom, pending identification of the sender. Someone finally noticed the name on the letter and sent it over to Rose Mary in the West Wing with a note saying, "The President's niece must have written this."

The letter read, "Dear Uncle Dick, I'm glad you were elected President. I'd like to come and live with you at the White House. Please write and tell me when I can come."

As soon as we were seated, Dick came aboard. (Pat had not accompanied him on that trip to San Clemente but had remained at the White House.) After a flight of only four hours, Air Force One landed at Andrews Air Force Base. Then we boarded the Marine One helicopter and flew to the South Lawn at the White House.

Dick led us into the oval-shaped Diplomatic Reception Room on the ground floor, where President Franklin Roosevelt delivered his fireside chats during the Great Depression and World War II. Situated in the center of the White House on the ground floor, the room serves both as the place where Presidents welcome diplomats and foreign dignitaries and as the first family's main entrance and exit. Beth and Amy got a history lesson as they viewed the mural wallpaper of early American scenes and the furniture from the Federal Period (1780-1810).

Gay admires Lincoln Bedroom

~White House Photo

Addressing the girls, Dick said, "Now, look around. There are phones everywhere in the White House. If you need something, all you have to do is pick up one of the black phones and say who you are, where you are, and what you want. You won't have to dial anything. Somebody will answer as soon as you pick it up. That's it. Now, let's go up and have some dinner." He was getting hungry.

Beth, who by that time was ten, piped up, "But, Uncle Dick, how will I know where I am?"

"Don't worry. I'm going to show you the whole place. Come on. We'll have the full tour, and then we'll have dinner."

So, for the next hour Dick led us around through every room, telling stories as he went. Talk about a royal tour! First he showed us around the floor that tourists see—the East Room, State Dining Room, Green Room, Red Room, and so forth. On the second floor, he took us to the First Family's residence, the Queen's Bedroom, and the Lincoln Bedroom.

Then he showed us the third floor, where most of the house-guests stay. Amy and Beth were assigned to what Amy refers to as "the King's Bedroom," decorated with padded red and cream toile fabric on the walls and several eighteenth-century antiques, including George Washington's marble-topped, mirrored shaving table, which Amy used for a mini-vanity.

On the top floor just off the main hall, Dick led us down a gentle slope into the Solarium, situated above the South Portico over the Truman Balcony. He said, "Girls, President Roosevelt, who was crippled, you know, used to roll his wheelchair down this ramp before dawn to wait for the sunrise and to enjoy this beautiful view of the Tidal Basin. Now let's go back down to the second floor." So, we proceeded to the Family Dining Room for dinner.

Before we even knew about the White House invitation, Gay had been instructing Amy and Beth on dining etiquette, including the uses of all the different forks, spoons, knives, and glassware. The girls had absorbed this information and at our White House dinner remembered their table manners, right down to using fingerbowls after the last course. The delicious dinner included hearts of palm as the appetizer, salad, roast pheasant, rice pilaf, peas and onions, and dessert. Both girls ate everything without their usual "picky-eater" attitude and learned to try new things without a fuss. Dick discussed each course with them and talked about the food and its preparation.

After dinner, while Pat, Gay, and I chatted over a cup of coffee, Dick gave the girls a special private tour of his personal rooms on the family floor. Amy recalls being led down a long walk-through closet, where all his suits and shoes were organized by color.

Finally, the girls settled into bed, but Beth, the curious one, couldn't sleep right away. She jotted notes in her little book, as her mother had encouraged her to do. Even though she had experienced ostracism at school, Beth still hoped to tell about the trip when she returned to class, feeling her classmates would want to hear about the White House. After a brief sleep, she awoke about 5 a.m. and retraced her steps to the Solarium. There she sat, waiting for the sun to rise and trying to see the Tidal Basin—just like President Roosevelt. After a while, she decided to try Dick's suggestion: She picked up the phone and said, "Hello, this is Beth. I'm in the Solarium, and I'd like some creamed corn and a Coke." Not long afterward, the butler, a polite, well-dressed African-American gentleman, obliged her with a bowl of warm creamed corn and a glass of Coca Cola served on a silver tray.

Recently Amy shared with me her memories of our White House visit. With her good artist's eyes, she described the decorations in detail—colors, and all:

> The third day at the White house, Tricia took Beth and me on a tour, showing us secret rooms and hidden stairways (usually used by staff to move cleaning equipment between the floors). On the second floor, she ushered us into the Treaty Room, decorated in a beautiful hunter green with deep burgundy draperies and accents. My sister and I admired the long, leather-covered table with matching chairs, over which hung a gigantic crystal chandelier. Then Tricia surprised us by pressing a nearly invisible line on one of the walls. Out popped the wall, revealing a charming secret powder room with hunter green and burgundy tiles and a dark green toilet and sink. To this day, Beth and I still talk about that little bathroom. Another secret panel in the Treaty Room remained locked, because Tricia didn't know

Amy and Beth
playing dress up at the
White House,
spring 1971
∿White House Photo

the whereabouts of the key. For decades, Beth and I have speculated about the mysterious room, trying to imagine what could be hidden behind that door.

Tricia also showed us her suite and closets—and then the fun began. In one of her closets, we discovered a row of beautiful gowns. With Tricia's encouragement, we spent hours trying on several of the gowns. Since Tricia was so petite, her gowns nearly fit us.

The next day, Aunt Pat asked us to put on the gowns again. Then we posed in various rooms all over the White House while a photographer took pictures, some of which ended up in the newspaper, saying we were "practicing for Tricia's upcoming wedding"—a story that must have been contrived. We had only been playing dress up!

Wedding in the Rose Garden

Tricia's marriage to Ed Cox on June 12, 1971, provided a joyful respite from the political turmoil that year, especially for Dick and Pat. I had often thought how wonderful it would have been had Dad and Mom lived long enough to see their grandchildren marry: Julie to David Eisenhower in December 1968, then Don and Clara Jane's daughter Lawrene to Tom Anfinson in June 1970, and now Tricia. Everyone in the family would have been delighted to witness Tricia's big day no matter where it took place, but her wedding in the White House Rose Garden took the cake.

The evening before the wedding, Dick and Pat hosted a rehearsal dinner at the historic Blair House across the street from the White House. The wedding party and guests sat in groups of ten at three tables. As the senior relative at my table, I was expected to make a toast, but feeling uncomfortable in that kind of situation, I could not assemble the words I had hoped to say. Suddenly the banquet ended before I could raise a glass. I later apologized to Ed and Tricia Cox for failing the rules of protocol. Much to my relief, they graciously waved it off.

At the dinner, my family and I enjoyed becoming better acquainted with Colonel Howard Cox and Mrs. Cox, Ed's parents. We remember them as extraordinary people. Anne exuded kindness and graciousness, never seeming to think of herself, but rather inquiring about other people. She reminded me a great deal of my mother in that respect. And the Colonel epitomized what Mom would have considered a stately, good-humored gentleman.

The rain let up long enough the afternoon of June 12 for the wedding ceremony to take place in the Rose Garden. Junior bridesmaids Amy, age thirteen, and Beth, age eleven, preceded Tricia down the white-carpeted aisle, looking lovely in their gorgeous lavender "Priscilla of Boston" gowns. Harry Winston, the famous jewelry designer, had made them each an elegant pin of colored gems to accent their dresses.

During that trip, my family and I stayed at the home of Mrs. Gladstone Williams, Director of the Protocol School of Washington for State Department wives, newly arrived congressmen, and anyone else who wanted to avail themselves of the finer points of etiquette. In the early 1960s, when we lived in Arlington, Virginia, Gay had taken a course at the Protocol School. She had always admired Mrs. Williams' extraordinary courtesy and welcomed this opportunity to visit with her again.

Brothers of the President

Despite the increasing demands of his official schedule, Dick tried to avoid seeming aloof toward family and personal friends. He never lost sight of them, but initially some of the family didn't grasp his total lack of spare time. All too often, I heard of long-time friends having disappointing encounters with the young White House staff sincerely trying to keep the President's daily agenda on schedule. From the start, I reminded everyone seeking easier access to the Oval Office of the enormous tasks Dick had to confront. The demands on his time never subsided.

Although we had less contact with Dick during his presidential years, Don and I still talked with him brother-to-brother. Dick made an effort to telephone us on special occasions or just to say hello and inquire about our families and us. Sometimes he asked our feelings on important issues, using us as a sounding board.

Junior Bridesmaid Amy
at Tricia Nixon and
Ed Cox's Wedding,
June 12, 1971
∾White House Photo

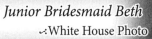
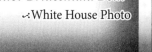

Junior Bridesmaid Beth
∾White House Photo

Tricia and her dad
∾White House Photo

The family in west end of White House residence floor,
June 12, 1971
Lawrene Nixon Anfinson; Don, Beth, Clara Jane, Rick, and
Amy Nixon; Julie Nixon Eisenhower; Donnie, Pat, Ed, and
Gay Nixon; Tom Anfinson

⌐White House Photo

As a result of Dick's presidency, Don and I embarked on exciting adventures but also faced special challenges. All my adult life, Dick had been in the public spotlight, but now that he held center stage, the pressure from governmental officials, reporters, and corporations mounted on Don and me to participate in briefings, interviews, and ventures. People sought us out for our Nixon name and the influence they thought we carried. "Oh, let's take him on. He can be influential."

In this regard, very early in Dick's first term, I received some surprising advice from Husang Ansary, a former Iranian ambassador to the U.S., who invited me to visit him at his suite in the Waldorf-Astoria in Manhattan. "You will be approached by many people wanting you to serve as a doormat to your brother's office," he predicted. "To avoid that, you should register as an agent for a foreign country. Then you can respectfully decline such appeals due to conflict of interest."

Of course, I didn't take his advice, but in later years, when I reflected on Ambassador Ansary's remarks, I wondered whether he was reacting to concerns Dick had expressed about people trying to take advantage of Don's and my connection to the White House. Realizing our precarious situation as brothers, he wanted us to know what to say, what not to say, and how to avoid getting involved with personal appeals from friends or strangers who might try to make inappropriate or illegal deals. Dick implored us not to promise anything involving the White House. He made it clear to everyone that personal appeals would have to pass through official filters before reaching the Oval Office.

I had to evaluate each opportunity that came my way with great care. Could I offer something substantial, or would I just be asked to provide special access to the White House? If I could not contribute more than my name, I would not accept the offer. Moreover, one thing I was clear about: I would decline on the spot any requests to intercede directly in the Oval Office. Dick and I had agreed to that from the beginning.

In many ways, Don took the brunt of having a celebrity in the family. From the time Dick reached the national spotlight and incurred enemies along the way, people accused Don of totally unfounded misdeeds. The critics tried to get to Dick by hurting Don. He became the whipping boy for reporters wanting to oust the President, or maybe they thought a carefully contrived scoop would earn them a better-than-average living. But the tabloid generators were barking up the wrong tree.

Don worked as an account executive for Virgil Gladieux, a Toledo businessman, entrepreneur, and food concessionaire who was later bought out by Marriott. Because his job involved extensive travel, Don befriended many people nationwide and became a significant influence in the New York scene. His friendliness had an element of innocence and gullibility. Having a heart of gold, he genuinely desired to help people involved in worthy causes—a trait from his Quaker upbringing as well as part of his own personality. But many of his friends attempted to use him to gain access to the President. When people would ask him for help, he would try to arrange a meeting with Dick. At other times he would call me and ask, "What do you think about this? We've got to tell Dick and see what he can do."

I would respond, "No, you don't want to tell Dick. It's just a business venture, and he can't do anything about it. He doesn't have time for that stuff. Dick made that perfectly clear. "

Compared to the treatment Don received, the media let me off easy. In fact, it was not widely known nationally that Dick had another brother. By trying to keep a low profile, I seldom appeared on the tabloid radar screens. However, those reporters who did know me remained curious about my supposed influence with Dick. They apparently thought I wielded clout that in reality I did not have.

PENTAGON BRIEFING

Soon after Dick's inauguration, Admiral Elmo "Bud" Zumwalt, Chief of Naval Operations (CNO), arranged for one of my fourteen-day active-duty-for-training periods (Navy ACDUTRA) to be carried out on a tour of the Sixth Fleet in the Mediterranean for the purpose of familiarization and education. My tour of duty began at the Pentagon with several briefings by top Navy brass. Admiral Zumwalt wanted the President's brother to be in the know, so he briefed me himself. An officer of my rank wouldn't normally receive such attention. Later, Vice Admiral Tom Connolly, Deputy Chief of Naval Operations for Air Warfare and father of the F-14 Tomcat, and Vice Admiral James

Holloway, III, foremost promoter of the $2-billion-nuclear-powered aircraft carrier, also briefed me in person.

To begin the cruise portion of the ACDUTRA tour, I departed Naval Air Station Patuxent River, Maryland, aboard a Lockheed P-3 Orion configured for antisubmarine warfare duty. In addition to the flight crew, Captain Reginald Armistead, our group leader, Captain Meyer Minchen, and Commander Dick Ford were on board. The plane landed for refueling in the Azores, then proceeded on to Rota, Spain. From there we received an introduction to Mediterranean operations of the Sixth Fleet. Admiral Isaac Kidd briefed us aboard his flagship cruiser and arranged introductions with the submarine fleet to include a short cruise on a diesel boat.

A few weeks after I returned from the cruise and concluded my ACDUTRA, Admiral Zumwalt invited Don and me to his Pentagon office for a personal and private briefing to explain subtle geopolitical situations impinging on U.S. military operations. In a small room adjacent to his main office, the CNO gave us a view of the world that few were allowed to see. Classified information is always strictly limited to those with a need to know, and we could see that in matters of such strategic concern, the whole picture could not be revealed. Obviously, we had to keep our mouths shut regarding what we did see and hear.

RICHARD NIXON FOUNDATION

Don and I readily accepted the opportunity to serve from 1969 to 1973 as two of the twenty-five trustees of the original Richard Nixon Foundation. At the first board meeting in San Clemente, California, in August 1969, we discussed the future presidential library and the documentation that would be most beneficial and historically significant to include.

Whittier and Yorba Linda had been on the potential site list from the beginning. After Dick won the 1968 election, six Yorba Linda businessmen established the Richard Nixon Birthplace Foundation in hope of attracting the presidential library. Also under consideration were Whittier College; San Clemente; the University of Southern California, Pat's alma mater, in the Exposition Park section of Los

Angeles; Duke University, Dick's law school alma mater; and Artesia, California, where Pat grew up. Each location offered a variety of pros and cons ranging from academic resources to accessible tourist facilities, attractions, and distractions.

The prominent Irvine family, for whom the city of Irvine was named, had offered to donate land for a prime Pacific Coast site between Newport Beach and Capistrano Beach. James Irvine, Jr. owned a land grant ranch and had been well acquainted with Dad, Mom, and Don from the early days. William Pereira, a renowned San Francisco architect, presented a superb plan for development of a library complex on that site. All the trustees acknowledged the aesthetic appeal of the architecture in the beautiful rendering. While the site seemed ideal, it held no historic or sentimental value for Dick and Pat, so several trustees from Whittier expressed reservations about that location.

About the same time, William Harrison, Whittier architect and father of my boyhood friend Billy, had prepared an attractive design for development on a hilltop site offered by the city of Whittier.

At the first board meeting, however, a minor dispute emerged regarding the location and the selection process. Several "executive suggestions" from trustees W. Clement Stone and H. Ross Perot brought that meeting to a close with a mark of indecision regarding site selection.

Subsequently, John Ehrlichman, counsel to the President, suggested I survey all existing presidential libraries and conduct a review of the proposed sites for the Nixon library, being as thorough as possible in considering the appeal of each alternative and the concerns of their promoters.

For me the search began in earnest during the summer of 1970. Along with trustees Clint Harris and Hubert Perry, Dick's friends from Whittier, and William Harrison, I began my tour of all the American presidential libraries then in existence. Clint picked up a new Toronado at the Oldsmobile factory in Lansing, Michigan, and met us at Chicago's O'Hare Airport. From there we drove to the four presidential libraries in the Midwest: Herbert Hoover's in West Branch, Iowa; Harry Truman's in Independence, Missouri; Dwight Eisenhower's in Abilene, Kansas; and Lyndon Johnson's in Austin, Texas.

I especially enjoyed visiting the Hoover Presidential Library and Museum, having admired Hoover since high school. The Hoovers had purchased his birthplace cottage in 1935 and had it restored and moved to its original location on the grounds of the Herbert Hoover National Historic Site. The town of West Branch had undergone a meticulous restoration as a Quaker village settled by pioneer families beginning in the 1850s.

The other three sites had features to commend them but drawbacks as well. Truman's was the first presidential library and museum constructed under the Presidential Libraries Act of 1955. Although not his birthplace, Truman called Independence his hometown. I don't believe the site, which the city donated, had any historic significance for Truman. The one-story building with a full basement did not impress me as a model to follow for Dick's library.

I liked the fact that Abilene did hold historic significance: Eisenhower's boyhood home is located on the library and museum property. The museum, constructed of Kansas limestone, seemed a fitting tribute to Eisenhower's years of service to our country.

Johnson's Presidential Library and Museum provided an example of a facility connected to an institution of higher learning—the University of Texas. I thought the architect had erred in selecting travertine for the exterior of the monolithic structure, because it would discolor and weather over the years.

Following that mid-continent road tour, I visited the Franklin Roosevelt estate at Hyde Park, New York, and the Rutherford B. Hayes home in Fremont, Ohio. Although it received some state and local assistance, the Hayes facility was the only presidential library not supported with federal funds. The Roosevelt and Hayes mansions contained interesting artifacts of their lives and presidencies, but the homes weren't useful models for the Nixon Foundation.

As the competition between several prospects intensified, I decided to take aerial photographs for a bird's-eye view of all the Southern California sites. Val Giannini, my former business partner in the early 1970s, arranged the fly-over and piloted the private plane from Fullerton to San Clemente, then up the coast to the Irvine family's proposed Laguna Hills site, then inland to Whittier and Yorba Linda. My nephew Don assisted me in taking pictures.

*Manolo Sanchez at San Clemente
with Don, Dick, and Ed, c. 1972*
∽White House Photo

Nixon brothers at San Clemente, c. 1972
∽White House Photo

Back in Washington, D.C., I presented my findings to the board, showing them slides of the sites we had toured and other potential sites. I did not draw any conclusions but exposed the trustees to the options. As I recall, my presentation engendered no enthusiasm among the directors.

Dick had avoided revealing any personal preferences. He just wanted the new facility to be a valuable legacy for many generations beyond his lifetime. His only criteria were that the site be readily accessible and a place for scholarly retreat. However, I knew that Pat's memories of her life in Artesia and Whittier were not as happy as those from her later years and that she was averse to having the library located in either of those cities. Although Dick was always a loyal alumnus of Duke University, its faculty had been politically unfriendly. They were only interested in housing the archive papers.

Meanwhile, the family memorabilia collection, which Don and Clara Jane faithfully maintained, had far outgrown the capacity of their two-car garage. Therefore, when the Yorba Linda Birthplace Foundation came to the rescue, storing and even restoring some of the old furniture, another appealing point accrued to the Yorba Linda bid.

Dick's resignation in 1974, however, brought work on the site selection to a temporary halt. The original project had been federally funded under the Presidential Libraries Act, but when he resigned, that funding ceased. Then in the early 1980s, George Argyros, a prominent businessman and owner of the Seattle Mariners baseball team, spearheaded the effort to form a private foundation and raise funds to build the library.

The long process of seeking opinions, finding facts, exploring, examining, comparing, and evaluating culminated in the selection in 1983 of San Clemente as the preferred location. The Library Foundation gave the city a deadline of July 1, 1987, to approve the site, but that deadline passed without action. Then Yorba Linda officials offered to donate Dick's birthplace and the adjacent land. The foundation accepted their offer in October, and ground was broken on December 2, 1988.

I heartily approved of the site selection. A presidential library should be located where scholars and students can work efficiently with the archives, and a presidential museum merely needs to be readily accessible and attractive to the public. But Yorba Linda is an ideal location, because it marks the exact geographic coordinates where Dick began his life and spent his first nine years. He was the only one of five brothers born in that little house our father built.

The foundation and structure of the house were restored and the interior refurbished, making the house safe and presentable to the public. Thanks to Don and Clara Jane, original family heirlooms and furniture, including the bed where Dick was born, show visitors how the home appeared when our family lived there. Dad probably would have been upset, however, if he had known the amount of money spent on the restoration project. He was a frugal man—as he had to be.

On July 20, 1990, the Richard Nixon Library and Birthplace opened at a cost of $25 million provided entirely by private funds.[60] More than fifty thousand people packed the grounds during the ceremony, which included appearances by Presidents Nixon, Ford, Reagan, and Bush and their wives. Gay and I were not able to attend that day but were grateful to the many loyal friends and supporters who brought the beautiful facility to fruition.

ORAL HISTORY PROJECTS

In conjunction with my work on behalf of the Richard Nixon Foundation, in 1973 I initiated an oral history study of Dick's early years and collected data relevant to his heritage. Whittier College agreed to sponsor a history professor to facilitate the project on the early life of my brother. Dr. Fred Binder, president of the college, appointed Dr. Richard Arena to conduct the interviews. Tom Bewley, Dick's former law partner, relayed the request from Drs. Binder and Arena, asking me to help introduce Dr. Arena and open doors to the people who knew Dick before he entered public life.

Funding from Leonard Firestone, a major supporter of the project, enabled Dr. Arena to interview and record people's recollections all over the country. He interviewed relatives and professors at Whittier

---

60 The original Richard Nixon Library and Birthplace Foundation operated the existing facility with a $5 million annual budget without any government support. In 2007, when it joined the National Archives and Records Administration as an official member of the federal system of Presidential Libraries, it was renamed the Richard Nixon Presidential Library and Museum with responsibilities shared between the private foundation and NARA.

College and even went to North Carolina to interview Dick's law professors at Duke University. Evlyn Dorn, Dick's first secretary, and Loie Gaunt, his secretary at the time, transcribed hour upon hour of those taped sessions. Both ladies were loyal to Dick to the nth degree. The resulting transcripts filled many bankers' boxes. The originals are stored at the National Archives repository in Mission Viejo, California, with copies at Whittier College.

Although I would have preferred less introductory material "setting the stage for free and open responses" on the tapes, nevertheless, the transcripts revealed many gems. Dr. Paul Smith at Whittier College described how he and Dick several times had discussed theories regarding the relative effect of events on history versus the effect of great leaders. The "great man" theory—that a leader can affect events of history rather than events themselves controlling the situation—always fascinated Dick. (I also had heard him discuss the historical significance of great leaders.) Another noteworthy interview was of Douglas B. Maggs, Dick's law professor at Duke University, who forthrightly shared his recollections of Dick as an extraordinary young man. And Maggs had a reputation for being blunt and intimidating, but Dick rose to his challenges and gained the professor's admiration.

In addition, Dr. Harry Jeffrey, a history professor, conducted the Richard M. Nixon Oral History Project at California State, Fullerton, focusing on Dick's and Pat's pre-political years before 1946. Relatives, friends, and colleagues were interviewed mostly during the period between 1969 and 1971. Over two hundred of those interviews have been transcribed, edited, and bound. They are available for research at the University Center for Oral and Public History at California State, Fullerton.

WHITE HOUSE TOUR GUIDE

Presidential siblings don't normally enjoy full access to the White House. But John Davies, special assistant to the President and director of the White House Visitors Office, suggested I be granted this privilege, so I could conduct personal tours. Early in Dick's first term, John, an affable, hospitable gentleman, requested a security badge for me to verify my identity already evident from my resemblance to the President. Dick signed off on the plan, knowing I would never abuse the privilege. At any gate, I could use my pass to take visitors through on tours. Although the White House staff maintained tight control, visitors had more access than is possible today with all the threats to security.

Unless Dick or Pat personally invited me, I avoided their second floor residence, but they always made my family and me feel welcome when we were guests. Elsewhere, I could pretty much come and go as I wished, taking family members and friends of Dick's and Pat's on tours of the West Wing, including the Oval Office, Cabinet Room, and Roosevelt Room at times that would not interrupt official business. I rather enjoyed leading those tours.

Expanding Opportunities

A Job in Alaska?

Back in 1962, after I had finished my seven years of active duty in the Navy, Gay, our daughters, and I traveled from our Seattle home to Alaska via the Alaska Highway. I drove everywhere the roads would allow. The state fascinated us with its geological and living natural resources and its rugged beauty. Although the trip was largely for pleasure, I also explored work opportunities. Expecting to find an expanding use for helicopters in Alaska, I contacted a helicopter company based in Anchorage and active regionally, but nothing resulted from my meeting with the owner.

Then in the spring of 1969, Maurice Stans, Secretary of Commerce, asked me to consider an appointment as director of the Federal Field Committee for Economic Development in Alaska. I expressed interest. I knew very little about the position except that it called for economic evaluation of natural resources and for development of proposals for legislation to resolve Alaskan native claims. I already had other business involvements and was not looking for a patronage position, but if that job could utilize my skills, I would consider it. My family and I had enjoyed our Alaskan experience in 1962, so Gay and I thought the prospect of living there sounded altogether agreeable.

Senator Ted Stevens (R-Alaska), Secretary of the Interior Walter Hickel, and representatives of two Native Alaskan groups met with

me in Anchorage. We discussed some of the problems they were facing and considered ways the federal government could help. The most
contentious question involved the Alaska Native land claims issue.
The more I learned about the job, the more attractive the position
appeared. So, the next day I explored the housing market in case I
accepted the offer.

Within forty-eight hours of my meeting, John Ehrlichman called
me from the White House, expressing concern that Senator Ted Kennedy and six others were heading to Alaska as a delegation to study
the same problems I had been asked to consider. Ehrlichman said,
"We have inside information—let's say a tip—that Kennedy's going
to release a statement regarding your prospective appointment to the
Federal Field Committee." He expected Kennedy to say my appointment would be illegal because a rider on the Post Office Appropriations Act of 1967 for the first time precluded members of a family
from working in the same government department. The legislation
was intended to prohibit postmasters from hiring their wives or close
relations, but Ehrlichman warned me the language could easily be
construed to say, "A brother of the President should not work anywhere in the executive branch of the federal government."

"John, I'm glad you warned me," I said. "I'm not here to cause
any embarrassment. I don't really need to accept this job for myself. If
I could do some good, I would, but because of the political noise, I'd
have limited opportunity."

Wally Hickel and Ted Stevens urged me to take the job, but I
didn't think it worth causing a political furor that would only benefit
the media and Dick's opposition, so I headed back to Seattle.

Within thirty minutes of my departure from Anchorage, reporters from *The New York Times* and other newspapers left messages on
my "unlisted number" at home. Ehrlichman also called Gay at work.
Her principal insisted she leave the classroom and come to the office
immediately to answer a call from the White House.

"You must issue a statement to the press explaining that you
really do not want to go to Alaska," Ehrlichman told her.

"But I do want to go to Alaska. I like the state with its wide-open
spaces. Alaska would be a great place to explore with my horses. I
don't particularly want to go to Washington, D.C. In fact, if Ed goes

to D.C., I won't go!" Gay hung up, leaving Ehrlichman to compose his own statement. I don't remember the contents, but the press had a minor heyday with that little story.

When I arrived home, I found our phone unplugged. Gay greeted me with: "I'll put the phone back on the wall. You call them!"

I got through to Ehrlichman and said, "I don't know how the word got out, but it shouldn't have. Government offices are too much like a colander with holes everywhere."

NAVY RESERVE DUTIES

By now I realized that government service was out of the question for me, at least during Dick's presidency. However, I did continue as an officer in the U.S. Naval Air Reserves and, at that time, as executive officer of a reserve helicopter squadron at the Seattle Naval Air Station.

In October 1969, Captain Glen Wallace, my flying partner during my first tour of sea duty eleven years earlier, asked me to travel to Memphis to review the graduation ceremonies at the Naval Air Reserve Training unit, which he commanded in Millington, Tennessee. Captain and Mrs. Wallace and Captain and Mrs. J. E. Godfrey met me on arrival.

As the reviewing officer, I greeted sixty-two basic training graduates and their parents and then toured the station's training facilities. Both the trainers and recruits were doing a superb job, considering the Vietnam War had both shortened and accelerated their training period from ten weeks to four. With that schedule, the Naval Air Station was graduating one company each Friday. I was pleased at how good they looked in such a short time.

At the reception that followed, Captain Wallace presented me with a portrait of myself in uniform and a Naval Air Reserve Training Unit plaque.

Reporters, as usual, questioned me about my influence with the President and my views on his administration. Once again, I assured them I had no influence. I defended Dick's efforts to end the war in Vietnam with honor, stressing that he was totally committed to ensuring there would be no more wars like this one, but he had to listen to a number of experts and review all opinions and strategies.

VOYAGE ON THE S.S. MANHATTAN

While on Navy Reserve duty, I had attended two training sessions at the Pentagon in 1969 and 1970. There I met some fellow officers from Houston, Texas, who were well connected to the oil industry and also affiliated with Project Apollo. My newfound friend, Meyer Minchen, a Navy Reserve captain and self-employed civilian in the oil business in Houston, had set up a luncheon where I met with Apollo 11 Astronaut Buzz Aldrin and Mike Wright, then Chairman of Humble Oil.

In my Apollo days, I had been a mere administrative employee of Bellcomm, working as a technical employment officer, so I felt overwhelmed and honored to be included in that meeting. At the time, Buzz Aldrin had the fame, and I had only a recognizable surname, so why was I there? Reflecting later, I realized that my résumé included reference to my strong interest in energy sources coupled with concerns for the environment. Meyer must have suggested I accompany Rusty Curtis, vice president of Humble's maritime operations, on an evaluation tour aboard the Manhattan, an oil tanker on her second voyage through the frozen Arctic from Baffin Bay in the East to Prudhoe Bay on the north coast of Alaska in April 1970.

The year before, the Manhattan had been the first commercial ship to navigate the Northwest Passage. Humble Oil had leased the extraordinary vessel for three years from Greek shipping magnate Stavros Niarchos. During that time, the company revamped the ship with the understanding that it would have to be restored to its original condition as an open sea supertanker after completion of the project. Humble Oil's modifications included reinforcing the hull and replacing the bow with an icebreaker design, plus myriad other changes.

Humble Oil's mission was to conduct a feasibility study to determine the most efficient, economical, and environmentally friendly way to transport oil from the North Slope: maritime shipment to the East Coast or an oil pipeline south to the Gulf of Alaska. Humble executives, as well as Canadian and U.S. scientists and environmentalists, were all concerned about potential environmental impacts and the pros and cons of each option. In an ocean covered with sea ice, oil spills posed an obvious risk. A spill from a fully loaded ship the size of the Manhattan would be disastrous.

Although I stayed aboard the ship only three days, just getting there from Seattle provided an incredible experience: enjoying clear weather all the way to Bangor, Maine; rendezvousing there with Rusty Curtis and several others; and proceeding in a four-engine Lockheed Jet Star to Goose Bay, Labrador, to refuel. With the skies still clear, we again refueled at Frobisher Bay on Baffin Island and then flew to Thule Air Base on the northwest slope of Greenland. There we disembarked and boarded the ship's helicopter for the final leg of the trip to touch down aboard the Manhattan, which had just started its journey west toward Bylot Island and Lancaster Sound.

Being the President's brother always invited VIP treatment, which I did not want, expect, or need to accomplish my objectives. I certainly did not look for special consideration on this trip either, but there it was in the form of lavish accommodations. After I returned home, Meyer Minchen informed me that I had occupied the stateroom usually reserved for Mr. Niarchos' friend, the grand opera diva Maria Callas.

Representatives from a Canadian environmental group had boarded the ship when I did, and we had many thoughtful discussions with officers of Humble Oil and with each other regarding the advantages and disadvantages of commercial development of the Northwest Passage. Concerned about the environmental impact, the Canadian government wanted to maintain regulatory control of waters under its jurisdiction.

The Humble helicopter provided easy transfers to the Canadian heavy icebreaker, the CCGS Louis S. St. Laurent, which at times sailed ahead and at other times alongside the Manhattan. From the vantage point of the Canadian ship's bridge, we observed the behavior of the ice under stress from the Manhattan's bow—an impressive phenomenon. Four-foot thick sheets of sea ice bent down, turned on edge, and then thrust aside as the Manhattan's sharply raked ice-breaking bow plowed ahead.

A curious fact about sheets of sea ice is that their behavior resembles tectonic plates in the crust of the Earth. The ocean currents play a part, but the wind is the strongest force moving the floating sheets. Pressure ridges form where ice sheets collide, resembling miniature mountain ranges. In comparison, the Earth's crust is a relatively thin layer of solid rock, the lithosphere, floating on a mantle of molten magma. The plates of solid rock forming the crust appear like the ice sheets on the Arctic Ocean in that they also move, but much more slowly and by gravitational forces from the Moon and internal forces in the depths of the Earth.

The Manhattan voyages in 1969 and 1970 proved ships of that type could navigate the Northwest Passage almost year round. The Manhattan easily broke through ice three to four feet thick at up to twelve knots (fifteen mph). Under the enormous mass and power of the ship, the ice just rolled aside, and much thicker ice could be made to yield with more propulsive power. Occasionally, large pressure ridges slowed the ship's progress, but only temporarily. So, ice proved not to be a dangerous obstacle.

However, submerged pinnacles of rock in the uncharted waters of the passage did pose a real risk. The passage had not been charted sufficiently to alleviate concern that the ship could ram into an unseen pinnacle below the surface. Potential damage from a major oil spill in the frozen Arctic would cause long-lasting environmental harm and far greater expense than a similar spill in open water. Mother Nature eventually cures all disasters, but that can never justify stretching the eventuality beyond a human lifetime.

Another consideration was that the project would require a whole fleet of ships like the Manhattan. The expense to build enough ships each 1,000 feet long with a 70-foot beam and propelled with 43,000 horsepower would have been prohibitive. The Manhattan produced more horsepower per foot of beam than any other commercial vessel.

But the pipeline alternative also posed potential problems. Many environmentalists needlessly worried that a pipeline would harm the caribou and other wildlife. The decision boiled down to economics, however; building the pipeline was more cost-effective than a fleet of tankers.

After completing the three-day tour with the Humble Oil executives on a westward cruise of about three hundred miles aboard the Manhattan into Lancaster Sound, we boarded the helicopter for the flight back to Thule. When the Lockheed Jet Star refueled in St. Louis, Missouri, I parted company with the Humble crew and proceeded home to Seattle on TWA.

OCEANOGRAPHIC FUND

In my civilian life, I spent the next several years developing diverse commercial interests and many associations. Although Ted Kennedy's interpretation of a rider on the Post Office Appropriations Act of 1967 led me to decline the Federal Field Committee job in Alaska, I continued to interact with government officials in the course of conducting business. They were there to do a job and to serve the public—but not to employ me.

After the Alaska debacle, I received a call from Secretary of the Navy J. William Middendorf, who suggested I contact Austin Colgate, his former partner in the Wall Street investment firm of Middendorf-Colgate. I readily accepted Mr. Colgate's invitation to join the board of directors and to serve as a sales consultant for the Oceanographic Fund, a publicly traded mutual fund established to find investors in ocean-related industry.

From 1969 to early 1972, I spent about 20 percent of my time working for the New York-based Oceanographic Fund, evaluating the profit potential of specific companies involved in ocean-related activity: oceanic research, development of equipment, and evaluation of sustainable use of resources. Most of my efforts involved traveling from city to city to conduct public forums on ocean industry and to promote interest in this work. I believed then, and still do, that one of mankind's most pressing needs is to continue exploring and developing the oceans—below, within, and above the surface. The United States can and should maintain strong leadership in the seas.

One of the corporations taking on these ventures was Tenneco Oil Company. I visited Deepsea Ventures, Inc., its subsidiary, to investigate the methods they were developing to mine significant quantities of manganese nodules from the seabed. Discovery of mineral resources at the bottom of the ocean had inspired several prospecting endeavors and raised my own geological curiosity. Nodules strewn across vast areas of the deep seas presented an economic prospect that at first seemed worthy of the Oceanographic Fund's consideration for investment. However, exploitation of such a remote resource would depend on the success of Deepsea Ventures' initial efforts. Soon after my first visit to the operations base in Hampton Roads, Virginia, I suggested that objections from a few concerned scientists and uncertainty over legal issues would discourage any substantial investment in harvesting the ocean bottom. Together with similar recommendations from others, the Oceanographic Fund opted to drop the project.

I also worked with Tap Pryor, an Oceanographic Fund Board member, inventor, and marine scientist as well as a fellow Naval Aviator. He had arranged for the Oceanographic Fund Board of Directors to convene at his father Sam's Hana Ranch Resort on the east end of Maui. Not far from the resort, Sam Pryor, Pan Am Airways' co-founder and former president, lived in a beautiful private villa perched on a promontory overlooking the churchyard where Charles Lindbergh was buried. Sam and Charles had been close friends through the years and neighbors for the last six years of Lindbergh's life. During our stay, he told us some fascinating stories about Lindbergh.

Affiliation with the Oceanographic Fund opened a whole new world of associations for me. Jon Lindbergh, Charles and Anne Morrow Lindbergh's son, also served on the board. A Naval officer and a marine biologist, he had considerable experience in aquatic life science. Gay and I went to dinner at his home on Bainbridge Island, Washington, where he had set up an experimental fish farm, a new industry in those days.

SEA GRANT ADVISORY PROGRAM

Ron Linski, the director of the National Water Resource Institute, nominated me to serve as one of the advisors to the University of Southern California's Sea Grant Program in 1969. In this advisory role, which involved only a small percentage of my time, I was asked to comment on their list of prospective projects.

Nationwide, a network of university-based Sea Grant Programs focuses on issues related to coastal marine and Great Lakes research and education. These universities work in partnership with private industries, states, and the National Oceanographic and Atmospheric Administration (NOAA).

LAW OF THE SEA COMMISSION

In 1970 or 1971, Dr. Martin Anderson asked me to recommend candidates to serve on a presidential commission studying law of the sea. Dr. Arthur Burns, a prominent economist and Dick's appointee as chairman of the Board of Governors of the Federal Reserve System, was heading up the commission. Burns, who influenced Milton Friedman's free-market economic theory, believed in strengthening private industry, so he wanted to recruit commission members with industry experience to counterbalance the academics. He hoped the businessmen would provide perspective on how academic suggestions would affect businesses.

Because of my experience on the Oceanographic Fund Board of Directors, I suggested Ed Shannon, former chairman of Santa Fe Drilling Company, and F. Ward Paine, founder of the Oceanographic Fund and president/managing partner of Ocean Science Capital Corporation, a Palo Alto, California, based venture capital partnership. I felt those two mavericks would likely offer refreshing ideas, because they were not part of academia. Burns agreed with my assessment and appointed them.

ECOFORUM

The week after my brother took office, a major environmental disaster occurred. A subcontractor's error had led to a natural gas blowout at a Union Oil Company platform off the coast of Santa Barbara, California, on January 28, 1969. Tragically, the spill could have been prevented if the contract driller had set the casings in tight rock at 5,000 feet below the ocean floor rather than in the permeable rock at 3,500 feet. The resulting spill covered an 800-square-mile area that killed and injured thousands of birds and other marine wildlife.

Visiting the site on March 21, Dick said:

> ...what is involved is something much bigger than Santa Barbara; what is involved is the use of our resources of the sea and the land in a more effective way and with more concern for preserving the beauty and the natural resources

that are so important to any kind of society that we want for the future.

I don't think we have paid enough attention to this. All of us believe that, all of us who have watched America grow as it has grown so explosively since World War II.

Looking toward the end of the century in the next 25 years—and the decisions we make now will affect the next 25 years—that is why I have set up within the Cabinet a Cabinet group for the environment which will consider not only problems like this, but the broader problems like the use of our resources in a away that will see that we have all the material progress that we need, but that we have that material progress not at the cost of the destruction of all those things of beauty without which all the material progress is meaningless.

That is what we believe, and I think that the Santa Barbara incident has frankly touched the conscience of the American people. It made headlines in Santa Barbara. I can assure you it made headlines in Washington and New York and all over the nation.

As a result of that, we are all thinking, in this administration, of this problem and we are going to do a better job than we have done in the past. It is up to the Federal government to provide the leadership, and I know in the state here we will have all the cooperation of the state and the city.[61]

Many say the catastrophe spawned the modern environmental movement and paved the way for the National Environmental Policy Act of 1969 and the establishment of the Environmental Protection Agency in 1970. In 1970, Dick signed a law making oil spills

---

61   "Remarks Following Inspection of Oil Damage at Santa Barbara Beach: March 21, 1969," *The Public Papers of the Presidents—Richard Nixon 1969* (Washington, D.C.: Office of the Federal Register, National Archives and Records Service, General Services Administration, 1972) 233.

a federal crime, for which the responsible companies had to pay the costs of cleanup.

◡: ◠

I, too, was concerned about how people and corporations could preserve our natural resources for the future and was working on a concept I called EcoForum, the objective of which was to provide a venue to discuss, exchange, and debate facts, opinions, issues, and challenges relating to the Earth's fragile ecology.

At the time I was serving on the Board of Directors of the Oceanographic Fund, Dr. Richard Fleming, chairman of the University of Washington's Oceanography Department and a fellow director of the Oceanographic Fund, introduced me to Val Giannini, who was running another ocean science capital company named "Northwest Oceanographers," of which Dr. Fleming was also a director.

Val and I met and came away of one mind that a great deal of the emerging angst and controversy over pollution and its regulation could be dissipated by having knowledgeable people share information, views, and concerns publicly in an orderly manner.

Val and I joined forces, changed the name of Northwest Oceanographers to EcoForum, Inc., and designed a TV panel show on which there would be one or more industry representative(s), a scientist or environmentalist, and perhaps a state or federal government representative to discuss ecological issues in a structured setting. I would moderate the show as a facilitator, not as an advocate of any position. We had also enlisted the help of Winter D. Horton, Jr., a TV film producer and cofounder of KCET public television.

I had a policy of telling Dick before doing anything with public exposure, and he usually referred me to John Ehrlichman for his opinion. In this case, Ehrlichman vetoed the TV panel show plan.

Next we proposed documentary films on environmental issues, such as cinematic versions of reports (e.g., the voluminous University of Southern California report on the Santa Barbara oil spill) or films for industrial companies recounting the extent of their considerable pollution control efforts, for which they were receiving scant credit.

One company I felt could have benefited from public exposure to its cleanup efforts was Union Oil (now a part of Chevron). The corporation had to spend huge amounts in both time and money to cap the oil rupture caused by its subcontractor's negligence and to clean the Santa Barbara harbor and beach. Their efforts, along with those of volunteers, actually left the beach cleaner than it had ever been. Not commonly recognized is the fact that oil has been seeping from the coastal shelf onto the beaches of California for eons. Certainly the magnitude of the human error far outweighed the natural seepage, but the reaction of many to stop drilling at all costs was not prudent.[62]

However, with so much uncertainty and fear in the private sector about regulatory and legal issues, corporations didn't want to court publicity. Industry executives weren't ready for that degree of public candor on the subject of pollution control, and EcoForum's documentary film initiative never got off the ground. "Green advertising" came decades later.

EcoForum went on to perform studies for large clients that included Bechtel, Weyerhaeuser, Armco Steel, Bendix, and Pacific Gas and Electric. But EcoForum never achieved its original goal of providing an open forum for environmental information, ideas, and opinions.

I bowed out of the company when I went to work on Dick's reelection campaign in early 1972, and EcoForum disbanded in 1976 when Val was appointed deputy special assistant to President Carter.

J-TEC ASSOCIATES

While I served on the Oceanographic Fund Board, Ward Paine introduced me to the world of venture investment specializing in technology companies like J-TEC Associates of Cedar Rapids, Iowa.

Robert Joy, a physicist extraordinaire, had teamed up with Theodore Johnson, a World War II veteran with a law degree. In 1968, they founded J-TEC, a small business in Cedar Rapids that manufactures sensors and metering devices used in atmospheric and oceanographic science and in chemical, industrial, aeronautical, and

---

62 After the spill and the resulting environmental restrictions on drilling imposed by the State of California and the federal government, new oil drilling came to a standstill. An unintended consequence of these restrictions is the growing U.S. dependence on foreign oil, a topic debated in the 2008 presidential and congressional campaigns. I believe technology and environmental regulations have greatly reduced the risk of such disasters. Oil drilling and a clean environment can coexist.

mining engineering. The company developed very elegant solid-state flow meters and anemometers to measure liquid or gas flow with extreme accuracy—right down to barely moving. Being solid state, the device has no spinning propellers or any other fragile moving part. The Army's M-1 tank makes use of the technique with the anemometer in its fire control computer system. The National Data Buoy System called for their installation on all buoys at sea to measure wind flow. Flow meters also are used in industrial processes and chemical plants.

The company captured my imagination when I joined in 1969. For five years, I worked as director, sales consultant, and product dealer. In fact, before ever visiting China, I sold some sensors and related equipment to the China National Technical Import/Export Corporation. The Chinese Ministry of Coal Mining wanted to test the flow meter as a mine draft sensor to detect dangerous accumulations of explosive gases in coal mines. When the air stops moving in an underground coal mine, methane gas builds up, and methane becomes very explosive when mixed with oxygen. Mine safety, especially in coal mines, demands careful monitoring of underground atmosphere as well as an awareness of structural stability in the country rock, the matrix surrounding the valuable ore. Being able to serve a worthy cause made my job most gratifying.

World Travels

Dick had always encouraged me to become aware of geopolitics and to get involved in world affairs, so I jumped at every reasonable opportunity. I've completed six journeys around the world, traveling in both directions, and have taken many other foreign trips, nearly all on business.

Europe

My first experience with foreign travel as a civilian came at the invitation of Dick Hansen, founder and president of Soladyne, a company in Cedar Rapids, Iowa. Ted Johnson had become well acquainted with Hansen and recommended that I accompany him on an upcoming business trip to Europe in 1969. Soladyne had developed a new telecommunications technique and needed to find a suitable partner such as Siemens in Bavaria, Thomson CSF in France, or Lucas in Britain before attempting to enter the competitive marketplace. Hansen garnered some interest in his proposals, but we returned home with more doubts than encouragement.

That trip served as a whetstone, sharpening my curiosity about what Americans could offer government-controlled industries like Deutsche Bundespost. I didn't see innovations in the nationalized telecom systems like I had witnessed at Bell system companies such as Bell Labs and Western Electric. Bureaucratic inertia in Europe impeded modernization, while American private enterprise maximized creativity and efficiency, thus promoting a robust economy.

However, for me the cultural side of the trip made up for much of what we found lacking in our business meetings. First, an executive tour of the Mercedes Museum in Sindelfingen; next, a self-directed excursion to the Notre Dame Cathedral in Paris; and finally, a box seat for a performance of *The Great Waltz* at London's Drury Lane Theater.

ETHIOPIA AND ASIA

Wayne Field, my good friend in Minnesota, had dreamed of owning a professional football team in Seattle, proposing to call it the "Seattle Kings," and he had envisioned them playing in the Kingdome, which was under construction at the time. Bolder investors outbid him for ownership of the team, however, and the Seattle Seahawks emerged instead.

Unable to acquire the football team, he decided to explore investments around the world. He loved to travel, so we got along well on that score. In April 1973, Wayne asked me to bring Gay and accompany him and his wife Delores to Ethiopia. He had found an opportunity there: Emperor Haile Selassie had a 12,000-acre experimental farm to propagate improved strains of cotton. Wayne wanted to see whether he could participate in developing it beyond the experimental stage.

Departing the States on Pan Am Airways, we arrived at London's Heathrow Airport on April 17 for an overnight and then flew to Amsterdam where we obtained visas for Ethiopia. We took advantage of our brief time to visit the miniature village of Madurodam in The Hague. Austin Colgate had suggested we stop there, thinking the village might serve as a model for a display at the future Nixon museum. We enjoyed the tour, marveling at the minute detail of the airport, shops, houses, canals, and Dutch landmarks, built on a scale of 1:25, but the idea of a miniature city or White House didn't fit into the plans for the Nixon Library.

We checked out of the stately Amstel Hotel for an early flight to Rome with a four-hour layover before continuing to Ethiopia. Don, who worked for Marriott at the time, had arranged for an old friend and Marriott employee in Rome to take us on a quick tour of the city. He picked us up at Fiumicino Airport in a big old Mercedes 600 and drove us on a whirlwind tour. With such a short time before our flight to Addis Ababa, we certainly could not do justice to Rome, but at least we got an introduction to the vastness of the city and some of its artifacts.

In Addis Ababa on April 20, we checked into the Hilton Hotel, where Don intercepted us by message, telling me to contact the U.S. Embassy. The next morning I called the American ambassador, who said, "You must stay at the Embassy." So, we spent only one night at the Hilton. A relentless promoter, Wayne had let it be known at the Embassy that President Nixon's brother was with him to survey the experimental farm.

Immediately the Embassy notified the Emperor's staff of my arrival. Dick and Emperor Selassie held each other in high regard. The Emperor had visited the White House early in Dick's first term. He saw to it that one of his sons, Ras Mengesha Seyoum, Prince and Governor of Tigray Province in northern Ethiopia, would drive us to the countryside. In his Mercedes sedan, we headed east of Addis Ababa to the Awash Valley game preserve, where we saw lions, giraffes, and many other animals and birds native to the region.

When we returned to Addis Ababa, Wayne rented a twin-engine aircraft to accommodate the four of us on a fly-over to survey the Emperor's plantation. From the air, we took some pictures, so Wayne could better visualize the opportunity for investment. Whether or not he visited the experimental plantation, I do not remember. Gay and I never saw the site.

Spending only three days in Addis Ababa, we noted that, in spite of the country's poverty and drought, Ethiopia also had much to commend it—friendly people, abundant wildlife, ancient culture, and a university doing avant-garde medical research on parasitic ailments like schistosomiasis, a disease conveyed to humans by a species of snail prevalent in tropical streams and rivers.

The highlight of the trip was our audience with Emperor Selassie, who was in the waning days of his reign, although no one knew it then. During our long visit, he pleaded with me to convey to President Nixon how much distress his country was suffering because of the Sahel drought, a periodic occurrence in that part of Africa that devastated agriculture and killed thousands of people and livestock. "We are able to pump water and irrigate that plantation," he said, "but my people are suffering terribly, because they have no technology to lift them up, and we need technical help. We need aid—not so much money but assistance in developing the technology—to bring water to the surface, so the people won't have such a hard life. We're going to be overtaken if nothing is done. The Communists are right outside the door. Please be sure to convey our need to your brother, and tell him we are a great friend of the United States and want to continue our close relations."

Before our scheduled departure from Addis Ababa, Don sent me a message saying he wanted Gay and me to meet him in Tokyo on the way home to explore East Asian business prospects. I rearranged Gay's and my tickets to continue around the world to Tokyo via Bombay (now Mumbai), Bangkok, and Hong Kong, so a lot more travel lay ahead. Meanwhile, Wayne and Delores flew home via Europe. After further evaluation of the prospect, Wayne decided not to pursue an investment in the experimental farm.

~: ~

Gay and I arrived at the Bombay airport late at night. On the ride to the Hotel Surf-n-Sand at Juhu Beach, we agreed we wouldn't want to visit that dismal place again soon. Perhaps we were traveling through the poorest part of Bombay, but what we saw depressed us all the way to the hotel. We felt deeply for the plight of the people.

Wading in the Indian Ocean fulfilled a dream for Gay, who has always been crazy about sandy shores. Fortunately, the middle of the night provided balmy air for a brief stroll. We had only a few hours before the continuing flight eastward. Unfortunately, I made the mistake of eating a raw salad at the hotel restaurant, and for several days, I paid the price.

From Bangkok, we flew on to Hong Kong, where we stayed overnight at the Peninsula Hotel—one of those elegant, overpriced antiques. Then, on April 25, we flew to Tokyo and checked in at the Hotel Okura across the street from the American Embassy. By that time, I was really sick from the Bombay salad, so the hotel called in their house doctor, who, of course, was Japanese, and spoke no English. Gay discovered that he spoke some Italian, however, so with her introductory knowledge of the language, she determined that the diagnosis of _non stitiketsa_ in Japanese-Italian simply meant "traveler's revenge."

In Tokyo, I recovered enough for a meeting with Don and his attorney, Stanley McKiernan. We also met with Don's future business partner, Toshiaki (Aki) Kawaguchi, who a few years earlier had been the Japanese secret service agent responsible for protecting Prime Minister Kishi during visits from foreign dignitaries. Aki had approached Don to help him launch some new businesses in Asia and elsewhere. Feeling uncomfortable with business proposals involving technology, Don assumed I could help him steer clear of scams. He persuaded me to come on board.

❦ ❧

After returning home, I relayed Emperor Selassie's message to Dick, as had the ambassador through the State Department. Dick, of course, was well aware of the dire situation in the Sahel, a region of savanna stretching from the Horn of Africa to the Atlantic Ocean. He responded, "Don't worry about it. I'll do all I can."

The U.S., in fact, was already sending aid to nations hit hard by the drought. But I was wary of how much more support the U.S. could render. Regardless of what the President might have suggested, foreign assistance had always suffered the vagaries of congressional lethargy, and the U.S., of course, had other pressing priorities. I never learned whether Congress approved additional funds for Ethiopian drought relief.

In May 1973, Emperor Selassie returned for another state visit to the White House, but his days as Ethiopia's leader were numbered. On September 12, 1974, a group of Marxist government officials and soldiers deposed the Emperor in a violent coup, ending his reign of nearly forty years. Placed under house arrest in Addis Ababa, he died under suspicious circumstances on August 28, 1975. A disaster ensued when the Communist forces led by Mengistu Haile Mariam came to power, imposing a military dictatorship and a reign of terror.

I considered Haile Selassie a great leader, absolutely loyal to his people and a true friend of the United States. But no matter how great a leader one is, he or she will always have detractors and pretenders to the throne. Dick and I grieved his loss and the loss of many innocent lives in the wake of Mengistu's ruthless takeover of Ethiopia.

~: CHAPTER 9 :~

"NIXON NOW MORE THAN EVER"

Being President in the midst of the Vietnam War and a politically volatile situation in the U.S., Dick had little time to focus on his 1972 election campaign. He had no choice but to rely on staff and volunteers to run the day-to-day operations. Former Attorney General John Mitchell and I served as the national cochairmen of the Committee to Re-elect the President (CRP). My position was nominal; Mitchell actually managed the campaign.

At the campaign headquarters in Washington, D.C., I got to know Jim McCord, a former CIA security officer, and G. Gordon Liddy, counsel to the CRP finance committee and former FBI agent. (Both were later arrested for the Watergate break-in.) In fact, Liddy had interviewed me when I first joined the campaign. After reviewing my curriculum vitae, he advised me to resign from the University of Southern California's Sea Grant Advisory Committee, because it sounded too much like a government position, which it was not. "There can be no conflict of interest here," he said.

Failing to see how my role in the program could ever be construed as a conflict of interest, I ignored his suggestion. Nevertheless, as I reflect on subsequent events, I realize there is virtually no limit to the desperate contrivances of political enemies. Therefore, the CRP had to be very careful to avoid any appearance of divided loyalties and influence peddling.

I moved back to D.C. in February, but Gay and the girls stayed home, so they could continue with work and school. During the campaign, I went home for a brief visit about once a month.

Anne Dore, my public relations advisor, trained me on planning effective presentations and coached me on public speaking and getting all the talking points down pat. She advised me to answer questions willingly, even those posed by political opponents. Reiterating what Dick had told me on many occasions, she said, "You'll get questions that are fully loaded. Be sure to unload them before you try to answer. Don't give closed answers to open questions."

ON THE SPEAKING CIRCUIT

From mid March to just before Election Day, the committee kept me on the road most of the time as a surrogate for the President. Although political assassinations had occurred in the 1960s and the country was still rocked by violence in 1972, I traveled without security protection.

For the most part, people treated me with respect, enthusiasm, and eagerness to hear what I had to say. Because Dick and I shared a similar political philosophy, I seldom consulted with him about my speeches. On the road, I related memories of growing up with Dick as my much older brother and surrogate father, and I told the crowds why we needed "Nixon now more than ever"—a major campaign theme.

During my amateur campaign speeches in 1972, my message often included Frank Nixon's nineteenth century republican philosophy, blended with a strong dose of Milhous reserve. I presented a simple yet forceful reminder that Americans were increasingly threatened with the extinction of essential ingredients underlying the success of our form of government.

The opposition was twisting the meaning of the founding fathers' words, so I'd refer to that beautifully succinct statement of purpose embodied in the Preamble to the Constitution: "We the people, in order to form a more perfect union ..." Remembering what Dad had taught my brothers and me, I'd say, "The verbs in that series of infinitive phrases need to be taken seriously. Where it says 'to provide for the common defense' and 'to promote the general welfare,' we should not try to reverse the meaning. Since the Great Depression and the New Deal, we've gone in the other direction, and it's time to reverse the trend. Of course, we have to do it carefully. Socialism develops out of a need and strong inclination all of us have to take care of one another. But help should come privately through churches, individual contributions, and genuine personal compassion rather than through big government programs. If people are really crippled, strictly limited government aid can help them, of course, but we don't want to give crutches to someone who's not lame, thus teaching him to walk with a limp."

～ ～

Event organizers would call the headquarters, asking for a speaker to present Dick's positions. Rob Odle handled surrogate programming and schedules. An advance man would make all the arrangements for my flights, ground transportation, hotels, contacts, room set up, and so forth. In all cases, Ron Walker took charge of the advance operations. With his skills, he readily found employment as a special assistant to the President following the election, and he eventually founded what became known within the administration as the "Advance Man's College."

I crisscrossed the nation, visiting 45 states—8 trips to Pennsylvania alone—and 165 cities, towns, and villages. With the goal of covering the whole country, the committee launched me on 155,000 miles of air travel—more miles than anybody else in the campaign amassed. One advantage of spending so much time on airplanes was that I could learn people's thoughts on issues of the day. I would strike up friendly conversations with fellow passengers. Sometimes they refused to believe I really was President Nixon's brother, but the "Nixon nose" usually settled the question. There's no mistaking that nose.

With United Airlines being the predominant carrier to my most common destinations, I frequently laid over at its hub at Chicago's O'Hare Airport. The year before, I had purchased a lifetime membership to the United Red Carpet Club, because I could foresee extensive travel in my future. When I flew for the campaign, a beautiful United hostess named "Carol" always met me at the plane. Every one of them was named "Carol." For the whole year, a Carol would walk me to the Red Carpet Room.

I didn't campaign in Alaska, Arkansas, Mississippi, North Dakota, or Rhode Island. The Republican Party in Alaska felt their state was so solidly in the Nixon column that a trip wasn't necessary. Polls also showed North Dakota firmly for Nixon. In the two southern states, political contests were brewing that the CRP wanted to avoid, so I stayed away. Although I drove through Rhode Island more than once on campaign swings, the committee scheduled no activities there.

Perhaps all my traveling wasn't necessary with the election looming as a landslide for my brother, but the CRP wouldn't take any chances, because the outcome was so crucial for the country and the world. We believed a McGovern victory would have meant capitulating to Communist forces in Southeast Asia.

With all the international and domestic pressures Dick faced in 1972, he could not take time from his executive duties. My serving as his surrogate not only freed him from devoting much time to campaigning, but it also provided political and community organizations with an acceptable alternative: a speaker who shared the Nixon name, appearance, voice, and philosophy.

Most of my stops were goodwill appearances—ceremonial openings of campaign headquarters, ribbon cuttings, state fairs, parades, business and industry gatherings, Chamber of Commerce meetings, factory tours, ethnic celebrations, breakfasts, dinners, and so forth. Some of the more interesting or unusual events included a luncheon with petroleum industry employees' Desk and Derrick Club in Oklahoma City, the one-thousandth Boys Club opening hosted by Mayor Richard Lugar in Indianapolis, and a community fair called the "Bean Soup Festival" in McClure, Pennsylvania.

Although I hit the campaign trail in March, my first surrogate speaking assignment was to fill in for Martha Mitchell, wife of Attorney General John Mitchell, in a speech at the Indiana Republican Women's Conference on April 19. She had refused to appear, complaining of stomach cramps, so I spoke to the ladies in Indianapolis. They were curious about Martha, who had a reputation for being outspoken. From what I heard, it seemed that she was suffering from severe emotional problems. I felt sorry for her and her family. John Mitchell eventually resigned to care for his ailing wife.

Other troubles began to surface in the 1972 campaign. Some of the campaign staff wanted Don out of public view for fear the paparazzi attention that had plagued him in the past would return. Unbeknownst to Don, the Secret Service or possibly the FBI had tapped his phone in 1971 to protect his family and him from the intrusion of some unscrupulous opportunists trying to get themselves out of trouble by gaining access to the President. I don't know who they were or what they were up to, but the wiretap exposed them to the proper authorities. And the U.S government's knowledge of their identities did ward off the intrusion.

In this and other crucial cases, wiretaps were warranted to protect personal privacy as well as national defense. The press, however, played up the fact that Don's phone had been tapped, as if he had been the one under investigation instead of the one being protected. More than a potential distraction to campaign plans, nasty media could destroy the reputations of the most honorable and loyal citizens.

Another opportunist who attempted to use Don's influence was Robert Vesco, a recent billionaire who had wrested control of the Investors Overseas Services from Bernard Cornfeld, the company's founder. Vesco also tried to implicate me in one of his shady schemes because of my relationship to President Nixon.

Howard Cerny, Vesco's attorney in New York, called me at my office in Washington, D.C., and said, "You've got to come up here today. Fly into Newark. We'll pick you up and take you out to Bobby Vesco's office here in New Jersey. He wants to meet with you personally."

I asked, "What for?"

"We'll tell you when you get here. Come on up."

So, having no speeches to make in the next couple of days, I said, "Okay. I'll come." Sure enough, Vesco wanted to get himself quickly and quietly identified with a contribution of $250,000 to the CRP and get some recognition in return. At the time, I had no idea as to his motives, but if any transfer were completed after April 6, anonymity would be out of the question. On April 7, 1972, the Federal Election

Campaign Act of 1971 would take effect. The new law mandated more stringent disclosure requirements for federal candidates.

"You'll need to talk to Maurice Stans," I said. "I can't accept any contributions. I'm not in the fund-raising game at all. I don't even acknowledge gifts. The Campaign Finance Committee handles that function. I'll try to find him."

Stans had resigned as Secretary of Commerce to head the committee and raise funds for Dick's reelection campaign. A CPA and an experienced government official, he had excellent credentials. Dick considered him a master financial manager. The several times I met him, he was exceptionally kind and helpful to me.

I called his office in D.C. and explained the situation to Arden Chambers, Stans' personal secretary. "Arden, I refuse to get involved in this, but these fellows want to reach Mr. Stans today. They're up against a tight deadline, you know, and they want to do something right away."

"Well, he happens to be en route to New York right now," she said. "He'll be staying at the Metropolitan Club as usual."

Vesco, who was listening on a speaker phone, interjected, "My chauffeur can take you by limo to where Maury will be going."

"If Maury calls his office when he lands, please tell him I'll be waiting for him at the Metropolitan Club to explain what's going on," I told Arden.

"I'm sure he'll call. I'll tell him you'll be looking for him in the bar. Just tell the server who you're waiting for and order some refreshments. You can sign the check to Mr. Stans' account."

I did as instructed, arriving about forty-five minutes before Stans. While waiting, I ordered a Bloody Mary. That signed check for the drink at the Metropolitan Club would prove to be a golden spike in confirming my testimony at the infamous trial of Mitchell, Stans, and Vesco in 1974.

When Maury arrived, I relayed Vesco's message. Then I called Vesco's office from the club's pay phone and said I had spoken with Stans, and it didn't matter to him whether the contribution was in cash or by check, so long as it was received before April 7.

That was the extent of my involvement. I left it up to them to communicate directly. Returning home to Washington, D.C., I had no knowledge of what transpired with respect to any contribution.

~: ~

I had been with the campaign for about three months when one day in May, Tina Karalekas, my assistant at the Nixon campaign headquarters across from the White House, told me that many of the volunteers and paid staff felt overburdened, ignored, and depressed; the White House staff was not giving them the time of day.

Tina said, "We really need to get someone to improve the morale here, and the President is the best one to do that. Some of the volunteers have never met Dick, and they certainly want to."

It's hard for people to realize the President's schedule is so tightly packed that even a slight deviation sometimes requires a presidential decree. Agreeing with Tina that her request was appropriate, I called Bob Haldeman, Chief of Staff, to ask for an appointment with Dick. Steve Bull, a White House staff aide, intercepted my call and referred me to Rose Mary Woods. They both inquired why I wanted to speak to the President directly. I didn't say but assured them they need not worry.

When I finally got access to my brother, I said, "Dick, you need to break away and visit the staff at the CRP. Morale is low over here."

Dick showed up at the headquarters the next day at 10 a.m. First he checked in with John Mitchell in the office below mine, and then he went to the third floor for a brief tour. As we walked through, I introduced Dick to the campaign staff and volunteers. He expressed sincere concern and appreciation for the workers' long hours, and they were delighted he took time to visit. Just by walking through those rooms, Dick lifted their spirits to a renewed level of vigorous commitment, and he provided each of them a lifelong memory of meeting the President.

~: ~

On May 26, I had the privilege of attending the Charlie Duke Day in Lancaster, South Carolina, an event honoring Charles M. Duke, who had a distinguished record as Brigadier General in the U.S. Air

Force and NASA astronaut. Duke, who grew up in Lancaster, served as CAPCOM, the head of the command center on the ground that communicated with the Apollo 11 astronauts for the first landing on the Moon; as backup lunar module pilot on Apollo 13; and as the lunar module pilot on the Apollo 16 flight to the Moon, April 16-27, 1972. Apollo 16 was the first to inspect, survey, and sample materials from the Moon's surface. Duke also served as backup to Eugene Cernan, the lunar module pilot for Apollo 17.

At that event, I ran into a belligerent heckler. While I respect those who oppose violence to the extent they revere life, I can't say the same for the many self-defined pacifists during the Vietnam War who were not peaceful at all toward those with whom they disagreed. Lancaster proved an unfriendly place for an anti-military demonstrator to act up. The audience erupted in a noisy uproar, which ended the man's effort at disruption. As the authorities abruptly evicted him, derisive laughter from the crowd filled the air.

The next event on the campaign trail brought me to Camillus, New York, a small city near Syracuse named after a Roman general. Camillus claims to be the true birthplace of the Republican Party.[63] In 1852, a group of businessmen and government leaders drew up a proclamation protesting the Fugitive Slave Law. The principles outlined in the document formed the basis for the new political party.

There I attended the May 30 Memorial Day ceremonies and rode in the parade. At Camillus Cutlery, founded in 1894, I accepted two gift sets of very fine kitchen knives, one for Julie and one for Tricia. The gifts were processed at campaign headquarters with instructions to thank all the supporters in Camillus for their generosity.

On June 11, I spoke at the first Italian Cultural Festival, a huge gathering in Central Park, New York City. A man in the crowd yelled, "Hey, Nixon, tell your brother to get us out of Vietnam!" Someone else wanted to silence him, but I had access to the loudspeakers and interrupted, "Let him talk. My wife is of Italian descent, and I always let her talk." The Italian Americans roared their approval, putting an end to the heckling that day. A speaker with access to a public address

---

63   Ripon, Wisconsin, and other northern cities also claim to be the Republican Party birthplace based on organized opposition to the Kansas-Nebraska Act, allowing those territories to determine whether to allow slavery within their borders.

Italian Festival NYC Central Park, June 11, 1972

system has a distinct advantage, whereas in South Carolina, the audience took control to silence the protester.

When demonstrators demanded my brother withdraw all our troops from Vietnam immediately, I'd ask them, "Do you want to abandon all those Vietnamese people? We've got to finish honorably and leave in the right way. If we do it right, we can support the South Vietnamese with a unified commitment here at home, so they can develop the means to defend themselves."

Another event I'll never forget was the Victor Awards banquet for sports achievement in Las Vegas on June 17. Susan Davis, the advance person for that engagement, set me up in an exotic suite at the MGM Grand Hotel. When I saw the accommodations—mirror on the ceiling, a heart-shaped tub for two, and pink fabric everywhere—I said to the bellman, "You should give this to a couple on a honeymoon. My wife isn't here!" On rare occasions, Gay could join me, but her full-time teaching job that year precluded much travel.

One of our volunteer speechwriters, had offered me some lines for the event. He was very accomplished—full of ideas—but sometimes the rush of meeting deadlines and trying to handle an unscheduled press interview left me no time to proof a speech before delivering it. That should have raised a red flag. Dick always stressed the importance of getting acquainted with the speech material and the audience, knowing beforehand what to say rather than just reading words from a page.

When I realized I was sharing the stage with Bill Cosby, I thought, "Oh, oh. I should try to be light and humorous here, but there's no time now to prepare, and how can I compete with Cosby anyway?" So, I read the prepared lines verbatim—a big mistake! The speechwriter had written one line saying my efforts in the campaign would probably guarantee an appointment to our embassy in Bangladesh. I really had no idea why he put that in. Maybe he meant it as a joke, but it drew no laughter—only a glare from Cosby. At that point, I immediately resolved never again to read from the podium what someone had written for me without checking it first.

On June 20, I toured a factory and met city officials in Albuquerque. At one of the speaking engagements, Tom Bolack, former governor of New Mexico (1962-1963), introduced me to Pete Domenici, mayor of Albuquerque and Republican candidate for the U.S. Senate. He praised Domenici's expertise in government management—skills readily acknowledged in New Mexico and badly needed in the U.S. Congress. Before departing D.C., I had heard Domenici portrayed as a very sharp, up-and-coming candidate. I could not disagree. That year he won a U.S. Senate seat from New Mexico, which he held longer than any U.S. senator from that state.

The advance man for an event in Texas arranged for me to speak at the National African Methodist Episcopal (AME) Convention in Dallas on June 21. I had planned to tell what I referred to as a *Friendly Persuasion* story of how my mother's forebears and other Quaker relatives in southern Indiana and Ohio had helped slaves from the South escape through the Underground Railroad in the mid-nineteenth century. Howard Marshburn had discovered that William Milhous, our ancestor, had operated a way station at his farm in Benton County, Ohio. Many people passed through that farm. The Milhouses welcomed everybody, no matter who they were or where they came from.

Mom and her sisters had often told stories of Mag, perhaps a former slave or a descendant of a slave, who took care of them as children. In recalling those deeply personal experiences with Mag, they revealed the family's profound commitment to the equality of all humans. Hearing someone use the term "race" had no significance to us beyond a description to visualize a person's physical appearance. I thought those stories of love and respect might help make it clear to the delegates that our Milhous blood and Quaker heritage had produced a firm commitment to the exercise of fairness and goodwill.

Unfortunately, I did not get to address the convention. In every campaign, unexpected and ugly moments do occur, but I have never experienced an event as hostile as the AME convention. The bishops accompanied me as I walked from the wing onto the stage. One of them started to introduce me but couldn't be heard over the uproar. The delegates, mostly women, greeted me with instantaneous screams of "No Nixon! No Nixon! No Nixon!" while waving their hands and shaking their fists in anger.

I told the bishops, "Look, they're not ready for any words from me. I wanted to relate some stories our elders told us during our youth. I had hoped to persuade these delegates to be less antagonistic toward Richard Nixon, but our story will come out in due time. I'm disappointed but won't worry about it. There will be other opportunities to clear the air."

The bishops apologized and expressed their gratitude for my effort to avoid more useless noise. I bade the audience farewell with a wave from the stage and a smile. The angry crowd booed in response.

Outside the auditorium, the embarrassed advance man apologized. I told him, "You couldn't have anticipated this situation without interviewing the delegates beforehand. There will always be a demonstrator or two acting on his or her own, but this appears to have been organized. If you get reprimanded, put it aside. You interacted with the bishops of the AME church, and they gave you no forewarning that the delegates might react with such angry, adolescent behavior."

Moving on to San Antonio, I attended a Hispanic fund-raising dinner as the featured speaker on June 23. There I told stories about growing up in Southern California and hearing Spanish most of my young life, which gave me a point of connection with the audience. Alex Armendariz, a loyal supporter and campaign volunteer, had been looking forward to my visit. Some other staunch supporters came for the event, but Alex apologized for the disappointing turnout.

I said, "Alex, eventually, the Republicans' friendship with the Hispanic world will come around. As far as the Nixons are concerned, friendly persuasion will prevail, and I'm confident our neighbors will see who we are and where we stand."

In Louisville, Kentucky, on June 27, I attended a reception for campaign volunteers. They needed to see someone connected to President Nixon walk through those doors. Speaking to the volunteers, I thanked them for their dedicated efforts and encouraged them to keep rolling for victory.

Meanwhile, I kept rolling; there could be no idle time in my schedule. That evening, in Berwyn, Illinois, I spoke at the conclusion of the International School of Music Concert, complimenting the teenage accordionists who had just performed. I admired the discipline it took to play as well as they did. Virginia Abatacola, sister-in-law of Mario Lanza, the great American operatic tenor and movie star, had invited me to the event. One of her children played in that accordion band.

July began with my attendance as a delegate at the Washington State Republican Convention in Olympia. I was nominated as one of the state committeemen from Snohomish County. I told the enthusiastic group of recruiters, "You know, this is really not my game. Chemistry and physics interest me much more than politics." My plea didn't work. The delegates elected me anyway, undoubtedly because of my famous name rather than my meager political qualifications.

My campaign schedule separated me from my family for weeks at a time, so I welcomed the opportunity for Gay and the girls to accompany me on a car trip to Oregon. On the Fourth of July, we attended the Timber Carnival in Albany, where I gave a speech on behalf of my brother. Then, my family and I watched in amazement as contestants cut through logs three feet in diameter, seemingly with the ease of slicing butter. Our front yard still contains some souvenirs of the "Hot Saw" event—wafer-thin slices of huge trees, products of that competition.

I then drove from Albany south to our next stop in Eugene for the Olympic Trials at Autzen Stadium. At both Oregon events, I had to use a large public address system—my first experience with such powerful audio amplification. The delayed echo distracted me, making it surprisingly difficult to keep speaking.

Tina, my assistant, and Spike Karalekas, her husband, both former residents of Massachusetts, arranged my visit to Boston to address the Business and Industry for the President Committee on July 17. Following the Boston event, I delivered ten more speeches at Business and Industry fund-raisers around the country. Don Kendall, the Chairman of PepsiCo, directed the effort. He took time from his corporate duties to volunteer on Dick's campaign.

WATERGATE BREAK-IN

As the summer progressed, journalists began to question me about the break-in at the Democratic National Committee headquarters in the Watergate Office Building on June 17. Having no firsthand knowledge of what had transpired, I usually answered, "Look, I really don't know what's going on back in D.C., but I do know how hard my brother has tried to find the best people to do the work of his administration.

The Committee to Re-elect the President is also comprised of good people, but in a political campaign, mistakes are unavoidable, and sometimes partisans become overzealous. I believe my brother would never directly order such a stupid and illegal action. The break-in should be kept in perspective, especially because the opposition has sought every contrivance imaginable to discredit my brother's administration. You'll probably find irregularities if you're proficient at 'picking the flyspecks out of the pepper,' but I don't see anything that warrants diverting the President's attention from more important matters of state at this time."

In the spring of 1972, I had become acquainted with Jim McCord, one of those arrested in the incident. Jim and his cohort Gordon Liddy were good, loyal Americans, I thought, but somebody had been determined to discover something. I didn't know what they were after, and I never tried to find out.

When the bungled attempt to bug the headquarters occurred, Dick was vacationing in the Bahamas. Returning to Key Biscayne the following day, he learned of the break-in from an article in *The Miami Herald*. He could see no reason why anyone would do such a foolish thing. Back at the White House, he questioned his aides about involvement of people in the CRP and the White House. They all denied having any part in the break-in or of having known about it beforehand. Dick took them at their word.

With the increasing complexity of domestic and global problems, modern Presidents require a lot of time for thoughtful contemplation and privacy, which is difficult to attain because of their crammed schedules. Along with heightened security, these conditions have led to unprecedented isolation and dependence on selective intelligence. Even though in the public spotlight, a President can become a virtual prisoner in the White House. Dick was always open to new ideas, but he became more and more dependent on the information the staff prepared for him. Many felt he relied far too much on Bob Haldeman to filter information and deny access to people who should have rendered advice to Dick. People in privileged internal positions wanted to press their own ideas and wanted to please "the boss." Too often they slanted information and left out important facts. So, in the beginning of the Watergate debacle, Dick did not have a clear picture of what had happened and who was involved. As time went on, however, he realized certain administration officials and campaign staff had not been honest with him.

After their ties to the break-in began to unfold, Dick did not want to destroy those people for having made serious errors in judgment. He was personally loyal to his friends, close associates, and aides. My guess is that he learned that trait from our mother. And, certainly, he did not want a scandal involving the CRP and his administration splashed all over the press. Such a scandal during the heat of the campaign could have swayed citizens to vote for the Democratic ticket in protest, leading to a McGovern victory followed by defeat in Vietnam. Dick feared that secret diplomatic efforts and national security would be jeopardized.

REPUBLICAN NATIONAL CONVENTION

Arriving in Miami for the Republican National Convention to be held August 21-24, I soon noticed the contrast between the 1968 and 1972 events. This convention lacked any suspense about the identity of the presidential nominee, but it didn't lack excitement. The wrath that had been hurled at the Democratic Party and President Johnson in 1968 over the Vietnam War now turned against the Republicans and President Nixon. Left-wing elements, which had taken control of the Democratic Party and nominated George McGovern in July, showed up in force in Miami. With the President appearing at our convention, security had to be heightened. Miami police and Secret Service agents kept on high alert, dealing with bomb threats and finding homemade incendiary devices, firecrackers, and a black powder bomb in the convention area. They used tear gas to control angry mobs decorated in "peace" symbols and carrying antiwar and "Impeach Nixon" signs. One group marched with a live elephant pulling a casket in an attempt to stigmatize the Republican Party for the lives lost in Vietnam. While some demonstrators remained nonviolent, others caused extensive destruction—all in the name of peace.

The evening of August 22, Dick appeared at an open-air Young Voters for the President rally at Marine Stadium, which Karen Anderson and Dennis Olson, her future husband, attended. That group of well-groomed, well-behaved, young people stood in stark contrast to the unruly demonstrators outside. As Dick walked on stage, the audience chanted, "Four more years! Four more years!" Sammy Davis, Jr., the star performer, led the crowd in singing "Nixon Now More Than Ever" and gave Dick a spontaneous hug. More than any other event at the convention, the youth rally encouraged Dick.

On August 23, delegates and guests were alerted that only people arriving on designated buses would be allowed into the convention because of the danger of riots. Karen described the experience:

> While Dennis and I were waiting in the bus in front of our hotel, a small band of protesters charged the vehicle and shook it in an attempt to prevent us from reaching the convention. We believed they planned to slash the tires and let out the fuel, as some had done to other buses. But they didn't get the chance. Dennis and several other young men jumped off the bus and chased the demonstrators, who fled in surprise.

> The trip to the convention was shocking and frightening. Protesters were demanding rights but denying the right of assembly to us. They broke shop windows, slashed tires of Miami citizens' cars, and turned over bus stop benches, as well as impeding traffic and harassing delegates. One woman who boarded the bus told of a demonstrator knocking out the teeth of a delegate from her state—a man who had had open heart surgery a few months earlier.

> Although our hotel was just a few blocks away, the bus trip to the Convention Hall took about an hour of inching through the rioting crowds. Fortunately, they couldn't prevent us from seeing President Nixon nominated and hearing his acceptance speech in which he said:

> ...I express the appreciation of all of the delegates and of all America for letting us see young America at its best at our convention. As I express my appreciation to you, I want to say that you have inspired us with your enthusiasm, with your intelligence, with your dedication at this convention.

You have made us realize that this is a year when we can prove the experts' predictions wrong, because we can set as our goal winning a majority of the new voters for our ticket this November.[64]

BACK ON THE ROAD

Following the convention, I spoke on August 26 at the Latin Chamber of Commerce in Miami, adding a few comments in the limited Spanish I knew. While many Hispanics tended to vote for Democrats, the Cuban businesspeople in Miami usually favored Republicans. I commended the local entrepreneurs for creating good jobs, telling them that my brother's opponents did not understand the importance of business for the nation and that the Democratic candidate would likely welcome Fidel Castro with open arms. My brother, however, understood that a country cannot be free unless it is strong and stands up to oppressive rulers. Judging by the many good write-ups in the Hispanic press, my speech apparently met with approval.

After a ribbon-cutting ceremony in Annapolis, I traveled to Cincinnati to cut the ribbon for William Keating's congressional campaign on August 30. Again reporters plied me with their standard questions. The publisher of *The Cincinnati Enquirer* strongly endorsed both my brother and Keating, and my appearance received mostly positive reviews.

Out West, I visited the Navajo Reservation in Window Rock, Arizona, on September 10. Peter McDonald, the leader of the Navajo Nation and a gracious host, invited me to its big powwow, which included Native Americans and supporters from Utah and New Mexico as well as Arizona. I had the opportunity to make some remarks at the event. While there, Former Governor Bolack introduced me to Congressman Manuel Lujan, who later became Secretary of the Interior under President Reagan. Bolack, whose range of operation extended beyond his own state, supported efforts of the American

---

64 John T. Woolley and Gerhard Peters, *The American Presidency Project* [online]. (Santa Barbara, CA: University of California (hosted), Gerhard Peters (database.) <http://www.presidency.ucsb.edu/ws/?pid=3537> accessed 23 July 2008.

Indian population to assimilate into the U.S. culture while continuing to honor their native heritage.

When I told Don about the powwow, he asked how many of my acquaintances from the campaign, like Bolack, might be willing to donate a stone specimen from their home state to build a small monument at Dick's birthplace in Yorba Linda. Bolack provided a beautiful piece of banded sandstone from New Mexico for the display. Don and I succeeded in collecting a stone from each of the other forty-nine states, and Don had them assembled. Unfortunately, fifteen years later, during construction of the Nixon Library and Birthplace, workers unaware of the display's significance demolished the fifty-state monument. Don had recently passed away, and no one in the local area knew the origins of the memorial.

∿ ∿

During the 1972 campaign, I accepted invitations to speak on several college campuses. On the evening of October 2, students at Drake University, a top-ranked private school in Des Moines, Iowa, eagerly challenged me on some details of recent history. I explained that my brother's sense of history had not automatically transferred to me, and I encouraged those interested in the past to keep good personal records for the benefit of future generations. As I was speaking, John Parker, the advance man for the event, recorded the following summary of my words:

> Here's a personal appeal to students everywhere. Pour your attention into the mold of history. Make a casting. If you cast yourself into that imperfect frame of reference, the casting will help you appreciate your own identity. It may even allow you a glimpse of the future. Others before us have created an approximate image of the past by recording what they perceived about the dynamics of their own experience. They may not be called "historians," but most certainly they will have preserved some pieces of history. Thus, if you describe your observations as you work, the result will be an improved image for posterity to use.

*Stone Monument, Yorba Linda, CA –
Specimens from all 50 States*

∽Don Nixon collection

The next day, I spoke at the Women's College of Washington University in St. Louis, Missouri. I encouraged the students to present their questions and then tried to help them see the truth behind the allegations against my brother. Unlike students on many campuses, these women were friendly to me and favorable to the Nixon Administration's plan to end the Vietnam War with honor without retreating from tyranny, as the left-wing opposition seemed to demand. But one young lady, who introduced herself as a professor, asked, "How can the United States justify staying in Vietnam when so many people have been murdered?"

I said something like, "Can you imagine what the North Vietnamese and the Khmer Rouge in Cambodia would do if we were not there?" The students cheered. After responding to another question, I looked around. The professor had disappeared.

My swing through the Northeast began in Bangor, Maine, on October 10. There I met William Cohen, a Republican candidate for the Senate, who later became Clinton's Secretary of Defense. Of course, all of us surrogates in the reelection campaign tried to promote and support Republican candidates wherever we could be helpful. As I continued through the Northeast, speaking at an event in Nashua, New Hampshire, and another in Rutland, Vermont, I could feel the momentum growing in support of "four more years."

Then on October 12, Mayor Stan Makowski met me at the airport in Buffalo, New York. Driving into the city, he ventured some advice regarding my scheduled appearance. He said, "Now, Mr. Nixon, I want you to keep in mind that it's a very ethnic area in and around Buffalo. We have a lot of Polish people here."

"Yes, I've heard that," I said.

"You know why so many Poles have names that end in 's-k-i'?" he asked.

"No, why is that?"

"Well, 's-k-i' stands for 'skill, knowledge, and intelligence.' I recommend you avoid Polish jokes while speaking here."

I got a big kick out of that and heeded his serious advice delivered with a smile. In those days, Buffalo was strong Republican country, and I didn't have any Polish jokes to tell anyway.

The rest of the month and early into November, I made whirlwind stops in Delaware, Maryland, Washington State, Oklahoma, Kansas, Nebraska, South Dakota, Minnesota, Wisconsin, Massachusetts, West Virginia, Washington, D.C., Pennsylvania, Virginia, Illinois, Oregon, Indiana, Florida, Wyoming, and Montana. Some of the states I visited more than once during that period.

Generally, the press treated me with respect and didn't bother me during the 1972 campaign, but on a few occasions, I was besieged by reporters. Even the *National Enquirer* succeeded in setting me up for an exclusive interview on November 3. Prior to my departure to Florida, Dick once again reminded me, "If you're bothered by reporters' questions, you should keep in mind, they're just trying to earn a living. Answer their questions if you can, and if it's not appropriate, say, 'Beg off.' But treat them kindly."

Traveling with Bob McCune, one of our most generous and helpful campaign volunteers, I visited the *National Enquirer* editorial staff and a group of reporters in their headquarters in Lantana. Bob knew one of the editors. To my surprise, I found a relaxed atmosphere at the editorial offices, and reporters pursued quite a decent line of questioning. Instead of focusing on Watergate or the war, they asked about the personal side of my brother—the side few people knew. That gave me the opportunity to tell them of Dick's "deep, loving concern for his family," his valuing of our ideas, and his warmth and humor. I also talked about my close relationship with Dick. The article appeared in the December 24, 1972, edition, so it didn't influence any votes, unless I persuaded some of those reporters.[65]

ELECTION LANDSLIDE

Seventy-two hours before Election Day, November 7, I drove home from Washington, D.C., by way of a brief campaign stop in Billings, Montana, to vote in my precinct and then flew back to D.C.

The Watergate allegations did not affect the outcome of the 1972 election. With prospects of peace in Vietnam on the horizon and an improving domestic economy, Dick and Ted won in a landslide with

---

65 "Edward Nixon Visits The Enquirer and Talks About His Brother, The President," *National Enquirer*, Vol. 47, No. 17, 24 December 1972: 14.

520 electoral votes and 60.7 percent of the popular vote. They lost only Massachusetts and the District of Columbia with a total of 17 electoral votes to George McGovern and Sargent Shriver. Republicans, however, failed to gain a majority in either house of Congress, so Dick still faced an uphill battle to get his legislative agenda passed.

⌁ CHAPTER 10 ⌁
A TERM CUT SHORT

The beginning of 1973 ushered in an exciting and hopeful time, both for the nation and for our family. In anticipation of the two hundredth anniversary of our country's independence during his second term, Dick selected "The Spirit of '76" as the inaugural theme. He even had "The Spirit of 76" painted on "Air Force One."

At that time, Amy, age fourteen, in ninth grade, and Beth, age twelve, in seventh grade, were attending the same junior high school. When they were together at school, Beth seemed to fare better, because Amy would come to her rescue if anyone tried to bully her on account of her last name being Nixon.

Gay and the girls joined me in Washington, D.C., for the inauguration on January 20, 1973, and many of our extended family members who had attended in 1969 made the trip again. Others, who had missed the first opportunity, decided to attend since this might be their last chance to participate in a presidential inauguration.

I had sent inaugural invitations to several old friends and was pleased that two of my fellow Duke alumni came with their wives. Dr. Ed Howard had become head of the Geology Department at Campbell College, and Bob Hope—not *the* Bob Hope, but Dr. Robert Hope from

North Carolina—had earned a Ph.D. in paleobotany, following in the footsteps of our beloved Doc Berry.

Chief Justice Warren Burger, a Nixon Supreme Court appointee, administered the oath of office on a bitterly cold Saturday. Karen Anderson stood on the lawn among a group of Young Voters for the President from Washington State to witness the culmination of many months of volunteer work on behalf of the reelection campaign.

In Dick's inaugural speech, he began on an optimistic note, saying the nation stood "on the threshold of a new era of peace in the world." But he stressed that although the United States would continue to defend peace and freedom, other nations must do their share. In fact, much of his speech dealt with the need for shared responsibility:

> We have lived too long with the consequences of attempting to gather all power and responsibility in Washington.
>
> Abroad and at home, the time has come to turn away from the condescending policies of paternalism—of "Washington knows best."
>
> A person can be expected to act responsibly only if he has responsibility.... So let us encourage individuals at home and nations abroad to do more for themselves, to decide more for themselves. Let us locate responsibility in more places. Let us measure what we will do for others by what they will do for themselves.
>
> That is why today I offer no promise of a purely governmental solution for every problem.
>
> We have lived too long with that false promise. In trusting too much in government, we have asked of it more than it can deliver. This leads only to inflated expectations, to reduced individual effort, and to a disappointment and frustration that erode confidence both in what government can do and in what people can do.[66]

---

66 "Richard Milhous Nixon Second Inaugural Address," *Inaugural Addresses of the Presidents of the United States* Vol. 2, 141.

Dad would have been happy to hear Dick utter those words before a worldwide audience. In fact, he probably would have glowed, knowing that Dick had learned so well the lessons he had taught him from early childhood, and now Dick was passing his philosophy on to all who would listen. How I wished our father could have been there.

Concluding his speech, Dick said:

> Let us pledge together to make these next four years the best four years in America's history, so that on its 200th birthday, America will be as young and as vital as when it began, and as bright a beacon of hope for all the world.

> Let us go forward from here confident in hope, strong in our faith in one another, sustained by our faith in God who created us, and striving always to serve His purpose.[67]

That evening, my family and I and other guests celebrated the climax of the inaugural festivities at one of the five balls around the city. In 1973, the Youth Ball was added for young people between the ages of eighteen and thirty. David and Julie Eisenhower and Ed and Tricia Cox presided over that event, which Karen and her friends attended. President and Mrs. Nixon and Vice President and Mrs. Agnew made appearances at all the venues.

AGNEW'S RESIGNATION

Sadly, the optimism of the 1973 Inauguration quickly faded as Agnew's legal troubles and the Watergate investigation took center stage. During Agnew's term as governor of Maryland (1967-1969), he had gotten involved in some questionable money matters that came back to haunt him. A U.S. attorney in Maryland began investigating allegations that he had received kickbacks from campaign contributors awarded state contracts. Agnew viewed the contributions as a help to meet his legitimate expenses in his role as governor—not as bribes to influence his decision-making. He claimed—and rightly so—that governors commonly received contributions from contractors. Furthermore, the

---

67 "Richard Milhous Nixon Second Inaugural Address" 143.

contractors who had contributed to Agnew were all well qualified for the state contracts and received them on the basis of merit.

Seeing the futility of continuing to fight, however, Agnew entered a nolo contendere plea for failing to report $29,500 in cash contributions on his 1967 income tax. He resigned as Vice President on October 10 and was fined $10,000 and put on three years probation. The press displayed a lot of vitriol toward Agnew, but I always liked him and was sorry to see him leave Dick's administration.

Following Agnew's resignation, Dick wisely decided to nominate Congressman Gerald Ford for Vice President because of his long experience in the U.S. House of Representatives and his reputation across party lines as a man of integrity. Dick felt he possessed the qualifications to fulfill the duties of President, if that became necessary, and he would face no undue opposition in congressional confirmation hearings. Ford was sworn in as Vice President on December 6, 1973.

CHRISTMAS FIRESIDE CHAT

The following week, on December 15, Dick and Pat invited me to the White House for a private pre-Christmas dinner before I returned home for the holidays with my family. Although I never celebrated Christmas at the White House, on several occasions I did visit during the Christmas season. The guest list that night included the Reverend and Mrs. Billy Graham, David and Julie Eisenhower, Congressman Leslie C. Arends (R-Illinois) and Mrs. Arends, Congressman George H. Mahon (D-Texas) and Mrs. Mahon, Senator Robert Dole (R-Kansas), and Senator Carl T. Curtis (R-Nebraska) and Mrs. Curtis. In honor of Helen Mahon's seventy-third birthday, Dick accompanied us on the piano as we all sang "Happy Birthday." Afterwards, Pat took the women aside, and the men retired to the Treaty Room on the family floor.

Dick said, "Manolo, let's have a fire, and we'll sit around the green table in here and reflect on a few things in the world." Manolo Sanchez, Dick and Pat's private butler/valet, always kept wood in the fireplace ready to light. Manolo and his wife Fina, Cuban refugees of Spanish descent, served faithfully and loyally for twelve years as personal household staff.

The fire soon blazed too hot for our comfort, so we extended the semicircle back against the wall. Without missing a beat, Dick continued to expound on the future role of the United States in the community of nations. No other nation or group of nations could even come close to the influence the U.S. had at the time, so he felt it imperative that it maintain its leadership. He commented on the uniqueness of our country—the only nation with a government and a population composed of a cross section of every nation in the world.

We sat spellbound at Dick's knowledge of world affairs and his strategic thinking as he reviewed the regions of the globe and the current and potential leader nations in each. To the best of my recollection, he talked of the Arab world facing serious internal divisions. The Russians had launched a communications satellite for them called ArabSat, but the owner nations couldn't even agree on who was going to program it. The Asian nations were traditionally at odds over resources, both natural and human. For example, Indonesia, a country rich in natural resources with a very large population, and Japan, nearly as populous with a stronger industrial base, had been enemies in World War II. North and South Korea, as well as North and South Vietnam, were in conflict. The People's Republic of China, in spite of its vast territory and teeming population, had not even emerged yet, but they had their sights set on annexing Taiwan and spreading communism. The peoples of the U.S.S.R. and Eastern Europe, hidden by their paranoid leaders from benefits of freedom, needed more exposure to and cooperation with the democratic nations of the continent. Closer to home, Dick noted that stronger ties between North America and Latin America would further enhance prospects for peace through mutually beneficial cooperative ventures. He expressed his belief that the developing countries of Latin America needed to rely more on free-market economic policies in order to overcome their rampant poverty.

For about forty minutes, Dick summarized his views nonstop except for an occasional comment from Bob Dole, who remarked that Dick had a grasp of history and geopolitics matched by no one else in the government.

On other occasions, Dick talked to me privately about world leaders, such as Golda Meir of Israel, Charles De Gaulle of France, and

Konrad Adenauer of Germany, whom he had met long before my own world travels. They were leaders who had a mission, and "They made a difference, not because they wished it, but because they willed it." Dick liked to make a point of that. On the back wall of the Leaders Room at the Nixon Library, these words of Dick's are boldly inscribed.

WATERGATE INVESTIGATION

The Watergate fiasco increasingly dominated the news in 1973 and 1974, with talk of impeachment escalating. Central to the controversy were the tapes of conversations recorded in the Oval Office. I felt sorry for Alex Butterfield, the aide at the White House who spilled the beans about their existence. Why did he even mention the taping system at the Watergate hearings? If we had had a different scenario, future historians could have poured over those recordings, seeing something much different from the reports that emerged during the foul atmosphere of the Watergate era.

Dick had a side few people understood—a fascination with technology. He was not skilled in that field, but when he pressed the button at the 1959 American Exposition in Moscow to show Khrushchev what he could do with a tape, he became enthralled with the prospect of recording events for future generations.

When I visited Dick in New York in 1966, he had asked me to set up a sound system to play classical music on tapes or vinyl records in his study. He appreciated the completed system, because I had installed very high-quality components with a powerful amplifier, AR speakers, and tape and record players. I'll never know if our talk of taping systems had much effect on Dick, but sometimes I blame myself for encouraging him to record tapes. He probably would have figured it out anyway, however, because Roosevelt, Kennedy, and Johnson had used taping systems at the White House, and Eisenhower might have as well.

Reaching his decision early in 1971 regarding the Oval Office taping system, Dick said, "Well, let's do it. The system will be totally out of sight, out of mind. Just let things fall where they may." Voice-activated recording allowed Dick to forget the tapes were running. He didn't have to push a button like Kennedy and Johnson did to turn on their systems.

Dick had intended the tapes to be kept private for his use in writing his memoirs, but he believed historians in the future would find them useful when analyzing his presidency. Documentation, he felt, would lessen the opportunity for them to write revisionist history. He had the system installed not to pry on unsuspecting visitors or to embarrass anyone, but to record all the Oval Office history as it unfolded. History was his most revered subject. He didn't destroy the tapes because of his sense of history. And, of course, Len Garment, counsel to the President, nixed any serious consideration of tape destruction.

Not only were the tapes damaging when not understood for what they were—mainly recordings of brainstorming and bull sessions—but also they were poor quality and difficult to transcribe. Many people do not realize how hard it is to transcribe tapes accurately, especially when several people are talking. Who said what? Did he really say …? Where should the punctuation go? Voices override each other; voices fade in and out. Background noise degrades clarity. Tones of voice are not taken into account in transcriptions. People often speak in fragments rather than complete sentences, and they fill their speech with meaningless utterances (*uh, eh, hmm*). Transcribers must make judgment calls, and they are not always correct. Sometimes they hear what they want to hear, their biases coming into play. Other times they simply misunderstand.

According to Joan Hoff, historian and author:

> As important as they are for studying the Nixon presidency, the inaccuracies in the existing transcripts and the difficulty of faithfully transcribing the unreleased ones mean that, well into the next century, the White House tapes will continue to pose more questions for the conscientious researcher than they answer…[68]

More recently, Conrad Black wrote:

---

68 Joan Hoff, *Nixon Reconsidered* (New York: Basic Books, 1994) xv.

The newly released tapes do not remove previous ambigui-
ties, and, as Henry Kissinger has accurately stated, Richard
Nixon is much better understood reading what he wrote
than listening to the idiosyncratic and inconsistent flow of
what he said to his subordinates.[69]

Another side of Dick few people understood was his bluster. Like
our father, Dick would often say things just to evoke a response, challenging his staff at every turn. And under the extreme pressure of the
presidency, he would let off steam when angry and disgusted with
the shortsighted opposition. Dick stressed the need to be tough and
strong. To relieve stress and to play the devil's advocate, he would say
things that sounded harsh when taken out of context.

The main problem I saw in Dick's relationship with some of his
staff was that at times they took him literally when he did not mean for
them to act upon what he said. They simply missed the point and pursued a shortcut to disaster. The astute ones, however, understood his
methods, knowing the man well enough to realize he often sounded
off with the intent of bringing his mind into sharp focus and laying
out all the possibilities, thus stimulating more free and open discussion with his staff.

MITCHELL-STANS TRIAL

Early in 1974, I answered a subpoena to testify at the infamous trial of
John Mitchell and Maurice Stans in New York. The year before, Mitchell
and Stans had been indicted on charges of conspiracy, obstruction
of justice, and perjury in connection with Robert Vesco's $200,000
contribution to the CRP. Although Vesco had mentioned to me that
he wanted to donate a quarter of a million dollars, he actually gave
$200,000 on April 10, 1972, three days after a new campaign finance
law took effect, making large anonymous contributions illegal. I didn't
know it at the time, but he had intended the contribution to influence
a Securities and Exchange Commission investigation into his activities.
His donation, however, didn't curtail the SEC investigation into his
embezzlement of millions of dollars from Investors Overseas Services.

---

69   Conrad Black, *Richard Nixon: A Life in Full* (New York: PublicAffairs, 2007) 1095.

In the press, a reporter accused me of having been the bagman who transferred the check from Vesco to Stans. The charge was completely unfounded. I had no involvement after my brief meeting with Vesco in 1972, and I never touched his money. I never even saw it.

My testimony on April 5, 1974, as the first defense witness at the trial contributed to the doubt regarding Stans' involvement. I said that Vesco had called me, not Stans, to his office and that I had waited for Stans at the Metropolitan Club. When Stans arrived, I had relayed Vesco's message to him. The receipt I had signed that day for the Bloody Mary at the Metropolitan Club bar corroborated my testimony. Also, I confirmed that Stans' message for Vesco was that it didn't matter to him how he paid—by cash or check, but a cash contribution would have to be received before the April 7 deadline. Apparently, my statements helped convince the jury of the honorable efforts of Stans and Mitchell to abide by campaign finance law. They were both acquitted. Facing other counts, Vesco failed to appear at his trial. He reportedly passed away in Cuba in 2007.

Don was called as a prosecution witness at the trial before I testified, but he had nothing to contribute. He knew Vesco and Mitchell, but that was the extent of it.

Watergate Subpoenas

In the Watergate days, anyone connected with the President, especially his close associates and family, was considered fair game by the press and the Senate Watergate Committee. Don and I both were subpoenaed to testify in June 1974. I don't remember why they were even interested in us, except that Herbert W. Kalmbach, Dick's former personal attorney, had told the committee that Don and I had received and passed along part of a $100,000 campaign contribution from Howard Hughes and that Rose Mary Woods was involved. Neither Don nor I had received any money, and we told that to the committee in no uncertain terms. Regarding Watergate, we had no firsthand knowledge of the break-in or anything that followed. I think the committee was on a fishing expedition, trying to make a case against Don. Being close to the President, he was a target for people trying to make a name for themselves in their efforts to implicate Dick.

At first, Don and I refused to appear in Washington, D.C., but the committee demanded that we answer the subpoena. When we finally appeared before the committee, all they did was swear us in. Then they took a break for lunch—a long lunch.

Elmer Stone, one of Don's very good friends, had volunteered his time to represent us as our legal counsel. During the lunch break, Don, Elmer, and I walked out of the hearing room. Elmer wanted to find an exit that would bypass reporters. He said, "We're going back to the hotel."

"Hold it, Elmer. The committee wants us here for the afternoon session," I replied.

Elmer, a smart and persuasive attorney, disagreed. "No, we will respond in writing to any questions they have. They must submit their questions in writing. After we get your statement on paper, you will appear in person and swear to the facts as written. We don't need to respond to any further subpoenas or questions. We have nothing to add."

As we left the hearing room, I spotted Senator Ted Stevens' office and told Don and Elmer to follow me in. I asked the receptionist, "Does the Senator have access to the basement, so we can bypass the mob of reporters and photographers waiting in the hall to shoot us?"

"Just go out to your right and turn right again. There's a single elevator," she said.

We made our getaway and returned to the hotel, where we worked on the statement we submitted to the committee. But the committee was not yet finished with us. They arranged to meet Don and me in Los Angeles for another interview. Elmer had told us not to do anything unless we were sworn in by a senator.

Senator Daniel Inouye (D-Hawaii), a member of the Senate Watergate Committee, stopped in Los Angeles, supposedly to interview us, but I think he had no intention of doing so. He was actually en route home, so he swore us in and turned the interrogation job over to committee staff. While they kept Don under the gun for close to six hours, they questioned me only about ninety minutes. I don't remember what they asked, but at the time I didn't think the questions pertinent. The staff members were just fishing for anything to embarrass the President, but the fishing line ended up with no fish. We left them with a hook in their mouth.

One fact I refused to divulge was my home phone number. The staff interrogator asked why. I told him the story of my wife being hounded by the press in 1969 while I was en route from Alaska. "How did they get our unlisted number?" I asked. "Was it Senator Kennedy? Was it someone on your committee? Was it someone on a senator's staff? That was a pure leak, and you know it. Sure, I could tell you my phone number, but I'm not going to volunteer it."

The inquisitor quit pressing me. I guess I showed some contempt, a dangerous thing to do, but I was feeling stubborn—the Frank Nixon in me talking back.

After my testimony appeared in the *Congressional Record*, I received several requests to autograph copies of the transcript. Funny the souvenirs people want.

The Watergate investigation took a toll on Don, our families, and me, financially as well as emotionally. I incurred substantial legal fees. Don's final costs were twice mine.

Back in Washington State, I tried to avoid the limelight, keeping as low a profile as possible. With my name and striking resemblance to my brother, however, I couldn't always hide. Out in public, people would recognize me and ask what I knew about Watergate. To protect our privacy, we installed a burglar alarm system and a telephone answering machine—fairly uncommon at the time. Calls from reporters were not returned. I even considered putting a steel fence around our house to discourage reporters and curious sightseers. People actually trespassed on our property to catch a glimpse of our house and me. My family and I just wanted to be left alone during that very difficult time. I didn't realize until many years later just how much our daughters suffered from the notoriety.

During that time, I began to use the analogy of sunbathing. A person unknown to the public can go to the beach, lie on a towel undisturbed, and get a tan. When a celebrity goes to the beach, he or she basks not only in the sun's rays, but also in the public spotlight. At first the attention might seem warm and enjoyable, but such intense scrutiny can quickly inflict a burn more harmful than that of the sun.

The risk of getting burned is especially high for political celebrities who acquire enemies due to the nature of political competition. Families cannot avoid being harmed by the vitriol hurled at their loved ones, and children are especially vulnerable. While some family members may withstand the attacks, many others are devastated. Such constant attention leads them to seek an effective "sun screen." Some go on the attack, finding a good offense to be the best defense. Some distance themselves from the public through spokespersons and bodyguards. Still others turn to addictions to escape the public stares and glares.

That celebrities and their families are put in this position at all is unfortunate. Everyone needs privacy and balance, tempered, of course, by the public's need for certain information. There must be a better way for the public to give celebrities and their families the space to live normal lives. Understanding and keeping a respectful distance are first steps.

STATE LUNCHEON HONORING CROWN PRINCE FAHD

On June 6, 1974, Don and I attended our last event in the White House State Dining Room, a luncheon in honor of Crown Prince Fahd of Saudi Arabia. In the receiving line, Prince Fahd's hand felt warm, but I detected a lack of spirit in his handshake. While lively conversations filled the room during the luncheon, at the head table, the Prince looked very serious and appeared to be suffering from a great deal of jet lag. Nevertheless, he rose to the occasion during an exchange of toasts aimed at maintaining good relations between the two nations. A moderate Muslim, Prince Fahd espoused pro-Western views and became an important ally of the United States when he became king in 1975.

I was seated to the left of Brent Scowcroft, who had replaced Alexander Haig as Henry Kissinger's deputy. Not having been briefed on who he was or where he had been, initially I remained silent and listened, but later he engaged me in a stimulating conversation. As an expert on foreign affairs and foreign policy, he knew the world inside out. Anyone with such knowledge and experience could always get my full attention, and I could see why Dick held him in such high regard.

A few days after the luncheon, Dick departed on a goodwill trip to the Middle East, including stops in Egypt, Saudi Arabia, Syria, Israel, and Jordan, in hope of improving America's strained relationships with those nations and promoting peace in that volatile region. Wes Kewish, a second cousin by marriage on the Milhous side and a resident of Cairo, sent Don and me a message that Dick's trip had been a resounding success in Egypt. Millions of well-wishers had lined the sides of the railroad tracks along the route of President Anwar el-Sadat and Dick from Cairo to Alexandria, waving signs of "Long Live Nixon!" in English and Arabic.

END OF A LONG DREAM

In July 1974, I attended a National War College seminar at Fort Leslie McNair in Washington, D.C. During the final session, a small band of wisenheimer naval officers tried to pin me down on what was going to happen with Watergate. I told them, "You good folks don't have to worry. The Constitution will prevail, and the people will continue living their lives. The United States of America will survive."

At the end of that two-week tour of duty, Don met me in D.C. for a visit with Dick in the Oval Office—the last time we saw him in the White House. He commented that Don and I were holding up well under difficult circumstances. We, however, were concerned about how Dick was faring. Obviously distraught, he opened the top left drawer of his desk and said, "Here are some souvenirs for you. I won't be able to hand out many more of these."

At noon on August 9, 1974, Don's thirty-second wedding anniversary, Gerald R. Ford was sworn in as the thirty-eighth President of the United States. Dick and Pat were airborne somewhere over Missouri heading home to California.

While Dick made mistakes in handling the Watergate affair, he recognized that the office of the President is above any man. Rather than drag the country through a tumultuous impeachment process, which would have diverted attention from crucial foreign and domestic issues, he decided it would be best to let Gerald Ford lead the nation, trusting he would hold a steady course toward their shared goals.

The Watergate era was a bad time for America, but the Constitution did prevail, the presidency was preserved, and the country remained strong. I believe my brother resigned in honor as a painful example to be considered by all future holders of the office. A fighter throughout his life, he lived by the motto "Never give up," but he knew when to put the interests of the country ahead of his own and walk away from the office he revered. As he wrote in *RN: The Memoirs of Richard Nixon*, "This was the nightmare end of a long dream."[70]

---

70   Nixon, *RN: The Memoirs of Richard Nixon* 1088.

❧ CHAPTER 11 ❧
THE NIXON LEGACY

It is true that no one knew the world better than Richard
Nixon. As a result the man who was born in a house his
father built would go on to become this century's greatest
architect of peace. But we should also not underestimate
President Nixon's domestic achievements.[71]

❧The Hon. Robert Dole
April 27, 1994

Entire books have been written solely on Dick's presidential years, and Dick chronicled this period of his life in much depth in his memoirs. My intent is not to recap or analyze all he accomplished but rather to summarize the highlights, many of which I suspect have been forgotten or remain unknown to the general public today.

Cynical citizens often comment that candidates can't be trusted: They campaign on a platform just to get elected and then break their promises once in office. Or they flip flop in the political wind, changing with every new public opinion poll. While some politicians operate in this manner, Dick stayed true to his promises if at all possible. His presidential initiatives closely correlated with his campaign position papers and speeches.

---

71 *Richard M. Nixon: Late a President of the United States: Memorial Tributes Delivered in Congress* (Washington, D.C.: U.S. Government Printing Office, 1996) 7.

A CHALLENGING TIME

Every modern-day President bears a heavy load, but Dick faced an especially daunting situation when he took office. Internationally, the Soviet Union and China threatened the security of the free world at the height of the Cold War. The United States was being torn apart internally by violent divisions over the Vietnam War, in which approximately 31,000 Americans had already died. Students led angry revolts against school and government authorities, and racial tensions erupted across the nation. Political and civil rights leaders, police, and rioters were gunned down on the streets of America. Making matters worse, the economy had entered a downturn spurred by spending on the war and President Johnson's Great Society programs. Inflation and unemployment were rising at an alarming rate. The environment had been largely neglected through decades of industrialization with its resulting pollution and scarring of the landscape. All these areas needed serious attention, but to accomplish any of his agenda, Dick had to gain support from the Democrats in Congress, because they controlled both houses. Few Presidents in the history of the United States have faced such tumultuous conditions upon taking office. Despite Watergate, Dick left the country in far better shape at the time of his resignation.

As Walter A. McDougall, professor of history at the University of Pennsylvania, Senior Fellow at the Foreign Policy Research Institute, and Pulitzer prizewinning historian and author, stated: "Indeed, Nixon deserves enduring credit just for being willing to serve as president in 1969, and enormous credit for achieving as much as he did."[72]

True to character, Dick relished the challenges he faced, tackling his new responsibilities wholeheartedly. He devoted nearly every waking hour to the pressing issues of the day and then had to squeeze in the more mundane ceremonial functions of the office. He worked late into the evening and rose early in the morning to resume his work.

Steve Bull, Dick's personal White House aide, wrote:

---

[72]   Walter A. McDougall, "Why I Think History Will Be Kind to Nixon," 16 August 2004, <http://hnn.us/articles/6709.html> accessed 4 November 2006.

The intellectual and psychological demands on a President are enervating enough without sleep deprivation being added. It would seem that the physical demands of the Presidency would require a young man for the job. Yet Mr. Nixon was nearly 60 when he assumed the Presidency, and he had more energy than a staff whose average age was almost half that.[73] His work ethic and the long hours he devoted to the discharge of his responsibilities were remarkable, and serve as one more reason why he was able to accomplish so much in such a relatively short period of time.[74]

FOREIGN AFFAIRS AND THE MILITARY

At Dick's funeral, Henry Kissinger said:

> In the conduct of foreign policy, Richard Nixon was one of the seminal presidents. He came into office when the forces of history were moving America from a position of dominance to one of leadership. Dominance reflects strength; leadership must be earned. And Richard Nixon earned that leadership role for his country with courage, dedication, and skill.[75]

Since Dick's trip to Europe as a congressman with the Herter Committee in 1947, he believed the United States had to take a leadership role in the world. The threats of communism, fascism, Islamic extremism, and nuclear proliferation made the twentieth-century world a dangerous place. Through extensive world travel and study, Dick developed strategies for promoting hardheaded détente and world peace. As President, he set out to implement them.

---

73 Dick actually had turned fifty-six shortly before taking the oath of office as President in 1969.

74 Steve Bull, "A Day in the Life of the President," Letters From Yorba Linda #59, *Richard Nixon Library and Birthplace*, 26 July 2006, <http://www.nixonlibrary.org/index.php?src=directory&view=letters&srctype=display&ba...> accessed 18 December 2006.

75 Dr. Henry A. Kissinger, 56th Secretary of State, *Richard Nixon Library and Birthplace* <http://www.nixonlibrary.org/index.php?src=gendocs&link=RNfuneral> accessed 17 January 2007.

VIETNAM WAR

Vietnam, of course, occupied a substantial amount of Dick's time as he sought to end U.S. involvement in the war while ensuring South Vietnam's freedom from Communist domination. As he had said in the 1968 campaign, one of his major efforts as President would be to train and equip the South Vietnamese to defend themselves—a process he called "Vietnamization." On July 25, 1969, at a press conference in Guam, Dick spelled out what became known as the "Nixon Doctrine": The U.S. would honor its treaty commitments, but from that time on, our nation would provide economic and military assistance only to countries willing to supply the manpower to defend themselves. However, if an ally were attacked by a major nuclear power, the U.S. would mount a nuclear response.

While Secretary of Defense Melvin Laird promoted Vietnamization and the Nixon Doctrine, Secretaries of State William Rogers and, later, Henry Kissinger, as well as others in the administration, pursued diplomatic efforts through the Paris peace talks, which opened just days after Dick's inauguration. To indicate the United States' sincerity in seeking peace, Dick halted bombing and offered to begin U.S. troop withdrawal. In September 1969, he ordered the return home of 35,000 soldiers. But he wasn't willing to gain peace at any price. Enduring peace had to be won with strength and honor.

Dick issued an ultimatum to the Communist government in Hanoi: By November 1, 1969, North Vietnam must indicate its desire for peace and pledge not to overtake South Vietnam militarily. If those conditions were not met, the U.S. would resume its use of force. In defiance, the North responded that the U.S. must cease its aggression and leave South Vietnam.

Following both the huge antiwar "Moratorium" demonstration in Washington, D.C., on October 15 and the rebuff by the North Vietnamese, Dick appealed directly to the American people in his famous "Silent Majority" speech on November 3. He felt the demonstration had, in fact, hindered the diplomatic peace process, because it encouraged the enemy to keep fighting. In his address, he called for the support of "the silent majority"—those Americans who weren't protesting in the streets. He reiterated his commitment to stay the course in

Vietnam until the North Vietnamese agreed to a fair and honorable peace or until the South Vietnamese could defend themselves.

True to form, most media commentators disparaged Dick's speech, but the silent majority responded with overwhelming support. The magnitude of that response surprised and encouraged Dick. His rating in the polls shot up to 77 percent. Subsequently, the U.S. House of Representatives passed a resolution backing his handling of the war effort.

By the end of 1969, Dick had cut U.S. troops by 115,000, while the South Vietnamese Army grew and assumed more of the combat role, as Dick had planned under his Vietnamization program. But in response, the Communists escalated their attacks, infiltrating Laos and Cambodia.

The situation in Southeast Asia further destabilized when pro-American General Lon Nol deposed Cambodia's Prince Sihanouk in a bloodless military coup on March 18, 1970, while the Prince was in Moscow.[76] The Kremlin, Red China, and North Vietnam suspected the U.S. of plotting and financing the coup. Dick, the CIA, and the State Department, however, had no inkling of Lon Nol's plan.

Meanwhile, the North Vietnamese continued to stall the Paris peace talks, so Dick made the difficult and politically unpopular decision to increase the military offensive in order to bring them back to the negotiating table. He felt the U.S. had to negotiate from a position of strength, and he wanted the North to realize the depth of our nation's commitment to ensuring a free South Vietnam.

In April 1970, the U.S. and South Vietnamese militaries routed the North Vietnamese sanctuaries in Cambodia (Parrot's Beak) and Laos (Fishhook), sites from which the enemy launched attacks in South Vietnam. In those narrow strips of land jutting into South Vietnam, the Communists had set up command posts perilously close to Saigon—just thirty and fifty miles away. Dick viewed the U.S. attacks not as an invasion of Laos and Cambodia, as North Vietnam had done, but as a necessary action to protect Saigon, to prevent the North

---

76 Prince Sihanouk then allied with the Communist Khmer Rouge movement led by Pol Pot, who later overthrew Lon Nol. Pol Pot's harsh policies were responsible for the deaths of an estimated two million Cambodians—one-fourth the country's population—during his reign from 1975 to 1979.

from gaining a stronghold in neighboring countries, and ultimately to hasten the end of this unpopular war. The successful incursion into Cambodia and Laos, which concluded on June 30, resulted in the capture of a large number of enemy weapons and equipment, destroying their ability to launch further attacks on South Vietnam.

In response to the U.S. offensive, more antiwar demonstrations and violence erupted across the United States. University campuses turned into hotbeds of unrest. Radicals bombed ROTC buildings, libraries, and other offices, and urban terrorists kidnapped college and government officials. At Kent State in Ohio, Governor James Rhodes called out the Ohio National Guard in response to the burning of an Army ROTC building and vandalism in town. Protesters pelted guardsmen with rocks and tear gas canisters. On May 4, some of the guard opened fire, killing four students, including two bystanders, and wounding nine others, which ignited a nationwide student strike and even more violent protests. On May 9, approximately 100,000 protesters descended on Washington, D.C. In the 1969-1970 school year, the toll of violence included an estimated "1,800 demonstrations, 7,500 arrests, 462 injuries—two-thirds of them were to police—and 247 arsons and 8 deaths."[77]

Again, Dick believed the increased dissent at home further emboldened the North Vietnamese, hamstrung his efforts to negotiate, and prolonged the war. He was convinced hostilities would have concluded sooner and with a more positive outcome had the United States been as united as in World War II.

Partisanship and political posturing by antiwar Democrats in Congress played a significant role in obstructing the peace process. Senator William Fulbright (Arkansas), Chairman of the Senate Foreign Relations Committee, spoke out strongly against the war and provided a forum for Vietnam veteran John Kerry to allege he participated in and witnessed atrocities committed by U.S. troops. Senator Mike Mansfield (Montana) denounced the war as "a tragic mistake." Senators Frank Church (Idaho), Eugene McCarthy (Minnesota), George McGovern (South Dakota), Wayne Morse (Oregon), and William Proxmire (Wisconsin) joined the criticism. On June 22, 1971,

---

77　Nixon, *RN: The Memoirs of Richard Nixon* 455.

the Senate passed a non-binding resolution calling for the withdrawal of all U.S. troops by the end of the year.

A few Democrats did support the war, however. Senator Henry "Scoop" Jackson (Washington) gained Dick's respect because he had consistently stood firm against Cold War communism. Understanding that the United States' primary mission is to protect its citizens, Scoop strongly supported adequate funding of the Department of Defense and U.S. military efforts to prevent this country from becoming a target. During international crises, Dick could also count on backing from Senators Richard Russell (Georgia), chairman of the Senate Armed Services Committee; John Stennis (Mississippi), ranking member of the committee; James Eastland (Mississippi); and John McClellan (Arkansas).

Throughout 1970-1973, Dick continued to pursue a course of Vietnamization coupled with U.S. troop withdrawal, peace negotiations, and offensives that included bombing North Vietnam. On November 30, 1972, all remaining U.S. troops withdrew from Vietnam, leaving 16,000 advisors and other personnel to aid the South Vietnamese military. When peace negotiations once again broke down in mid December, Dick gave North Vietnam an ultimatum to resume talks within seventy-two hours or face the consequences. And face the consequences they did. Dick ordered the bombing of military targets in Hanoi for a period of twelve days. His strategy worked, convincing the North Vietnamese to return to the negotiating table.

On January 27, 1973, a week after Dick's second inauguration, the official end of the long hostilities occurred when the U.S., South Vietnam, North Vietnam, and Viet Cong guerrillas signed the Paris Peace Accords. Under the agreement, the U.S. would halt military action and withdraw all military personnel within sixty days. The North agreed to an immediate ceasefire and release of all American prisoners of war within sixty days. The first POWS arrived in the U.S. on February 12. Among those landing on February 23 was Lieutenant Commander John McCain.[78]

Although South Vietnamese President Nguyen Van Thieu objected, he finally agreed to the provision allowing North Vietnamese

---

78 The only time I met Senator McCain, on an occasion in Washington, D.C., he expressed how deeply grateful he was to President Nixon for his freedom.

soldiers to remain in his country. Dick privately assured President Thieu that the U.S. would come to South Vietnam's aid if the North violated the peace agreement. The U.S. Congress, however, passed the Case-Church Amendment prohibiting further military involvement in Southeast Asia after August 15, 1973. This action predictably emboldened the North Vietnamese to invade the South without fear of U.S. reprisal.

The Vietnam War proved harder to conclude than Dick had hoped and predicted, but he accomplished what his predecessors had not: He extricated the U.S. from Southeast Asia through a negotiated settlement. The later collapse of South Vietnam should not be blamed on Richard Nixon, but on Congress's abandonment of our ally.

ENDING THE DRAFT

In 1968, Dick had campaigned in favor of ending the unfair and unpopular draft, which President Wilson had imposed in 1917 to supply troops to fight in World War I. With its economically skewed deferments, the system gave an advantage to Caucasian men with the financial means and academic ability to attend college. Others got around the system through draft evasion, fleeing to Canada, or claiming to be conscientious objectors. While draftees made up about 16 percent of the military at that time, they served in a disproportionate number of combat positions in Vietnam and suffered a disproportionate number of casualties.

Dr. Martin Anderson, my coworker at the 1968 Nixon headquarters, had persuaded Dick of the need to institute an all-volunteer military. After Dick's election, he appointed Martin as special assistant to the President. In this capacity, Martin helped establish the fifteen-member President's Commission on an All-Volunteer Force. Thomas Gates, Secretary of Defense under Eisenhower, chaired the committee, which became known as the Gates Commission. Members included free-market economists Alan Greenspan and Milton Friedman, as well as former generals, civil rights leaders, university presidents, businessmen, and a student. William H. Meckling, who strongly opposed the draft, served as executive director. At the outset, five commissioners supported an all-volunteer military, five opposed it, and five were undecided. Together these men hashed out the pros and cons and the impacts of a change. Concluding their work ahead of schedule and below budget, the commission on February 20, 1970, unanimously recommended ending the draft. On January 27, 1973, the day the Paris Peace Accords were signed, Secretary of Defense Melvin Laird announced that American men between the ages of eighteen and twenty-five would no longer be drafted. The legislation authorizing the draft expired July 1, 1973.

We must not forget what a momentous achievement Dick and his administration accomplished by ending the draft. Changing any bureaucracy presents enormous obstacles, but to have reversed a fifty-six-year-old policy demonstrated remarkable vision, tenacity, and skill, especially in the face of opposition from such notable people as National Security Advisor Henry Kissinger, Secretary of Defense Melvin Laird, and top military authorities.

As I can attest, the uncertainty of when or whether one's number is going to be called puts a hold on plans for the future. The Nixon Administration's decision to end conscription profoundly affected the lives of healthy U.S.-born males reaching adulthood since that date. Not having the draft hanging over their heads enables them to proceed with their lives, whether entering a trade, dropping out of college to go into business, as Bill Gates did to start Microsoft, or continuing with postgraduate studies. Many do choose to enter military service, of course, but whatever their decision, young men have had more freedom to decide their life's course since the end of the draft.

And the all-volunteer military proved a remarkable success. The pay raises accompanying the new system made the military competitive with the civilian job market and provided a viable career choice. With all servicemen enlisting rather than being conscripted, the U.S. military emerged as a stronger force than under the draft. For over thirty years, recruits have been better educated and more skilled than their demographic counterparts in the civilian population.

OPENING CHINA

Long before becoming President, Dick dreamed of ways to facilitate opening the Chinese mainland to contact with the United States.

Although an ardent foe of communism, he saw as early as 1954 that the isolation of the vast Chinese nation did not serve the interests of world peace or the citizens of China. Soon after Dick took office, he began overtures to China, including the relaxation of visa and trade restrictions and scientific and cultural exchanges. On July 15, 1971, Dick's announcement of his impending state visit to China aroused high hopes around the world.

Near the end of 1971, I had penned the following poem as a Christmas greeting, which prompted Dick to call from the Oval Office to express appreciation for my thoughts. When I wrote it, I had been focusing on the ideas in the last stanza, hoping to persuade some of my intended recipients on my Season's Greetings list to reflect more intently on the reason for the season. Dick certainly needed no such persuasion. He was way ahead of us all.

WINTER SOLSTICE

It's time for the low noon sun to rise.
Time to open perceptive eyes.
Time to declare what solstice means
Besides the glitter of glistening scenes.

The summer sun will soon be here
In just precisely half a year.
Winter will yield through spring, and then
The high noon sun will wane again.

Time goes around in many ways
To bring us back to these twelve days.
Nights are long this time of year,
Even longer up north of here.

Vision and light go hand in hand.
Yet, even at night in a colder land
Reason and sight are running through
On trains of thought, in clearest view.

To see the light in night's disguise

We must unveil our mental eyes.
Then tell the world what solstice means
Besides the glitter of glistening scenes.

More for thoughts that the season brings
And less to worship material things.
Time to forget the pagan ways.
Time to revise the holidays.
Time to remember where we've been.
Time for children—of kith and kin.
Time to reflect and look ahead.
Time to give thanks for daily bread.

Time to begin a meaningful search:
Time to discern the meaning of church;
Time to find ways for wars to end;
Time for diverging beliefs to blend,

Before the noon sun wanes again.

Ten weeks after writing these lines, I received a card from "RN and Pat" postmarked February 25, 1972, Beijing, where Dick was in the midst of his own meaningful search for peace. On February 21, after many months of negotiations, including Kissinger's July 1971 secret trip to Beijing, Dick made history as the first U.S. President to set foot in the People's Republic of China.

Since coming to power in 1949, Communist Party Chairman Mao Zedong had taken a hard line against the United States, and the Vietnam War only heightened his animosity. Therefore, I daresay no one expected him to agree to any U.S. proposal. Indeed, without Premier Zhou Enlai interacting patiently with Mao, China might not have been receptive to Dick's visit and efforts to normalize relations between the two countries. Zhou Enlai cut through diplomatic red tape, making things happen, even when it appeared negotiations would fall apart. After the U.S. and China became hopelessly deadlocked on a minor point of order, Premier Zhou knocked on Secretary of State William Rogers' hotel room door in Hangzhou. A Chinese Premier taking the initiative to talk directly to the U.S. Secretary of State definitely went against diplomatic protocol, but Zhou determined that the mutually desired objective could be achieved through direct communication. Following his bold action, the problem at hand disappeared.

The delicate negotiations resulted in the Shanghai Communiqué, a joint statement issued on February 27, 1972, by the U.S. and China, pledging to work toward normalized relations. The document clearly described the governing principles in their new relationship. On areas of disagreement between the two countries, the communiqué simply stated their differences, with neither side compromising its principles. Essentially, the U.S. and China agreed to disagree on certain issues, including the existence of an independent Taiwan. With this communiqué, the world stage suddenly revealed a revised balance of power and a new hope for friendship and peace.

DÉTENTE WITH THE U.S.S.R.

On the pragmatic side, Dick and the leaders of the People's Republic of China understood the strategic implications of the agreement. They knew that establishing diplomatic relations went beyond idealism to the recognition that both countries faced a threat from the Soviet Union. The Kremlin, in fact, closely monitored Dick's meetings in China with grave concern. They realized a strong American-Chinese alliance could undermine the U.S.S.R.'s expansionist goals.

Anxiety over the U.S.-China détente played a part in Leonid Brezhnev, General Secretary of the Communist Party, agreeing to a summit with the U.S., in spite of the escalation of hostilities in Vietnam at the time. As he had with China, Kissinger paved the way for Dick's meetings with the Soviet leaders. During the Cold War, the U.S. and the U.S.S.R. had engaged in a massive nuclear arms race. At the summit in Moscow in May 1972, Dick and the Soviet leaders hashed out ten agreements to lessen tensions between the two nations and reduce the risk of nuclear war. Knowing that war would destroy both nations, they tried to create incentives for deterrence. The outcome of the talks included: an Anti-Ballistic Missile (ABM) Treaty in which each side agreed to limit ABM systems; an interim Offensive Agreement temporarily freezing the number of each country's intercontinental ballistic missiles and submarine-launched missiles; an interim Strategic

Arms Limitation Treaty freezing the number of strategic missiles to those currently in existence or under construction; agreements to encourage cooperation in science, technology, health research, trade, and space exploration; and an agreement on twelve Basic Principles of U.S.-Soviet Relations—a code of behavior between the two nations.

MIDDLE EAST

A student of history, Dick realized that age-old conflicts in the cradle of civilization had the potential to explode into widespread violence. During his administration, militant Arabs in the Middle East seethed over the existence of the nation of Israel. Dick foresaw the dangers of Islamic extremism spurred on and financed by Soviet Union-backed Communists.

When Egypt and Syria led a surprise attack against Israel in early October 1973, trying to force Israel out of the territory it had seized in the 1967 Six Day War, the Nixon Administration came to the financial aid of the vastly outnumbered Israeli forces in what the Israelis called the "Yom Kippur War," and the Arabs called the "Ramadan War." Israeli Prime Minister Golda Meir attributed that aid to saving her nation.

The Organization of Arab Petroleum Exporting Countries (OAPEC) reacted by imposing an oil embargo against the U.S. on October 17, resulting in a critical oil shortage, increased prices at the pump, and long lines at gas stations. Although the U.S. suffered because of the embargo, Dick never wavered regarding his decision to aid Israel, which he felt had every legal right to exist and to be free from attack.

Following the cessation of military hostilities, Secretary of State Henry Kissinger went to the Middle East to guide the parties in settling their differences peacefully. These Nixon Administration efforts led to renewed diplomatic relations between the U.S. and Egypt after six years of estrangement. In June 1974, Dick traveled to Israel, Egypt, Syria, Saudi Arabia, and Jordan to cement the progress he and Kissinger had made and to pave the way for further peace efforts. Dick also strengthened U.S. ties with moderate Arab nations such as Morocco and Tunisia.

DOMESTIC POLICY

Some political analysts had predicted Dick would be a status quo President on domestic policy. They underestimated my brother. From day one, Dick took initiative and risks, accomplishing far more than many of his predecessors and successors in tackling complex problems with bold new approaches—not more of the same failed policies of the past. His agenda included expanding and enforcing civil rights, promoting environmental protection, supporting medical research, and reforming the federal government structure and the welfare system.

In evaluating his presidency, we must remember Dick inherited a legacy of big government from his predecessors, especially the New Deal from Roosevelt and the Great Society from Johnson, but those programs had not solved the grave social and economic problems plaguing the nation. In fact, the programs had become part of the problem; people had grown dependent on them. Rather than encouraging people to continue on the government dole, Dick sought to provide incentives so able-bodied people could leave the welfare system and experience the American dream of home and business ownership. Dick stressed the traditional values of volunteerism, individual responsibility, hard work, education, and the viability of businesses, especially small businesses, as the best means of raising the standard of living for all. He encouraged the private sector and individuals to get involved and to use their creativity to solve social problems.

Our parents and grandmother, along with our Quaker heritage, had instilled in Dick a desire to help the downtrodden—the true victims of injustice. Thus, Dick initiated efforts in the field of civil rights and welfare reform. While sympathizing with the plight of the poor, he felt that many of the New Deal and Great Society welfare programs increased family breakdown and contributed to a vicious cycle of poverty. He believed in requiring able-bodied people to work or get job training in order to receive benefits, unless the recipients were mothers of children preschool aged or younger. The Democrats blocked much of Dick's welfare reform package, however, but it laid the groundwork for successful reform in the 1990s.

In formulating public policy, Dick mixed ideology with pragmatism. He said, "We have to try things to prove whether or not the ideas are valid. Don't just let them sit there untested." Contrary to the image many people have of Richard Nixon, he encouraged the sharing of innovative ideas. He would say, "I want to hear from those who have something new to contribute, something that's not been beaten to death already." Had he not proposed legislation to deal with pressing issues, he would not have been elected and reelected. Once in office, a strong leader must stand front and center, but a losing candidate or a would-be leader can only make noise.

When ideas he implemented proved unsuccessful, such as wage and price controls in 1971, Dick acknowledged the error and set about to reverse course. Going against his better judgment and his belief in the free-market system, he took the then-popular action of proposing those controls to deal with skyrocketing inflation. But he phased out the controls over the course of his administration, noting that in the long-term the economy would have been better off with self-correction rather than government tampering.

BRIDGES TO HUMAN DIGNITY

In radio broadcasts during the 1968 campaign, Dick had proposed a series of "Bridges to Human Dignity." As President, his policies reflected his belief in the essential dignity of man. A strong supporter of equal opportunity for all groups, he began right away to extend rights and increase opportunities for people who, because of unjust laws or practices, had been unable to partake of the American dream.

To this day, I think people do not understand how responsive Dick was to racial minorities, women, youth, and the poor. Rather than just talking about problems, he tackled them head-on. His action-over-rhetoric approach helped improve the status of disadvantaged groups, bringing them more fully into the mainstream of American life. Through legislation and executive orders, the Nixon Administration made significant progress toward ending years of racial discrimination, thus opening doors so minorities would have equal access to employment, housing, voting, and education.

Although equal rights under the law provided essential protection, Dick realized these rights alone could not stem the tide of poverty and anger in the black ghettos. And he knew government handouts could provide food and shelter but do nothing to raise people out of poverty. Success of minorities in the job market, Dick believed, was an essential bridge to human dignity. Arthur Fletcher, an American of African descent whom Dick appointed as assistant labor secretary in 1969, became known as the "father of affirmative action." Leonard Garment, special consultant to the President on domestic policy, also deserves much credit for advocating civil rights reforms.

That year the administration established affirmative action programs, setting goals (not quotas) and timetables for hiring minorities. In 1972, Dick signed the Equal Employment Opportunity Act into law. Envisioning a day when the U.S. would be a color-blind society, he believed the need for affirmative action would fade as minorities participated more fully in all aspects of society. He viewed it not as a permanent crutch but as a temporary aid to free people from a cycle of despair and dependency.

Another bridge was black capitalism. Dick strengthened the Office of Federal Contracts Compliance Programs and issued an executive order creating the Office of Minority Business Enterprise in the Department of Commerce. Under his administration, the hiring of minority contractors for large federal projects increased.

During the 1950s and 1960s, the volatile school desegregation issue had angered blacks, parents, states' rights supporters, and school boards alike. When Dick took office, nearly 70 percent of African-American students in the South attended all-black schools. Although having opposed forced segregation laws throughout his political career, he did not support federally enforced busing to accomplish desegregation. Instead, he proposed locally controlled desegregation; those who were affected would participate in developing a solution. His administration's effort directed by Secretary of Labor George Shultz created biracial State Advisory Committees in 1970. By gaining voluntary cooperation of the local communities in seven Southern states, violence was averted, and at the end of that year, only 18 percent of African-American children still attended segregated schools in the South.

Regarding enfranchisement, Dick took a bold approach in not merely extending the Voting Rights Act of 1965, which targeted southern states, but in nationalizing voting rights protection and abolishing literacy tests in the Voting Rights Act of 1972.

NATIVE AMERICANS

In 1968, Dick had also campaigned against the shameful U.S. policies toward American Indians, including deprivation of their ancestral land and demeaning paternalism. With non-natives running Indian programs, Native Americans had lost initiative and morale. He championed their right of self-determination and promoted economic development and health-care improvement.

As President, Dick set out to implement his plan to reform the Bureau of Indian Affairs and U.S. policy toward Native Americans. In a special message to Congress on July 8, 1970, he laid out his plan to honor treaty commitments and reverse the federal government's termination of tribes, which had produced the unintended consequence of overreliance on the U.S. government. In Dick's words:

> The recommendations of this administration represent an historic step forward in Indian policy. We are proposing to break sharply with past approaches to Indian problems. In place of a long series of piecemeal reforms, we suggest a new and coherent strategy. In place of policies which simply call for more spending, we suggest policies that call for wiser spending. In place of policies which oscillate between the deadly extremes of forced termination and constant paternalism, we suggest a policy in which the Federal government and the Indian community play complementary roles.

> But most importantly, we have turned from the question of *whether* the Federal Government has a responsibility to Indians to the question of *how* that responsibility can best be furthered. We have concluded that Indians will get better programs and that public monies will be more effectively expended if the people who are most affected by these programs are responsible for operating them.[79]

Specifically, Dick called for increased funding for Indian Affairs and legislation to strengthen tribal governments and promote

---

79 "President Nixon's Special Message on Indian Affairs, July 8, 1970," *Public Papers of the Presidents of the United States: Richard Nixon 1970* (Washington, D.C.: Office of the Federal Register, National Archives and Records Service, General Services Administration,1971) 576.

economic development. In April 1971, he signed the Alaska Native Claims Settlement Act, which provided natives with 40 million acres of land, $500 million in federal compensation, and $500 million in mineral revenue from lands they gave up. Also, up to 80 million acres could be set aside for national parks, forests, and wildlife refuges.

WOMEN

Believing in equal opportunity for women, Dick increased the number of women appointed and hired in the Executive Branch. To help level the playing field in the workplace, education, and athletics, he established the Presidential Task Force on Women's Rights, included women under affirmative action regulations, and ordered that sex discrimination be added under the Department of Labor's guidelines for contract compliance. By signing Title IX, which prohibited sex discrimination at institutions of higher learning that received federal funding, he strengthened athletic programs for women.

EIGHTEEN-YEAR-OLD VOTE

Despite what young antiwar demonstrators thought of Richard Nixon, he was concerned about youth and wanted to encourage their participation in the political process. In the 1968 campaign, Dick supported extending voting rights to all citizens eighteen and older. The national party platforms of both the Republicans and Democrats, in fact, called for the eighteen-year-old vote. Proponents argued that if eighteen-year-olds could be drafted and serve in the military, then they should have a say in the election process; conscription without representation was unfair. Dick, however, said, "The reason the voting age should be lowered is not that 18-year-olds are old enough to fight—it is because they are smart enough to vote."[80]

In 1970, Congress extended the Voting Rights Act of 1965 to include the eighteen-year-old vote in all federal, state, and local elections, and Dick signed the legislation into law. The U.S. Supreme Court promptly ruled that Congress could establish regulations in federal elections but not at state and local levels. In record time, the states

---

80 *Nixon Speaks Out: Major Speeches and Statements by Richard M. Nixon in the Presidential Campaign of 1968* (New York: Nixon-Agnew Campaign Committee, 1968) 167.

ratified the act, leading to passage of the Twenty-sixth Amendment to the U.S. Constitution in 1971.

Many of the approximately eleven million newly eligible voters cast ballots for the first time in 1972, and despite the strident antiwar, anti-Nixon youth protests, Dick won a substantial proportion of the youth vote.

New Federalism

True to his conservative beliefs, Dick set about to implement "New Federalism"—a plan to reorganize the federal government and restore decision-making to the state and local levels. He believed the unwieldy, wasteful federal bureaucracy stifled business through overregulation and red tape. By dismantling many cumbersome agencies that had outlived their purpose and by consolidating overlapping organizations, Dick sought to diminish the role of big government. He promoted efficiency and effectiveness by insisting that all federal programs meet the Office of Management and Budget's cost-benefit standards.

Under his revenue sharing plan, federal matching funds were sent—no strings attached—to state and local governments, which best knew the needs of their constituencies. The State and Local Assistance Act of 1972 returned more than $83 billion in federal tax dollars to states and local governments. But many congressmen accustomed to handing out federal dollars for pork barrel projects opposed revenue sharing; after all, it decreased their influence back home. The program eventually died.

Judiciary

Regarding constitutional issues, Dick believed the Warren Court in the 1950s and 1960s had crossed the line into political activism rather than strictly interpreting the Constitution. Of course, no President can predict how a Supreme Court justice nominee will rule while on the bench, but Dick's criteria for nominees included strict interpretation. He also sought nominees with keen legal minds and broad experience as attorneys and appeals court judges. Dick nominated Chief Justice Warren Burger and Associate Justices Harry Blackmun, William Rehnquist, and Lewis Powell. Rehnquist, whom President Reagan elevated to Chief

Justice, remained the most stalwart conservative during his tenure on the Supreme Court from January 1972 to September 2005.

WAR ON CANCER

Dick knew firsthand how catastrophic diseases can devastate the afflicted and their families—physically, emotionally, and financially. Not only had he lost two brothers to tuberculosis, but he mourned the death of Elizabeth, his favorite aunt, who had succumbed to breast cancer at age thirty-three. Pat's mother died of cancer when Pat was thirteen, so she had to assume the housekeeping duties for her father and two older brothers. So, when Dick entered Congress, he supported measures to ease families' burdens during times of serious illness.

As President, Dick devoted himself to the War on Cancer, which he announced in his January 1971 State of the Union address. He proposed a $100 million research grant to the Department of Health and Human Services to create a system of National Cancer Centers and to work on developing a cure. Later that year, he directed that Fort Detrick, a U.S. Army biological warfare facility, be converted into the Frederick Cancer Research and Development Center. When he signed the National Cancer Act on December 23, 1971, he said to the Members of Congress: "I hope that in the years ahead that we will look back on this day and this action as being the most significant action taken during my Administration."[81]

While the war on cancer has by no means been won, significant strides have been made since Dick made it a priority.

SPACE EXPLORATION

Since his days as Vice President, Dick had enthusiastically supported space exploration—both for the sake of national defense and for the scientific knowledge that could be gathered. Continuing the Apollo programs of Presidents Kennedy and Johnson, Dick gave the go-ahead for the landing of the Apollo 11 spacecraft on the Moon on July 20, 1969. For a moment, people seemed to forget the troubles on Earth as they watched Neil Armstrong and Buzz Aldrin take their historic first

---

81 "Remarks on Signing the National Cancer Act of 1971, December 23, 1971," *Public Papers of the Presidents of the United States: Richard Nixon 1970*, 1205.

steps. There they placed an American flag and a plaque written by my good friend James C. Humes, a White House speechwriter:

> Here men from the planet earth
> First set foot upon the moon
> July, 1969 A.D.
> We came in peace for all mankind

Bursting with excitement, Dick spoke with Armstrong from the Oval Office by radio-telephone. He said, "Because of what you have done the heavens have become a part of man's world. And as you talk to us from the Sea of Tranquility, it inspires us to redouble our efforts to bring peace and tranquility to earth."[82]

When the Apollo 11 crew splashed down in the Pacific Ocean southwest of Hawaii, Dick greeted them on the aircraft carrier U.S.S. Hornet. From there he rejoined Pat to continue their eleven-day good-will journey, first to Southeast Asia with a stop in South Vietnam, and then to Romania and Great Britain.

THE ARTS

The strong influence of the arts on our family also translated into Dick's public policy. In 1969, he appointed Nancy Hanks to chair the National Endowment for the Arts, which had been established during the Johnson Administration. Under her capable leadership and with Dick's support, government and private funding for the NEA increased. The goal was to make the arts available to all Americans, including the disadvantaged and school children.

Dick favored granting artists and performers a kind of "royal commission" with government supporting only works of beauty and high standards that raise the human spirit, such as classical ballet, symphonies, theater, paintings, and historic architecture. He hoped the funding would result in art that eventually would qualify as enduring contributions to our culture. In later years, however, Dick expressed disappointment with some of the tasteless and profane projects funded by taxpayer money. He even suggested that the federal government could eliminate the NEA to help reduce the national deficit.

---

82 Nixon, *RN: The Memoirs of Richard Nixon* 429.

ECOLOGY

Some claim Dick had little interest in the environment, and that any accomplishments were motivated by political expediency or solely the doing of his aides. From one who knew him well, I can vouch for Dick's commitment to a clean environment. After all, we grew up in Southern California in the days when orange and lemon orchards, avocado groves, strawberry fields, and other produce farms occupied most of the land. Witnessing the Los Angeles Basin becoming an enormous sprawling "house orchard" with smog from industries and vehicles clouding the sky and polluting the environment, he knew government action would be necessary to preserve open spaces and restore clean air, water, and land. And I believe I influenced his views during our talks when I was in college about the destruction caused by harmful mining practices.

Drawing on our discussions and the advice of John Ehrlichman, John Whitaker, secretary to the Cabinet, Egil "Bud" Krogh, deputy assistant to the President for domestic affairs, and others in his administration, Dick addressed long-neglected issues and gave environmentalists a voice. Soon after taking office, he directed that environmentalists, business people, and scientists be brought to the table to discuss and propose solutions. As always, he favored a balanced approach, taking into account the concerns of all parties. He didn't want environmental legislation to unduly burden businesses; that would ultimately harm owners, employees, customers, and the economy. If Congress increased spending, making the program unaffordable, he would veto the legislation, even though he agreed with the intent.

Early in his first term of office, Dick set out to reform the government structure dealing with the environment. His first effort was to establish the cabinet level Council on Environmental Quality. In 1970, Congress approved his plan to create the Environmental Protection Agency (EPA) to promote a cleaner environment and public health. Ironically, liberal senators such as George McGovern, Edmund Muskie, and Ted Kennedy tried to derail those efforts.

In addition to the EPA, Dick's legacy includes passage of the National Environmental Policy Act, the Clean Air Act, the Marine

Mammal Protection Act, extension of the Endangered Species Act, and extension of the National Park system. Dick had long advocated for National Parks, and several new parks were added during his administration.

ENERGY INDEPENDENCE

Dick bears the distinction of being the first U.S. President to deliver a comprehensive message to Congress on the subject of energy, a message he deemed urgent. On June 4, 1971, he told Congress that the challenges were: "one, to find new sources of energy to fuel the economy; and two, to find sources of energy that will not pollute the environment."[83] With increased demand for energy and pressure on our fuel supplies, he predicted increased costs to consumers. To meet the country's energy needs while decreasing pollution, Dick proposed the following goals:

- To Facilitate Research and Development for Clean Energy
- To Make Available the Energy Resources on Federal Lands
- To Assure a Timely Supply of Nuclear Fuels
- To Use Our Energy More Wisely
- To Balance Environmental and Energy Needs
- To Organize Federal Efforts More Effectively[84]

In November 1973, three weeks after the onset of the Yom Kippur War and the ensuing Arab oil embargo designed to punish the U.S. for its aid to Israel, Dick addressed the nation, calling for America to achieve energy self-sufficiency. He named his plan "Project Independence," envisioning a major effort such as the U.S. undertook with the Manhattan Project to develop the atomic bomb and Project Apollo to put a man on the Moon. The Alaskan Pipeline Act, which Dick signed November 16, 1973, was an integral component of his plan.

Continuing the theme of energy independence in his State of the Union Address on January 30, 1974, Dick stated that for the first time in the history of these speeches, energy was the first priority. Although

---

83 "Remarks About a Special Message to the Congress on Energy Resources," *Public Papers of the Presidents of the United States: Richard Nixon 1971*, 703.
84 "Special Message to the Congress on Energy Resources" 704.

an end of the oil embargo looked promising, Dick called for voluntary energy conservation, greater transparency of information provided by oil companies and producers, and research and development.

> Let this be our national goal: At the end of this decade, in the year 1980, the United States will not be dependent on any other country for the energy we need to provide our jobs, to heat our homes, and to keep our transportation moving.[85]

◡ ◠

As I review my brother's accomplishments as President, I believe he profoundly affected our lives today, making the United States a more just society, leading the world toward the fall of communism, and awakening Americans to the need for clean, renewable energy alternatives. I agree with Walter A. McDougall in his assessment of Nixon's presidency. He cited evidence "that Nixon left a mighty legacy, but also that decades may pass before scholars, journalists, and politicians own up to the truth."[86] He continued:

> First, I would argue that Nixon's politics and diplomacy laid the foundations for victory in the Cold War. Nixon extricated the U.S. from the exhausting, divisive commitment of a half-million soldiers to a guerrilla land war in Asia. And even though the Paris Accords failed, for reasons we can debate, America's alliances and posture in the world survived that defeat.

> Indeed, Nixon left America in a far stronger geopolitical position thanks to his strategic alignment with China, which completed the encirclement of the Soviet Union.... The opening to China also ensured that after the Soviet Union collapsed, the result would not be new hot and

---

85 "State of the Union Address: Richard Nixon" (January 30, 1974) *Infoplease* (Pearson Education, 2000-2008) <http://www.infoplease.com/t/hist/state-of-the-union/187.html> accessed 21 July 2008.

86 McDougall 1.

cold wars in the Asia/Pacific, but stability and prosperity throughout the region. [87]

…Nixon's maneuvers at home and abroad made the best of a bad situation, and so helped to make possible the later achievements of Reagan.[88]

---

87 McDougall 2.
88 McDougall 4-5.

∿ CHAPTER 12 ∿
RETRACING FOOTSTEPS

But meaning in life does not derive from the station in life you attain, and the depth of personal satisfaction you feel does not depend on the height to which you rise. Fulfillment comes from dedication and service to a worthy cause, whether as a foot soldier or as the commander-in-chief.[89]

∿Richard Nixon

As Dick often mentioned, he had reached the pinnacle of success, holding the highest office in the land and the most influential in the world, yet he had also descended to the deepest valleys. No prior personal or political crisis could compare with the despair he felt following the resignation, knowing he would always be labeled the first—and maybe the only—U.S. President to resign the office. He could hardly bear the thought that he had let down his family, supporters, administration, and nation. Worst of all, he would not be able to complete the initiatives he had begun, especially his efforts to bring a more lasting world peace.

For Dick and those close to him, the problems didn't let up after he left office. He faced new legal challenges and mounting attorney fees. The press continued to hound him. New and increasingly virulent books spread innuendoes and lies. Supposed friends turned against him, and loyal ones like Bebe Rebozo were accused of all manner of evil. Dick watched with deep disappointment as one aide after

---

89 Richard Nixon, *In the Arena* (New York: Pocket Books, 1990) 44.

another was sentenced to prison. I believe what his friends endured hurt Dick more than the attacks against himself.

Of course, the tremendous stress took a toll on Dick's health. After President Ford pardoned him on September 8, 1974, "for all offenses against the United States," Dick suffered a life-threatening recurrence of phlebitis that sent him to the hospital, where he hovered between life and death following surgery. During his hospitalization and recovery, Julie kept us apprised of his condition.

Yet through all these trials, Dick did not succumb. As he regained physical strength little by little, his determination returned. I had always admired that resilience in my brother: political losses never ultimately defeated him. He would advise me and others, "Keep your spirits up. Keep fighting. When thing's are going against you, you learn life's important lessons." In *In the Arena,* he wrote a prescription—universal principles for overcoming defeats:

> Put the past behind you. Analyze and understand the reasons for your defeat, but do not become obsessed with what was lost. Think instead about what is left to do.

> Do not let your critics get to you. Remember that they win only if they divert you into fighting them rather than driving toward your goals.

> Devote your time to a goal larger than yourself. Avoid the temptation of living simply for pleasure or striving only to leave a larger estate.[90]

ROAD TO RECOVERY

In his hours of solitude in 1974 through 1977, Dick reflected on where he had been and how he could regain his ability to further "the causes of peace, freedom, opportunity, and justice, not only for the people of the United States, but also for all the people in the world."[91] By 1978, he had recovered sufficiently to rededicate himself to this mission

---

90 Nixon 43.
91 Nixon 44.

through writing books, speaking, and retracing his footsteps in countries around the world where he met with world leaders and citizens.

Watergate and the resignation had deeply affected Don and me as well, and we also needed time to heal. At first we sought solace in isolation, avoiding all media interviews. In the initial aftermath of Dick's resignation and during his recovery from phlebitis, Don and I both respected his need for privacy. Living nearby in Newport Beach, Don always kept the door open, saying, "Anytime you need me to do something, I'll be there." And Dick, of course, knew I'd be there for him too. However, it wasn't until after Dick launched into his massive memoirs project in 1975 that Don and I regained regular contact with him. Don visited him before I did, because he lived so close. I don't recall the occasion of my first visit during that period. The memory of that event more than a quarter of a century ago has faded into the recesses of my mind.

~: ~

The D.C. Beltway is notorious for people seeking proximity to those holding high office, trying to curry favor and advance their own agendas. With Dick no longer in a position of power, his political "friends" dropped by the wayside. But he never lacked true friends—those who stuck by him when he had no power to dispense—and they helped him along his road to recovery.

A myth has circulated since Dick's early years that he was glum, never laughing or enjoying himself and never sharing close relationships. In spite of the nickname "Gloomy Gus" bestowed on Dick first by Harold and Don, our more gregarious brothers, and then by his classmates at Duke, he certainly knew how to have a good time. Serious and reserved by nature, Dick generally kept the fun times separate from work and the public eye. But author Bill Adler compiled quotations that revealed my brother as a true American humorist, who had a sharp wit and could bring laughter to his audiences.[92] Even in the years following Watergate and the resignation, when Dick got together with friends, they all let their hair down and had a lot of laughs. Don would tell me stories of Dick enjoying the company of good friends so much that he

---

92 Bill Adler, *The Wit and Humor of Richard Nixon* (New York: Popular Library, 1969) 4.

would play the piano for a while to get everyone warmed up. Then he would stand on the piano bench and lead the crowd singing.

Dick's inner circle included Bebe Rebozo, Bob Abplanalp, and Gavin Herbert. Although reputed to be very different in personality and interests, the four together made quite a team. No matter how the political tides ebbed and flowed, Dick could count on their loyalty. After Dick resigned, they all spent time with him at San Clemente.

I didn't know any of them well, but I met Bebe several times at social events and Bob on one occasion for a business consultation. Gavin serves with me on the Richard Nixon Library and Birthplace Foundation Board of Directors. From my brothers, however, I heard stories about the three and the good times they shared.

Dick and Charles B. "Bebe" Rebozo, a Florida businessman of Cuban descent, became acquainted in 1951. A quiet host and entertainer, Bebe wasn't looking for anything except to be helpful. I think Dick appreciated him so much because he didn't say a lot. And Dick, not wanting to talk a lot either, would tell Bebe, "Drive the boat. I've got to think." Cruising for hours around Key Biscayne provided perfect privacy.

Bob Abplanalp, the son of Swiss immigrants, had made a fortune inventing and patenting an improved aerosol nozzle to dispense everything from spray paint to shaving cream. He first met my brother in 1963 when he retained Dick's law firm to handle legal affairs for his company, Precision Valve Corporation. At that time, Dick had just started his law practice in New York. The two developed a close friendship that soon extended to their families. Bob once described his two heroes as his father and Richard Nixon.

Always loyal and never using his friendship with the President to promote himself or gain anything in return, Bob performed many acts of kindness. After Dick's election in 1968, Bob loaned him money to buy the San Clemente property to be used as the Western White House. He also gave Dick and Pat access to his vacation home on a private island in the Bahamas and use of his yacht.

Gavin Herbert, the only one of the three still living, has diverse business and philanthropic interests. He founded and is chairman emeritus of Allergan, Inc., a California-based worldwide pharmaceutical company that manufactures ultrapure contact lens solution in

China. At the University of California, Irvine, he helped develop and has supported the Department of Ophthalmology.

Don, who met Gavin before Dick did, might have introduced the two. Having a green thumb, Don frequented Roger's Gardens, a large retail nursery that Gavin owns in Corona del Mar specializing in high-grade floral decorations. The two could talk for hours about flowers and ornamental plants. In his small yard overlooking Newport Bay, Don filled every available space with one plant or another. Roses were his specialty, with Double Delight—a white rose fringed with pink—being his favorite.

Don and Clara Jane's youngest son, named "Richard" for his uncle but known as "Rick," inherited the Milhous gift with plants. Watching his father transform the family garden, he became inspired, so Don helped him get a job at Gavin's nursery. There Rick learned the art of creating magnificent wire-framed hanging flower baskets potted in moss.

During the years Dick and Pat resided in San Clemente, Gavin volunteered his time to make sure the grounds of La Casa Pacifica, the former Western White House, remained exquisitely manicured. Wearing his climbing cleats, Rick pruned some very tall eucalyptus trees while Dick and Pat lived there. A bold kid, he scaled those trees without a worry.

When Dick and Pat moved from San Clemente in 1980, Bebe, Bob, and Gavin purchased La Casa Pacifica. Later Gavin bought out the other two, and he and his wife currently make their home there.

Dick also maintained a long-term friendship with W. Clement Stone, philanthropist, author, and trustee of the Nixon Foundation. Perhaps their friendship related to similar life occurrences. Each had suffered the early loss of close family members—Clement's father and Dick's brothers Arthur and Harold. Clement and Dick each had to take responsibility at a young age and contribute to the family income. Truly, each lived the American dream, rising from hardship and poverty to the top of his field. With an investment of twenty dollars, young Mr. Stone, a high school dropout, had bought an insurance agency and turned it into a multibillion-dollar insurance empire. Many people knew him best for his "positive mental attitude" aphorisms and his work-ethic philanthropy.

Clement and Dick shared an interest in Boys Clubs, supporting the organization through philanthropy and advocacy. They believed Boys Clubs to be an important way to keep youths off the streets and foster productive pursuits to prevent delinquency. Often Dick spoke of his desire for children to grow up in a better world, and he admired Clement's efforts to improve the lives of young people.

Dick also enjoyed Bob and Delores Hope's company. He and Bob had a good time poking fun at each other, comparing their noses and golf handicaps. Bob was a "doctor of humor," and Dick valued his friendship, especially his sincere kindness and the depth of thought behind the smiles.

Any list of Dick's friends after he left office undoubtedly would be incomplete, but some who cheered him up included Billy and Ruth Graham, John Wayne, Jimmy Cagney, Paul Keyes, Jimmy Stewart, Ray Price, Frank Gannon, Herbert Kalmbach, Jack and Helene Drown, Clint Harris, Hubert Perry, George Argyros, and Jimmy Roosevelt. These friends, along with Bebe, Bob, and Gavin, came from different walks of life—entertainment, politics, religion, and business—and different points of view. Dick enjoyed each one for his or her unique personality and perspective. Their loyalty played a crucial role in his recovery.

Family Visits

Dick visited us at our home near Seattle only once. The day before Amy's wedding in May 1981, the Secret Service drove him from the airport to our house. His earlier-than-expected arrival caught us by surprise—and not at home. In the flurry of pre-wedding preparations, Gay and I had darted out for some last-minute items for the party at our house that evening.

Answering the door in her slip, Beth hadn't anticipated seeing her famous uncle standing on the porch. Neither was she prepared for the sight of Secret Service agents prowling our yard. Embarrassed, she said, "I was just sewing up my maid of honor gown."

"Oh, excuse me," Dick apologized. Then he set her at ease. "That's okay. Just go on sewing. I'll make myself at home." Going into the kitchen, he poured himself a cup of coffee to pass the time until Gay and I returned.

Reflecting on that incident, Beth described her uncle as being "casual, down to earth, and very gracious—a Milhous trait."

When Gay and I drove up our driveway and saw Secret Service agents on guard, we knew Dick had arrived.

After greeting us, he said, "Riding north on I-5, I asked the Secret Servicemen the name of that beautiful yellow flower alongside the road. None of them knew. What is it?"

"That's Scotch broom, a very bad weed for hay fever sufferers."

"Well, it's beautiful, and someone ought to find a way to make it less troublesome."

Soon the guests began to arrive. We had sent fifty wedding invitations to our immediate family and local friends, but when word spread that Amy's uncle Dick would attend, suddenly two hundred other friends and relatives from around the country asked if they, too, could receive an invitation.

The evening before the wedding, guests filled every nook and cranny of our home. Don and Clara Jane drove up from California, making it one of the few occasions that all three of us Nixon brothers got together following Dick's resignation. The Milhous and Parsons cousins, also from California, arrived.[93] Tina Karalekas, my assistant in the 1972 campaign, Jeannie, her twin sister, and Heidi Hiltgen, a close friend, flew out from Washington, D.C.

Above the chatter, Dick said, "Well, now. Only five days ago, Ed turned fifty-one. It's not too late to celebrate. I think we should all sing 'Happy Birthday' to my kid brother." Pulling out the piano bench, he sat down and started playing. Although I'd seen him honor others on their birthdays, I hadn't expected him to think of me after my birthday had passed.

Later that evening, as the guests departed, a Secret Service agent drove Dick to the Olympic Hotel in downtown Seattle. Preferring classic hotels, my brother admired the Olympic's Italian Renaissance architecture and always chose to stay there when in Seattle.

About two hundred people attended Amy's wedding on Saturday, May 9, at the Rainier Club a few blocks from the Olympic Hotel. Fortunately, we had given Ellis Jones, manager of the club, sufficient

---

93 Lucille Parsons was the daughter of my aunt Elizabeth Milhous Parsons.

warning to accommodate the expanded guest list. Adding to the festive atmosphere, local musicians Phil and Pam Boulding played their Celtic harp and hammered dulcimer. In another room, Bob Gronenthal, Gay's music teacher, plucked his classical guitar, delighting guests with beautiful, soft compositions. In the Rainier Room, with its enormous walk-in fireplace, people mingled while enjoying an abundance of superbly prepared hors d'oeuvres.

Rising to the occasion, Dick chose an appropriate time to address the whole group to pay tribute to the bride and groom. Then he shared a few impressions of Seattle and the Pacific Northwest, even noting the beauty of Scotch broom: "My brother here tells me that yellow flower along the freeway isn't good for us, but I wish it could be. It's beautiful." Only a nonresident would exhibit such an appreciation for our ubiquitous Northwest weed.

The following day, Dick spoke at an event at the Olympic Hotel sponsored by the King County Republican Party. Never passing up an opportunity to see him when he came to Seattle, Karen Olson attended and got a hug from my brother in the receiving line as they reminisced about how quickly the years had passed since his visit to the Anderson home in 1962. She brought him up to date on her family and activities. That was the last time they met.

A couple of women I had worked with during the 1972 campaign had flown from Washington, D.C., just to see Dick. "Would it be all right if we got in the receiving line even though we've met him before?" one of them asked me. Apparently those considerate ladies hesitated to take up more of his handshaking time, knowing how tiring it can be for a celebrity.

Seeing their eagerness, I encouraged them. "Go right ahead, even if you've met him before!" So they worked their way through the line, met the man face-to-face and hand-to-hand, obviously gratified and excited.

Whenever I traveled to New York or thereabouts on business, I would visit Dick and Pat. I happened to be there on my fifty-second birthday, May 3, 1982. Ray Price, who would turn fifty-two May 5, and W. Clement Stone, who would become an octogenarian May 4, joined us that evening for a birthday dinner Dick hosted for the three of us at the 21 Club, a former speakeasy converted to a renowned restaurant in Manhattan. Among the guests were Roy Cohn, chief counsel (1953-1954) to Wisconsin Senator Joseph McCarthy, and Bill Simon, who had served as Secretary of the Treasury under Presidents Nixon and Ford. Later he became a financial advisor to the Nixon Library and Birthplace Foundation. Bill immediately impressed me with his kind offer of personal assistance in my business pursuits.

~: ~

On another occasion, I attended a party Dick and Pat hosted at their home on East 65th Street in New York in honor of their Secret Service agents. Dick made some opening comments and proposed a toast. Then he said, "If you notice that the fellow standing at the far end of the room bears a resemblance to me, it's because we had the same parents." The agents responded with hearty laughter. I think they all knew me anyway.

One of them standing nearby said, "You know, we like this man because he treats us well and levels with us. We feel comfortable with him, and for that, we admire and respect your brother."

Dick always maintained good relations with the Secret Service, and they appreciated him long after he left office. He showed consideration for the personnel through kind words and thoughtful acts. If they had only twenty minutes or less left on their shift, he never would ask them to drive him somewhere. Instead, he would wait for the next shift. Maybe it was his Navy training: "A good officer always takes care of his men."

In 1984, Pat gave up Secret Service protection, and Dick discontinued it in 1985, saving U.S. taxpayers over $3 million a year. Mike Endicott, the Secret Service agent assigned as his driver, retired and joined Dick's staff to provide personal security and serve as chauffeur.

After one of my visits with Dick at his office in Manhattan, he had an appointment uptown so offered me a ride back to my hotel on the way. Getting out of the limousine, I stepped right on Mike's foot as he held the door open for me. Even today, I'm embarrassed to remember that incident.

VIEWS FROM OVERSEAS

Following Dick's resignation, I began a new career in real estate but didn't find it suitable to my skills or interests; sales did not appeal to me. I also became discouraged by the sneers of those who couldn't resist making derogatory comments about my brother. Finally, I decided to seek employment outside the U.S., where the Nixon name was still highly respected. I embarked on several overseas ventures, traveling to lands Dick had visited. In the Middle East, Africa, Asia, and Europe, people would ask, "Aren't you President Nixon's brother?" When I'd answer yes, they'd tell me of their great respect for him, not understanding why he had to resign.

Don also traveled extensively overseas during this period—often with me. For both of us, retracing Dick's footsteps brought healing. Everywhere we traveled, we saw evidence Richard Nixon had been there. We received positive receptions because our brother had cracked open new doors and windows. Even after Watergate, his popularity around the world remained strong.

When we returned to the U.S., we shared with Dick the words of admiration we had heard. That buoyed his spirits and encouraged him to travel to some of the countries he had visited while in public office.

JAPAN

The change in plans that had rerouted me from Addis Ababa to Tokyo in 1973 eventually resulted in a three-year job evaluating technical aspects of projects for Donald Nixon Associates Corporation (DNA) based in Newport Beach, California. I served as executive vice president and consultant to Don and his partner Toshiaki "Aki" Kawaguchi. The DNA Corporation focused on developing prospects in foreign trade with various manufacturers worldwide. On behalf of the company, Don and I made many trips to Japan, visiting such corporations as Nippon Electric (NEC), Ishikawajima Harima Heavy Industries (IHI), Kanebo Silk Company, and Marubeni—one of Japan's largest trading companies.

Iran

In 1977, I accompanied Don and Aki to Tehran, Iran, representing Mikimoto, a Japanese company that specialized in cultivating, sorting, grading, and marketing cultured pearls. With the objective of developing new markets, the company asked DNA to explore venues in which to display the pearls as fine art. In Tehran, we met Husang Ansary, former Iranian Ambassador to the U.S., who had warned me early in Dick's presidency that people would want to use me to gain access to my brother. Now he said he could do nothing to assist us in our specific quest, but he suggested we visit the new art museum and meet the director and his staff, who were preparing for a fine arts show. The ambassador admired the director, because he displayed artwork of all kinds—not just the geometric mosaics permitted under Islamic law.

I found the design of the museum impressive. The architect had employed innovative techniques using indirect lighting, so sunlight never fell right on the works of art. Through this effective method of display, the public could view the paintings or other objects without risking ultraviolet deterioration of the art.

In Tehran, Don and I stopped at a Persian carpet shop. Cyrus, the Jewish proprietor, proudly showed us his guestbook, pointing to the recent visit and sale of a carpet to actress Elizabeth Taylor. Then he showed us his fine inventory of prized carpets woven in the cities of Isfahan and Kerman. Don paid a considerable amount for an exquisite wool and silk carpet inscribed with the weaver's name and appraisal at the foot, the end placed farthest from Mecca during prayer time.

Feeling frugal as usual, I said, "They're beautiful, but I don't want to pay that much for a prayer rug, because I'm not going to pray on it."

"But I have a really beautiful silk Ghom carpet for you at a bargain price," the rug merchant said, not wanting to lose the opportunity for a sale. Ushering Don and me into his back room, he unrolled and spread out a magnificent rug in tones of brown, gold, ivory, and green. He told me he couldn't sell it—or even display it—to Muslims, because the carpet portrayed "graven images." The artist's name could not be revealed, so the whole bottom row had been stripped off. Those animals and trees painstakingly woven in the intricate design didn't bother me. I had no intention of worshipping the images, so I paid Cyrus's "deeply discounted price" and bought that Ghom.

Many years later, I learned that the design of my carpet is typical of those woven in Ghom, a Muslim holy city south of Tehran, and they are, indeed, highly prized.

ᴖ᛬ ᛬ᴖ

Our visit occurred during the reign of Shah Mohammed Riza Pahlevi, a pro-Western monarch who had instituted a program of socio-economic reform, including land redistribution, promotion of literacy, and emancipation of women. His secular government encouraged a more open society. Dick, a long-time friend of the Shah's, applauded his progress in bringing Iran into the twentieth century. However, Dick had confided to me his concern the Shah was moving too fast toward modernizing a country steeped in theocratic tradition. Making matters worse, the Carter Administration was pushing him to reform Iran at an even faster pace. Dick worried that radical Islamists would incite rebellion against the Shah's policies, thus turning back the clock.

Unfortunately, Dick's prediction came to pass. When Ayatollah Khomeini seized control of the government in 1979, he cracked down against everything Western and undid the Shah's reforms. Shortly after the Shah's ouster, he and Dick met in Mexico, where he expressed bewilderment and disappointment that, after trying to comply with President Carter's wishes, the U.S. government let him down. As Dick wrote:

> The United States and the West have lost a staunch friend in an explosive area of the world where we desperately need friends who will act as a stabilizing force. . . . Iran has lost an effective leader.[94]

Dick strongly believed in supporting friendly governments overseas, even though they did not meet U.S. standards of democracy and human rights.

> Especially when a key country like Iran is involved, we must never forget that our choice is usually not between the

---

94 Richard Nixon, *The Real War* (New York: Warner Books, 1982) 299.

man in power who is our friend and somebody better, but between him and someone far worse.[95]

EGYPT

From Tehran, Don and I traveled on to Cairo, my first of several business trips there over a two-and-a-half-year period under the auspices of the DNA Corporation, which represented several large Japanese companies doing business in Egypt. Don assigned me the job of organizing a field office in Cairo to assist our clients in Middle East trade matters. On numerous occasions, he would join me in Cairo, and at times I would meet with him at the DNA headquarters in Newport Beach.

Our work in Egypt occurred during the administration of President Anwar el-Sadat, successor to pro-Soviet President Gamal Abdel Nasser, who died in office in 1970. Nasser had virtually destroyed the entire infrastructure in Cairo while building an army sympathetic to the Soviets. We saw remnants of Nasser's socialist debacle everywhere—rubble in the streets and a barely functional telephone system that at one time had rivaled systems in Europe.

For example, I could lean out the window of my sixth-floor flat and motion to a young volunteer courier loitering on the sidewalk below. Eager for a tip, he would quickly ride the elevator, if we had power that day. Otherwise he would run up six flights of stairs and appear at my door. I'd then hand him a message to deliver to a business contact across the street. With a big smile, he would dash off, thankful to have earned some money. I could communicate faster by sending the messenger than by dialing the person on the telephone.

Nasser certainly had left Egypt in shambles, and Sadat had an enormous clean-up task. Don's enthusiasm for DNA's involvement in Egypt stemmed mainly from his admiration of Sadat's modernization efforts. As our primary objective, Don and I assisted a consortium of Japanese clients in bidding on a contract for a telecommunications retrofit to repair the damage caused by neglect during Nasser's regime.

---

95 Nixon 299-300.

Realizing his country's future would improve by allying with the United States rather than the Soviet Union, Sadat took courageous steps toward a negotiated peace with Israel and liberalization of economic policies in Egypt. Dick, who had met with Sadat in Cairo in June 1974, regarded him highly as a man of integrity and vision. But Sadat's policies, like those of the Shah, incurred the wrath of Islamic extremists, one of whom assassinated him in 1981. My brothers and I were deeply saddened by the loss of this great leader.

My second objective in Cairo was to assist IHI in their bid to build and operate a ship-breaking facility in Alexandria. The job would entail dismantling old, retired steel ships of all kinds and retrieving and recycling the metals and other items of value.

During one of our early trips to Cairo, Don and I were staying at the Le Meridien Hotel downtown on Al-Gazeera Island in the middle of the Nile River. As I walked out of the hotel restaurant ahead of Don, a Westerner stopped him. Introducing himself as Dennis "Denny" Freed, high school principal of Cairo American College, he said, "I couldn't help but notice the striking resemblance of the man ahead of you to Richard Nixon. Is he the President's brother?"

Don answered, "Why, yes he is, and so am I."

At that point, I turned around and met Denny. During our conversation, I discovered that he, his wife Ellen, and their young sons Joshua and Aaron also resided in the Pacific Northwest when not in Egypt. We exchanged contact information, and on several occasions, the Freeds hosted us at their condo in Maadi, an upscale suburb south of Cairo.

Because my work often involved long separations from my family, we planned for Gay, Amy, and Beth to spend their 1978 summer vacation with me in Cairo. First, Gay escorted a group of high school students, including Beth, on a People-to-People European tour ending in Vienna. Then Amy and I flew from Seattle, staying overnight in Copenhagen. There I escorted her on a fun-filled stroll through Tivoli Gardens—her first tour of the amusement park. After rendezvousing with Gay and Beth at the Vienna airport, we all flew to Cairo.

There we lived in the flat on Dr. Taha Hussein Street I had occupied on prior trips. As part of our business arrangement, Aki had researched the Zamalek District for potential housing and rented the apartment for me. Located on Al-Gazeera Island, this popular residential neighborhood was convenient to our business interests and much safer than other residential prospects he had considered. From the window of our sixth-floor apartment, we would watch as the Egyptian military patrolled in front of the American ambassador's residence directly across the street.

We relished the opportunity to explore Egyptian history with its innumerable antiquities, some predating the birth of Christ by more than three thousand years. In Cairo, Judeo-Christian and Islamic history permeates everything. Everywhere we went, my family and I bumped into it. We toured Saladin's Citadel, one of the city's largest attractions with its Mohammad Ali Mosque. Before entering, we washed our feet and then walked around barefoot according to the rules. Next, with our shoes on, we explored the ancient Christian Coptic Church of St. Sergius, one of the oldest Christian churches in the world, built in the fourth century A.D.

Of course, no trip to Egypt would be complete without a visit to the famous pyramids at Giza, the only remaining structures of the Seven Wonders of the Ancient World. The majesty of the pyramids and the astounding feat of building such structures without modern equipment impressed us so much that we returned several times.

In the cool, dark early morning hours, we would drive by car twelve miles or so southwest of metropolitan Cairo to Giza City on the west bank of the Nile. There we would rent four horses and ride a few miles to Sahara City, a small oasis where an Egyptian sold drinks under an open-air cabana with a roof of palm fronds. Enjoying a cup of coffee or a 7-Up, we would watch a picturesque scene unfold. The sun rising on the horizon illuminated the pyramids in the foreground against the backdrop of the Cairo skyline. Over the Nile River valley hung a misty fog—or smog. Out on the desert, however, nothing obstructed our view. Then, while the sun was still rising, my family and I would ride horses into the Western Desert. Before returning to Giza, we would stop at the cabana again for a cool, refreshing 7-Up.

On one of our trips to Giza, Gay announced, "I've always dreamed of riding a camel across the desert, and this is the day!"

The camel keeper boosted her up onto the back of a one-humped dromedary as it knelt in the sand. An expert horsewoman,

Gay thought she could quickly master the art of camel riding, but it proved more difficult than she expected. Camels don't run like horses. In fact, they don't even walk like horses. Aptly called "ships of the desert," these great beasts rock back and forth, back and forth. Although the ride made her feel seasick, she found the experience thrilling nevertheless.

Seeing Gay's discomfort, the camel keeper finally persuaded her to dismount and rent a horse. She soon caught up with the rest of us.

Denny, Ellen, Joshua, and Aaron accompanied us on a couple of horseback riding tours to the pyramids. Like Gay, Denny loved horses and thoroughly enjoyed those trips.

Through an Egyptian friend, Denny arranged for a special tour for our two families of the Step Pyramid, so named for its six stepped levels. The architect Imhotep had the massive structure, the oldest of the pyramids, built for Pharaoh Djoser about 2630 B.C. Having to crawl down a dark, stuffy tunnel to the burial chambers made Amy and Beth feel squeamish and reluctant to proceed, but Gay and I encouraged them onward. Always the adventurer, Gay wanted to see it all.

Reaching the end of the tunnel, our guide explained that the antiquities ministry prohibited him from carrying an artificial light, which might damage the priceless relics, so he had covered two boards about thirty inches square with aluminum foil. Placing them in just the right positions, he directed some sunlight from the entrance to reflect on a well-preserved mummy perched on a ledge. I don't know who that mummy was—not Pharaoh Djoser anyway, because only his mummified left foot remains.

During Ramadan, my family and I vacationed in Alexandria, known as "The Pearl of the Mediterranean," on the northern rim of the Nile Delta. In 1974, Dick had traveled there by train with Sadat. Throngs of well wishers had greeted them. Some carried signs saying, "We trust Nixon." Knowing of the rousing reception Dick had received added to my admiration of Alexandria and its inhabitants.

Our host, a physician and brother of one of our friends in Cairo, talked about the great Library of Alexandria as if its tragic destruction had occurred in recent history. Still proud of that great center of research and learning, he and other Alexandrians liked to speculate on who had carried out that reprehensible deed and when it had occurred. They had their theories, blaming everyone from Julius Caesar in 48 B.C. to the Muslim conquest in 642 A.D.

I had already been to Alexandria on business with Don and Aki, so I knew the lay of the land and could show Gay and the girls the sights, including Aboukir Bay, of special interest to me since I had taught midshipmen about Lord Nelson's great victory over the French there in 1798. My family's priority, however, was a trip to the white, sandy seashore. Because Muslims were celebrating Ramadan, we thought we would have the beach pretty much to ourselves. How wrong we were.

Deciding to take a dip in the calm Mediterranean Sea, seventeen-year-old Amy and fifteen-year-old Beth splashed around in water chest deep, having a great time—until a couple of Arab boys swam underwater and grabbed them by the legs. The girls jumped out of the water screaming.

"What's the matter? What's the matter?" Gay yelled from shore.

"Those boys are feeling us under the water!"

So, Gay waded out. When the boys started touching her, she jabbed them with her elbows and made quite a ruckus. Leaping from the water, they beat a hasty retreat. Even after they were out of sight, Beth and Amy refused to reenter. By the time I returned to the scene with some soft drinks, my family let me know they had already had enough time on the beach.

On the way home to the U.S., we stopped in London. There I rented a car and drove Gay and the girls to northern Scotland to visit the heritage museum in the highland town of Aviemore. Discovering that ancient Scots by the name of Nixon were related to the Armstrong and Wallace border clans, Beth developed a fascination with William "Braveheart" Wallace, whom she determined must be a distant ancestor. If true, that's probably where the Nixon stubbornness and perseverance originated.

After returning home in late summer 1978 in time for the girls to start school, I made numerous business trips to Newport Beach to consult with Don. From Seattle or Los Angeles, I also traveled to the East Coast and to Tokyo and the Middle East several times. For the DNA Corporation, I circled the globe on four occasions. Don, too, traveled extensively. He loved to go. If Aki mentioned the possibility of a flight on Japan Airlines, Don would jump at the opportunity.

"Where are we going, why, and when?" he would ask, eager for another trip.

~: ~

During the summer of 1979, Amy stayed in Seattle to take care of our home and look after her widowed grandmother, who lived across the street, while Gay and Beth joined me in Cairo. They both have a facility with languages and had already mastered some essential Arabic shopping vocabulary. Wanting to increase their skill, they tried to enroll in an Arabic class at the language school, but the class had already begun with maximum enrollment. They persuaded the teacher to let them join an Italian class, however. Although Gay and Beth started two weeks late, they finished at the top of the class. Mastering a Romance language proved easier for them than for the Arab students, who had to learn a whole new script.

That summer, our friendship with the Freed family deepened as we continued to spend time with them in Cairo. One day, Denny asked me a favor: Would I meet with Yehya Omar, the father of Tarek, one of Denny's students? Upon learning of my relationship to Richard Nixon, Tarek had asked Denny to arrange an introduction. I agreed to a meeting, so Denny set it up.

Omar, a Libyan expatriate, had a fascinating story to tell. He had been like a son to King Mohammed Idris al-Sanousi. After Colonel Muammar Qaddafi rose to power in a bloodless military coup on September 1, 1969, while the king was undergoing medical treatment in Turkey, Omar had fled for his life because of his close association with the deposed monarch. A U.S. Air Force general arranged to ship Omar in a crate aboard an Air Force plane. Escaping with a large sum of money, he then acquired villas in Geneva, Rome, Athens, London, and Washington, D.C. With substantial investments in several places around the world, including the Canning Basin Oil Field in Northern Australia, his worth amounted to several million dollars. At the conclusion of our meeting, I asked Omar, "Is there anything you would like me to do for you?"

Without hesitating, he said, "Yes, I'd like to meet your brother, Richard Nixon. Can you introduce me?"

"That's not something I would normally do," I responded, "but I'll give it a try."

Over the years, many people had made that request of me. Being in Cairo at the time, I had no idea whether an opportunity would ever arise for Omar and Dick to meet.

IRELAND

At the end of the summer, on our way home to Washington, Gay, Beth, and I stayed overnight in Paris. The next day, we flew to Ireland in search of the Milhous ancestral home in County Kildare near the town of Timahoe. We wanted to locate the cemetery, the final resting place of our forebears, where Dick had placed a memorial stone in October 1970.

Renting a car in Dublin, I quickly relearned to drive on the "wrong" side of the road. Heading southwest into County Kildare, we came to a sign, "Timahoe 4 miles," so we turned down the road. To our surprise, about three miles later, another sign appeared: "Timahoe 2 miles." Puzzled by the signs, we continued until we spotted three cottages and a vacant lot at a crossroads. On the roof of one of the houses, a man was repairing thatch. In the front yard, a lady was pulling weeds, perhaps for the thatch roof.

I rolled down the car window and asked in my best Irish brogue, "Excuse me, ma'am. Can you tell me where's Timahoe?"

"Aye, this is Timahoe," she said.

"Well, can you tell me where's the cemetery? My ancestors are buried there."

"And who'd they be?"

"They'd be the Milhous family, ancestors of President Nixon."

She peered in the car and stared at my profile. "Oh, I see you are related. Right down the road apiece just before the bend in the road, you'll come to an old sign all covered with weeds. If you peek through those weeds, you'll find the cemetery. You'll see the large stone President Nixon placed there not so long ago. I remember it well."

Timahoe Memorial Stone – Ireland, 2001
~Author's collection

In the middle of the old burial ground, we found the memorial Dick had dedicated October 5, 1970—a marble slab placed atop two stones to form a bench. Our cousin Jessamyn West McPherson, a Milhous family historian and Irish enthusiast as well as a famous author, had joined Dick and Pat for the ceremony.

When Beth saw the old cemetery and a headstone with the Milhous name nearly obliterated, she sat down on that bench and cried. Her tears touched me deeply.

Ireland has always held a certain attraction for my family and me—its green rolling hills, fertile pastures, and lush vegetation, the rugged seacoast and the mild, misty climate, the people's respect for the land and their love of horses. The word *atavism* took on meaning for us. Jessamyn had told me that visiting the place our ancestors left behind and walking in their footsteps would evoke an overwhelming sense of familiarity, and she was right. We immediately felt comfortable, at home, part of the country and its people. Somehow, we belonged in Ireland.

Dick also had a special place in his heart for Ireland and was proud of our Irish heritage. When he visited the Emerald Isle, he could relate it to the intriguing stories Grandmother Almira had told him during his youth—the stories she had heard as a child passed down from generation to generation. Being her youngest grandchild, born when she was eighty years old, I remember Grandmother's stories of Ireland only as recounted by my aunts, uncles, and older cousins.

Muslim Views

Shortly after returning home, I decided to dissolve my relationship with Aki Kawaguchi. The business prospects had not come to fruition, and he had depleted his financial resources. I continued to work with Don, however, helping him evaluate the constant flow of business prospects. Don maintained his affiliation with Aki for a while but eventually discovered that promotion of ventures dependent on foreign capital was not in his best interests. Don then closed the DNA office.

In late 1979, I returned to Cairo to finish business and say goodbye to the many friends and acquaintances I had come to enjoy and respect. Our Japanese clients appreciated DNA's efforts on their behalf, but they had not succeeded in their competitive bids. The consortium of Japanese telecommunication experts from Fuji, NEC, etc., lost the bid to retrofit Cairo's telecommunications system to a Dutch consortium headed by Phillips and Siemens. Even the U.S. consortium of AT&T, General Telephone, and others lost out. My second objective— to aid IHI in its bid to build and operate a ship-breaking facility in Alexandria—also failed. The Danes won that one. Americans, myself included, found it difficult to compete in the Middle Eastern system of commerce in which paying baksheesh was the accepted practice.

Although my ventures in Egypt did not prove profitable from a business standpoint, I gained many intangible benefits from a deeper exposure to Muslim culture than would have accrued from mere tourist travel or meeting Muslims in the United States. Living and working among those kind and helpful people provided me the opportunity to form friendships and gain understanding of their religious beliefs and political philosophy.

In Cairo, I heard the Muslim viewpoint on the politics of the Middle East. My friends, especially Hassan El-Abd, his wife Zizi, and her father Hassan Baraket, talked freely about their animosity toward Israel, although they expressed high regard for American ways. As our conversation progressed, I realized their grudges weren't so much against Israel as against the Balfour Declaration, a 1917 letter from British Foreign Secretary Arthur Balfour to Lord Rothschild, a British Zionist, stating Britain's support of the idea of a Jewish homeland in Palestine. Between World War I and World War II, Britain administered the territory of Palestine. In 1947, the United Nations passed a resolution calling for the establishment of a Jewish state in part of Palestine and Transjordan. The following year, Israel was declared an independent nation, founded on the goal of freedom and justice for people of all races and religions.

My Muslims friends, however, could not get this perceived affront out of their system. While they got along fine with individual Jews, they could not accept what they viewed as the great eviction of so many Arab brothers from their homeland of a thousand years.

Interestingly, my friends expressed a positive view of Richard Nixon, and I don't think it was motivated by my being his brother. As moderate Muslims, they didn't blame him for defending the state of Israel. They just didn't like what led to the nation's founding, and no one could fault Dick for that.

Hassan seemed a perfect match for his great city. Both he and Cairo epitomized cosmopolitanism, with cultures from all over the world intersecting and conducting business. The El-Abds owned a very large home in the heart of the city where they entertained diplomats, ambassadors, and heads of state. When Don and I arrived at their home for some business discussions, we found he had organized a party and invited U.S. Ambassador Hermann Eilts to join us. The ambassador, a career diplomat, had served in Saudi Arabia prior to his tour in Egypt from 1973 to 1979.[96] That evening, the liquor flowed freely, and Hassan's guests, many of whom were Muslim, all imbibed. Attending an international party seemed to liberate those Muslims from their cultural inhibitions against alcohol.

France

Although I never traveled overseas with Dick, we did cross paths in Paris in April 1980 at the Hotel de Crillon, a former palace converted into a hotel. My good friend Donley Brady and I had arranged to meet him there on our way to Guinea to investigate diamond mining prospects. Dick had chosen Paris to announce the release of his book *La Vraie Guerre*, first published in French, then German, and Spanish. Finally, the English version appeared in the U.S as *The Real War* later that year.

I can only speculate why this book was first published in France, but I do know that Dick always had a good reputation there. He had been friends with former presidents Charles de Gaulle and Georges Pompidou, and he admired their command of diplomacy. The French always seemed inclined to avoid conflict by negotiating and then negotiating some more—as long as there was something to negotiate—but they also knew when to defend themselves.

---

96 Because of Ambassador Eilts' prominence as an American and his close association with President Anwar el-Sadat, Qaddafi ordered an unsuccessful attempt to assassinate him during the Carter Administration.

In *The Real War*, Dick argued for a balance between negotiation, competition, and deterrence. Focusing on the threat from the Soviet Union and the Communist bloc, he maintained that World War III had begun after the end of World War II without most of the world taking notice. This new war was being fought in ideological, political, economic, and technical arenas as well as in military conflicts. In the book, he pointed out the fallacy of thinking that if the U.S. and Western democracies would be kind to the Communists, they would recipocate.

Dick also realized the threat of Muslim extremism and anti-Western dictatorships. On a prophetic note, he wrote:

> Radical Iraq is now the most powerful military force in the Gulf. Its military strength is overwhelming in strictly regional terms.... Even without any further Soviet support, the Iraqis could move with impunity anywhere they decided to: in Kuwait, Saudi Arabia, or Iran.[97]

Instead of continually appeasing brutal regimes, Dick proposed a response: leadership through strength and determination. He based his theory on what Charles de Gaulle, Winston Churchill, Franklin Roosevelt, and other world leaders learned in World War II and how they would have handled the current international threats. Envisioning a common goal for the future, Dick proposed strategies to prevent a war of annihilation.

In our hotel room, Donley and I watched as Dick delivered his speech on French television. I thought how statesmanlike he appeared. Because the broadcast was directly translated into French, one of Donley's good friends interpreted for us. As I remember, Dick warned viewers of the threat of communism and shared ways France and other democratic nations could prevail in the Cold War. Reporters then interviewed him regarding his new book and other subjects as well.

Donley wanted to know the reaction of the press. "Are they being critical of Dick?"

---

97   Nixon, *The Real War* 93.

"No, no," our interpreter assured us. "They like what he has to say very much."

~: ~

A few months earlier, Donley had acted as tour guide for Ahmed Sékou Touré, the Communist president of Guinea, when he visited California at the invitation of the Overseas Private Investment Corporation (OPIC). A quasi-federal agency under the guidance of the Secretary of State, OPIC was established during Dick's presidency in 1971 to help U.S. companies invest in emerging markets overseas, thereby fostering free-market development in Third World countries. Donley, a board member of the agency, had been assigned the task of escorting Sékou Touré. A gracious host, he gave him the royal tour up and down the Central Valley. During that time, Sékou Touré urged Donley to come to Guinea. Convinced an absolute fortune lay beneath the surface of his country, he offered to grant Donley the diamond exploration rights in about one-tenth of the land, supposedly in appreciation for his hospitality.

An attorney with no knowledge of diamond mining, Donley jumped at the opportunity. When he asked me to accompany him, I doubted whether I could be of any benefit, because I had no expertise in diamonds either. Seeing my hesitation, he suggested I call my brother and ask his advice. That was one of the few times I agreed to consult with Dick on a personal matter. Donley, who had coordinated Volunteers for Nixon in the Western states in 1972, met with Dick and me in San Clemente. He asked Dick about taking me along as a geologist to evaluate the diamond concessions.

Dick thought it would be a worthwhile experience for me, even though I lacked a background in diamonds. Donley remembers him saying, "Ed will be really good for you, because he's the smartest of us all."

I couldn't disagree with Dick that the trip would be a worthwhile experience, but I declined his compliment. Certainly, he had more than proved his intellectual capabilities.

~: ~

At the Hotel de Crillon, Colonel Jack Brennan, Dick's aide-de-camp, called: "Your brother would like you to come down to his room. He has some suggestions and some books he wants you to take to Africa."

Donley and I also wanted to discuss with Dick how we should approach President Sékou Touré.

In his hotel room, Dick appeared in high spirits. Returning to the public spotlight to expound on world affairs had given him a much-needed emotional boost—as did the enthusiastic response among the TV audience, including the French press.

Dick inscribed and autographed two books: one to Sékou Touré, president of Guinea, and another to Félix Houphouét-Boigny, president of Côte d'Ivoire (the Ivory Coast). Then he gave Donley and me some good advice about how to approach those men. As Vice President in 1960, Dick had escorted Sékou Touré to the White House, and he was well aware of the dire political and economic situation in Guinea.

My brother's grasp of history and current events never failed to amaze me. No matter the countries involved, he could analyze historical events and relate them to present-day conditions. Comparing Guinea and Côte d'Ivoire, he noted that these two former colonies of France had pursued radically different paths to independence. Sékou Touré, the son of a poor Muslim farmer, had risen to political power in 1958 on an anti-French platform, leading the resistance to Charles de Gaulle. Driving out the French with ferocious attacks, the rebel forces destroyed nearly everything in their path, including many of the country's treasures. Sékou Touré proclaimed, "We prefer poverty in liberty to riches in slavery."[98]

And poverty without liberty is what the country got. Although the ground contained much wealth, the people lived in increasing deprivation because of his tyrannical rule, corruption, and failed socialistic policies. Sékou Touré's regime had forced some ethnic groups into exile, and he was responsible for killings, tortures, imprisonments, and mysterious disappearances. By granting the Soviet Union nearly all the options on his country's bauxite, the chief source of aluminum, Sékou Touré supplied the Russians with the natural resources to build

---

98 "Ahmed Sékou Touré, Guinea (1922-1984)." University of Florida, <http://www.uflib. ufl.edu/cm/africana/sekou.htm> accessed 10 December 2004.

airplanes and an arsenal of weapons, thus aiding their cause in the Cold War.

Dick preferred the positive approach when dealing with foreign despots. Rather than lambasting communism, he thought it more effective to present the positive alternatives of democracy and free enterprise. Knowing the dictator had a lot of blood on his hands, Dick advised us, "In Guinea, tell President Sékou Touré you're hoping to offer the people something to dream about and something to work on that will benefit all the people. Given the right opportunities, communism will eventually cease to be so attractive. When the people are freely allowed to see what liberty can provide, their new vision will enable tyranny to die."

My brother, however, greatly admired President Houphouët-Boigny and what he had done for his country. In addition to having hosted Houphouët-Boigny at the White House in October 1973, Dick maintained contact with him through diplomatic channels, including Henry Kissinger and Timothée Ahoua N'Guetta, the Ivorian ambassador to the U.S., whom Dick greatly respected. Among the topics they had discussed were the Soviet threat in Africa and the Biafran war for independence from Nigeria.

In contrast to Guinea, Côte d'Ivoire had been far more peaceable and orderly about claiming freedom. Houphouët-Boigny, the first president after the country gained independence from France in 1960, encouraged a slow process of Africanization along with foreign investment and French aid. A political moderate, he maintained his membership in the French Parliament and cooperated with commercial ventures in his country, inviting businesses from America and Europe to invest. Under his leadership, the country prospered due to sound planning and management as well as the country's thriving cocoa industry. In fact, Côte d'Ivoire became one of the most prosperous nations in sub-Saharan Africa.

When Donley and I left the U.S., we had no intention of traveling to Côte d'Ivoire, but Dick strongly advised us to go to Abidjan to personally deliver the autographed copy of *La Vraie Guerre*. He assured us we would have no problem entering the country without a visa. While we were in Paris, Jack Brennan communicated with President

Houphouét-Boigny's office and arranged for the president's aide to meet us at the airport and take us directly to the presidential palace.

GUINEA

On April 24, 1980, Donley and I landed at the outdated airport in Conakry, Guinea. Despite being there by invitation of the president and having nothing to declare, we had to stand in line an inordinate amount of time before clearing customs. First we waited outside in the sweltering heat. Then we entered the terminal, disappointed to find that it lacked air conditioning. If my memory serves me correctly, we saw fans, but without electricity they sat motionless, unable to circulate the hot, humid air. Apparently the power plant could generate only enough electricity to light a sixty-watt bulb hanging above the counter.

After we finally cleared customs, our driver took us through town to the Guinea Iron Mining Company (MiFerGui) guesthouse for foreign businessmen. Looking out from the balcony, we realized we had been locked in—literally. Stern sentries stood in guardhouses at the front and back of our accommodations, which resembled a jail more than a hotel. Obviously suspicious of us, those Communists weren't going to give us the opportunity to snoop around. When a guard about two hundred yards away spotted Donley shooting photos from the balcony, he glared and shook his finger in warning: "Photography Prohibited!" Fortunately nothing came of the incident.

Our second-story room contained few amenities—just a couple of low-wattage electric lights and intermittent running water. After the long wait in the humid airport, we anticipated a refreshing shower. But to our disappointment, the water barely trickled. Without a telephone, television or even a radio in our room, we had no means of communication with the outside world.

Then I had an idea: I had brought a small portable multi-band radio. Untwisting some metal coat hangers, I constructed a long antenna. When the coast was clear, I hung it out our window, making sure to align the chain along the corner to minimize the chance of detection.

Donley said, "If they ever find this, Ed, you can imagine what they'll do to us!"

Fortunately, my improvised antenna worked, bringing BBC programs to our room to help pass the time. Either the noise from our conversations muffled the broadcasts, or the distance between our room and the guardhouse prevented the sentries from hearing my radio. We even got so bold as to sing along with a radio broadcast of *La Marseillaise*, the militaristic French national anthem, which would have riled the French-hating Communists had they heard us.

After our hosts freed us from about three days of captivity, we spent several days negotiating with the bureaucrats at the Ministry of Mines, discussing details, and setting terms for Donley's diamond deal. Soon we realized our hosts had an ulterior motive: They wanted foreign assistance to explore the concession area. In return for all the diamonds Donley could extract, the ministry asked him to bring in a team of geologists to provide more accurate geologic maps of the area. The few Guinean geologists, who had been trained at the Sorbonne in Paris, needed help with that task. Because Sékou Touré had driven out the French, they had no desire to come back to assist on the project. The Russians only paid a pittance for the bauxite, iron, and other resources they mined, so Sékou Touré thought Americans, like Donley, could be much more lucrative friends.

Ministry officials later invited Donley to return to Guinea to visit the countryside and to inspect a section of his concession. Having read the reports, I declined the invitation. "There's no need to go out to the field," I said, "because at this time, a diamond mine in Guinea is just a trench where they're digging alluvial diamonds. You might experience the excitement of finding a diamond on the bank of a stream, but you want to see what the experts have dug over months of searching and mapping. That's where the evidence is."

During his field trip, Donley learned that most of the diamonds could be used only for industrial purposes. Although the concession contained a variety of valuable green diamonds, premium quality gems were rare.

One day before our scheduled departure, our driver took us to the presidential palace where we waited in a large lobby to meet with President Sékou Touré. While sitting on an overstuffed chair, Donley spotted little pyramids of what looked like sawdust on the floor. Pointing, he whispered, "What in the world are they?"

"That's from termites," I said. "They're probably all over the place."

Finally, the guard ushered us in to meet with the president, and I presented him with my brother's book. He acknowledged it grudgingly, but when he noticed it was printed in French, the official language of Guinea, and personally autographed by Richard Nixon, his demeanor brightened. He claimed to admire my brother and even seemed pleased to meet me. Following my presentation, Sékou Touré and Donley conducted their business.

Côte d'Ivoire

From Guinea, Donley and I flew to Abidjan, Côte d'Ivoire, as Dick had suggested. That was one time I shouldn't have listened to my brother. I hadn't been around the world as much as he had, but my instinct told me that entering an airport without a visa, especially in a Third-World country, could land us in hot water.

To our relief, the airport at Abidjan was much more modern than Conakry's. To our dismay, however, no one met us. Making matters worse, the airport security supervisor promptly confiscated our passports. We tried to explain to the man, who spoke passable English, that we had traveled to Abidjan on quick notice at the request of my brother, former President Richard Nixon, and that he had arranged for us to be picked up at the airport and taken to meet with President Houphouét-Boigny. Not swayed by our explanation, he led us into his office and sat us down on a bench. Then he opened the curtains covering a big Plexiglas window, so we could see the scene taking place on the other side. Guards with what looked like black rubber garden hoses were whipping the legs of a man with his pants down, wearing only shorts. Other men awaited their turn for a similar beating. Apparently, airport staff handled security problems by inflicting corporal punishment. The supervisor probably thought he could encourage us to confess to avoid meeting the same fate.

Tense and upset, Donley and I sat there looking at each other. Not knowing the man's crime, nevertheless, we felt sorry for the harsh treatment he was receiving. We resorted to humor to help relieve our anxiety. He leaned over to me and whispered, "What has your brother gotten us into? Are we next?"

"I don't know, but we need to think of something fast to get out of this mess."

"Ed, you'd better take your pants down pretty soon. You've got longer legs than I do, so they'll have more time with you. Let them work on you first."

In his most authoritative voice, Donley then turned to the supervisor and tried again to convince him: "I am an attorney, and this is Edward Nixon, brother of President Richard Nixon. You're making a big mistake detaining us."

Once more the supervisor rejected that unlikely story.

Turning to me, Donley said, "Ed, stand up and turn sideways." Then he asked the supervisor, "Does he look like the former President of the United States or not? I'm telling you right now to call President Houphouét-Boigny's office and find out whether he's expecting us before you take any further action."

"Look at my passport," I added. "It lists Richard Nixon as my next of kin." What my nose couldn't accomplish, my passport finally did. After detaining us for about an hour, he finally broke down and called President Houphouét-Boigny's office. The color nearly drained from his face as he hung up the phone. Suddenly his bravado evaporated, and he looked like one scared guy.

Soon a presidential aide came to the arrival area and picked up our checked luggage. He directed the supervisor to send us down immediately. Close to tears, the supervisor grabbed Donley's briefcase in an offer of assistance, but Donley grabbed it back, saying, "I'm going to carry that."

The supervisor probably feared we would report him, but we had no intention of getting him in trouble. We were just relieved to be free. I don't know what his superiors did with him, or what happened to the driver who failed to pick us up in the first place.

The president's aide drove us to the Hotel d'Ivoire where he waited for us to check into our rooms and take a brief tour of the facilities, escorted by the assistant manager. The hotel, a member of the Intercontinental chain, featured an ice-skating rink in the basement plus all the amenities typical of five star hotels in Europe and America—a welcome change from our last stop at the guesthouse in Conakry.

The aide then led us to the executive office building. Georges Ouégnin, President Houphouét-Boigny's chief of protocol, officiously but with courtesy, ushered us into the president's reception room.

"You have fifteen minutes only," he said. "Many people are waiting for an audience with the president."

"Okay, that's fine. We just want to present this book, *La Vraie Guerre*," I replied.

The Hotel d'Ivoire had offered the services of Regis Nadeau, a friendly young manager, to translate for our meeting. A French-Canadian, he spoke both French and English fluently.

The president apologized for his driver's failure to meet us at the airport and explained that the men on the other side of the window there were illegal aliens. He noted that his country attracted many such people seeking a better life. From time to time, his government would round them up and detain them in facilities like that little airport jailhouse.

As our meeting progressed, Houphouét-Boigny made it clear that he was a staunch ally of the United States and that he greatly admired Richard Nixon. No way would he let us leave after fifteen minutes.

"Mr. President," I said, "my brother applauds your work in bringing Côte d'Ivoire into the modern world. Because of your effort to maintain friendly international relations, he holds you in high regard among world leaders."

Houphouét-Boigny informed us of the serious problems plaguing his nation. "We have nothing here in Côte d'Ivoire compared to the rich mineral resources in Guinea. All we have is agriculture, industrious people, and good schools."

I corrected him. "You also have freeways and the Hotel d'Ivoire with its ice-skating rink and amenities I haven't seen in any other tropical country."

"Those are just European things," he said. But I could tell he was proud of his country's accomplishments by the way he glowed at my compliments. He then added that Wrangler manufactured all their jeans in Côte d'Ivoire.

Several times during our meeting, Georges interrupted, reminding us of the people waiting to see the president. Houphouét-Boigny just waved him off.

When we left after our hour-long meeting, we saw Georges's reason for concern. The anteroom resembled a doctor's waiting room with patients seated on all available chairs. Regis explained to Donley and me what had transpired in the French dialogue between Georges and the president. Houphouét-Boigny clearly told him he wanted to give us his full attention.

Deciding we should spend an extra day in Côte d'Ivoire, Donley asked me to rearrange our flights in order to find a more convenient schedule. Regis had done such an extraordinary job interpreting for us that I enlisted his help to change flights. The francophone Africans seemed to appreciate French Canadians more than they did the Parisian French, and they especially liked Regis. Happy to interpret again, he took me to the airline ticket counter.

A young chap behind the counter inspected my passport and then looked at me. Seeing I had listed Richard Nixon as next of kin, he said, "You are related to President Nixon?"

When I told him he was my brother, he responded, "In Côte d'Ivoire, we cannot understand what is wrong with the American people. Why did they let a man as good as your brother go?"

"I've wondered that myself," I replied. "Because perfect strangers in other parts of the world have made comments similar to yours, I have to conclude that most citizens of other nations don't read U.S. newspapers with all their exaggeration and innuendo. If only there were a way to educate journalists so they would write the facts without the bias, the world would be a better place."

My response satisfied him, and he gave me Donley's and my tickets via Air Afrique—the quickest way out of town. We flew east to Lagos, Nigeria, and then home via Paris.

Brussels to Guinea

Donley and I traveled to Guinea again later that year. In Brussels, our first stop, he introduced me to Steve Mayeur and his family. The Bradys had become acquainted with them on a recent skiing trip in Switzerland. Learning of my relationship to Richard Nixon, the Mayeurs immediately treated me as a VIP. Whenever situations like that occurred, I felt embarrassed, because the real VIP was nowhere in sight.

"It's our tradition for the honored guest to open the champagne bottle by whacking the cork with a sword," they told me.

"But I don't know anything about that," I protested.

"You know how to use a sword, don't you?" asked Steve.

"Well, I don't ..." The next thing I knew, I was standing in the Mayeurs' backyard with a sword in my right hand and the champagne bottle in my left. "Wouldn't it be easier just to uncork it?" I asked, knowing my question would be to no avail.

Steve replied, "Easier maybe, but that wouldn't be traditional. Besides, you don't want to get cork in your champagne."

No, but neither did I want tiny slivers of glass in my drink, though I kept my thoughts to myself. Not being an experienced swordsman, I took a few whacks before I finally opened that bottle. Everyone cheered. I don't remember whether I drank any champagne. I might have been too suspicious of finding shards.

∽ ∾

Aki Kawaguchi and his prospective investor, a retired dentist from Tokyo, joined Donley and me in Guinea. The dentist's expedition in search of investment opportunities in gems and other mineral resources ended abruptly when he decided the opportunities didn't match his investment criteria. Thanking his hosts, he quickly arranged a return flight to Japan. Donley also opted out of his diamond project after our second trip to Guinea, figuring the cost of remapping and mining would likely exceed any significant profit. We both returned home, discouraged but wiser.

That trip typified my ventures into overseas investment. Many of the businessmen I represented had plenty of money to speculate. Hearing about a prospect in Africa, they would say, "Let's go have a look. Maybe we'll see a lion while we're there."

Ever since Dick became President, people had approached Don and me with diverse requests and business prospects. Going anywhere in the world with Don, I would learn of some new "hot venture." Don got more involved in the investment world than I did. He was more willing to pursue other people's ideas, but I felt increasingly uncomfortable in that arena.

Stanley McKiernan, our attorney, had advised me to form a corporation for tax purposes and as an umbrella for evaluating and following up on worthy endeavors that better fit my area of expertise.

NIXON WORLD ENTERPRISES

Therefore, in May 1980, I had founded Nixon World Enterprises, Inc., an ongoing international business consulting company based in Washington State, which specializes in developing technically oriented commercial trade and investment opportunities. As president of the company, I have investigated and evaluated a wide range of prospects for clients in Japan, Korea, Taiwan, Hong Kong, Macao, the People's Republic of China, the Philippines, Pakistan, Egypt, Turkey, Uzbekistan, Russia, Guinea, Côte d'Ivoire, Denmark, Britain, Germany, Spain, Portugal, Monaco, France, Italy, Canada, Jamaica, Panama, Bolivia, Chile, and Uruguay. My activities have included advisory support for startup companies in the U.S. and development of original equipment manufacturers overseas; promotion of international satellite communications; marketing of agricultural products; transportation improvement; pollution abatement; and support of sister cities and other cultural exchange programs.

Nixon World Enterprises has given me the opportunity to focus on developing innovative methods for the clean extraction of earth resources and to pursue Dick's and my dream of energy independence. As a geologist, I've concentrated on the technical evaluation of metal mining prospects with new techniques in metallurgy and hazardous waste disposal. I encourage innovations in thermo-voltaic and photo-voltaic electric power generators and the development of hybrid electric power plants combining conventional and alternative energy resources.

OMAR

After returning to the U.S., Denny Freed contacted me in 1980, asking me to come to New York to meet with Omar, who wanted to follow up on our initial visit in Cairo the year before. By that time, Denny had left his position with Cairo American College to work for Omar as one of his office staff—the "token American" as Denny described himself. While his job focused first on some projects on the Red Sea and later on USAID matters, he also worked with several men associated with high officials in the Egyptian government and the former Libyan government who were involved in military procurement.

Omar primarily wanted to meet my brother, and he asked my assistance in arranging it. I knew Dick would be interested in talking to him about the situation in Libya, but I hesitated to pursue this request. Not wanting to be a doormat or to burden Dick, I had shunned such solicitations. And this one made me even more nervous, because Omar insisted on paying me for setting up the meeting. That was not in keeping with my modus operandi, but he said he always compensated people for their efforts on his behalf.

Sharing my dilemma with friends, I said, "I don't want to get paid for introducing someone to my brother. That's not something I do for a living,"

Disagreeing with my reservation, several people assured me that a finder's fee was appropriate.

Finally, I agreed to consider Omar's offer.

I explained to Dick, "This man's an expatriate from Libya, and he has quite a story to tell. He'd like to talk with you in person about the future of Libya."

Being well versed on Qaddafi's rise to power and his repressive socialist government, Dick could not resist that kind of introduction, so without hesitation he said, "Have Nick schedule it."

Nick Ruwe, Dick's chief of staff at 26 Federal Plaza in Manhattan, suggested that Mike Sotirous, a Greek-American attorney friend, would be willing to help me conclude the deal with Omar. He told me, "Greeks are superb negotiators, especially in deals with Muslims."

When I expressed reluctance to Mike regarding my potential value to the client, he said, "I'll go with you and do the negotiating."

Mike and Omar settled the deal in a matter of minutes. Omar also wanted to employ me as a consultant to research some of his investments to see how they might be enhanced, so Mike proposed an annual retainer for me to represent Omar for two years. Omar countered with an offer for two years paid in annual installments after the introductory meeting with my brother.

Mike said, "No problem. It's a deal."

I agreed to Omar's generous offer. Shaking my hand, he paid me cash on the spot. As was the custom among wealthy Arabs, he carried huge sums of cash in his suitcase, which he dispensed for business deals.

On March 30, 1981, our agreed-upon meeting date, Omar and Denny arrived in a limo at Dick's classic four-story, brownstone home on East 65th Street in Manhattan. I had expected to see Omar dressed in his typical Arab robes, but instead he wore a Western suit. Omar's attorney, Bill Casselman, who formerly served as counsel to President Nixon, attended as well.

The meeting began with Dick and Omar exchanging pleasantries. In an apparent attempt to impress, Omar offered his jet to Dick if he should travel to the Middle East.

Dick responded, "Oh, you have a plane?" His polite reply showed he understood Omar's intent but refused to fall for the ploy.

As Dick was very good at doing, he asked all kinds of questions. Naturally, one of them was "How long do you think Qaddafi will remain in power?"

I believe Omar responded, "It shouldn't be more than a few months."

Eventually Omar shared his long-held desire to overthrow Qaddafi and his willingness to commit resources to reach that goal.

About fifteen to twenty minutes into the conversation, Dick's Secret Service agent opened the door and interrupted, "Mr. President, you have an urgent call from the White House!" Dick excused himself and went into his office to answer the red phone, a special line to the Oval Office.

Looking shaken, Dick returned to announce, "President Reagan has been shot." Soon Julie, who happened to be at her parents' home, entered, obviously upset over the assassination attempt. Her father stepped out of the room for a few moments to comfort her and then came back to our meeting.

Denny suggested, "Perhaps we should pray for President Reagan."

As a Quaker, Dick didn't pray publicly but rather conversed privately with God. He didn't have time to act on Denny's suggestion anyway, because the Secret Serviceman informed Dick that the White House was on the line again.

After the call, he said, "Gentlemen, I'm afraid we'll have to postpone our meeting. I'll need to be on the line for quite some time with Alexander Haig."

Haig had served as President Nixon's White House Chief of Staff and at that time was Secretary of State under President Reagan. Like a good general, Haig took initial control at the White House, pending Vice President George H.W. Bush's return to Washington, D.C. Haig called Dick, as well as former Presidents Ford and Carter, to apprise them of the situation.

So, we all departed, anxious to hear news of President Reagan's condition. Reporters and photographers lined the street outside Dick's home. Appearing nervous, Omar jumped into the limousine parked in front, only to discover that it belonged to Dick—an understandable mistake because the vehicles looked identical from the exterior. He quickly extricated himself from Dick's limo and got into his own.

A little later, Denny called Ellen, who had just seen the television broadcast of former President Nixon being interviewed in front of his home with Pat by his side. She told him that Dick had said, "The only thing we can do for President Reagan is pray."

As far as I know, Dick did not reconvene that meeting.

∿ ∿

My job with Omar required a move to Washington, D.C. At first, I subleased an apartment from a friend and later bought a condominium. Gay stayed home in Washington State to continue working as a math teacher.

After all his efforts to secure my services and my efforts to accommodate him, Omar rarely contacted me, so I worked on my own energy projects while in his employ. I did investigate a few investment leads he wanted me to look into, however, but he never pursued them. To my knowledge, his interest in developing further investments in Australia didn't materialize. He asked me to meet him once in Rome and once in Geneva.

On the trip to Rome, Denny met me at the Cavalieri Hilton, a resort hotel located in a fifteen-acre private park high upon the hill overlooking the Vatican and the historic city center. "Have you ever been to the Vatican?" he asked. "If not, let's go down and have a look."

Because I hadn't seen it, we hailed a taxi. Strangely, we walked right into Sistine Chapel without waiting in line for a tour. Having the chapel almost to ourselves, we gazed at Michelangelo's masterpiece ceiling in almost eerie silence. As we exited the building, we realized why no crowds were inside. In St. Peter's Basilica, the Pope was addressing an enormous audience in honor of Children's Day. People had brought their sons and daughters for the Pope to bless. Denny and I proceeded to the back of the cathedral. Seeing that some boys and girls had piled up rickety old benches to obtain a better view of the Pope, we, too, improved our view by stepping up on an available bench.

Walking through the Vatican, Denny and I couldn't help but marvel at its magnificence. Among the many works of art, we spotted the display of gifts of state, including the Boehm bird sculpture that I believe my brother presented to Pope Paul VI on his visit to the Vatican in 1969 or 1970. Not a connoisseur of art myself, nevertheless, I greatly admired the exquisite porcelain sculpture by Edward Boehm, especially because I knew how enamored Dick was with Boehm's masterpieces.

Omar hosted a private dinner party in his suite, which Denny and I attended along with the CEO of Alfa Romeo. My memory of the event is a blur, but Denny recalls Omar challenging the CEO to manufacture a fully armored car to defend against large capacity weapons—a matter of urgent concern to wealthy businessmen at risk of being shot in the wake of recent attacks. Omar probably feared for his life too.

My final meeting with Omar occurred in Geneva, Switzerland, in 1982 following my vacation with Gay in Spain. If my memory serves me correctly, Gay and I parted company in Madrid, and she proceeded on to Santiago de Compostela and La Coruña, where she visited Manolo and Fina Sanchez, Pat and Dick's former household staff.

At Omar's invitation, I met him at his elegant villa in Geneva, where he paid me the final installment of the retainer. It has always amazed me that he fulfilled his commitment on the basis of a handshake alone. Honorable in his business dealings with me, he remained true to his word without any contract or formal agreement.

Omar then gave me a new assignment: Travel to Monaco to set up a working relationship with Tarek. From the concern Omar expressed, I suspected he wanted me to get his son involved in business pursuits to distract him from the temptations of women and gambling in Monte Carlo. I called Tarek at his locations in Monaco as well as Geneva. Receiving no response, I could not follow through on my assignment.

I awaited further instructions from Omar but heard nothing from him again. Never had I been paid so well for doing so little. Because I was just spinning my wheels, however, I welcomed the termination of our business relationship. I had made many new friends and established helpful business contacts in Washington, D.C., but I decided to return to California and focus full time on building a "domestic highway" to sustainable alternative energy derived from transient retrievable resources. I would devote all my efforts to promoting clean extraction of mineral resources and developments in alternative energy—an area that had fascinated me since my school days.

TRIAD AMERICAN ENERGY

In the early 1980s, my nephew Donald A. Nixon had formed a small company called Triad American Energy, Inc., which I joined in 1983 because of my deep interest in lessening dependence on fossil fuels. To encourage investment in alternative energy, the U.S. Department of Energy, under the Carter Administration, had instituted tax write-offs until the end of 1985. One of those alternatives, wind energy, had already been developed to a certain extent in California; but with the incentive of tax write-offs, the idea really took off.

Excited by the idea, Don, Jr., engaged Leonard Berman and his son Bruce to help get the funding underway to erect and sell windmills north of Palm Springs, California. The company focused mainly on acquiring property rights.

Triad American Energy promoted a two-bladed windmill—a fifty-kilowatt machine mounted on pedestals. The company installed several wind-powered electric generators that could feed directly into the Southern California Edison utility lines. On Californian ridges like Altamont and Tehachapi and mountain passes like San Gorgonio, from time to time we measured the wind using the J-TEC anemometer with a handheld device, because, without a certain amount of wind,

*Triad American
Energy -
50 kW Turbines –
California, 1983*
~Author's collection

Nordtank Wind Turbine – Jutland, Denmark, 1983
~Author's collection

no generation was to be had. We also evaluated the lay of the land and made sure we got the windmills up and running by December 31, 1985, the deadline for claiming alternative energy tax breaks. That day we erected our last tower, a 200-kilowatt windmill at Tehachapi.

At that time, Southern California Edison's projects in the Palm Springs area and the San Gorgonio Pass were at the end of the power line, where they had peak demands in the summer for air conditioning. So, wind energy, or any other alternative source of energy that could be pumped into the end of the line, would reduce the load of the regular Southern California Edison demand. Many of those windmills are still operating, but some have fallen into disrepair and are too expensive to run. Advanced technology has made many of them obsolete.

Concurrent with our efforts in Southern California, Leonard Berman had responded to an invitation to investigate prospects for wind farms in Jamaica. He sent me on several trips to that Caribbean nation as a guest at Lady Sarah Churchill's estate above Montego Bay. With Lady Churchill's assistance and the cooperation of the government, I surveyed by car and helicopter the most promising sites for a wind farm. I considered the ridge above the town of Mandeville to be the most suitable site because of its consistent wind and proximity to an electric station. However, with expiration of the short-lived investment fever back home, the prospect soon lost the support needed for a more thorough evaluation.

On behalf of Triad American Energy, I visited wind turbine equipment manufacturers in Europe, including the Nordtank facility in Jutland, Denmark, to obtain firsthand knowledge and to assess their systems. Upon returning to California, I reported the results of my trip and my positive impressions of the Nordtank system.

Seeking to enhance the efficiency of wind energy systems, Don, Jr., also engaged John Laing, a German inventor specializing in fluid dynamics, to optimize the windmills. When we met, I asked Mr. Laing how Triad American Energy could make a more efficient design and generate more electricity. He took the request home and thought about it overnight. The next day he came back with all kinds of drawings of different ways to arrange the windmills.

"Wind energy is worth pursuing, but there's far more energy to be harnessed directly from the sun," he told me. "I envision a huge floating platform that I'll call 'Solar Marine.' It would rotate to follow the azimuth of the sun during the course of the day and optically concentrate the beam radiation directly onto photocells."

Pyron Solar, Inc.

The Laing concept soon evolved into a research and development company based in San Diego. The Laings urged me to take on a directorship in the company to help get it registered in California as Pyron, Inc. In 1983, I agreed to do that on a temporary basis to launch the company.

Spectrolab, a Boeing subsidiary in California, manufactures the photocells used in spacecraft and also those used by Pyron. Operating photocells in the ultracold environment of space offers the efficiency of a ready-made heat sink. The solar exposure is hot but dissipates rapidly. The trick to doing it on Earth is to keep the cells cool. That's where Laing's floating platform comes in. The temperature of the cells, even under high concentration of the sun's rays, can be maintained and stabilized by mounting them on a rotating array of photo-voltaic conversion modules that floats on a shallow pond of water.

In the late 1980s, I was asked to introduce the Pyron concept in China and to present it to one of the four Ministers of Energy—the one responsible for electric power. However, since the project was not yet well-developed, and clean energy had not yet gained a high priority, the minister didn't share my enthusiasm. The Ministry never responded following my presentation.

In May 1993, with the help of Senator Pete Domenici, I escorted John Laing to present his project at the Sandia National Laboratories, a U.S. Department of Energy facility in New Mexico responsible for research on emerging technologies aimed to meet national energy and safety needs. Fifteen years later, following considerable improvements in design, the ultrahigh efficiency of the Pyron system has received much praise for its promising solar energy conversion technology.

Pyron Solar, Inc., a new company under the leadership of CEO Doug Carriger, is preparing a new product to be manufactured in San Diego for sale to domestic electric utilities and for export to the emerging alternative energy markets worldwide.

Pyron–
Early Concept
  ❧Author's
  collection

Pyron Solar
Triad model
at Pyron Solar
Headquarters–
New Product
  ❧Author's
  collection

Pyron Solar –
Platform Assembly
A Rotating Stage
for Mounting the
Array of Photo-
voltaic Conversion
Modules
  ❧Courtesy of
  Stephanie Aretz,
  Pyron Solar, Inc.

I continue to be involved as a consultant and advisor. Two decades after my first presentation in Beijing, we have finally begun to have traction in the Chinese market.

CHINA

While I was pursuing business prospects, Dick had resumed an ambitious schedule of overseas travel, beginning with a trip to England in 1978 to deliver an address at Oxford University. In April 1982, to commemorate the tenth anniversary of his historic visit, he retraced his steps in China accompanied by several friends, including Gavin Herbert, Ray Price, and Jack Drown.

Mr. Chen Jinhua, former Vice Mayor of Shanghai, hosted a banquet in Dick's honor. Addressing the guests, Dick said:

> … as a result of what happened in 1972, Shanghai now has a special place in the history books because, if Premier Zhou Enlai and I had not agreed on the famous Shanghai Communiqué in 1972, we would not be here tonight. That was the beginning of a new relationship between the Chinese people and the American people.
>
> And in the past ten years, significant progress has been made in the relations between our two countries. Thousands of American tourists have had the opportunity of coming to Shanghai, and we have been privileged to receive thousands of Chinese students in the United States.
>
> And then in the material sense, we have seen great progress. Ten years ago there was virtually no trade between the United States and the People's Republic of China. Now it is over $5 billion.…
>
> Through economic cooperation, through cultural cooperation, scientific and educational, we can do so much for each other and for the whole world.[99]

---

99 Transcription of Former President Richard Nixon's speech at the banquet hosted by Former Vice Mayor of Shanghai, Mr. Chen Jinhua, at Jin An Guest House on 12 April 1982, Shanghai, People's Republic of China. Transcribed by Karen Olson.

Following that event, Dick and his friends went on to visit Hangzhou, Beijing, and other cities.

Introduction to Business in China

For ten years following Dick's first trip to China, I had been asking him if I should go there to promote various business prospects. He said, "No, not yet. Not ready. Don't go in too soon. Wait for others to explore and get things started. See how fast the Chinese are willing to move beyond the Cultural Revolution before you go in."

I didn't realize Dick might have been including me in "not ready." But by 1984, he felt he had prepared me to make my first trip. Stanley McKiernan had introduced me to a potential client who wanted me to help him find a manufacturer in China for his newly patented invention—a simple hydraulic device called a "safety jack." I met Dick at his office in Manhattan to discuss the prospect. "I know you suggested I not rush into a venture in China," I said, "but I think I have a product that makes sense now. We should offer the Chinese something they can manufacture and sell around the world. We have to open that door, so they can experience a bit of liberty. For them to participate in a market economy would benefit all concerned."

"Sounds like a good idea, but let's check it out. Why don't we ask Bob Abplanalp?" So Dick got Bob on the phone.

Responding with an immediate offer of consultation, Bob said, "I'll send the car right down. Have Ed meet me at the entrance to the building."

We rode in his limousine to a midtown location where we discussed the prospect and how to get it off the ground.

"Your client has got to be strong enough to defend his invention before he starts making too much noise about it, or somebody will come in and jump it before he gets it well protected," Bob advised.

I passed along that sound advice to my client, and I'm sure he gave it careful consideration.

During my next conversation with Dick, he said, "I want you to go to China, and when you do, you should carry a tribute to your Chinese hosts." Following up on Dick's advice, I asked for suggestions from Bud Krogh, an attorney who had served as staff on Dick's Domestic

Council and in other capacities. He volunteered the assistance of Nina Quan, his law firm associate, who composed a beautiful set of tributes inscribed on high-quality parchment paper to present to each official host on my trip. The tributes related to the theme, "Seize the Moment," espoused by both Dick and Chairman Mao.

Dick also told me, "The Chinese will give you red carpet treatment everywhere, but to make the most of your trip, you've got to have a plan and know what you're running into. I'll set up a proper, thorough advance for you like I'd do if I were traveling. The advance-man will go ahead of you and introduce the project."

Dick enlisted Bud's assistance. Because he was planning to participate in a lawyers' convention in Shanghai and Hong Kong, Dick asked him to advance the trip for my client and me. Bud did a superb job finding four prospective locations in Beijing, Shanghai, Chongqing, and Chengdu that could compete in manufacturing the device.

My brother also called ahead to Han Xu, at that time the Chinese Vice Minister of Foreign Affairs in Beijing. Serving in the absence of an ambassador, he had headed the first People's Republic of China legation in Washington, D.C.[100] Han Xu and Dick had become close friends and often visited in each other's homes. They felt at ease talking about all manner of topics, including the differences between their two countries. During Dick's trip to China in 1982, they had met again.

Before I left the States, a Chinese-American friend warned me, "Americans do not find all the food in China palatable. Some can cause gastric distress; others are unappetizing. Keep in mind the rule: If unsure of the menu items, order a bowl of steamed rice and a bowl of broth—any kind. Make sure they've been heated to boiling. Then mix the two. That's a fine meal. You can live on it. But if you attend a banquet at a reputable hotel, enjoy the tasty morsels. Don't worry about their safety."

I thanked my friend for his advice, assuring him I would keep that in mind.

---

100   China had no official ambassador or embassy in Washington, D.C., until President Carter granted diplomatic recognition to China in 1979, much to Dick's disapproval, because recognition meant breaking diplomatic relations with Taiwan. Carter's communiqué stated that the United States acknowledged one China and that Taiwan was a part of China.

Along those lines, Dick advised, "When you get to China, you're going to be asked to toast with some high-powered alcohol, like Mao Tai. Let me tell you, all you need to do is follow this procedure: Tip the glass, tap the glass, and touch it to your lips. Finally, lick your lips. That's all you need."

Apparently Dick had learned the hard way.

When my client, his associate, and I arrived in Beijing, we checked into the very small but clean and comfortable Jinglun Hotel operated by a Japanese hotel chain. On behalf of Han Xu, an official from the Foreign Ministry called to invite us to dinner at the Diaoyutai State Guesthouse, one of eighteen private, secluded villas reserved for heads of state and notable foreign visitors. The name *Diaoyutai* means "Fishing Terrace." In the enclosed, guarded complex near the Imperial Palace that long ago served as the vacation home of emperors, visitors can actually cast a line and reel in carp. During Henry Kissinger's secret mission to China in 1971, he stayed at one of the villas where he met with Zhou Enlai.

Han Xu, two other Chinese officials high in the Foreign Ministry, my client, his associate, and I attended an elaborate twenty-five-course banquet equaling any White House state dinner. We sat sixty degrees apart at a big, round table with a lazy Susan in the center. I remembered my Chinese-American friend's advice about the safety of hotel food as the waiters served us platter after platter of Chinese delicacies that chefs had fashioned into works of art. Back and forth almost silently the waiters paraded through the kitchen door, bringing us more edibles. No way could we even sample them all, and the staff and our hosts didn't expect us to either. Dick had been correct in predicting we would receive the red carpet treatment in China.

At the end of the banquet, Han Xu asked, "How did you like the tea?"

"I'm not normally a tea drinker, but this is extraordinary," I said.

"Let me tell you why. This tea comes from the prized tender tips of the tea leaves during their early growth in the spring. They are picked only by girls up to the age of sixteen who have passed a very special eye exam. These girls have much better eyesight than other humans. They can distinguish subtle shades of color, texture, and transparency that older eyes miss, and boys cannot detect. They harvest only a small quantity of these golden tips, so the tea is very rare and very expensive."

I then felt guilty for having guzzled it as if it were just an ordinary cup of tea. I could really tell the difference though. The tea from the young leaves with a touch of jasmine had a more delicate aroma and flavor than the standard beverage in the States.

"If I could afford this tea, it would be the only type I'd drink from now on," I told Han Xu.

During the following weeks, my client, his associate, and I toured the factories Bud had lined up in the four cities. As a marketing tool, we showed a video of how the device functioned and then discussed the possibility of manufacturing it there. Eager to win the contract, each of our gracious hosts demonstrated his factory's capability to do the job. They bent over backwards to provide whatever we needed.

I thought the factories in Chongqing and Chengdu in Sichuan Province offered the best prospects. We had to obtain special permission to visit the site in Chengdu, an aircraft manufacturing plant where they modified Russian MIGs, because it was forbidden territory to foreigners.

At my client's request, we went to Hong Kong so he could carefully consider his options, promising to return to Beijing after he reached a decision. Finally he signed a contract with the Chengdu factory but later backed out in favor of a manufacturer in Taiwan.

CIRCUS PANDAS TO AID WILD COUSINS

At least since the seventh century, Chinese emperors had practiced "panda diplomacy," presenting those unique animals as goodwill gifts to leaders of other lands. On April 16, 1972, Ling Ling and Hsing Hsing[101] arrived in Washington, D.C., as a gesture of peace and friendship from Mao Zedong following Dick's trip.[102] For many years, the panda pair delighted millions of visitors to the National Zoo.

So, when Stanley McKiernan, Don's attorney, asked me to help Kenny Feld of Ringling Brothers Barnum and Bailey Circus bring a

---

101   Ling Ling lived to the age of twenty-three and Hsing Hsing to twenty-eight, longer than the twenty-year normal life expectancy for wild pandas.

102   Panda diplomacy ended in 1984 with passage of a Chinese law making it illegal to give pandas to entities outside China. Pandas could only be loaned for ten years for a fee of $1 million per panda pair per year.

performing panda to the United States, I found the idea intriguing. Feld, who inherited the circus from his father, had watched a panda entertain at the Shanghai Circus and wanted to bring it to the U.S. for a nationwide tour to raise money for the Wild Panda Preserve in Western Sichuan Province. One of the rarest animals in the world, giant pandas feast on bamboo trees, a rapidly diminishing habitat. At the preserve, pandas are bred, nurtured, domesticated, and researched. Thinking Feld's offer had merit, I agreed to help.

In preparation for the trip, I met with Feld in Washington, D.C. He told me the details of Ringling Brothers' plan to put the panda on one of their two circus trains that toured the U.S. each year. In return, Ringling Brothers would pay the Wild Panda Preserve at least $2 million and any additional sums they could gain from the tour. My assignment was to encourage the Chinese to change their policy regarding a panda tour in order to significantly benefit the threatened animals and their wilderness habitat.

First I traveled to Beijing on August 15, 1985, and the next day to Shanghai with George Yeoung, the Chinese interpreter and guide Stanley had hired. A bright, aggressive businessman—Shanghai style—George did all in his power to promote the project. In Beijing, we had breakfast with the mayor of Chongqing, whom I had met on my first trip to China, and with his assistant, the deputy director of the Foreign Affairs Office of the Chongqing Municipal People's Government.

Then on August 16, George and I visited the Shanghai Circus on behalf of Ringling Brothers. A marvelous performer, the panda Wei Wei could ride a bicycle around the ring, deal cards, eat with a knife and fork, and dance with the trainer. Despite his bulky frame, he could perform feats of great agility.

At the hotel in Shanghai, I met with Yuan Huei Quo, head of the Foreign Affairs Division of the Shanghai Bureau of Culture, his assistant, and Yang Lu, president of Shanghai International Ventures and Consultants Corporation. Mr. Yuan told me the Ministry of Culture handled the panda's scheduling, and the circus could never grant permission for Wei Wei to leave China. He also pointed out that the panda was allowed only one trip per year and had already been scheduled for a tour in Japan in 1986. Ringling Brothers would have to submit a proposal for 1987, which would require approval by a number of bureaucracies.

Discouraged by the bureaucratic red tape and the inability of the Shanghai Circus to schedule Wei Wei, we flew to Hong Kong on our way home. There we had dinner with a recent acquaintance, Wang Guang Ying, chairman of China Everbright Corporation, who told me, "You know, Wei Wei is not the only performing panda in China. You should go over to Fujian Province and find one. Four or five pandas there can perform just as well as Wei Wei. The curator of the Fuzhou Zoo is a renowned veterinarian, and he trains all the pandas."

Taking the old gentleman's advice, George and I flew to Fuzhou for a brief visit on August 17. There we met first with Mr. Chen Tian Guan, deputy director of the Foreign Affairs Office of Fuzhou, and his assistant. Mr. Chen then took us to the zoo, where he arranged our meeting with Mr. Chen Yu Chu, the zoo's curator. Messrs. Chen told us about the zoo's four performing pandas, Bass, Tao Tao, Qing Qing, and Dong Dong, and showed us a video of Bass's recent performance at Hong Kong's Ocean Park.[103] They said a panda could be borrowed, but the central government would have to approve the plan. Neither knew the proper procedures.

The highlight of the trip was meeting Tao Tao, who performed his repertoire of tricks for me. He rode a bike, swept the floor, and danced with the trainer. George took this picture of me posing with Tao Tao, whose fur felt like fine steel wool, in spite of his soft, cuddly appearance.

I returned home with a plan to pursue the loan of a panda from both Shanghai and Fuzhou. Ringling Brothers wrote a proposal to the Ministry of Forestry, because the pandas in Sichuan Wild Panda Preserve were under its auspices. Stanley McKiernan, his partner John Edmunds, and I followed up with a trip to China that fall to discuss the plan with the Ministry of Forestry, but we also met with the Ministry of Culture. As our negotiations progressed, Ringling Brothers decided to pursue a contract with the Ministry of Forestry as the more productive of the two options.

---

103 When a Chinese name is repeated (Tao Tao, Qing Qing, etc.), that indicates a diminutive. Bass, with one name, was the big guy.

Tao Tao, the performing panda – Fuzhou Zoo, China, 1985
～Courtesy of George Yeoung, Project Assistant

On a third trip to China, I delivered Ringling Brothers' proposal. They had created an extraordinary scale model of the panda's exclusive railcar, which even included growing bamboo. The Ministry of Forestry received the plan with much enthusiasm, and everything appeared a go—until an official of the World Wildlife Fund caught wind of it, I was told. The WWF had worked in China to preserve pandas since 1979, but this official objected vigorously to the idea of transporting a wild panda, or any wild animal for that matter, to be put on display and perform in a circus.

Our efforts weren't entirely wasted, however. Instead of a panda, the Ministry of Culture eventually sent Ringling Brothers a troupe of acrobats. As guests of the circus, Stanley and I had the pleasure of watching those outstanding athletes perform in Madison Square Garden.

REACTIONS TO THE TIANANMEN SQUARE TRAGEDY

In the fall of 1989, following the pro-democracy Tiananmen Square uprising in June, Dick and I traveled separately to China—he to meet with Deng Xiaoping and other officials in Beijing and I to attend the eight hundredth anniversary of Chongqing, Seattle's Sister City, because I served on the Sister City Association Board of Advisors. Before departing, Dick and I discussed our trips. I asked, "In light of the tragedy at Tiananmen Square, what should I say? I don't want to encourage or excuse that type of crackdown on dissidents in any way."

"No, just tell them where we stand. You don't condone government-led violence to solve a problem that's been festering for years."

And Dick stood his ground when he met with Deng Xiaoping, telling him in front of the media that the civilized world was outraged over the killing of the protesters, causing a crisis in the relationship between China and the U.S. He said that China would have to remedy the situation. In private, Deng admonished Dick that he would not tolerate public ultimatums from foreign dignitaries, but he would discuss the matter behind the scenes.

During my trip, the mayor of Chongqing told me that Deng privately had indicated the massacre went against his better judgment, but the People's Liberation Army had overruled him in their repressive crackdown against the dissidents. He could have stopped the slaughter, though. No excusing that!

◡˙ Chapter 13 ˙◡
Final Journeys

Applying my geology training, I cofounded Great Circle Resources in 1986 with Sergej Schachowskoj, a former U. S. Marine of Ukrainian descent, to assist clients in acquiring rare earth oxides mined from large deposits in Inner Mongolia and processed in a Shanghai refinery. Also under the auspices of Great Circle Resources, Sergej and I became involved in the McCaw Space Technology project in 1986-1987. During that time, I traveled extensively, completing my sixth and final trip around the world. On the road so often, I regretted not having more time to spend with my family, including Don and Clara Jane and Dick and Pat.

Don

Don, who had always loved to travel and would go anywhere at the slightest suggestion, started cutting back on his business trips in 1986. With his health deteriorating, he could no longer maintain his rigorous schedule. He was diagnosed with non-Hodgkins lymphoma shortly after he retired from the DNA Corporation. I had already branched out into other business pursuits, so I did not take over his company. My interests lay elsewhere.

Near the end, Don suffered a great deal of discomfort and pain. The last time I called him at Hoag Memorial Hospital, he could barely talk. I've always wished I had visited him before he passed away on June 27, 1987.

Gay and I flew down for Don's memorial service on June 30. Dick's doctor had advised him to avoid travel following surgery, so Tricia flew from her home in New York to represent Dick's side of the family. The morning before the memorial service, Don's body had been laid to rest at Rose Hills Cemetery in Whittier, where he had planned for his final resting place high on a hill above the Milhous gravesites.

PAT AND DICK

Following a trip to Washington, D.C., on behalf of Pyron, on May 1, 1992, I drove to Dick's office in Saddle River, New Jersey. Dick was laid up with a sprained ankle, so he asked Kathy O'Connor, his assistant, to drive me to his home in nearby Park Ridge. Dick was upset with himself that he would not be able to deliver a speech in Chicago. At the age of seventy-nine, he still kept active and grew impatient when forced to rest.

Not needing my briefcase, I had left it downstairs. A short while later, Pat arrived home. Frail and in poor health, she got off the elevator on the fourth floor of their townhouse where Dick and I were meeting in his office. She handed me my heavy briefcase, thinking I had forgotten it. Just as cheerful as always, Pat greeted me with her usual "Hi, Eddie!"

Gracious Victorian lady that she was, Pat left Dick and me alone, so we could enjoy a private discussion. I appreciated her thoughtfulness, as I wanted to talk about a difficult topic that day. No matter where I traveled, people would invariably ask me about Watergate and Dick's resignation. I wondered how he felt about his decision after nearly eighteen years.

"People keep asking why you resigned rather than face the trial in the Senate. As time has passed, how do we view the resignation in the light of history?"

Dick said, "Look, the Constitution is foremost. The office of the President is the most honorable any man can occupy. If you don't fulfill it to the nth degree, you must respect the honor of the place and move on. You're just a man. Leave it to the next one to learn from the mistakes you made and carry on. What happened is still difficult—always will be. But I'm not too worried about it."

So, my brother respected the honor of the presidency—the office—and that made him decide to resign rather than fight—even if he thought he could win in the Senate. Who knows? He might have, but it was better for him and the country that he move on.

～ ～

The next time I saw Dick turned out to be the last. Our extended family gathered for Pat's funeral at the Nixon Library and Birthplace on June 26, 1993. With Dick, Tricia, and Julie by her side, she lost her battle with lung cancer on June 22—the day after their fifty-third wedding anniversary. The epitaph on her tombstone reads, "Even when people can't speak your language, they can tell if you have love in your heart." Pat certainly did.

After Pat's death, I kept in contact with Dick by telephone. During one of our conversations, he encouraged me to pursue his mission of keeping the country free, clean, and independent. Although my brothers and I had pursued very different paths—politics, business, and geology—in this respect, our missions converged. Dick, Don, and I had long been concerned that America could not continue consuming domestic reserves of basic resources indefinitely, both from the standpoint of diminishing supplies and because of the volatile politics of the Middle East threatening the oil supply. Each of us had viewed the challenges and mission from a different perspective, however. As a geologist, I had spent much of my higher education and career out in the physical world, studying the Earth, while Dick, had worked in Washington, D.C., and Manhattan, directing foreign and domestic policy and later writing about policy issues. Don, the businessman, had been the go-getter, always intrigued by others' ideas and ready to jump on their bandwagon. I remember him saying, "We've got to do something!"

With Don gone and Dick in his declining years, I realized he was passing the baton to me and that soon I would be carrying out my mission alone without his wise counsel that I had so valued over the years.

On April 17, 1994, Julie called from the Cornell Medical Center of New York Hospital to tell me her father had suffered a stroke.

"How bad is it?" I asked.

She said, "It was a hard hit. He's unable to talk, but as I left his room he signaled thumbs up."

Five days later the last of many long journeys brought Dick from New York to Yorba Linda, California, where he was interred next to Pat only a hundred yards from his birthplace.

Now as I complete my story, I hope the legacy of Richard Milhous Nixon may find new meaning. It is truly a matter of understanding what President Clinton proclaimed in his eulogy at the Nixon Library on April 24, 1994.

Oh, yes, he knew great controversy amid defeat as well as victory. He made mistakes, and they, like his accomplishments, are a part of his life and record. But the enduring lesson of Richard Nixon is that he never gave up being part of the action and passion of his times. He said many times that unless a person has a goal, a new mountain to climb, his spirit will die. Well, based on our last phone conversation and the letter he wrote me just a month ago, I can say that his spirit was very much alive to the very end.

That is a great tribute to him, to his wonderful wife, Pat, to his children and to his grandchildren, whose love he so depended on and whose love he returned in full measure. Today is a day for his family, his friends, and his nation to remember President Nixon's life in totality.

To them, let us say: may the day of judging President Nixon on anything less than his entire life and career come to a close.

May we heed his call to maintain the will and the wisdom to build on America's greatest gift, its freedom, and to lead

*Ed meeting President Clinton at Dick's Funeral with Former
First Lady Barbara Bush and
Former President Gerald Ford in background*
∻Courtesy of William Jefferson Clinton Presidential Library

a world full of difficulty to the just and lasting peace he dreamed of. [104]

EULOGY TO MY BROTHER

On April 26, I stood before faculty, students, and local citizens at Whittier College to deliver a eulogy to my brother. Struggling to maintain my composure, I recounted stories of my youth in Whittier and how Dick had encouraged me to study and learn—a habit he continued the rest of his life. Rather than lecture, he would guide me by asking a series of questions, waiting patiently for me to solve the problem myself.

During the eulogy, I noted my belief that Dick was a great teacher, although most people don't think of him as such. But any great leader does teach. Dick spent nearly half a century as a public figure, traveling to more than eighty nations and meeting with all the major world leaders of his era except Stalin. He spoke and wrote prolifically about those experiences and his belief in the superiority of free governments and markets. Although he is gone, we can still learn from his vast knowledge and wisdom.

"Yes, we will miss him," I told the audience, "but he left us with a legacy, bequeathing to the world a whole new set of challenges. We'd better rise to the occasion…. Every one of us has a mission to carry out. Read those books he wrote. At least read some of them, because there's a strong message in every one."

I concluded the eulogy with a poem I had written in 1984 that reminded me of my brother's extraordinary service to the country he loved so dearly. It also expressed my hope that future generations would persist in their missions, as Dick had in his.

THE FINGERPRINTS OF GOD

May we always be willing to give
even what we cherish most
to make the world a safe haven
for future generations

---

104 "Bill Clinton, 42nd President of the United States" <http://www.nixonlibrary.org/index.php?src=gendocs&link=RNfuneral.> accessed 17 January 2007.

as their missions of curiosity
approach the limits of understanding.

May those who succeed us
persist in the journey
with care and concern
no matter how difficult or long.

And when we depart
this realm of space and time
to approach the infinite and eternal,
may we leave behind
only footprints of love
among the fingerprints of God.

A TOAST TO DICK AND PAT

Nearly three years later, on February 17, 1997, the Richard Nixon Library and Birthplace hosted a major address by Dr. Henry Kissinger to commemorate the twenty-fifth anniversary of Dick and Pat's historic trip to China. A few hours before my flight to California for the event, Kathy O'Connor, assistant director of the Library, had called, asking me to propose a toast to my brother at the luncheon following Dr. Kissinger's speech. I gladly accepted her invitation.

After the main course of beautifully prepared Cantonese cuisine catered by the Hyatt Regency, John Taylor, director of the Library and master of ceremonies, introduced me. Approaching the microphone to deliver my pre-toast remarks, I surveyed the audience of about 150 of Dick's long-time supporters and then spoke these words:

As we look out these windows past the row of kumquat trees and the First Lady's Rose Garden, we find two memorial markers just this side of that little house my father built where Dick was born. Marks of memory in a place like this, though perfectly appropriate, are but a small sample of the reminders that we encounter around the world today.

Everywhere I've traveled on five continents, evidence of their passing is ubiquitous. I've seen it not just in Beijing, Shanghai, Xi'An, and many other cities in China, but elsewhere—places like Sydney, Canberra and Cairns; or La Paz, Cochabamba, and Santiago; or Cairo, Alexandria, Addis Ababa, Conakry, and Abidjan; or Karachi, Islamabad, Tashkent, and Samarkand; or Moscow and hundreds of points west. My family name is magic in all those places, not because of anything I have done, but because Dick and Pat had passed that way before.

Tracing the footsteps of these two peacemakers, we can now see the world as a much friendlier place. So from the rest of us here today, let us raise a glass in toast to Dick and Pat Nixon, to their memory and their legacy.

∻ CHAPTER 14 ∾

CHALLENGES

The world is a dangerous place—
not because of those who do evil—
but because of those who look on, and do nothing.

∻Albert Einstein

Three weeks before his death, Dick completed his final book *Beyond Peace*. In fact, he suffered the massive stroke while proofing the galley for the book.

Beyond Peace hadn't yet been published when I delivered the eulogy at Whittier College. Later, as I read his book, I reflected on what I had been thinking during the eulogy and my call for a more serious consideration of his writings. The applicability of what he wrote in his final book seems ever-more significant today. With an appreciation for our nation's past, Dick set forth a platform for the present and a vision for the future. Writing at the end of the Cold War, he also warned that without a strong, unified, growing America, the twenty-first century would be "another grim century of tyranny and war."[105]

Now, nearly fifteen years since Dick's death, the United States is embroiled in a global war on terror and is facing serious domestic problems. People often ask me, "What would your brother have done to address these issues?" Some of them probe deeper: How would he have handled the war in Iraq if he had been President? How would he have deterred Iran and North Korea? What could the U.S. do to encourage

---

105   Richard Nixon, *Beyond Peace* (New York: Random House 1994) 173.

the People's Republic of China to promote human rights more openly? How could our country lessen its dependence on foreign oil? What advice would he have given on health care and the economy? What would he have said regarding the moral decay in our country?

In *Beyond Peace,* Dick, touched upon many of these issues, giving clues to what he might have done.[106] With great prescience, he spelled out the challenges the United States would confront in the twenty-first century, both at home and abroad, including the threat of Islamic extremism and the need for energy independence. My brother urged Americans to consider his vision of our country's destiny, calling for a return to our founding principles and a renewal of the American spirit.

As I read Dick's final message, I could feel the influence of our parents and grandparents on my brothers and me. I could hear the appeals passed down from generation to generation in the Nixon and Milhous clans to base our lives on timeless virtues: "honesty, fidelity, thrift, hard work, patriotism, diligence, self-discipline, gratitude, and a belief in liberty, religious freedom, and equality of opportunity."[107]

In the ideas Dick espoused in *Beyond Peace,* I could identify Mom's idealism and her Quaker beliefs. As the reconciler in our family, Mom shunned violence and promoted peace by the example she set. She taught us the need for faith, hope and charity as the foundation for life. Dad also taught us those values, but in his chosen role as the contender, he vocalized his opinions at every opportunity regarding the role of government and the pressing issues of the day. I could see Dad's particular influence in some of Dick's positions. In his books and in his life, Dick wove the two strands of our Nixon-Milhous heritage into what he called, "hardheaded idealism and enlightened realism."

Dick understood we can never change human nature or totally eliminate poverty, racism, or war. We must avoid utopianism or change just for the sake of change, or we'll wind up with change in our pockets but no real money as the government consumes more and more of our income. And worse, we will continue down the road of an

---

106   In the appendix to my book, I share some of Dick's thoughts in *Beyond Peace* that speak to the challenges we face today.
107   Nixon 236.

unhealthy dependence on government to provide what once was our responsibility and that of our families, churches, and communities.

But we can all do our part in our own sphere of influence to make this world a friendlier place. My hope is that people, especially youth, will read Dick's books and become inspired to explore, ask tough questions, and think critically and creatively to find real solutions to the problems confronting us.

Dick concluded *Beyond Peace* with a challenge to each one of us to strive for excellence and to recover the sense of mission that made this country great. As he wrote:

> Our challenge today is a positive one—a challenge to build, not to destroy, a challenge to be for, not just against, a challenge to be driven not by our fears but by our hopes.[108]

---

108 Nixon 250.

EPILOGUE

While writing this book, an ocean of memories flooded my mind. Through the successes and the defeats, including Watergate, Dick encouraged us to keep forging ahead. Never get discouraged to the point of quitting. Just keep moving on. Never give up. Keep on fighting the battle that you believe in and make it real for your children so the country will not age so fast. That was Dick's philosophy, and it has been mine, too.

The pets, the cousins, the girl friends, the trips—our life was not particularly different from that of any other family. When people ask me about Dick as a child, they always expect to discover a magic ingredient in his background that produced the thirty-seventh President of the United States.

It doesn't work that way. Dick had special qualities, to be sure. But like other children, he played, he had fun, he enjoyed athletics. The difference, probably, is that he more strongly developed the traits one looks for in a leader. Dick was the most self-disciplined person I have known, and the most objective. As a child, he was perhaps more serious minded than others, and I think the great amount of reading he did influenced that, as did the early deaths of our brothers. He accepted responsibility—in fact, sought it more readily than most his age. And he had a desire to educate and develop himself as much as one person possibly could.

How does a President of the United States happen? No one, including the most astute sociologists and psychologists, will ever be able to tell you. Many common factors make us what we are, but unique experiences make us what we become. Certainly, our family environment was conducive to the development of a leader, and I know this was a factor. But a leader of Dick Nixon's strength and capacity is the product of a unique mix of hundreds of unpredictable elements, including genes, environment, and circumstances.

How did Richard Nixon reach the highest office in the land? I watched his development from a special vantage point, but I cannot tell you. I'm just thankful he did.

APPENDIX
RICHARD NIXON
ON THE ISSUES

From Richard Nixon's final book *Beyond Peace*, we selected the following quotations that give insight as to how he might have addressed the challenges facing our nation in the twenty-first century:

FOREIGN POLICY

PERSIAN GULF

- Our strategy toward Iran should be to contain its influence inside and outside the Persian Gulf. We should keep open the possibility of directly exploiting Iran's weaknesses if it continues its campaign of terror and intimidation against Western interests. Iran has turned state-sponsored terrorism into a science. If it persists with its subversion and terrorism, we should be prepared to assist ethnic and religious factions in Iran that oppose the Tehran regime, thereby weakening its ability to threaten our interests abroad. (146)

- With their vast oil wealth, and in view of the weakness of Saudi Arabia and the other Gulf states, the Iraqi and Iranian regimes will be in a position to threaten the Gulf indefinitely. Consequently, the United States should assume the responsibility of guaranteeing Gulf security with its military power. . . . The United States must accept the fact that it is the only Western power with the military resources to project force and block Iranian and Iraqi advances in the region. (148-149)

ISRAEL

- The United States has a critical interest in the survival and security of Israel. The United States and Israel are not formal allies, but we have a moral commitment that transcends any security agreement. (143)

CHINA

- We should strongly protest China's human-rights abuses whenever and wherever we can. But punishing China's leaders for human-rights abuses by restricting and reducing our economic contacts does not serve the long-term interest of those Chinese who want more political freedom. (126)

TAIWAN

- While we should not risk jeopardizing our relations with Beijing by formally recognizing Taiwan diplomatically, we should recognize Taiwan economically by strongly supporting its efforts to become a member of such organizations. And we should begin extending to Taiwan government officials the diplomatic courtesies that the leaders of one of the world's major economic powers deserve. The best guarantee of Taiwan's security is our relationship with the People's Republic of China. The Chinese will not launch a military attack against Taiwan as long as Beijing knows such an action would jeopardize their relationship with the United States. (134)

NORTH KOREA

- Until it ceases to be a threat, we should continue to treat it as the pariah nation that its leaders still persist in making it. (136)

VIETNAM

- …we should keep the political relationship in a deep freeze as long as Hanoi continues to treat as second-class citizens the millions of South Vietnamese who were our allies in the war. We should follow the administration's decision to lift the trade embargo with vigorous efforts to encourage investment in Vietnam and draw it further into the global economy, not to help the present Vietnamese regime but to strengthen the forces of change. (137)

RUSSIA

- The promotion of human rights and political freedom should be an important American objective. But the pursuit of freedom in the explosive Russian environment, with its unique traditions and circumstances, cannot be based on the ideal Western notions that may have little to do with local circumstances. (71)

CUBA

- It is time to shift the central focus of our policies from hurting Cuba's government to helping its people. (137)

- … our best service to the Cuban people now would be to build pressure from within by actively stimulating Cuba's contacts with the free world. (138)

DOMESTIC ISSUES

VALUES AND CULTURE

- The violence, discord, viciousness, and slovenliness that so mar the quality of life in America are products of the spirit, and they require answers of the spirit. These are behaviors, not conditions. We will get America back on the path of civilization when Americans once more respect and demand civilized behavior.

  From the 1960s on, our laws and our mores have been driven by the cultural conceits that took hold during the heyday of the counterculture, including a denial of personal responsibility and the fantasy that the coercive power of government can produce spiritual uplift, cure poverty, end bigotry, legislate growth, and stamp out any number of individual and social inadequacies. (174)

- The founders created a land of opportunity. For more than three centuries, opportunity was enough because the culture conditioned people to take advantage of it. But we have now created a culture in which appallingly large numbers ignore the opportunities offered by work, choosing instead those offered by the interwoven worlds of welfare and crime. Our task now is not to invent opportunity, but to enforce honest work as the route to it. We need to get America back on track before it sails off into the abyss. (176)

ROLE OF GOVERNMENT

- The founding fathers were not utopians but were practical idealists. Recognizing that man is inherently flawed and driven by self-interest, they sought to devise a system of government that took these realities into account. Their intent was not to create a new man, to supply meaning to empty lives, to redistribute wealth, or to run the economy. Rather, their aims were limited but lofty: to create a system able to maintain the conditions of freedom against internal and external threat, to administer the nation's laws effectively, and to encourage rational deliberation and choice on the part of a self-governing people. (180)

- Waging war and providing for national security are among those tasks for which governments are designed. Governments are incapable of running an economy, picking winners and losers in cutting-edge industries and technologies, transforming the nature of human beings, or creating a social utopia. The fallacy of contemporary liberalism is its assumption that every problem has a government solution. It does not. (183)

- We hear too much today about how to reinvent government and not enough about how to reduce it. (183-184)

- In trying to do too much that it has no business doing, government does too little to meet its primary responsibility—to protect the lives, liberty, and property of the people, and to maintain those conditions under which a free economy can best create new prosperity. (184)

- Our problem today is not too little direct democracy but too many politicians who pander to the ephemeral mood swings of popular fashion. (185)

- Public opinion is a fickle mistress. What is popular is often not what is right. But what is right and unpopular can often be made popular if statesmen have the courage and foresight to lead. (185)

EQUAL OPPORTUNITY

- The founding fathers believed that civil rights belonged to individuals, not groups. The principle of natural rights embodied in the Declaration of Independence defined our goal as equality of opportunity, which rejects distinctions of legal status and privilege defined by race, religion, ethnicity, tribe, language, or sex. Everyone is the same in the eyes of the law. But insisting on equality of opportunity is the opposite of demanding equality of result. (187)

- This institutionalization of preferential treatment, with the theory of group rights it represents, undermines the basic principles of our Constitution and a free society. It repudiates the idea of merit essential to a competitive and fair society. It often has the unintended consequence of encouraging rather than overcoming failure. It leads the beneficiaries to think of themselves as passive victims whose fate depends on others rather than on whether they seize the opportunities available to all Americans. It also epitomizes the corrosive entitlement mentality that increasingly pervades American society—one of the greatest threats to our fiscal health, our moral fiber, and our ability to renew our nation. (188-189)

- The entitlement mentality has been created by politicians who promise more than government can afford and professional liberals who demand that government do that which it is not competent to do. It threatens to destroy the virtues of self-reliance, individual responsibility, initiative, and enterprise that built our country and will be indispensable in any effort to renew it. All Americans should have an equal opportunity to earn the good things of life. But except for those who are unable to do so, they are not entitled to receive those good things from the earnings of others. (189-190)

IDEALISM AND REALISM

- The founders believed that representative government presupposed a high degree of civic virtue, an insight that modern libertarians do not appreciate. (190-191)

- The grisly history of the twentieth century demonstrates tragically the evil that can be done by governments that try to change human nature. (191)

- … the American combination of hardheaded idealism and enlightened realism has built a record of world leadership, prosperity, and essential decency that no nation, past or present, can match. It has enabled us to lead abroad and achieve a remarkable degree of prosperity and social justice at home, not on the basis of narrow and selfish interests but through the appeal of high ideals and common values. (191)

- Idealism without realism is naïve and dangerous. Realism without idealism is cynical and meaningless. The key to effective leadership at home and abroad is a realistic idealism that succumbs to neither utopianism nor despair. (192)

ECONOMY

- They [deficits] distort our economy over the long run by siphoning off for short-term consumption funds that could have gone toward long-term capital investment. They confer benefits on the present generation and burdens on future generations. While sustainable in the short term, and even justifiable in recession and war, deficits act like water, eroding the foundations of a strong economy. (199)

- Savings and investment are central to our ability to finance industrial expansion and productivity growth. Capital gains taxes are taxes on savings. Income and payroll taxes are taxes on production. All three reduce the ability of American companies to compete in world markets. (204)

- Sensible tax policies would therefore shift the balance toward taxing consumption more and production less. That is why a value-added tax would be preferable to income and payroll taxes. (204)

- The bottom line is that America cannot tax its way to prosperity; it cannot spend its way to prosperity. If we want prosperity, we need to shape our policies to foster growth. (205)

HEALTH CARE REFORM

- The litmus test applied to every federal program should be whether it advances freedom or restricts freedom.... America's health care system does need improvement, but it does not need replacement. (207)

- We have the world's best medical care because we have free markets in a free society. To throw that away in an orgy of politically correct egalitarianism would be a self-inflicted wound for which there would be no cure. (210)

- Any sensible reform of the nation's health care system must start with the patient, not with the government. The most powerful force inflating health care costs has been a system of insurance that removes the patient's own incentive to shop for value. We should increase, not diminish, the patient's role in choosing his own providers, his own level of service, his own balance between expenditures for health care and for other goods and services. (210)

- We need instead to control exploding medical costs primarily through market forces that will ensure that the quality of American medical care remains high. We should devise a system that includes greater emphasis on preventive care, sufficient public funding for health insurance for those who cannot otherwise afford it, and competition among both health care providers and insurance providers to keep down the cost of both. We also need to reform the perverse legal liability and medical-malpractice standards, which have sacrificed patient protection in favor of protecting the physician or hospital against staggeringly costly lawyer-instigated lawsuits. (211)

EDUCATION

- If America's public schools are to do their job, they must again be civilized places of learning rather than free-fire zones. Discipline in the classroom is fundamental if learning is to be possible. Beyond that, personal, social, and intellectual discipline are all key elements of learning itself. Yet for decades, many if not most of our public schools have been progressively abandoning the trust that parents and communities have placed in them, giving up on discipline and often yielding to mob rule. (213)

- The home is the key ingredient in a child's education. Habits learned there persist for a lifetime. Children from homes where knowledge is prized and reading is encouraged come to school eager to learn. Those from homes where learning is not part of life enter the schoolhouse door with two strikes against them. Couch-potato parents are likely to produce couch-potato children. (217)

- Setting standards and expecting them to be met are what too much of our public education system has abandoned in its prolonged fit of patronizing and egalitarianism. (217)

- Aging 1960s radicals who now dominate the faculties of many universities have helped power the movement for political correctness, which punishes truth, penalizes merit, promotes faculty on the basis of quotas, and suffuses the campus with an atmosphere of abysmal, inflammatory ignorance.... (218)

- Unless those responsible for our great universities ... take forceful and determined measures to restore their institutions' standards of educational integrity, they will have grossly violated their basic trust. And we as a nation will have failed our first responsibility to the next generation: to transmit to them the values, the history, and the traditions of a humane civilization, together with the knowledge and understanding to bring those values to life. (218)

URBAN PROBLEMS

- To the reflexive liberal mind, urban problems are poverty problems, and the way to meet them is to throw money at them. For thirty years the United States has been doing just that. The Great Society was given a blank check. The liberals claimed it bounced because of insufficient funds. The real answer is that the check should not have been written at all. (219)

- Poverty is a symptom, not a cause, of our urban decay. The rot in our cities is a spiritual, ethical, cultural, and behavioral rot, which causes the poverty, the crime, and the degradation and abuse of public facilities. (219)

- The liberal approach to welfare—spend more and demand less—means well but is tragically misguided. Its self-defeating incentives perpetuate poverty by rewarding illegitimacy, entrenching dependency, encouraging fathers to abandon their children, and thus undermining the stable family. (220)

CRIME

- Our criminal justice system has abysmally failed to deliver what should be the first freedom: freedom from fear. Young thugs openly thumb their noses at a system that operates a revolving door, often sending those who get caught back out onto the streets at a rate that clearly carries the message that crime does pay. But the more fundamental problem is the social corrosion that creates the criminals in the first place: the breakdown of value structures, the lack of discipline, the absence of any sense of right and wrong among many young Americans... (223)

- The cop-out of blaming crime on poverty is morally corrupt and intellectually vacuous. When I was growing up during the Depression, there was far more poverty but far less crime. The difference was that our families and communities enforced civilized standards. (224)

RACE

- It is essential that all people have the opportunity to study their own roots, which make our national tree so strong. But those who say that skin color alone entitles minority groups to an alternate set of national icons strike at the heart of what it means to be an American.... Being American is not about being white and Christian, or black and Muslim, or Asian and Buddhist. It is about being dedicated to a country that in principle offers virtually limitless opportunity to all, regardless of their background. (227)

VIRTUES AND SPIRITUAL RENEWAL

- The more the federal government steps in and does things for people, the less they are going to do for themselves. The best spur to initiative in the private sector is to let people know that if they want something done, they had better just do it. The best role for the federal government is to create conditions conducive to doing it. Our growing reliance on government to fix every social ill has given us a shrinking conception of the concept of public service. Too often we equate it solely with being in government, even though those in private enterprise provide all the funds to pay for our public servants. The public benefits from the work of every good plumber, doctor, salesman, window washer, artist, teacher, and homemaker just as much as it does from those who are paid by the taxpayers. (235)

- One of this nation's great strengths is that we are a diverse nation, with many competing convictions and interests....There are, however, some basic virtues that all Americans of goodwill can share: honesty, fidelity, thrift, hard work, patriotism, diligence, self-discipline, gratitude, and a belief in liberty, religious freedom, and equality of opportunity. While government cannot ensure these indispensable virtues, it can at least stop weakening them. (236)

- Ultimately, the American people must look mainly to religion, the family, and themselves as the driving forces for spiritual renewal. Politically, conservatives must make the case for traditional values and individual accountability in a way that transcends both the mushy moral relativism of modern liberals and the inquisitorial instincts of a few religious zealots. If they do, the vitally important themes of religious renewal and family values can appeal to the vast majority of Americans rather than divide them. (237)

- But the evidence suggests powerfully that the best way to raise educational standards, to eradicate poverty, to increase upward mobility, and to promote civic virtue is to strengthen the healthy two-parent family. (240)

MISSIONS AND GOALS

- Our great goal should be to rekindle faith in freedom, not only abroad but at home. In the coming century, preserving freedom will require far more than "eternal vigilance," though that will be needed. A free society needs a muscular determination to make its institutions work. It requires that free people take on the responsibilities that go along with freedom.... If we backslide on our responsibilities, we invite the alternatives to freedom. (245)

- Extreme nationalism, racism, and religious fanaticism are running rampant in the world.... If we do not find a way to keep nations together, they will fractionalize and the Cold War will be followed by scores of bloody, smaller wars. America has the responsibility and the opportunity to provide the example of how a nation with many races, religions, and nationalities can be held together by a great idea that transcends them all. (247)

- Unlike the goals of previous superpowers or empires, America's goal is not to conquer the world by our arms or our wealth, but to lead by our example. (249)

- We are the heirs of the traditional values that have been the bedrock of America's goodness and greatness. We should preserve and renew them, and make them once again our guides to national and individual conduct. The success we have enjoyed in the past and the success we believe we can achieve in the future should bring not a sense of lulling contentment but rather a deep and enduring realization of all that life has offered us, a full acknowledgment of our responsibilities, and an unwavering determination to show that under a free government, a great people can thrive best, materially and spiritually. (250)

- Our status as the world's only superpower is meaningless unless it is driven by a higher purpose. We should reach into the soul of this nation and recover the spirit and mission that first set us apart. We do not aspire to a perfect, problem-free society, but we will demand more from ourselves. We must improve ourselves at home so that our example shines more brightly abroad. (251)

We encourage people to read *Beyond Peace* in its entirety.

BIBLIOGRAPHY

BOOKS

Adler, Bill. *The Wit and Humor of Richard Nixon*. New York: Popular Library, 1969.

Aitken, Jonathan. *Nixon: A Life*. Washington, D.C.: Regnery Publications, Inc., 1993.

Ambrose, Stephen E. *Nixon: The Education of a Politician 1913-1962*. New York: Simon and Schuster, 1987.

Angelo, Bonnie. *First Mothers: The Women Who Shaped the Presidents*. New York: Harper Collins, 2000.

Arnold, William A. *Back When It All Began: The Early Nixon Years*. New York: Vantage Press, 1975.

Black, Conrad. *Richard M. Nixon: A Life in Full*. New York: PublicAffairs, 2007.

De Toledano, Ralph. *Nixon*. New York: Henry Holt and Company, 1956.

------*One Man Alone: Richard Nixon*. New York: Funk and Wagnalls, 1969.

Eisenhower, Julie Nixon. *Pat Nixon: The Untold Story*. New York: Simon and Schuster, 1986.

Fraser, George MacDonald. *The Steel Bonnets: The Story of the Anglo-Scottish Border Reivers*. London: Harper-Collins Publishers, 1995.

Garment, Leonard. *Crazy Rhythm: My Journey from Brooklyn, Jazz, and Wall Street to Nixon's White House, Watergate, and Beyond* ... New York: Times Books, 1997.

Gellman, Irwin F. *The Contender: Richard Nixon The Congress Years 1946-1952*. New York: The Free Press, 1999.

Herndon, Booton. *Praised and Damned: The Story of Fulton Lewis, Jr.* New York: Little Brown and Company, 1954.

Herschensohn, Bruce. *Taiwan: The Threatened Democracy*. Los Angeles: World Ahead Publishing, 2006.

Hoff, Joan. *Nixon Reconsidered*. New York: Basic Books, 1994.

Inaugural Addresses of the Presidents of the United States, Volume 2: Grover Cleveland (1885) to George W. Bush (2001). Bedford, MA: Applewood Books, 2001.

The Inaugural Book –1973 "The Spirit of '76." Washington, D.C.: 1973 Inaugural Committee, 1973.

Kornitzer, Bela. *The Real Nixon: An Intimate Biography*. New York: Rand McNally and Co., 1960.

Kotlowski, Dean J. *Nixon's Civil Rights: Politics, Principle, and Policy*. Cambridge: Harvard University Press, 2001.

Mansfield, Stephen. *The Faith of George W. Bush*. Lake Mary, Florida: Charisma House, 2004.

Mazo, Earl. *Richard Nixon: A Personal and Political Portrait*. New York: Harper and Brothers, 1959.

Nixon, Richard. *1999: Victory Without War*. New York: Simon and Schuster, 1988.

----- *Beyond Peace*. New York: Random House, 1994.

----- *In the Arena: A Memoir of Victory, Defeat and Renewal*. New York: Pocket Books, 1990.

----- *Leaders*. New York: Warner Books, 1982.

----- *RN: The Memoirs of Richard Nixon*. New York: Grossett and Dunlap, 1978.

----- *Real Peace/No More Vietnams*. New York: Simon and Schuster, 1990.

----- *The Real War*. New York: Warner Brothers, 1980.

----- *Seize the Moment: America's Challenge in a One-Superpower World*. New York: Simon and Schuster, 1992.

----- *Six Crises*. New York: Doubleday and Company, 1962.

Nixon Speaks Out: Major Speeches and Statements by Richard M. Nixon in the Presidential Campaign of 1968. New York: Nixon-Agnew Campaign Committee, 1968.

Price, Raymond. *With Nixon.* New York: The Viking Press, 1977.

Rosen, James. *The Strong Man: John Mitchell and the Secrets of Watergate.* New York: Doubleday, 2008.

Setting the Course: The First Year—Major Policy Statements by President Richard Nixon. New York: Funk and Wagnalls, 1970.

Stans, Maurice H. *The Terrors of Justice: The Untold Side of Watergate.* New York: Everest House, 1978.

Wilson, Richard, ed. *The President's Trip to China: A Pictorial Record of the Historic Journey to the People's Republic of China with Text by Members of the American Press Corps.* New York: Bantam Books, 1972.

GOVERNMENT PUBLICATIONS

"President Nixon, Special Message on Indian Affairs, July 8, 1970," *Public Papers of the Presidents of the United States: Richard Nixon 1970.* Washington, D.C.: Office of the Federal Register, National Archives and Records Service, General Services Administration, 1971. 564-567, 576.

"Remarks About a Special Message to the Congress on Energy Resources. June 4, 1971." *Public Papers of the Presidents of the United States: Richard Nixon 1971.* Washington, D.C.: Office of the Federal Register, National Archives and Records Service, General Services Administration, 1972. 703.

"Remarks Following Inspection of Oil Damage at Santa Barbara Beach: March 21, 1969." *The Public Papers of the Presidents of the United States: Richard Nixon 1969.* Washington, D.C.: Office of the Federal Register, National Archives and Records Service, General Services Administration, 1970. 233.

Richard M. Nixon, Late a President of the United States: Memorial Tributes Delivered in Congress. Washington, D.C.: United States Government Printing Office, 1996.

"Special Message to the Congress on Energy Resources. June 4, 1971. *Public Papers of the Presidents of the United States: Richard Nixon 1971.* Washington, D.C.: Office of the Federal Register, National Archives and Records Service, General Services Administration, 1972. 703-714.

INTERVIEWS

Brady, Donley. Telephone interview by Edward Nixon and Karen Olson. 2 December 2004.

Edmundson, Theodore. Telephone interview by Karen Olson. 25 June 2008.

Jeffrey, Professor Harry J. Telephone interview by Karen Olson. 12 March 2007.

Marshburn, Howard. Telephone interview by Edward Nixon and Karen Olson. 9 May 2008.

Martin, Philip. Personal interview by Karen Olson. 10 May 2006.

Neely, Sylvia. Telephone interview by Karen Olson. 24 June 2008.

Paldanius, Elizabeth Timberlake. Personal interview by Edward Nixon and Karen Olson. 5 October 2001. Telephone interview by Edward Nixon and Karen Olson. 2 December 2004.

Price, Raymond. Telephone interviews by Edward Nixon and Karen Olson. 25 and 26 August 2008.

Wright, Bill and Marygene. Personal interviews by Edward Nixon and Karen Olson. 5 October 2001 and 12 November 2005.

CORRESPONDENCE

Cox, Dorothy. Letter to Edward Nixon. 30 March 2006.

Dolby, Bill. E-mail to Edward Nixon. 25 May 2005.

Freed, Denny. E-mail to Edward Nixon. 17 July 2007.

Freed, Denny. E-mails to Karen Olson. 22 and 27 October 2007.

Howard, C. Edward. E-mail to Edward Nixon. 4 July 2005.

McPherson, Jessamyn West, Letter to Edward Nixon. 2 August 1968.

Price, Raymond K. E-mail to Edward Nixon. 26 August 2008.

NEWSPAPER ARTICLES

"300 California Families Flee Flood Waters." *Chicago Daily Tribune* 7 February 1935: 1.

Arnold, Martin. "Edward Nixon Rebuts Stans Prosecution." *The New York Times* 6 April 1974: 1, 15.

Bell, Eleanor. "Nixon Visits Seattle Girl Kept At Home By Ailment." *Seattle Post-Intelligencer* 11 August 1962: 14.

Berkow, Ira. "Coach 'Chief' Newman Recalls Presidential Aspirant As Gutty 155-Pounder: Nixon Got 'Tattoos,' No Letter For Whittier Football." *The Register* 6 August 1968: C1.

"Edward Nixon Visits The Enquirer and Talks About His Brother, The President." *National Enquirer* 24 December 1972: 14.

"Jane Hampton Collins, Nixon Secretary." *Washington Post* 25 January 2001: B7.

Kelly, Charles. "Nixon: The Prescott days." *The Arizona Republic* 10 December 2000, F1, F5.

Kennedy, Lou. "Jane Collins, Nixon's secretary, dies at 79." *Sarasota Herald-Tribune* 6 January 2001: 6B.

Lloyd, Patricia. "Public Sentiment Grows For Ike Budget—Nixon." *Pensacola News-Journal* 2 June 1957: 1, 6.

McLellan, Dennis. "Robert Abplanalp, 81; Tycoon, Loyal Friend of Richard Nixon." *Los Angeles Times* 3 September 2003: B10.

"Milhous – Nixon Brilliant Event." *Whittier News.* 26 June 1908. (retyped article)

Muhlstein, Julie. "Nixon on Nixon: 'There's a lot there.'" *The Herald* 18 February 2002: B1-2.

"Other Nixon Has Mind On Sea And Under." *The Commercial Appeal* 25 October 1969: 17.

Raleigh, Sally. "Here's Pat Nixon," *Seattle Post-Intelligencer* 9 August 1962: Women's Section 6.

Robbins, Jerry. "Nixon's Navy Brother: 'I Never Intercede.'" *Memphis Press-Scimitar* 24 October 1969: Second Section, 17.

"Seattle Girl Visited by Pen Pal—Nixon," *The Seattle Times 11* August, 1962: A1.

Sheh, Kevin and Richard W. Kimball. "Nixon's tie to Prescott," *The Daily Courier,* excerpted in *The Blue Heart Bulletin*, Vol. 17, No. 6, January 2007: 2.

Shribman, David M. "Nixon's mastery of change explains his durability." *The Salem News* 2 August 2008: 3.

Thimmesch, Nick. "A soft-selling campaigner." *The Seattle Times* 19 September 1972: A13.

Wolfe, Ellen. "Ed Nixon 'In Hiding': President's Shy Brother Ducking the Limelight." *Palm Beach Post-Times* 21 July 1974: D20.

Online Sources

"1969 Oil Spill." University of California Santa Barbara. <http://www.geog. ucsb.edu/~jeff/sb_69oilspill/69oilspill_articles2.html> accessed 30 July 2008.

"Ahmed Sékou Touré, Guinea (1922-1984)." *University of Florida George A. Smathers Libraries.* <http://www.uflib.ufl.edu/cm/africana/sekou.htm> accessed 10 December 2004.

"American Experience/The Presidents/Richard M. Nixon." PBS.org. <http://www.pbs.org/wgbh/amex/presidents/37_nixon/printable. html> accessed 9 November 2006.

Ancestry.com. *1900 United States Federal Census* [database on-line]. Precinct 10, Larimer, Colorado; Roll: T623 126; Page 24B. Provo, UT, USA: The Generations Network, Inc., 2004. Original data: United States of America, Bureau of the Census *Twelfth Census of the United States,* 1900. Washington, D.C.: National Archives and Records Administration, 1900. T623, 1854 rolls. <http://search.ancestry.com/cgi-bin/sse. dll?rank=1&gsfn=Francis+A.&gsln=Nixon&=&_82...> accessed 8 October 2008.

Ancestry.com. *1910 United States Federal Census* [database on-line]. Los Nietos, Los Angeles, California; Roll: T624_85; Page 9B; Enumeration District: 281; Image 964. Provo, UT, USA: The Generations Network, Inc., 2006.Original data: United States of America, Bureau of the Census *Thirteenth Census of the United States,* 1910. Washington, D.C.: National Archives and Records Administration, 1910. T624, 1,178 rolls. <http://search.ancestry.com/cgi-bin/sse.dll?rank=1&gsfn= Francis+A.&gsln=Nixon&=&_82...> accessed 8 October 2008.

Ancestry.com. *1920 United States Federal Census* [database on-line]. Placentia, Orange, California; Roll: T625_123; Page 4A; Enumeration District: 361; Image 1004. Provo, UT, USA: The Generations Network, Inc., 2005.Original data: United States of America, Bureau of the Census *Fourteenth Census of the United States,* 1920. Washington, D.C.: National Archives and Records Administration, 1920. T625, 2,076 rolls. <http://search.ancestry.com/cgi-bin/sse.dll?rank=1&gsfn=Franc is+A.&gsln=Nixon&=&_82...> accessed 8 October 2008.

Ancestry.com. *1930 United States Federal Census* [database on-line]. Prescott, Yavapai, Arizona; Roll: T63 126; Page 6B. Enumeration District 26; Image 404.0. Provo, UT, USA: The Generations Network, Inc., 2004. Original data: United States of America, Bureau of the Census *Fifteenth Census of the United States,* 1930. Washington, D.C.: National Archives and Records Administration, 1930. T626, 2,667 rolls. <http://

search.ancestry.com/cgi-bin/sse.dll?rank=1&gsfn=Francis+A.&gsln=Nixon&=&_82...> accessed 8 October 2008.

"Astronaut Bio: Charles Duke 05/94." *Lyndon B. Johnson Space Center.* <http://www.jsc.nasa.gov/Bios/htmlbios/duke-cm.html> accessed 11 December 2004.

"Bill Clinton, 42nd President of the United States." <http://www.nixonlibrary.org/index.php?src=gendocs&link=RNfuneral.> accessed 17 January 2007.

"Boehm Gallery: History." <http://www.modelhorsegallery.info/B/Boehm/Boehmstory.html> accessed 27 August 2007.

"A Brief History of Yorba Linda." *City of Yorba Linda.* <http://www.ci.yorba-linda.ca.us/history.asp> accessed 27 April 2005.

Bugbee, Linda Waldron. "RN's Birthplace: I lived there, too!" Letters from Yorba Linda #65. http://www.nixonlibraryfoundation.org/index.php?src+directory&view+letters&refno=134... accessed 27 June 2008.

"Casa Pacifica: The Western White House." *San-Clemente-Beaches.com.* <http://www.san-clemente-beaches.com/Casa-Pacifica.html> accessed 11 June 2007.

Cumming, Greg. "The Silent Majority at 35: Letters from Yorba Linda #45" posted 27 October 2004. *Richard Nixon Library and Birthplace Foundation.* <http://www.nixonlibraryfoundation.org/index.php?src=directory&view=letters> accessed 29 October 2004.

"Fine Porcelain Collectible Sculptures—Boehm." <http://www.wildlifewonders.com/boehmporcelain. html> accessed 27 August 2007.

"First Inauguration." *The Eisenhower Presidential Library and Museum.* <http://www.eisenhower.archives.gov/PAGE1.HTM> accessed 28 March 2006.

Henderson, David R. "Thank You, William H. Meckling." *David R. Henderson Collection.* <http://www.davidrhenderson.com/articles/0199_thankyou.html> accessed 4 November 2006.

"Historical Background and Development of Social Security." *Social Security Online History.* <http://www.ssa.gov/history/briefhistory3.html> accessed 2 September 2005.

"The History." *Yorba Linda, California – Community Guide.* <http://www.orangecounty.net/cities/YorbaLinda. html> accessed 30 May 2008.

Hoff, Joan. "Re-evaluating Richard Nixon: his domestic achievements." *The Nixon Era Center at Mountain State University.* <http://www.nixonera.com/library/domestic.asp> accessed 29 March 2006.

"Houphouët-Boigny, Félix." *Encyclopaedia Britannica Online.* <http://www.britannica.com/eb/article?tocid=9041189> accessed 9 December 2004.

"Houphouët-Boigny, Félix." *Fact Monster.* <http://print.factmonster.com/ce6/people/A0824299.html> accessed 10 December 2004.

"Images of Robert the Bruce." <http://www.magicdragon.com/Wallace/Bruce3.html> accessed 5 July 2005.

"In Our Path: Essay: 1983." <http://www.outtacontext.com/iop/essay-1983.html> accessed 21 December 2004.

Jordan, C.C. "The P38." <http://www.yarch.vc.net/mil/p38.html> accessed 12 August 2006.

"Long Beach Earthquake: 75th Anniversary," *Southern California Earthquake Center.* <http://www.scec.org/education/08-307longbeach.html> accessed 4 September 2008.

"Map showing Operated Lines of Pacific Electric Railway." <http://www.usc.edu/isd/archives/la/historic/redcars/redcar_map.jpeg> accessed 20 December 2004.

"Memorandum of Conversation, Abidjan, Ivory Coast, February 24, 1970." *Foreign Relations*, 1969-1976, Vol. E-5, Documents on Africa, 1969-1972. <http://www.state.gov/r/pa/ho/frus/nixon/e5/54806.htm> accessed 31 August 2007.

"P-38 Lightning—All About It." <http://www.all-about-all.info/catalog/P-38%20Lightning> accessed 5 July 2005.

"Pacific Electric Railway in brief." <http://www.uncanny.net/~wetzel/whatispe.htm> accessed 21 December 2004.

"The Pacific Electric Railway System." <http://www.outtacontext.com/iop/redcar.html> accessed 21 December 2004.

"Pacific Electric Whittier Line." <http://www.erha.org/pesw.htm> accessed 21 December 2004.

"Presidents and Popes." *Someonespecial.com.* <http://www.someonespecial.com/cgi-bin/someone/Boehm/boehmstory.html> accessed 27 August 2007.

"Principal Achievements of President Nixon and his Administration." Richard Nixon Library and Birthplace. <http://www.nixonlibrary.org/index.php?src+gendocs&link+RN_Achievements&category=...> accessed 1 November 2006.

"Pyron Solar." <http://pyronsolar.com/US/home.htm> accessed 8 April 2005.

"The Red Cars of Los Angeles." <http://www.usc.edu/isd/archives/la/historic/redcars/> accessed 21 December 2004.

"Richard Nixon for President 1968 Campaign Brochures: 'The Nixon Stand.' *4President.org*. <http://www.4president.org/brochures/nixon-1968brochure.htm> accessed 11 April 2006.

"Richard M. Nixon Panel Addresses President's Evolving Legacy." *Duke Law News & Events*. <http://www.law.duke.edu/features/news_nixon_panel.html> accessed 16 January 2003.

"Second Inauguration." *The Eisenhower Presidential Library and Museum*. <http:/www.eisenhower.archives.gov/PAGE1.HTM> accessed 28 March 2006.

"Shanghai Communiqué Issued (Feb 27, 1972)." *The American Experience*. <http://www.pbs.org/wgbh/amex/china/peopleevents/pande08.html> accessed 4 November 2006.

State of the Union Address: Richard Nixon (January 30, 1974) *Infoplease* (Pearson Education, 2000-2008) <http://www.infoplease.com/t/hist/state-of-the-union/187.html> accessed 21 July 2008.

"The Status of Human Rights Organizations in Sub-Saharan Africa: Guinea." *University of Minnesota Human Rights Library*. <http://www1.umn.edu/humanrts/africa/guinea.htm> accessed 10 December 2004.

"Treaty Between the United States of America and the Union of Soviet Socialist Republics on the Limitation of Anti-Ballistic Missile Systems." *U.S. Department of State*. <http://www.state.gov/www/global/arms/treaties/abm/abm2.html> accessed 23 July 2008.

"The Vietnam War – The Bitter End 1969-1975." <http://vietnamwar.com/timeline69-75.htm> accessed 29 December 2006.

Widner, James F. "Radio Days – Fulton Lewis Jr." 2003 <http://www.otr.com/lewis.html> accessed 14 November 2004>.

"Will Rogers." <http://www.willrogers.org/> accessed 9 December 2004.

Woolley, John T. and Gerhard Peters, *The American Presidency Project* [online]. (Santa Barbara, CA: University of California (hosted), Gerhard Peters (database.) <http://www.presidency.ucsb.edu/ws/?pid=2698> accessed 27 May 2008.

----- *The American Presidency Project* [online]. (Santa Barbara, CA: University of California (hosted), Gerhard Peters (database.) <http://www.presidency.ucsb.edu/ws/?pid=3537> accessed 23 July 2008.

----- *The American Presidency Project* [online]. (Santa Barbara, CA:University of California (hosted), Gerhard Peters (database.) <http://www.presidency.ucsb.edu/ws/?pid=3575> accessed 23 July 2008.

----- *The American Presidency Project* [online]. (Santa Barbara, CA: University of California (hosted), Gerhard Peters (database.) http://www.presidency.ucsb.edu/ws/?pid=3962 accessed 23 July 2008.

Young, Mark. "A little history….." <http://genforum.genealogy.com/nixon/messages/1475.html> accessed 9 December 2002.

OTHER

President Richard Nixon's Daily Diary, 22 February 1970 and 15 December 1973.

Nixon, Richard M. "'Bridges to Human Dignity' Part II Through Free Enterprise." An Address by Richard M. Nixon on the NBC Radio Network, 2 May 1968.

Richard Nixon Library and Birthplace Docent Guild's Fact Book.

PERIODICALS

Dmohowski, Joseph. "From a Common Ground: The Quaker Heritage of Jessamyn West and Richard Nixon." *California History*, vol. 73, no. 3. Fall 1994: 215-255.

Ertel, Laura. "Ed Nixon: Newest Ralston Recipient Bridges Geology and the Environment," *Duke Environment Magazine*, Spring 2004: 40.

Kelly, John. "Let's Get Rid of Management." *Alaska Airlines*, March 2001: 7.

TRANSCRIPTION OF CASSETTE TAPES BY KAREN OLSON

Ed Nixon interview by Sylvia Neely in Prescott, Arizona. Sharlot Hall Museum Tape #1530. 18 February 2007.

Edward Nixon's speech to Docents at the Nixon Library and Birthplace, 22 March 2001.

Edward Nixon's speech to Orange County Republicans at Italian Restaurant in Costa Mesa, California, 17 September 2001.

Former President Richard Nixon's speech at the banquet hosted by Former Vice Mayor of Shanghai, Mr. Chen Jinhua, at Jin An Guest House on April 12, 1982, Shanghai, People's Republic of China.

Grace Foudy interview by Mona McCroskey. Sharlot Hall Museum Tape #1119. 21 March 1996.

VIDEOS AND CDS

Larry King and Julie Nixon Eisenhower Tour the Richard Nixon Library and Birthplace. 50 min. Videocassette Cable News Network LP, LLLP, 2001.

Nixon's Boyhood Home: A Personal Tour With Julie Nixon Eisenhower and Huell Howser. Huell Howser Productions, 2004. (CD)

The Real Richard Nixon: Early Life. Interview of Richard Nixon by Frank Gannon. 66 min. Videocassette. Central Park Media, Raiford Communications, Inc. 1995.

CREDITS

PHOTOS

Clinton Presidential Library and Museum, photo of President Clinton and Edward Nixon, April 27, 1994, at President Nixon's funeral: 415.

Time & *Life* Pictures, Joseph Scherschel, photographer, Getty Images, "Nixon-Woods Marriage At Pensacola Naval Air Station: 196. Also, thanks to my friend George Karalekas for his efforts in obtaining permission.

The Seattle Times, photo of Richard Nixon, Karen Anderson, friends, and family, by Richard S. Heyza, August 10, 1962: 213.

Sharlot Hall Museum, Prescott, Arizona, photos of Clows Rest Home and Hannah Nixon, c. 1928: 40, 43.

QUOTATIONS

Charisma House, *The Faith of George W. Bush* by Stephen Mansfield, 2004.

Joseph Dmohowski, "From a Common Ground: The Quaker Faith of Jessamyn West and Richard Nixon," *California History*, Fall 1994.

Walter McDougall, "Why I Think History Will Be Kind to Nixon," online article, August 16, 2004.

Perseus Books Group, *Nixon Reconsidered* by Joan Hoff, 1994, and *Richard M. Nixon: A Life in Full* by Conrad Black, 2007.

Eloise Price, *Descendants of William Milhous, Jr. and Martha Vickers*, 1996.

The Seattle Times, "Seattle Girl Visited by Pen Pal—Nixon," August 11, 1962.

The Whittier Daily News, "Milhous-Nixon Brilliant Event," June 26, 1908.

Tricia Nixon Cox and Julie Nixon Eisenhower for permission to quote from the books authored by their father Richard M. Nixon, including *Beyond Peace, In the Arena, RN: The Memoirs of Richard Nixon, The Real War,* and *Six Crises.*

INDEX

Note: In this book, "Dad" refers to the author's father, Frank. "Mom" or "Mother" refers to Frank's wife Hannah, a Milhous. "Grandmother" refers to Almira Milhous. The index follows the author's use of the names "Eddie" or "Ed" and "Dick" in the book (versus given names Edward and Richard, respectively).

R